IT'S NOT HARD TO APPLAUD
[SADOWSKY'S] SPUNK, DRIVE
. . . AND HUMOR."
—*Booklist*

"I wanted to tell my mother how wrong she was about Bernie. How he respected me. . . . She was afraid that Bernie would take advantage of me. I couldn't tell her that I was getting worried that he wouldn't."

———————

"We were in the car. The white mink stole was lying on the front seat between us. Bernie said, 'You hate it.'

"I said, 'No, I just don't love it. It's fabulous, but not for me.'

"We were waiting for a traffic light on Park Avenue. An elderly, heavyset black woman was at the curb. 'Okay,' Bernie said, 'it's not for you. Maybe it's for her. Here,' he called to the woman. He tossed her the mink. The light changed. We drove away . . ."

———————

"He talked in his sleep. He didn't just talk. He fought, cursed, and yelled. 'You bastard, I'll kill you . . .' "

WEDDED
TO CRIME

My Life in
the Jewish Mafia

WEDDED TO CRIME

My Life in the Jewish Mafia

SANDY SADOWSKY
WITH H. B. GILMOUR

B

BERKLEY BOOKS, NEW YORK

The following is a true story. In some instances names have been changed to guard the innocent or for reasons of legal and personal protection. Hattie Prince, Reefer May, Peter Knossos, Muttel Diamond, Bea Spizer, Lila Navarro, Peter Von Shlemme, Milty Heinz, Tom Sullivan, Tony and Charlie North, Ziggy Schwartz, Chalky Lefkowitz, Giorgio the Jaw, Iris, Enid and Lido are pseudonyms.

WEDDED TO CRIME

A Berkley Book/published by arrangement with
Daniel Weiss Associates, Inc., and Chardiet Unlimited, Inc.

PRINTING HISTORY
G.P. Putnam's Sons edition/June 1992
Published simultaneously in Canada
Berkley edition/March 1993

ISBN: 0-425-13764-3

A BERKLEY BOOK ® ™ 757,375
Berkley Books are published by The Berkley Publishing Group,
200 Madison Avenue, New York, New York 10016.
The name "BERKLEY" and the "B" logo
are trademarks belonging to Berkley Publishing Corporation.

PRINTED IN THE UNITED STATES OF AMERICA

10 9 8 7 6 5 4 3 2 1

ACKNOWLEDGMENTS

It would never have occurred to me to write a book, except for a fabulous happening on a rainy day at the hairdresser's. I was telling a story about one of the funnier episodes in my life as a gangster's wife, and two other women came out from under their hair dryers to listen. One was Lee Klein, a neighbor, who said, "If you were a book, I would read you"; and the other was Bernice Chardiet, a well-known book producer, who said, "You *should* write a book and I'll *help* you work on it. You have a terrific story to tell." From the moment we met, Bernice had faith in me and in my story, not only for its "insider" view but for what it might say to other women. I'm very grateful to Bernice and her partner, Daniel Weiss, for their diligent efforts to make this book a reality on my behalf. I would also like to thank Lisa Wager, my editor at Putnam, for her enthusiasm and her wonderful editing skills, and H.B., my collaborator, for her wit and humor, and her dedication to this project.

And to all my dearest family and friends, who have been there for me and shared my life, a very special thank you, and all my love!

To Jeffrey, the greatest! My joy,
my friend, my beloved son, and to
Tillie, my mother. Wish you were here!

Contents

WEDDED TO CRIME

Prologue

"I've got a little business to take care of before we hit the Copa, kid," Bernie Barton said, ushering me into the back of the limo that had been waiting to pick us up at his Greenwich Village supper club.

It was an unusually warm June night in New York. We were on our way uptown to catch Billy Daniels's opening at the Copacabana—the popular singer was a personal friend of Bernie's—and I was dressed for the occasion in five-inch heels, a tight little black cocktail dress, and a single strand of pearls. My thick auburn hair was pulled back in a high ponytail. Between the heels and piled-up hair I was just about Bernie's height. And I was wearing my makeup the way I'd learned to during my brief stint as a Vegas showgirl—bright red lipstick, thickly drawn doe eyes, and spiky false black lashes.

It was about a week before my twentieth birthday and a week after Bernie's forty-first.

"Stop at Chesty's, the cocktail lounge over on Thirty-eighth Street," he told the driver.

I'd only been dating Bernie Barton for about a month, but already I knew better than to ask what business he was going to take care of.

"This is Sandy Sadowsky," he introduced me to the four men waiting for us at a table at the back of the bar. Despite the oppressive weather, they were all in suits. Diamonds flashed when they shot their cuffs. Diamond-studded gold watches glinted at their *wrists. Diamond rings—one in the shape of a horseshoe—circled their pinkies.*

Two of the men were bookmakers, one tall, nervous, skinny; the other short, fat, and bald. The third person at the table looked like a fireplug in a sports jacket. He was the bodyguard. And the body he was guarding belonged to the fourth man at the table, Tommy Dio, a stocky, immaculately groomed man with thick worker's hands and manicured fingernails.

Tommy was known as the nice Dio—compared to his brother, the celebrated Teamster boss, Johnny Dio. The Dioguardi boys were "labor relations experts," soldiers in the Lucchese crime family. They were also the cherished nephews of James Plumeri, better known on the pages of The Daily News *as the mobster Jimmy Doyle.*

"Uncle Jimmy," who was several years older than Bernie, was a friend of his from way back, from when Bernie was a spunky, blue-eyed kid driving bootleg trucks for Meyer Lansky on the Lower East Side. It was probably Uncle Jimmy who had suggested the sitdown meeting with Tommy Dio. Tommy was considered a gentleman. If anything needed straightening out in New York's Garment Center, he was the man to talk to.

What needed straightening out that night was a debt some woman owed to the Mutt and Jeff book-making shylocks across the table. They had fronted a girl named Bunny several thousand dollars in betting capital—at the going mob rate of interest. Bunny lost the bets. The vigorish, the interest, was mounting like mad. By this point it was about five times the original loan.

"I don't want no more fuckin' jewelry," the tall, nervous bookie said, then shot me an apologetic glance. "Excuse my language." Then he turned back to Bernie. "I got jewelry coming out my ass already. I ain't a fence. I don't work on Forty-seventh Street. I want the cash, or her old man's going to be shitting out of a second asshole. Excuse me," he said again to me.

Bernie reached for my hand under the table and gave it a little squeeze. I smiled at him, then ducked my head and went back to stirring my screwdriver.

"BB, what's your interest here?" Tommy Dio asked Bernie.

"Bunny's an old friend. Her husband's a nice guy, Tommy. Small potatoes. Straight. A dress manufacturer—"

Tommy Dio glanced at the short bookmaker. "You went up to see him last week, am I right? What did you do, you threatened the man?"

"Tommy, Tommy," the bald guy said, mopping his brow with his paisley silk handkerchief. *"The broad owes us up the wahzoo. It's going on months already. What do you want me to do?"*

Tommy Dio brushed imaginary crumbs off the white linen table-cloth and shrugged at Bernie, waiting for his response.

"I'm godfather to their kid," Bernie said. *"Just stop the clock on the vig, that's all. Give her some time to clean up the loan . . . to handle the vig she's already run up."*

"The woman is still betting," the short, fat guy said.

"She can't bet no more," Tommy Dio decreed. *"That's the first thing."*

"Okay," Bernie agreed.

"This girl, this Bunny—you used to fuck her, right?" the tall bookmaker asked Bernie. *"Excuse me,"* he said again to me.

Bernie's hand tightened on mine. *"So?"* he said softly, in his ge-nial, gravelly voice. But I knew he'd come close to swinging at the man.

"So, you still shtupping her? That's why you're so concerned?"

"Watch the mouth," Bernie warned, still smiling. *"Here's what I'm asking,"* he said. *"The woman's a friend of mine and she's in trouble. Stop the clock on the vig. Now. Today. Give her a year to pay up. Leave her old man alone. And take the goddamn jewelry she's offering as collateral. Give the woman a break."*

"Done," Tommy Dio said. *"BB, you're personally responsible that she holds up her end. It's a done deal."*

"He's still fucking her. Got to be," the short, fat guy laughed.

"Don't talk that way in front of the kid, okay?" Bernie said. This time, he wasn't smiling.

"Okay. Okay," the bookmaker said. *"No offense, kid, right?"*

I was the kid.

George Raft, the movie star, who was also a friend of Bernie's, always called me the kid. And when I was pregnant with Bernie's son, Raft said, "Look at that, the kid's going to have a kid."

Many Junes later, almost to the day, the kid's kid was graduating from college.

The 1989 graduating class of the John Jay College of Criminal Justice was so big that the ceremony was held in Carnegie Hall that year. And the day was so swelteringly hot that Carnegie Hall looked and sounded like the F train. Despite the air-conditioning, wilted parents were fanning themselves with graduation programs.

Little kids were squirming, shouting, tugging at the ties they'd been forced to wear or their new, too tight shoes.

I was glad I'd arrived early to get a decent seat. I'd hurried up the steps and through the lobby, not knowing whether it was my high heels or my heart making the racket. Before I'd even gotten to my seat, I'd felt tears brimming. But I made it, mascara dry, head held high, as if Bernie were gripping my arm, leading me through the chaos.

I lost it when the graduates marched in. The families and friends who'd waited so impatiently fell silent for a moment, awed. Then we all stood and started applauding wildly. I spotted my son among the capped and gowned graduates filing into the hall. That did it. The flood gates gave way. The tears came, the makeup streaked. I didn't care. Jeffrey looked so handsome, so much like his father—ramrod straight, with Bernie's muscular build and dark, good looks.

And how proud of him Bernie would have been, I thought, as the graduates took their seats. Jeffrey's father hadn't gone to college. He hadn't even graduated from grade school. Everything Bernie Barton had needed to survive as a kid, he'd learned on the streets of New York's Lower East Side. Back then, the neighborhood—from Allen Street to Avenue A—teemed with Jewish immigrants, and the streets stunk of herring, pickles, and poverty. When Bernie was a boy, Meyer Lansky ruled the Lower East Side and guys like Farvel the Stick and Red Levine could help a smart kid bring home a buck to his family instead of wasting his time in school. College? Where Bernie grew up, having a son in the sixth grade was a luxury most families couldn't afford.

Now, here was Bernie's son receiving a college degree in Criminology. Bernie's son, Jeffrey, sitting on the stage of Carnegie Hall as the president of John Jay talked about the graduates' futures in law enforcement. Some would join the New York Police Department, he said. Others would go into drug enforcement work, join the FBI, or go on to law school and perhaps become district attorneys, lawyers, judges. Today, there were more opportunities than ever in law enforcement, the president pointed out ironically, because there was more crime. And the young people graduating, he said, would be among those responsible for changing that daunting statistic, for fighting the war on drugs, for combating crime, for making our society safe and our country a better place to live.

Proud? You could practically hear the buttons popping off the parents' vests. I was *kvelling*, bursting with pride and joy. Bernie, I asked silently, did you hear that? That's your kid he's talking about, the one you never really got a chance to know.

What a party he'd have thrown today, I thought as I watched Jeffrey on the stage, waiting for his diploma. Bernie would have pulled out all the stops, jammed our Upper East Side apartment with friends and family. Cokey would have come down from Harlem. Uncle Vinny would have come up from Florida. Josh would have been there, the Park Avenue lawyer who—as Bernie had always warned him he would—had finally gotten disbarred for consorting with criminals. There would have been huge platters of food, champagne flowing, people singing and dancing and toasting, "Mazel-tov!"

The *gantse* wise-guy *mishpocheh* would have showed up for Bernie's boy. From Vegas, Detroit, Miami, Cincinnati, Chicago. Guys with $50 haircuts and $1,000 suits, diamond pinky rings, gold Rolexes, and shoes as soft and shiny as their silk ties. Mobsters with names like haberdashers—Manny, Moe, and Dave. Tough guys who talked business in the steam room of the Luxor Baths and then cried at Molly's on Rivington Street when the violinist played "My Yiddishe Momme." And it would never have occurred to Bernie Barton that there was anything strange about a room full of gangsters celebrating his son's graduation from a school for law enforcement.

Watching our son accept his diploma now, watching Jeffrey wave the rolled parchment over his head in triumph, I suddenly felt the terrible loss again. Right there in Carnegie Hall, at what should have been—and was, really—one of the happiest, proudest moments of my life, I needed Bernie beside me. Twenty-four years after his death, I still missed him.

Oddly, though, I noticed that I was not crying now. I shook my head, and smiled. Sandy, I said to myself, look at that—all you have to do is *think* of the guy and you go from wimp to stand-up broad again. I could almost hear him saying it: *Tough guys don't cry, baby. Stand-up broads don't, either.* His words, his thoughts, his way of life. When had they become mine?

I was a kid when I met Bernie Barton. And though I didn't know it at twenty, I'd been desperate for everything this man had to offer. His strength, certainty, and protection. His desire to mold me, teach me, turn me into his kind of woman, perfectly matched my need to be shaped, led, and loved.

I guess it was right there, in Carnegie Hall, the day of Jeffrey's graduation, that I began to understand. I seemed to have the beginnings of an answer to the question I'd asked myself countless times in a life where excitement, danger, and violence were as commonplace as Corning Ware: What's a nice Jewish girl like you doing in a place like this?

CHAPTER ONE

A Nice Jewish Girl

There's a joke about a little boy who comes home from school and tells his mother he was in the class play. "I played a Jewish husband," he says. "That's okay," his mother tells him. "Next time, you'll have a speaking part."

Contrary to belief, all Jewish husbands are not mild-mannered accountants.

My father was a gambler. He embezzled from his brother. Borrowed money from the mob. Had an affair with my mother's best friend. And, when I was fifteen years old, he ran off and left us penniless—my mother, Tillie, my eight-year-old sister, Marlene, and me. We were so flat busted that when the loansharks, the "shylocks," came to our house to collect the money he owed them, they felt so sorry for my mother that they gave *her* money. He got in touch with me months later and conned me out of a small inheritance that was in trust for me. His name was Sol and I worshipped him.

It was his father's old apartment in Flatbush that we moved to in 1949, when I was ten. It was near Ebbets Field when the Dodgers still played there, a big, airy apartment with high ceilings and lots of light in a tree-lined, middle-class Jewish neighborhood in Brooklyn. My sister and I shared a pink room. We slept in twin four-poster Colonial beds. At night, with the door open at the right angle, I could look into our dresser mirror and watch the living room TV.

We lived on the fifth floor of a six-story apartment building. Our neighbors down the hall were Enid and Mervin. Enid was a knock-out. She had false eyelashes, hairpieces, hats, and gloves for every occasion. She was a great cook. She drove her own car. Her husband Mervin didn't drive. He was kind of a *shlep*.

Enid taught my mother how to dress, how to put on makeup. My mother would sit at Enid's dressing table and Enid would powder, paint, and perfume her, show her how to use eyeliner, how to glue on the lashes, pluck a sophisticated arched brow, pencil in fuller lips. They'd try on clothes together. And whisper and laugh. I was wild for Enid. I idolized her.

After school, if my mother wasn't home, I'd go down the hall to Enid's for milk and cookies. Sometimes, I'd try on her shoes. She had more shoes than A.S. Beck's and Kitty Kelly's combined: suede ankle straps, open-toed wedgies, creamy, soft leather, and glass-smooth patent leather in "smart" colors, gay colors, with grosgrain bows and satin trim, and flat, medium, and break-your-ass high heels. Enid was our own Joan Crawford. I hung on her every word, and a couple I wasn't supposed to hear.

Sitting at her kitchen table, my chin in my hands, I'd listen to the confidences she shared with my mother . . . and, one day, discovered the secret of the shoes. Enid, glamorous wife of the *nebbish*, Merv, was a kept woman. Everything she had, from her home to her hairpieces, she owed to her lover, "a big man in the shoe union."

Enid and Mervin were my parents' best friends. The couples went out a lot together. Dressed to kill, they hit the New York night spots. They drank, danced, and dined together, had their pictures taken against zebra-skin-covered banquettes, toasted one another, argued over which couple would pick up the check and who should tip the hatcheck and cigarette girls.

My father loved the high life. He loved to see my mother done to the nines. Her beautiful, pale face brightened with red lipstick and amber rouge. Her hair swept up, held in place with fancy combs and crocheted snoods. Sol was one of the original slaves of fashion. He loved clothes, loved shopping, loved to spend lavishly on us, his girls. He'd take my mother and me into the city to carpeted dress shops on Madison Avenue, where he'd supervise our selections. A handsome, tall, and burly man with striking, prematurely white hair, he'd sit on little gilt chairs surveying us, squinting through the smoke of his ever-present cigar, as we modeled for him.

Clothes. Broads. Cigars. Gambling. Sol was passionate about

them. He borrowed the cash to support his passions wherever he could—whether it was from shylocks on the street or the till of the bindery he owned with his brother, Meyer. My father loved excitement, tumult, the wildness of the streets. From the time he was a kid, he always had to be where the action was. As a boy, he'd idolized gangsters. As an adolescent, he'd driven a bootlegging truck for Al Capone. He knew how to melt down gold. He hung out at the track. He loved the horses and could not keep a buck in the pockets of his elegant, double-breasted suits if there was one around to bet on. Clothes. Broads. Cigars. Gambling. He loved them. But most of all, he assured me, he loved me. Most of all, I was the love of his life. His favorite. His girl.

And the day he left was the day I stopped being a girl. February 1954. I was fifteen years old. On Friday night, my father packed a suitcase. It was no big deal. He kissed us goodbye. He was going out of town on business. It was bitter cold out. From the kitchen window, I watched him walking toward the Oldsmobile on Lincoln Road. Under the street light, I could see his coat blowing, the breath coming from his mouth as he opened the car door. He didn't look up at me or wave. It was no big deal.

On Monday afternoon, I walked home from Erasmus Hall High School. It was still cold out, but the books clutched against me were more an unconscious shield for my breasts than a way of staying warm. My legs were bare except for the bobby socks and white bucks I wore with my pleated navy skirt. My long, wavy hair was tucked into the hood of the white and plaid reversible parka my father had bought me in the fall. And if my lips were quivering with cold, they were quivering under the requisite Milkmaid pink lipstick we all wore that year.

I opened the door to our apartment. The warmth in the hallway felt good. I shook my head out of the parka hood. Something was wrong. From the vestibule, I saw men in the living room. They were waiting for me.

I recognized Dr. Horowitz first. "Is Mommy sick?"

My uncle Jakey was there. He answered before Dr. Horowitz could. "No, she's asleep." He was angry.

"The doctor gave her a shot," my mother's other brother Leo explained, nodding at Horowitz.

"She got a letter from your father today." Jakey said *your father* like it was the polite form of *that bastard*. "He must have mailed it before he left. He's not coming back."

"The money," Leo prompted.

"He took it. All of it. Every cent your mother had in the bank for his *fahcocktah* gambling. He owes 'the shylocks.' From his family's mouth he'll steal to pay the shylocks! Look," Jakey said, snatching up the letter that had been sitting on one of the end tables. He held it out to me. He smacked it with the back of his hand. "Look. This is what he says. I owe the shylocks. I'm not coming back. So Leo goes to the bank as soon as your mother calls and, sure enough. Nothing. *Gornisht.* He emptied the account. He left you to starve!"

Enid came out of the bedroom and put her arm around me. "Sit down, Sandy, honey," she said. She took the letter from Jakey and handed it to me. I skimmed it. I couldn't really focus on it. All I knew for certain was that it was addressed to my mother. It didn't mention my sister or me. I handed it back to Enid.

"It'll be all right, Sandy," she said. "You've got to be strong for Marlene and your mother. She came to my door sobbing. I called Dr. Horowitz and he gave her a tranquilizer. She's sleeping now, but she's going to need you when she wakes up." Enid took my hand and squeezed it. "It's okay, honey. Everything will work out. You'll see."

I didn't respond aloud. I became aware of a suddenly deafening pulse in my ears. It took a little while to realize that the sound was coming from the thudding of my heart. I don't know if anyone said anything else. I wouldn't have heard it. My mind was dead; my body, my emotions had taken over. All I felt was rage. As if I'd caught Jakey's anger like a cold.

I walked into the darkened bedroom where my mother was sleeping. I stood beside the bed, staring at her. I hated her. It was her fault that he'd left, that he'd left *me*. It had to be. I hadn't done anything, had I? I was the one he loved. He'd never have left me. I hated her. I hated her in the wedding picture on the dressing table, the one standing on the doily next to her glass perfume tray. I wanted to smash the picture of her holding calla lilies, standing next to him, in her long white satin gown.

She was seventeen years old in that wedding portrait; and he was twenty-six. They had been secretly married for more than two years.

My mother, Tillie, was only thirteen years old when Sol Sadowsky swept her off her feet. He was tall and handsome, armed with a quick smile, a facile phrase, and the raw energy and ambition of an American. A big man, relentless in pursuit of what he wanted. And, at thirteen, Tillie was it—a beautiful child, a refugee from Eastern Europe who spoke English gamely but haltingly, a pale, fragile-looking girl with blonde hair and coal-black eyes. To him she must have seemed a treasured and protected child, but at thirteen she'd already had enough sorrow and adventures to fill a normal lifetime.

Her mother and father had been murdered in a pogrom. At three years old, she'd gone to live with her mother's sister, Tohba, and her husband, Sholem. Orthodox Jews, they'd been forced to flee Russia, and Tillie's childhood was spent wandering through a Europe crushed by poverty and hostile to Jews. When finally her aunt and uncle managed passage to America, they adopted Tillie. Despite the fact that she was always called "the orphan child," she was adored by her adoptive parents and, reared in their Orthodox household, was considered pious, loving, and sensible. The brothers born after her, Jake, Marty, and Leo, had always been protective and respectful of her.

And she of them. So much so that although she was a married woman at fifteen, she went home to her aunt and uncle's house every night and told no one of the marriage until she turned seventeen. Then she announced that she was engaged to Sol Sadowsky. Everyone knew she'd been seeing him for years, knew how unaccountably constant he'd been, probably marveled that a man of his reputation had acted with such faithful restraint. Pleased and undoubtedly relieved for her, the family threw Sol and Tillie a mighty wedding. It was years before anyone discovered that on her wedding day, the orphan child was already married.

She was not a child anymore. She was, to me, that day and for years to follow, my enemy—the woman whose ignorance of fashion, coquetry, compromise had driven my father away. I turned from the wedding portrait remembering the nights they'd fought. It was her voice I remembered, her shrill, unforgiving anger. Her tears and outrage at his broken promises, the gambling debts, the increasing, unexplained absences. It was the terrible feeling of helplessness I remembered, of lying in bed and listening and knowing, somehow, that my future was being decided by my mother's unhappiness.

I left her—in the room that Monday afternoon and in the wreckage of my adolescent heart. I turned to Enid for consolation. And so did my mother. And Enid was always there for us, helping with a few bucks, a little food, words of comfort and encouragement. My uncle Meyer, from whom my father had stolen, also sent money and food. It was true what my mother's brothers had said:

Sol had cleaned us out. He'd taken every cent he could get his hands on. There was no money for rent, for clothes, for food. He'd left us to starve.

It was the end of normalcy. I'd never loved school, but I'd had friends there. If I wasn't a great student, I had other attributes. I was admired for my personality and spirit and sense of humor. I dressed well. I was tall and maybe a bit self-conscious about my height and developing body, but I was reasonably attractive and, under Enid's tutelage, getting good at making the most of my dark eyes and pale skin and dark, auburn hair.

Now, shame bowed me. My eyes were bloodshot and swollen from crying night after night, and dark from lack of sleep. My skin grew sallow. My shoulders were rounded with despair. I felt and looked like hell.

Shame kept me from my friends, too. Just being around kids who had normal, two-parent families caused me pain. I felt separate, different, cast out. My father had abandoned me. My flamboyant, high-living father had run off leaving us destitute. Potatoes mashed with *shmaltz*, eggs and onions became our nightly protein-balanced meal. My mother, half mad with grief, got a job in a dry-cleaning store, handling other people's dirty clothes. I worked part-time at a shoe store. Every cent we earned went toward helping us survive. And I thought everyone knew and everyone believed—as I must have in my deepest, secret heart—that I'd done something to deserve it.

My best friend, my only friend now, was Leona, who had, by my reckoning, as screwed up a family life as I now did. She was a Polish-Greek Catholic with three bizarre brothers—the nine-year-old walked around the house in high-heeled shoes—and a bus-driver father who made Ralph Kramden look like a Rhodes scholar.

I began to cut school regularly. I couldn't study or concentrate on anything. Almost every day, I'd break down crying in class. Run out, mortified. Find Leona. Go with her to Garfield's Cafeteria and smoke and drink coffee among the old men until it was time to go home. I had avoided my friends. Now they began to gossip about me, to shun me. Rumor was I stayed away from school because I was pregnant. There was no other way for them to explain my sudden tears or why I hid from them. And there was no way for me to explain the separateness and shame I felt.

Finally, the truancy and misery overwhelmed me and I dropped out of Erasmus Hall High. I had turned sixteen. There'd been no celebration, no sugar corsage or birthday cake. My father had left and taken my childhood with him.

From the lofty height of my high-heeled shoes, I looked down on my school girlfriends. I was still sixteen but I was a working woman now, wearing nylon stockings and earning $45 a week at the shoe store. I'd enrolled in adult evening classes to get my diploma. I contributed my salary to the household. Still, there was never enough money at home, and that was not the only scarcity. Energy, laughter, optimism, and joy were also in short supply. So that fall, at the invitation of my mother's cousins who had a big house in Beverly Hills and two kids approximately the same ages as Marlene and I, we moved to California.

If I'd felt like an outsider among my Brooklyn classmates, I felt like a Martian among the blue-eyed blondes of Beverly Hills, who drove their own convertibles to school, dressed like they'd stepped out of *Seventeen* magazine, and lived the kind of lives I'd only seen in movies. It was as if I were watching some blinding Technicolor extravaganza from the last row of a dark theater.

Nearly every morning I'd leave our cousin Helen's sprawling Tudor mansion and find a bench along the way to school. There I'd sit, in all my angry, adolescent New York-ness, cutting school, staring out at brilliant sunlight, turquoise cars, tanned people, palm trees. And I'd long to return to Flatbush, to drink coffee with Leona in the smoky comfort of Garfield's Cafeteria, to be back in Brooklyn where I knew who was who, what was what, and how to pronounce it.

One day, when we'd been in California about a month, I saw someone sitting on one of *my* benches. A kid hunched over like a little old lady, with a couple of school books and a loose-leaf binder beside her. As I got closer, I recognized the dejected little girl. It was my sister, Marlene, who was nine years old then. I was shocked to discover that she was as miserable and lonely in Beverly Hills as I was.

That night at dinner I announced to my mother that I was leaving. "With you or without you," I said, "I'm going back. I can't stand it here. I ask for a cup of coffee 'regular.' It's bad enough that I say, 'caw-fee' and they say, 'calf-ee.' But they think 'regular' means *black*—with milk on the side!"

"Big deal," she said. "You'll get used to it."

"I don't want to get used to it. I want to go home! If I have to beg, borrow, or steal the airfare I will. But I'm going back to Brooklyn."

"Stop it, Sandy." My mother shook her head and sighed. "You're just a kid. Who's going to take care of you? Where are you going to live?"

We'd given up the apartment on Lincoln Road. Home was no longer a place.

"I'll get my job back in the shoe store," I said. "I don't need you or anyone to support me. I can do it myself and I will."

Two weeks later, after a lot of screaming and fighting, my cousin gave me the airfare. I packed a suitcase and returned to New York alone. I got a job—in a training program at AT&T. I even re-enrolled in night school. And I lived with any friend or relative who'd put me up for a night or two. It was lonely and exhausting. I lived out of the single suitcase I'd brought with me. It was a fierce winter, and I was still in aching shock over the sudden destruction of our family. Between the weather, work and school, and the gypsy life I was living, I was constantly tired. And very relieved when, a couple of months before my seventeenth birthday, my mother and Marlene returned from California.

We moved into a single room with a kitchenette and bathroom a couple of blocks from our former, two-bedroom apartment. It was cramped and ugly, but I was grateful to have a home base, a place where I could finally hang up my clothes.

The relief and gratitude I felt were secrets I kept from my mother. I no longer trusted her. The shabby apartment where we all slept in one room I added to my list of grievances against her. I still held her responsible for my father's leaving, for the devastation of our family. Not only had he gone, but he might as well have taken her with him for all the good she was doing us now. She'd become useless, a depressed drudge incapable of anything but anger or tears. She clung to her family. She had no friends left. And, in my terrible, callow cruelty, I let her know it every chance I got.

I knew what would make her wince. "You drove him away," I'd shout at her. "He's probably found another woman."

Enid was no longer our neighbor. My mother stopped seeing her. And with work and school occupying all my time, I hardly ever visited our old building where Enid and Merv still lived. One day, I saw Enid's green Buick parked across the street from our new place.

"Sandy!" She rolled down the window and called to me. "Come over here, honey. I want to talk to you."

I climbed into the front seat beside her.

"Your father wants to see you," she said.

I was stunned. I turned and looked over my shoulder, half-expecting to see my father in the backseat. "Where is he? You know where he is? You've talked to him?"

She was lighting up a Pall Mall. Her manicured fingernails were blood-red against the white cigarette. She shrugged and stuck the lighter back into the dashboard. "He wants to see you, Sandy. I'll take you to him. But don't tell your mother. Okay?"

Dumbfounded, I nodded my head. "Where are we going?" I asked, as she pulled away from the curb. "How did he get hold of you? Did he call? Have you been in touch with him all along?"

"He's talked to Merv a couple of times," she said uncomfortably.

We parked on a Brooklyn street near a luncheonette my father had liked. As we walked toward the shop, I saw him. He was standing just outside the luncheonette, handsome as ever in a dark overcoat, his thick white hair ruffled by the wind. He was smoking a cigar and he gave me a crooked smile. "Hi, sweetheart," he said.

I ran to hug him, my heart bursting with joy and relief. He was back. His troubles were over. He was coming home!

But he turned to Enid who was standing a few steps off to the side and put his arm around her. "There's something you should know, Sandy," my father said. "Enid and I are in love—we have been for many years. We're going to get married as soon as our divorces come through."

I stared at him, incredulous. For years? "You were having an affair before you left us?"

My father nodded, the cigar bobbing merrily up and down.

"We didn't want to hurt you or your mother, Sandy," Enid said. "These things happen. I hope when you're older you'll understand."

I found myself nodding as if, sure, I understood. I couldn't speak. My main concern was that my father was going away again.

He pulled away from Enid and bent toward me, taking the cigar out of his mouth. "You'll always be my angel, Sandy," he said. "What happened between your mother and me has nothing to do with you. But now, I need your help. Can you help your old man, Sandy?"

I nodded again, waiting.

"Your grandfather left you a little money, sweetheart. Twenty-five hundred, right? I need you to lend me some. Not a lot. Just half of it. I'll pay you back, Sandy. Just as soon as I'm on my feet again. I promise."

"But I can't touch that money till I'm twenty-one—"

"You can with my consent. I'm your legal guardian," my father explained. He took my hand and we all walked to the bank together. Inside, he helped me fill out the necessary forms, told me what to say, and where to sign. And I withdrew half of my inheritance and gave it to him.

"Daddy," I asked him outside the bank, "do you think I could come live with you? I'm working now. I could help out."

"Sure," he said. "I'd really like that, sweetheart." He kissed me on the forehead. "I'll call you, Sandy. Soon."

I didn't see him again for twenty-six years.

My father had his gambling debts. My mother had her broken heart. And suddenly, I'd had enough of both of them.

For more than a year and a half, my life had been decided by *their* problems, their secrets and misery: where and how I lived, what I wore, who I saw, and who I hid from. I'd been shlepped from coast to coast, from security to destitution, from childhood to adulthood with no time out for adolescence. Sadness and anger had become my constant companions: They woke me in the morning and put me to sleep at night. Then, shortly after my father let the I-Love-Enid cat out of the bag, everything changed.

Fun was what I wanted. And I didn't care how fast or far I had to run to find it. Where there was a good time to be had, that was where I was going to be.

Garfield's Cafeteria on Church Avenue was just the starting gate. It was open twenty-four hours a day. You could sit around with a cup of coffee for at least twenty-three of them before someone would wipe yesterday's food off the table and give you the boot. After nine at night, the *alter kockers* and the squares cleared out and the cool crowd took over. Leona and I met there nearly every night.

After dinner—which I'd have at home to save a couple of bucks—I'd put my hair up into a long ponytail, pencil in thick black doe eyes, and slip into a cardigan sweater buttoned down the back and tight black Toreador pants. In black flats (which took me from my workday high-heeled five-ten—too tall for the neighborhood boys—to a nearly normal five-eight), I'd run to meet Leona at Garfield's.

Sitting at a table at the back of the blue-tiled cafeteria, we'd nurse our coffee and chain-smoke and alternate laughing too loudly with trying to look blasé—blasé was a cool thing to be. And blowing smoke rings was a blasé thing to do. Seductively, we'd pout circles of smoke into the air and stab at them with the lit end of our cigarettes. "Don't let it die a virgin," we'd laugh. Sometimes, we'd ask one of the guys for a light. Wreathed in blue smoke, we schemed and dreamed and watched the guys with Marlboro packs rolled up in their T-shirt sleeves, combing back their DAs—Duck's Ass hairdos—and hiking up the collars of their black leather motorcycle jackets.

It was 1956. I was almost eighteen. Brando had already won his first Oscar for *On the Waterfront.* Elvis had just made his movie debut in *Love Me Tender.* But for Brooklyn girls, the boy of the moment was our home-grown native son, Tony Curtis. And Arnold, who leaned over from the next table and lit my cigarette in Garfield's one night, was a perfect Curtis clone. Brilliantined black hair, swept back at the sides and cresting over his forehead. Blue eyes surrounded by thick black lashes. A smoldering smile. A Brooklyn accent. And he was in acting school in the city. *The* city—Manhattan. Arnold was irresistible. And of all the leggy, big-breasted girls in Garfield's, it was me he reached for through the smoke.

Arnold introduced me to Manhattan nightlife. His favorite hangout was Jilly's on Fifty-second Street. He knew everyone in the small, dimly lit piano bar where Nicky DeFrancis played "Fly Me to the Moon" and guys in sharkskin suits and pinky rings bought Manhattans and Seven-and-Sevens for Garment Center models. Arnold told me my body was as good as the suit-and-coat models' who hung out at Jilly's. Hell, I was tall enough, and I had a great bust, a tiny waist. I was a perfect size eight. And, come on, did I want to be a telephone operator for the rest of my life? Arnold was all for self-improvement. Hey, why did I think he was taking acting lessons?

The girls I met at Jilly's seconded the motion. Marilyn, who was twenty-one and modeling for Miller and Shulman Coats and Suits, thought I'd do great in the Garment Center. Judy, a hairdresser from Glasgow, Kentucky, who worked in a famous New York salon, absolutely agreed with her. "With yo' looks, honey," she'd drawl, "why you bustin' that pretty little butt for peanuts?" I was

earning about $65 a week at AT&T. Marilyn made twice that for
walking around a showroom looking pretty.

So I signed up for a night course at the Barbizon School of Modeling. And now when I walked into Jilly's to meet Arnold, I was
toting the round black patent leather Barbizon Model's hat box the
school had given me—along with lessons on how to walk, wear a
hat and gloves, diet, makeup, and exercise. In those days, exercise
meant getting strapped, with a sling around your butt, onto a machine that shimmied you till your breasts banged against your arms
and your teeth felt loose. And, boy, was I proud. I was studying to
be a model. I had a boyfriend who was going to be an actor, who
looked just like Tony Curtis, and knew everyone from the drop-
dead gorgeous greasers at Garfield's to the celebs at Jilly's. Arnold
even knew Cole Porter's bodyguard and masseur, Steve.

One night, the three of us went up to Porter's apartment in the
Waldorf Towers. A valet let us into a spacious entry hall that led to
a huge livingroom with floor-to-ceiling windows overlooking the
Manhattan skyline. A grand piano sat near the windows on thick
gold carpeting. The furnishings, like the scale of the rooms, were
oversized. Deep velvet club chairs and an enormous plush sofa.
Cole Porter looked almost lost in the upholstery. He hoisted himself out of the sofa to greet us. I was surprised to notice that he
limped. He was very gracious, very warm, and almost shy.

At Steve's or Arnold's suggestion, he showed me through the
suite. It was the first time I'd seen a private library—an entire
room filled with shelves of books, a leather-paneled desk, a
wooden pedestal on which stood a rotating globe of the world.
The bathrooms—any one of which was larger than our entire
apartment—were carpeted. There were gold-flecked mirrors on the
bedroom ceiling. Porter had his own massage room.

He offered us drinks, which his valet fixed. And, as I sunk sleep-
ily into one of the big club chairs in the livingroom, Cole Porter sat
at the piano and played "Begin the Beguine" and "Night and Day."
Later, I woke in that chair and listened to Steve, Cole, and Arnold
talking. I couldn't hear every word, but there was an intimacy in
their tone and manner. I remember thinking that they must all be
very good friends. I remember wondering whether Steve was
gay—queer, we called it then—and then, a fleeting, silly thought,
whether Arnold might be AC/DC.

When Cole Porter was out of town, Steve threw parties in that
magnificent eight-room apartment in the Waldorf. The crowd was
wild, mixed, young, and trashy. Broadway dancers, starlets,

whores. The women all seemed to be named Nikki, and came in carrying little dogs in their hands. The guys were gorgeous, mostly gay. I'd stand in a corner hanging on to a drink, my brown eyes as wide as they could get through the stinging smoke, staring at the scene and hoping Arnold would find me soon and take me home.

A few months before my nineteenth birthday, after I'd become a genuine Seventh Avenue showroom model, Arnold and I broke up. His mother stormed our Brooklyn apartment demanding back the friendship ring he'd given me.

Arnold got to keep the ring; I got to keep the terrific friends I'd made at Jilly's. A couple of nights a week I'd stay in the city at Marilyn's apartment—she was Jewish and still lived with her parents. Or at Judy's when her boyfriend, the guy who owned the renowned salon she worked in, went home to Scarsdale to spend a night with his wife and kids. He was paying rent on the apartment, which was just above his shop in the East Fifties. It was a simple arrangement. He paid the rent, he got first dibs on the bed. One of the things that made his salon famous was that it was open very, very late to accommodate celebrities, showgirls, call girls, and other clients who lived a reversed night and day existence. It was one of them, a stunning redheaded friend of Judy's, who decided at Jilly's one night that I had just what it took to be a fabulous Las Vegas showgirl.

Sure, it made sense to her, I thought. And if she drinks two more screwdrivers, she'll decide I ought to run for Miss Rheingold. "I don't sing, dance, or act, and I've got a Brooklyn accent," I reminded her. "And anyway, I'm making nice money modeling now."

So, okay, my legs were getting palsied from walking around in five-inch heels a hundred hours a day. My arms were starting to look like Charles Atlas's from lifting seven-pound coats—putting them on, taking them off, twirling, shlepping them back to the dressing room and reappearing a minute later in a five-pound, two-piece suit under yet another seven-pound coat. Ah, the glamour of the showroom model's life. But what the hell, I was taking home close to $125 a week, which in 1957, 1958, was a month's rent on a nice little three-room apartment in Manhattan.

"Showgirls don't sing and dance, silly. They just walk around in fabulous costumes and earn three hundred a week."

"Three hundred . . . A week?!" I was floored.

"Three hundred, three fifty . . . And that's just salary," Judy's friend explained. "They fly you there and you get room and board free."

"Over my dead body," my mother said when I told her.

I'd answered an ad. The Desert Inn wanted me. "Ma, I'll be able to send home about two hundred fifty a week. And it's like camp, for God's sake. We stay in *dormitories*."

"You know what a *courva* is?" she asked.

"A hooker. But Ma, I'm going to be a showgirl, not a hooker. I'll live in a dorm with other girls. We'll be supervised. I'll be as safe as if I were in a girls' boarding school."

"A showgirl. You'll walk around naked on high-heeled shoes with fruit on your head. This is a job? For *shiksas*, for *courvas* this is a job, not for nice Jewish girls," my mother said.

We were at the kitchen table. On the daybed behind us, my open suitcase was packed. All I needed to add before snapping it shut was the cosmetic case that pear-shaped Noah, one of my Garment Center admirers, who ran the drugstore in the lobby of the building where I worked, had given me as a going-away gift. I was stuffing cotton balls into the pretty pink case as fast as I could. My mother was pushing crumbs from our breakfast rolls around a plate, and shaking her head, and sighing with exasperation. "Las Vegas, *feh!*" she said. "Who knows what you'll meet there, the kind of men waiting to take advantage of a girl like you. A girl? No, a baby!"

She was right. In Las Vegas, I was a baby. I was not just chronologically younger than most of the girls I lived and worked with. Emotionally, I was an infant. From the moment I stepped off the plane into the white desert sunlight, I became a homesick, nervous wreck hiding behind a perpetual, dazed smile.

The showgirls and dancers lived behind The Desert Inn in a two-story annex that looked like a motel. I shared a room with a pair of tough little blonde Barbie dolls from the midwest who'd been in Vegas for a while, knew the ropes and how to wind them around the wallets of heavy hitters in the casino after hours. I thought three hundred a week plus room and board was sumptuous. Donna and Lureene thought it was chump change.

They, and some of the other more experienced girls, were very patient and protective with me. They teased me about my accent, my innocence, the bounty of my breasts. They taught me how to make up like a showgirl. Enid's false eyelashes and over-the-lip-line penciling was conservative, subtle compared to the bigger-than-life-showgirl look we were after. Max Factor Pan-Cake makeup slathered from the dark roots of your hair to the deep cleft of your cleavage—applied with damp sponges in which the makeup oils had long ago turned rancid. Soft, coal-black eye pencil drawn heavily across the top lids of your eyes, sweeping up half-way across your temples. Bright red lipstick emphasizing the brightest, whitest, seductive smiles money could buy.

We wore the makeup on stage a couple of hours a night. We wore it with our amazing sequined-and-spangled costumes, in Merry Widow corselettes that could cinch a twenty-two-inch waistline down to a mere nineteen inches—because looking great was more important than breathing. In flesh-colored tights and stiletto heels we moved into the blinding spotlight. We walked gracefully, desperately, under elaborate headdresses that soared up out of tiny sequined skull caps anchored with bobby pins that made you feel like a human pin cushion balancing a chandelier on your head.

I loved being on stage. After the initial terror had passed, of tripping or having the great plumed headdress tilt or tumble, moving into that spotlight, walking out of the wings to center stage, was a fantasy come true. A transformation. I was no longer Sandy Sadowsky of Flatbush, Brooklyn. I was a performer, a glamorous Vegas showgirl.

We wore the makeup on stage a couple of hours a night, but, more importantly, we wore it after the shows to let the big spenders in the casino know that we were showgirls.

The stage shows I'd been so apprehensive about turned out to be the easiest part of life in Vegas. I'd work until close to three in the morning, grab a quick, free meal at the casino coffee shop, sleep for a few hours, and then get up to rehearse for most of the day. It was a grueling schedule, even for an energetic nineteen-year-old. But the money was great—or so I thought until Donna set me straight.

"Three hundred bucks?" She looked at me and shook her head as though I were a drooling embarrassment.

We were putting on our makeup, sitting alongside half a dozen other girls at the long, mirrored table we shared in the dressing room. It was noisy, chaotic, and warm. And I'd said something about how nice it was to be making *real* money.

"Compared to what you could be raking in—with that body and those big brown eyes, Sandy—three hundred bucks is nothing," Donna concluded.

"Well, sorry. But I'm not a hooker," I said.

"Well, sorry!" She laughed. "I wasn't talking about hooking.

Listen, after the show, we'll change and walk through the casino and I'll show you what I mean."

That night, between the first and second shows, we walked out to the vast carpeted casino, past rows of clanging slot machines and green felt-covered blackjack tables crowded with players who were drinking, smoking, and betting with equal intensity. As Donna led me toward the craps tables, she gave me the drill: "Okay, now, you'll stand on one side of the guys and I'll be on the other. All you have to do is ask me if I'm going to play. Got it? We just mosey over and you give it a half a minute and then you say, 'So, Donna, are you playing tonight?' "

The craps table we stopped at was jammed with high rollers. There were guys standing behind piles of chips, pushing one, two, three chips, blues, reds, yellows, onto the numbers and watching the dice hit the felt and not even blinking as the croupier raked in the chips they'd lost. Donna moved toward a guy whose eyes were pinned to the table action. He had rolls of chips in his hands and he was toying with them, as if he couldn't wait to put them down on the next number. He polished off a glass of booze and ordered another from a passing waitress as Donna sidled up next to him.

I worked my way up to the table, a couple of players away from her. "Donna," I called, "are you going to play?"

She ran her fingers through her long blonde hair and gave a little shrug. "I can't tonight," she answered. "I don't have any money."

The guy standing next to her looked up. He gave her the once-over, then, boom, he pushed a stack of chips in front of her. "You're in, babe," he said, and turned back to the game.

My mouth fell open.

Donna slid a couple of the chips onto the felt. And, cautiously, quickly, scooped the rest into the little handbag she was carrying. She played the chips on the table, then moved on.

"See, the thing is these guys stop thinking of chips as real money. And it's part of the game to give chips to pretty girls, especially showgirls," she said, as we hurried back to the dressing room for the next show. "They're smoking, they're drinking, they're bombed, they get generous. On a good night, you can pick up an extra couple of hundred dollars . . . and, baby cakes," she added with a wink, "you don't have to unzip a thing."

Needless to say I did not mention this newfound skill to Tillie during my weekly phone calls home. And, to tell the truth, while it made me feel grown up and glamorous for a while to walk through the casino at three A.M. in full showgirl makeup, gold hoops dangling from my ears, in tight black Toreador pants, black ballet slippers, and a blouse unbuttoned to flash just enough Max-Factored cleavage to rake in a roll or two of chips, the game never countered my homesickness. Las Vegas was very exciting, very full of wise guys and easy money in the late fifties but, to tell the truth, the generous guys weren't always so befuddled with booze and gambling that they didn't want a pound of flesh for a handful of chips. And, to tell the truth, which I never did to my mother, Donna, Lureene, and some of the other girls who'd befriended me did "date" for money from time to time, and if they weren't certified hookers, they lived with a similar contempt and desperation for men and money. For the most part, the Vegas showgirls I met were there for one of two reasons: to land a husband or to move up in a performing career; and in both areas they were ruthlessly competitive.

Nights were days and days were nights. There were no rules. I was a nervous wreck most of the time. And twenty minutes a night in the spotlight didn't balance out the fear and loneliness I experienced daily.

So six weeks after I left New York, I telephoned Tillie and made her the happiest Jewish mother in Flatbush. "Ma," I said, "you were right. It's a *shiksa*'s life out here. I'm coming home."

CHAPTER TWO

The Velvet Room

In Vegas, the girls sometimes called me a bookworm because I'd stay in the Annex reading instead of cruising the casino at night. Some of them thought I was crazy. Most of them figured it was because I was Jewish and that along with having horns, killing Christ, and barbecuing gentile babies for Passover, Jews were just naturally brainy.

But I left my reputation as a bookish recluse in the desert. Back in New York, I jumped into nightlife with a new vengeance.

Judy or Marilyn, Patty or Nikki would say: "Okay, where are we going tonight?"

We'd be gathered around the piano bar at Jilly's, or filling little plates with steaming free hors d'oeuvres at the El Borracho on East Fifty-fourth, or fixing our makeup in the ladies' room at Billy Reed's Little Club.

And someone would call out the name of a nightspot in town. And within five minutes, we'd bat our eyelashes at whoever was picking up our tab and move on to the next, better, newer, hotter club. Then as now, many of them were owned, run, or frequented by the mob.

It was the spring of '59. Eisenhower was golfing away his last term as president. Nobody cared about Nixon, least of all Ike who, asked to name one of his vice president's outstanding accomplishments, said: "Give me a week and I might think of one." Hardly anyone outside of Massachusetts had heard of John F. Kennedy.

But if you walked into a Manhattan supper club or afterhours joint, you'd hear people whispering:

"Wow, there's Anthony Strollo, the one they call 'Tony Bender.' Runs the Jersey waterfront."

Or: "That's 'Tony Ducks' from the Teamsters, the blue-eyed guy in the horn-rimmed glasses."

Or: "Oh my God, is that Johnny Dio?"

And you'd stare in awe at the faces you'd seen on the front page of yesterday's *Daily News*. Celebrities.

One of the hottest new spots in town that boasted such "celebrities" was an elegant supper club in the Brittany Hotel on East Tenth Street in Greenwich Village.

"It's called The Velvet Room," Judy's redheaded friend Nina told us. "Right, baby?" She was toying with the suit lapels of a guy named Zippy, who had something to do with the International Ladies' Garment Union.

About eight of us had assembled at Jilly's, and now we were hungry and eager to move on. Noah the pear-shaped druggist, my old admirer from Seventh Avenue, was picking up the bill for Marilyn, Judy, and me. With one of the three little black cocktail dresses I owned, I was wearing the artificial pearls he'd given me a couple of weeks before—to celebrate my promotion from off-the-rack modeling to couture suits and coats.

"The Veyl-vet Room," drawled Judy. "Sounds sexy."

It was. A big, tufted black leather door opened onto a red carpeted entryway, behind which sprawled a long, polished mahogany bar. Walls flocked in a red and cream fleur-de-lis pattern were reflected in the huge, gold-specked mirror behind the bar. Chandeliers and crystal wall sconces bathed the room in a soft pink glow.

Beyond the lounge area, the dining room curled around a little piano bar and dance floor. An elaborate mahogany and glass divider separated the two rooms. The tables were set with white linen, candles, and flowers.

Nina's boyfriend, Zippy, had phoned ahead. The maitre d' led our party of eight to a long table at the edge of the dance floor.

We'd just gotten our drinks and were checking out the menus when, "Sandela! Yoo-hoo, Sandy!" a husky voice bellowed.

"Oh, shit," I said.

It was Helen, one of my mother's few still-loyal friends.

Although she was classically beautiful with fine chiseled features, deep-set eyes, and pale hair swept back in an elegant chignon, when Helen drank she became a wild woman capable of anything. I froze at the table and raised my eyes to heaven—or the nearest thing to it—the cream-colored ceiling of the dining room. God, please, I prayed, don't let her embarrass me.

It was too late.

"Who is that?" Judy asked as Helen careened from the banquette against the back wall toward our table, thudding against chairs, wine buckets, and waiters along the way.

"A friend of my mother's from Brooklyn."

"She's gorgeous," Marilyn said.

"She's bombed out of her gourd," said Nina.

"She's your mother's friend?" Noah, whose attention was riveted to the creamy front of Helen's low-cut dress, couldn't believe it.

"She used to live downstairs from us. She's ten years younger than my mother. About thirty, I think."

"Sandela! What are you doing here? You look gorgeous. Come, sweetheart. Come, *shayna*—" She grabbed my wrist and started pulling me to my feet. "I want you to meet my fiancé," she said, pointing to the man she was with. To avoid a scene, I got up and walked her back to the banquette. "Sandy, this is my fiancé, Bernie Barton," Helen said. "He owns the place."

The man in the booth smiled and rose slightly. The most amazing pair of baby blue eyes I'd ever seen fastened onto mine.

"Bernie," Helen said. "This is my friend Tillie's daughter, Sandy. Is she gorgeous, or what?"

Never taking his eyes off mine, he nodded, amused. "Hey, kid," he said. His voice was gravel. His hand in mine was soft and cool.

I sat with them for a few minutes. I don't remember what I said. Nice to meet you. Your restaurant is beautiful. I don't remember what he said, except that he made me laugh, made me feel comfortable and nervous at the same time: comfortable because I felt that he liked me; nervous because he was Helen's boyfriend, old enough to be my father, and I found him very attractive. People stopped by the table. People treated him with deference and respect. You could tell they were pleased when he kidded with them, or stood to shake a hand.

I excused myself and returned to my friends. "He owns the place," I told Judy. "He's a doll. He's funny and bright. I can't figure out what he's doing with Helen, though. She's been married and divorced twice already and she's got a new boyfriend every other day."

Sometime later, I went to the powder room. The banquette

where Bernie and Helen had been sitting was empty. Scanning the
room quickly, I didn't see either of them. I was disappointed.

To get to the bathrooms, you had to walk out of The Velvet
Room and into the Brittany's lobby through a corridor of telephone
booths. The booths were the old-fashioned kind that had wooden
doors with glass panels in the top half. There was a bald guy with a
phone to his ear in one of the booths. He wasn't speaking, just grinning. When I came out of the powder room, ten minutes later, he
was still leaning back against the wall of the booth, holding the receiver. He was still grinning, but his expression had changed to one
of glassy-eyed ecstasy.

Curiosity got the best of me and, as I passed, I peered cautiously
into the booth. And saw that he had company, a woman on her
knees who was giving him . . . reason to smile.

I kept walking and started to laugh.

"Hey, kid." The gravel voice stopped me in my tracks. Bernie
Barton was standing in front of me. "Give me your number," he
said. "I'd like to take you out."

There was no doubt in my mind that I wanted to see him again.
But it wasn't as easy as all that. "I can't," I said. "You're engaged
to my mother's friend."

Bernie laughed. He had big, perfect white teeth. His amazing
blue eyes crinkled at the corners. "Helen? Come on," he said.
"She's everyone's fiancée."

I tried not to smile but I knew what he'd meant.

I was wearing my highest heels that night and he was just a bit
taller than I, built strong and solid as a prize fighter, with thick dark
hair that was not exactly gray but lighter at the temples.

Bernie Barton took my hand. The shirt under his Glen Plaid suit
jacket was powder blue, almost the same shade as his eyes. The
collar and cuffs were white and, as I looked down at his hand holding mine, I noticed the monogram on his cuff, "BB." That's what
they had called him—"BB" or "Mr. B"—the guys, the cigarette
girl, who'd come by the table while I was sitting with him and
Helen.

"You've got to," he said, teasing. "I own the joint. You're on my
turf, you do what I say."

Under the grin was a will of iron.

He handed me a matchbook from the club and I wrote down my
number for him. "Okay," I said, "but I don't know if I can go out
with you."

"Sure, kid," he said, pocketing the matchbook. "I understand."

* * *

He called me the next day.

"I'm sorry, Mr. Barton," I said, "I told you yesterday. I'm not the kind of girl who goes out with another woman's man."

I wasn't trying to be coy or cute—I wouldn't have known how with this man. I'd seen him in action, on his own turf as he'd called it. The people who'd stopped by his table at The Velvet Room last night had done everything but bow or curtsy to him. He excited and intimidated me. He seemed so sure of himself, so determined about what he wanted. And that he wanted to see me seemed an enormous compliment.

But Helen had called him her fiancé and, no matter how we'd joked about it last night, I couldn't go out with a man who belonged to someone else. Not after what Enid had done to my mother.

"Listen, kid," Bernie said, with just a trace of impatience, "I told *you* yesterday that I'm not going with the lady. Now, why don't you give her a ring and ask her. I've got to get back to work. I'll talk to you later."

It took me an hour to get up the nerve to call Helen. I kept playing through the scene, imagining Helen as my naive and loyal mother and me in the evil Enid role. Finally, I stubbed out my cigarette and dialed the number.

"Bernie wants to go out with me," I blurted out, close to tears. "Is he really your fiancé?"

Helen burst out laughing. "Oh, baby, poor baby," she said. "No. Go out with him if you want to. I called him my fiancé? Oh, my God, he'll never speak to me again. You want to see him, be my guest. But, Sandy baby, listen—Bernie Barton is not someone to take seriously. You know how old he is, baby? Forty. And he's been around. He's a gangster. He was in the rackets. He's been in jail. For a good time, a little fun, he's fine. Just don't get serious with him."

So Bernie Barton was a gangster. What did that mean? Helen might just as well have said he's exciting, dangerous, he's a man with a past. That's what I knew about gangsters. They weren't real. They were celebrities. Stars. Bigger than life. The eight-inch black and white screen of the Philco television console in our old Brooklyn living room on which I'd seen the Kefauver hearings had seemed too small to contain them.

While other kids were mesmerized by Howdy Doody and Winky Dink, I'd watched Frank Costello's hands fooling with the water pitcher at the senate hearings table. And listened to guys "take the Fifth"—the Fifth Amendment—and respectfully refuse to answer questions on the grounds that the answers might tend to incriminate them.

What I remembered most of all about the hearings, which I'd catch when I came home from school, was Virginia Hill. She was a beautiful hillbilly who'd gone out with some top mobsters. They said she'd been Joe Adonis's girl and then Bugsy Siegel's. And there she was in her low-cut black dress and wide-brimmed black picture hat, in sunglasses with a silver fox jacket draped across her shoulders. Notorious, glamorous, mysterious were the words most used to describe her. And when they questioned her about the nightclub she owned and all her other assets, Virginia didn't take the Fifth. She said, "Men lahks to give me money."

I was only twelve or thirteen when the racketeering hearings were televised and that was what I remembered: Virginia Hill saying, "Men lahks to give me money." I thought she was sensational.

When Bernie called me later, just as he'd said he would, I agreed to go out with him the next night. He said, "Good. Okay, kid. I'll send a car for you." And when, at exactly eight o'clock, the doorbell rang and a well-dressed older man announced that he was Mr. Barton's driver and that the car was waiting at the curb, I kissed my frowning mother's face, gave my wide-eyed little sister, Marlene, a hug, and swept grandly out the door thinking, wow, this is the life.

Mr. Barton's driver held open the car door and for the first time in my life, I climbed into the plush backseat of a beautiful black limousine. Bernie was going to meet me at the club, but he'd sent flowers and arranged to have a bottle of champagne chilling in an ice bucket in the limo and Frank Sinatra crooning through the speakers. Feeling alternately sophisticated and like a kid playing movie star, I poured myself a glass of champagne and settled back against the velour seats for the trip from Brooklyn to Manhattan. A trip, I gleefully reminded myself, that I'd made countless times—in my unfortunate former life—by subway.

I had finished two glasses of champagne and was feeling pretty good by the time the limo pulled up in front of The Velvet Room. I smoothed back my hair and readjusted the black ribbon around my high ponytail. I smoothed down the snug black sheath I was wearing and adjusted my string of pearls so that the clasp was at the nape of my neck where it belonged. I slicked on a fresh coat of bright red lipstick, made sure the doe eyes weren't smeared or the false lashes hanging askew. But somewhere between the curb and the big tufted leather door I became suddenly stone-cold sober and very unsure of myself.

I was totally unprepared for the way Bernie Barton's eyes lit up when I walked into the lounge. He was at a table up front, in the bar. He was in conversation with another guy and he looked up, straight at me, as if radar had told him I was in the room.

He stood and came toward me. "You look great, kid," he said in his husky voice. He looked me up and down. "Beautiful, baby," he said, walking me over to the table. "Isn't she beautiful?" he said to the heavyset older guy he'd been talking with. It thrilled me to hear the pride in his voice. "This is Ziggy Schwartz," Bernie said. "We grew up together."

"We did a lot of things together," Ziggy said good-naturedly. He laughed and shook his head. "*Oy-oy-oy*, Bernie. You're gonna do time for this one."

"She's worth it," Bernie kibitzed back. "What're you drinking, kid?"

I asked for something fruity—I think grapefruit juice and vodka—and Bernie raised his eyebrows a little, then smiled. He snapped his fingers and someone was there in a second to take the order.

We sat down with Ziggy who, it turned out, was the head of a Teamsters local. He was a little drunk and said a lot of things that Bernie shook his head over, and told me a lot more about Bernie than he wanted me to know in the first fifteen minutes of our first date: They'd been to jail together. Bernie had a daughter my age. Bernie had been a big shot, a *macher*, in the union, but he'd screwed up, gotten popped for something stupid, something, Ziggy said, "only *shvartzas* get popped for."

Bernie was annoyed, but only once did he reprimand Ziggy Schwartz. That was when I said, "You know, my mother's maiden name was Schwartz." And Ziggy, with a cockeyed, drunken smile, shrugged and said, "Yeah? Maybe I fucked her."

"You don't talk to this one like that," Bernie said angrily.

Ziggy paled. Then he nodded, and grinned again. "I'm sorry, Sandy. I'm just a dirty old man. I don't remember how to talk to nice girls anymore."

We left Ziggy in the lounge and walked through the dining room toward the banquette, where he'd had dinner with Helen. People called out to Bernie as we passed: "BB, how's it going?" "BB, let me buy you a drink." "You robbing the cradle, BB?" And Bernie had a smile, a handshake, a wink, or a wisecrack for each of them.

At the table, too, we were interrupted by a constant stream of men—men dressed as elegantly as Bernie, with manicured hands, perfect hair, monogrammed cuffs, gold watches, platinum ID bracelets, diamond cuff links, star sapphire pinky rings. And, at least three times between the shrimp cocktail and the filet mignon, Bernie was called away to handle something in the bar, in the kitchen, in the backroom.

Once, he came back to the table and told our waiter, "See the guy at the bar with the shiner? Get him a raw potato from the kitchen."

'Yes, Mr. B," the waiter said, and took off.

"Are raw potatoes good for black eyes?" I asked.

Bernie laughed. "No. That guy, Joey, up there. He likes to do bar tricks. He's got one—where he pushes a straw through a raw potato. He gets them to bet him he can't do it. And he takes their money, too. The guy's a maniac. Holds up taxis on the way over here for drink money."

The guy at the bar was Joey Gallo. "I'm a tough guy," he used to say. He'd come into The Velvet Room with his brother Albert, who they called "Kid Blast," and a couple of other wise guys—they were like a little wolf pack, ferocious and unpredictable. Black eyes, skinned knuckles, scraped cheeks. But they wore suits at the club and if their fingernails weren't always spotless their long-collared white shirts and pocket handkerchiefs and silk ties were. "Crazy" Joe Gallo was their leader. "I'm tough. I'm a really tough guy." I remember him saying it all the time. And this was before he read Camus and Gide in jail and became the darling of swinging sixties café society.

"So what's a kid like you doing hanging around with Helen? She's got a few years on you," Bernie said when he'd returned to the table for the fourth time in fifteen minutes.

"She's a friend of my mother's," I told him. "Actually, she's ten years younger than my mother and ten years older than me. When she was falling apart over her second divorce, she'd come to my mother for advice. They became very good friends. She used to live in the same building as we did in Brooklyn."

"What'd she tell you about me?" he asked.

"Nothing," I said.

"Nothing?" He laughed.

"I mean, that you weren't her fiancé, of course. And that she didn't have any objections to my seeing you."

"I owe her one."

"And not to take you seriously," I added, staring down at the ravages of my steak and baked potato.

"Good advice. So what are you, Jewish?"

"Yes. Are you?"

"Sure," he said, then smiled. "You want to see proof?"

I laughed. "No, thanks. I'll take your word for it."

"Good girl."

"But 'Barton,' " I said, "that's not a Jewish name."

"Used to be Blaustein. You know who Barton MacLane is? He played the heavy in a lot of old gangster movies and cowboy movies. Him and Bruce Cabot—I used to love them. That's where I got Barton. From Barton MacLane."

"That's interesting—that you liked the bad guys, not the heroes," I said.

"They had more character. They were tough guys. Heavies always have more character, don't you know that? So, are you Orthodox?"

"My mother keeps kosher. I don't."

"That's nice. Coming from a good Jewish family is nice. So, listen, kid. I've got to do a little work in the back now. Order yourself a nice dessert, some coffee, cognac, whatever you like. The car'll be ready whenever you want to go back to Brooklyn."

He stood up. I couldn't believe it. He was leaving me. My heart sunk. I felt tears welling. And all I could think of was, moron, why did you tell him your mother keeps kosher? As if that had somehow been the deciding factor in his dismissal.

He tilted my chin up and, bending, kissed me lightly on the lips. "Same time tomorrow night?" he said. "I'll send the car."

My mother saw more of me now than she had in months. I came home every night after work to shower and change and get ready for my date with Bernie.

"Who is this man?" she wanted to know. "Where does he get the money to send a car all the way to Brooklyn twice a night?"

"He's a very nice man, Ma. He owns a supper club in New York."

These conversations would take place while I rushed around the cramped apartment, getting dressed, doing my hair, and putting on makeup.

My sister, Marlene, would be sitting at the kitchen table trying to study, but most of the time she'd get caught up in the Cinerama soap opera playing around her. She'd give me a wink or a grin or an A-OK circle if I got in a good line.

"A very nice man who is twenty years older than you. What kind of *very nice man* goes out with a girl young enough to be his daughter? And what do you have in common with this fine gentleman? He buys you malteds, maybe? He wants to hold your hand? And you, you ride him around his fancy supper club in a wheelchair?"

My mother would be at the sink or stove, preparing Marlene's dinner. She'd toss her remarks over her shoulder, casually, like someone flinging a scarf dripping acid.

"We have dinner, we talk— He's smart, Ma. He's lived a very interesting life."

"Oh, you talk. I see. And he's smart, your good friend with the car and the money and the fancy New York supper club. Of course, why didn't I figure that out. Of course, that's what he wants from you—conversation! Especially because he's smart, right? And he must be a very educated man to have such deep conversations and discussions with a high-school dropout."

"A high-school dropout who pays your rent, Ma!"

I was still contributing most of my salary to the family. As a showroom model in the Garment Center, I earned about four times what my mother did at the cleaning store. And Bernie was impressed with this—not that I was a model, but that I supported my family.

He'd done the same when he was a kid. His mother and her sister had worked twelve hours a day in the candy store on the ground floor of their tenement building on First Street and Avenue A. To help support them, Bernie had taken a job as a hat boy at Moe Penn's, an elegant men's shop on Grand Street. He was twelve years old at the time.

The haberdashery catered strictly to a moneyed clientele. And among those with cash to flash on the Lower East Side in the early thirties were some of the most notorious gangsters and gunmen of their day. At Moe Penn's Bernie got to know them. Two who took a special liking to him were Meyer Lansky's lieutenants, Sam "Red" Levine and Philly "Farvel the Stick" Kovolick.

Years later, I met them. They were in their late fifties, early sixties by then, which was ancient to me. But in their twenties—about the time Bernie was talking his way into that job at Moe Penn's— Red and Farvel were making big names for themselves in what used to be called "The Outfit."

Rumor had it that it was Red, using a squad of imported Jewish hitmen dressed as Federal tax agents, who engineered the 1931 murder of Salvatore Maranzano, the self-proclaimed Boss of all Bosses of the Italian mob.

Farvel, who was busted in '33 at a "crime conference" at the Hotel Franconia, along with Bugsy Siegel, Lepke Buchalter and Gurrah Shapiro, was known even among those strong-arm men as a shakedown artist of exceptional greed. He was called "Farvel the Stick" because he drove for Lansky—stick shift getaway cars and bootlegging trucks—and did anything else with a stick that Meyer needed done.

Another dapper dresser from the old neighborhood, another one of the well-connected "older" guys who shopped at Moe Penn's, was James Plumeri, better known as Jimmy Doyle, whom Bernie introduced to me two decades later at The Velvet Club as Uncle Jimmy. In the late fifties when I met him, Jimmy owned and lived above a nightclub on First Avenue called the Ali Baba—which Bernie always called The Bucket of Blood. In the sixties, Jimmy disappeared. Years later, pieces of him were still turning up in garbage cans all over New York.

Farvel, Red Levine, Jimmy Doyle. They were the guys Bernie met when he was twelve and working at Moe Penn's, the ones who taught him the ropes and had him running numbers and driving bootleg trucks when he was thirteen, the men who became his friends and called him "kid" for the rest of his life.

Bernie told me about them long before I met them. Not how they had made their reputations, but that they'd helped him out when he was young and needed to make money to help support his family. And, forgetting that I was supposed to be a sophisticated model in my little black dress and string of pearls, elbows on the table, chin in my hands, I hung on his every word.

I wanted to tell my mother how wrong she was about Bernie. How he respected me because I gave her money and was Jewish and came from a good Orthodox home. I wanted to tell her how wrong she was about why he liked me. She was afraid that Bernie would take advantage of me. I couldn't tell her that I was getting worried that he wouldn't.

Every night Bernie sent his car for me promptly at eight and every night for two weeks, after a chaste kiss, he sent me back home alone to Brooklyn.

And every night at his club I became more impressed with him, with the amazing range of people who were drawn to him, who'd known him for years and told me benevolent little secrets about how BB had bailed them out of a jam or done some thoughtful little thing for their sick mother or kid brother or cousin Shlomo from Delancey Street. And every night of those first two weeks I became more infatuated with Bernie Barton, every night a little more in love.

Then one Monday we'd finished dinner and were sitting at Bernie's table in the lounge, when two men came by to say hello. Bernie asked them to join us. One of them was a stocky guy he'd grown up with, who we'll call Milty Heinz. Milty, Bernie said, was one of Johnny Dio's right-hand men in the Teamsters. I'd heard of Johnny Dio. Anyone who picked up *The Mirror*, *The News*, or *The Herald Trib* had read about him at one time or other. He was one of the mob's "labor relations experts," who'd been accused of plotting the acid-throwing attack that blinded a newspaperman named Victor Riesel in 1956—supposedly to keep him from testifying before a special federal rackets grand jury.

The other guy, Steve Crane, a tall, attractive man who owned restaurants in California and New York, turned out to be the ex-husband of Lana Turner, the movie star. His daughter had recently gotten into trouble for knifing a small-time hood named Johnny Stompanato. The headlines had talked about an argument in the movie star's bedroom that escalated to violence, and the daughter had been acquitted on the grounds of justifiable homicide because she'd only killed the hood to save her mother's life.

So there I was, nineteen years old, resting my ponytail against the tufted leather banquette at Bernie's table in the bar, listening to Johnny Dio's right-hand man telling Lana Turner's ex-husband what a "ballsy bastard, a real stand-up guy BB is," when a good-looking, grinning man with a great tan swept into the place, a blonde on each arm, and hollered, "Mr. B—my main man!" And there I was looking right up into Billy Daniels's incredible smoky blue eyes. Eyes I'd only ever seen before in black and white, on television, where Billy was always introduced as "That Old Black Magic man," because that was the song that had become his trademark.

Billy set the blondes up at the bar and came back to our table. He teased Bernie with affection and familiarity and talked with Milty Heinz and Steve Crane for a while. Then he kissed my hand and returned to his girls.

"You know Billy Daniels, too?" I whispered, awestruck.

Bernie nodded, no big deal.

"How do you know him?"

"From uptown, from Fifty-second Street, jazz joints, around," he said. "Let's go up to the apartment."

"What?"

"The apartment. My place, dummy."

"Candy man, you've got to come see me at the Copa," Billy Daniels called after us as we left the club. "And bring the princess with you, baby."

CHAPTER THREE

———

Bernie's Princess

The apartment occupied the entire second floor of a beautiful brownstone on Seventy-ninth Street between Fifth and Madison.

"Oh, my God, I don't believe it," I said as Bernie led me through a gorgeous set of tall, solid wood double doors into a carpeted hallway.

"What's the matter?"

"My father used to take me shopping right around the corner from here."

"Yeah? That's nice."

"No, but I mean, you don't understand. This is the street I always wanted to live on. In this neighborhood. On this street. In a building just like this."

He was walking ahead of me, up a flight of red-carpeted stairs and down the hall. He stopped in front of the door to his apartment and glanced skeptically at me over his shoulder.

"Honest," I said, as he began working on the locks. There were at least six, including a thick deadbolt and a police lock. "Isn't that amazing? This is where I've always wanted to live."

"Maybe you should look around first," Bernie said, without cracking a smile. He threw open the door and I followed him into the apartment.

Then suddenly I thought about how I must have sounded, like I had my bags packed in the back of the limo and if he just gave me a minute, I'd move right in. I got very flustered.

"You want a drink?"

I followed Bernie into a huge room with a dining table and chairs in one corner and, in another, a lavish mirrored cabinet housing a TV, radio, stereo, and record collection. The room was tiled in black and white squares and, in front of the Murphy kitchen—a little hideaway closet that contained a tiny sink and half-refrigerator and stove—was a giant white tufted-leather standup bar.

"Listen, I didn't mean it like it sounded. I mean, it's true. We used to drive in from Brooklyn. My father used to take us shopping on Madison Avenue. I always loved this neighborhood—"

"You nervous?" he said, walking over to the bar. "Don't be nervous." He poured himself a drink, then handed one to me. "Come on," he beckoned with a hitch of his head.

A set of large black and white doors with etched-brass knobs led into the living room, a spacious room carpeted blood red. The ceiling was black, the walls were white and, at the far end of the room, two huge floor-to-ceiling windows looked out onto the wide street. The furniture was also red, white, and black, and there was a big fireplace with a white marble mantel.

Across from the fireplace, partially screened by a tall black lacquered cabinet, was a large mirrored alcove that held, like a diamond in a platinum setting, Bernie's king-sized bed. In which, I thought, the apartment I shared with Marlene and my mother could have laid down to rest. I took a big swallow of the scotch he'd poured me. "Wow," I said.

Bernie laughed and turned me around so that I was facing him. With a hand on each of my shoulders, he held me at arm's length and looked at me quietly for a minute. "So?" he said.

"So," I echoed, my voice breaking, my head bobbing philosophically like an old rabbi thinking it over: "Yeah, so . . ."

"You going to sleep with me, kid?"

"Yeah." My head was still bobbing, my brown eyes staring into his baby blues.

"It's late."

"You sleepy?" I asked.

Bernie turned me around and pointed me toward the bathroom. "Go." He laughed.

Forty-five minutes later I was wide awake staring up at my reflection in the mirrored ceiling above the bed. Bernie was sound asleep beside me. He hadn't laid a glove on me. Well, a glove maybe. A sweet, gentle, sexy hugging hand or two, yes. A pair of very nice loving lips, yes. And then, he'd said, very softly in that raspy, sexy voice, "Okay, baby. Sleep, honey." And rolled over. And that was that. He was out. I was up.

I spent the few remaining hours before dawn wondering whether I'd done something wrong, whether Bernie really cared for me, whether he found me attractive. I took breaks in the worrying by imagining what it would be like to live with him, to live in this apartment, to sleep every night with him in this bed.

It was the first time I'd ever spent the night with a man. I got up early in the morning for work and, when I had showered and dressed, Bernie was still asleep. I had no idea about the etiquette of the situation. I decided not to wake him. I spent a while composing a little love note to him, then left it on the pillow and tiptoed out of the apartment.

Later, he called me at work. "How you doing?"

"Fine," I said, grinning at just the sound of his gruff voice.

"Good. Listen, I'll see you later at the club. Only don't say anything, you hear me?"

"Sure," I said, not sure at all what he meant.

"You tell anyone about last night, I'll kill you."

"Oh," I said. "Oh, Bernie, of course I won't. But it was nice. You were sweet."

"Sweet?" he growled. "What's wrong with you?"

That night at The Velvet Room, we were very careful with one another, trying to behave as though nothing had changed between us. But every once in a while, we'd catch each other's eye across the table and I'd start to smile. And Bernie would shake his head like, cut the crap, kid. But you could see him trying not to grin. He'd turn away fast, or get into a sudden, intense conversation, or order someone around.

Another old union friend of his showed up close to closing time, a guy named Moishe Pickles. If Bernie had wanted to prove to me that night what a tough guy he really was, Moishe was the best PR man he could've asked for.

"What a temper this man has," Moishe told me, clapping his hands together and laughing. "You remember the shirt buttons?" he asked Bernie. "One night we're in a bar uptown. A shmuck, a square, a guy named Alby, right, Bernie? He comes over to the booth. BB's talking to a couple of people. He tells this customer, wait. But this Alby needs to see him. Right away. He don't get the message. Guy wanted money, a loan, something. Bernie says, 'Alby, I'm talking business here,' right, Bernie? The shmuck still don't get it. 'I gotta talk to you,' he said. Three times. Four times.

Finally, BB gets up. He's got that little nail-cleaning knife of his. He says, 'When I tell a guy to wait, he's supposed to wait.' And with one stroke, he moves down this Alby's shirtfront and one, two, three, he shaves every single button off this square's shirt. The guy went nuts. He took a swing at BB."

"What happened?" I asked.

"He went nuts," Moishe repeated. Then he shrugged. "Bernie broke his jaw."

"You broke his jaw?"

"And my thumb. You forgot that part, Moishela."

"Oh, yeah. It was disgusting. His thumb was hanging off like it didn't even belong to his hand. Watch out for this man, Sandy. What a temper!"

"Hang out. Have another drink. We're going home now," Bernie told Moishe.

When we got into bed, and I was curled up against Bernie, lying in the crook of his arm, examining his thumb, he said: "You think I'm a tough guy?"

"No."

"You're wrong," he said.

We made love that night. And every night after. I started hanging out at the apartment. I moved a few things into Bernie's closet. A couple of evenings a week, I bathed and changed there after work, then went down to meet him at the club. Flatbush Avenue was where my mother and sister lived. East Seventy-ninth Street was where I felt at home.

I loved walking around barefoot on the deep pile carpeting. I loved sitting at the tufted white-leather bar. I loved taking long, leisurely bubble baths with the stereo on in the living room and a glass of champagne on the rim of the tub. And, most of all, I loved being in love with Bernie Barton. I'd known him a little more than a month, but it was a new adventure every day.

One afternoon I was sitting in his apartment, waiting for him to get dressed. I was on the bar stool with my legs crossed, swinging my foot. Bernie crossed the room knotting his tie. "You've got a hole in your shoe," he said.

Embarrassed, I looked at the sole of my black pumps. "I'll have to get it fixed," I said.

"Forget about it. Tomorrow afternoon you meet me after work."

He called me at the showroom at three the next day. "I'll be at

Fifth Avenue and Forty-ninth Street in twenty minutes," he said. "Meet me."

"I don't know if I can leave so early."

"You want me to talk to your boss for you?"

Less than an hour later, we left The Ansonia shoe store. It was a beautiful, bright spring day and I was wearing a brand new pair of open-toed, brown-and-white, high-heeled spectator pumps. With my purse tucked under my arm, I stepped out of the store into the sunlight of Fifth Avenue swinging a stack of tied-together shoe boxes with each hand. A clerk, whose hands were similarly filled, followed me out to the curb. Bernie had bought me *twenty-seven* new pairs of shoes!

"Who's Enid?" he asked. He had hailed a cab and was peeling off a couple of bills to hand the clerk.

I hadn't even realized I'd said her name aloud. I settled into the backseat of the taxi surrounded by stacks of shoe boxes. "Oh, a woman I knew a long time ago who loved shoes," I said.

A few days later, I walked into Bernie's apartment after work. A man I'd never seen before was sitting on the black sofa in the living room with a big brown paper shopping bag at his feet. He glanced up, grinned, and toasted me with the tall glass in his hand.

He was a light-skinned black man with a little mustache and slicked-back red hair. He was wearing a bright Hawaiian sport shirt, orange linen slacks, and pointy light brown alligator shoes. I had never seen anyone like him in real life. He looked like a cross between Cab Calloway and Nathan Detroit.

"You've got to be Sandy," he said.

Bernie was nowhere in sight and I must have looked as nervous as I felt.

"He's in the bathroom. He'll be right out. Relax. I'm an old friend," the man said pleasantly.

I'd never known a black man before, never seen one sitting back with a drink in his hand in a white man's living room calling himself an old friend. This was in the fifties. The Civil Rights movement was still a couple of years and several states down the road. Blacks couldn't vote in the South, couldn't go to the same movie theaters or drink from the same water fountains as whites. They were expected to step off the curb to allow a white person to pass. Up North, and certainly in the Brooklyn Jewish world I came from, there was another kind of segregation that kept us just as separated, just as ignorant and prejudiced about the people we politely called Negroes and more familiarly called *shvartzas*.

Billy Daniels, with his blue eyes and $600 silk suits, didn't count. He wasn't a man, anyway. He was a star.

Bernie walked into the room before I found my voice. "Baby, this is Red. Red, Sandy." He was in a terrific mood.

"Hello," I finally said.

"Hot Dog here is my main man. Wait till you get to know him, Sandy. You're going to love this guy."

Red nodded modestly.

"Hot Dog?"

They laughed. "That's what they call me," he said. "My real name's Harrison Allen."

"You know at baseball games, how they'll pass a hot dog hand to hand and by the time it gets to you it's ice cold and you missed five great plays? That's Red. That's how he blows a joint." Bernie could see I was confused. "Smokes tea . . . marijuana," he explained. "The time it takes for him to pass it to you, man, the crowd's gone home and they're rolling up the infield."

They both thought that was pretty funny. "Excuse us a minute, baby," Bernie said, signaling Red to follow him into the alcove.

"You didn't lie, man," Red said, chuckling, hauling his skinny self up from the couch. "She sure is a fine-looking girl." And off they went behind the black lacquered cabinet, laughing up a storm.

I didn't know whether they were laughing at me or had been smoking funny cigarettes before I'd gotten there or what was going on, but there was a bond between them that made me feel naive and left out. I walked out of the living room, over to the bar.

"Listen, baby," Bernie called to me. "I need you to work for me tonight. At the club."

I couldn't believe it. I'd just spent a full day on my feet in a Seventh Avenue showroom and now he wanted me to work another shift. He had never ever even suggested such a thing before. What was going on here?

"The cigarette girl can't make it. I need you to fill in for her."

He and Red were still in the alcove and I was close to tears. But I said, "Okay. Whatever you want."

"Your uniform's in that shopping bag Red brought over. That's all you're going to wear. Go on, get it. Try it on."

I walked over to the couch and looked into the shopping bag. At first all I saw was a swatch of silky fabric. I reached into the bag to get the uniform. Bernie and Red poked their grinning heads out of the alcove in time to see me pull a gorgeous Breath-of-Spring mink stole out of the brown paper bag. The fur was soft and thick, light as a feather, and lined in exquisite pale satin.

I thought I'd gotten the wrong bag. "Bernie?"

"What's the matter? You don't like it?"

"Like what? This is a mink stole, Bernie."

"It's your new uniform, baby," he said. "And there's something for you on the fireplace."

In a little white jewelry box on the marble mantel was a pearl and sapphire ring.

"So? You like it?"

"Oh, Bernie, it's gorgeous." A ring, I was thinking. Oh, God, he's given me a ring. And a *mink stole*! I ran to him and kissed him. "Thank you," I whispered.

"Thank Red," he said. "He went shopping for me. Of course, if you don't like it," he teased, "we can always send it back, right?"

"We aim to please," Red said, delighted.

And they meant it, too. Through the years a lot of shopping bags and boxes showed up. Bernie loved to surprise me. And, for the most part, I loved his gifts. Nothing ever came close to that first Breath-of-Spring mink, though. Once he got me a long white mink stole. He thought it was sexy and fabulous. I thought it looked like something a stripper would wear. I mean, it was *white* and long. Tall as I am, I could've wrapped it around me twice.

We were in the car. The white stole was lying on the front seat between us. Bernie said, "You hate it."

I said, "No. I just don't love it. It's fabulous, but not for me."

We were waiting for a traffic light on Park Avenue. An elderly, heavyset black woman was at the curb, waiting to cross the street. "Okay," Bernie said. "It's not for you. Maybe it's for her. Here," he called to the woman. He tossed her the mink. The light changed. We drove away.

Bernie's birthday was May twenty-eighth, just a couple of weeks before mine. And only a couple of days after he gave me that first mink stole. I was nineteen years old and, believe me, I wore that little mink every chance I got. That first night, I wore it to the club and never took it off for a minute, not through dinner or drinks after. I hugged it close to me all night. It was the most glamorous thing I had ever owned, the most extravagant gift I'd ever received. It was practically a pet. And when Bernie told me we were going to the Copacabana for his birthday, the mink and I were in seventh heaven.

The Copacabana was famous as a celebrity hangout. Almost every gossip column you read in the morning covered who was seen with whom at the Copa the night before. Plenty of FBI files were filled with the same information. Not all the Copa celebs were movie stars.

The club was owned by Julie Podell, a little Jewish man with a voice like landfill. There was enough gravel and ground glass in it to bury New Jersey. Downstairs at the Copa, in the main room, Julie used to stand at the back of the club watching his people work. He didn't mix much unless he knew you and then it was mostly, "How's it going? You got everything you need?"

Bernie introduced me that first night as his lady. Julie gave me a little nod, said, "Nice to meet you, Sandy." Then, "Everything okay, Bernie? You got a table? Carmine, take care of Mr. Barton."

I don't remember who was playing in the main room that night. It might have been Joe E. Lewis or Jack E. Leonard or Steve Lawrence and Edie Gorme. They were the headliners of that time. Or it could have been Billy, whom we saw there several times and who never failed to get an embarrassed smile from Bernie by teasing him, shouting out affectionately from the stage: "There he is, one of the good bad guys . . ." Or, "One of my dearest friends . . . a nice white Jewish man." But I remember we just peeked in on the main room, that night, then went upstairs to the lounge.

Ruby Stein waved us over to his table. I had never met him before. I had never even heard of him, but by the 1960s, Ruby and his partner, Jiggs, were notorious as big loanshark bankers. They lent money to some of the most dangerous shylocks on the street. Guys who paid them one and one-half percent interest and, in turn, lent the money at five times that rate to doctors, lawyers, stockbrokers, and corporate types desperate to cover gambling debts or other emergencies. Ruby's clients included guys who used leg breakers as enforcers, guys who'd threaten whole families to get their "vig" or take over a man's business if he couldn't pay up, and suck it dry of cash and into bankruptcy in a couple of months.

As I said, I didn't know anything about Ruby the night of Bernie's birthday. He was just a nice Jewish man to me, about ten years older than Bernie, wearing glasses. His well-groomed hair was brown with pronounced reddish highlights. He was a perfectly ordinary-looking guy—except for one thing. Ruby had a twitch, an eye tic that looked like he was winking at you. The more he drank, the worse the tic got.

He was with Jiggs Forlano that night at the Copa when he called us over to his table. Jiggs was a black-haired Italian, as tall, dignified, and silent as Ruby was drunk and wild. The night was young for Bernie and me, not quite midnight, but Ruby had obviously been drinking for a good couple of hours. He always drank brandy. And when Bernie introduced me to him, he started winking at me. This made me extremely nervous. Not only did Bernie have a temper, but there was a big bosomy blonde rubbing up against the sleeve of Ruby's sharkskin jacket, and who knew what kind of temper she had.

Bernie said, "This is my lady, Sandy."

Ruby said, "Hiya, kid," and winked. He was too far gone to remember his friend, so she introduced herself. "I'm Beryl," she said pleasantly. "Glad to meet you." And Ruby winked at me.

"Beryl. That's my Hebrew name," Bernie said.

"Look at that, he's my namesake," Beryl told Ruby. He winked at her.

Jiggs, who was known as "the shylocks' shylock," talked softly to Bernie for a while. Then Ruby and Bernie started talking ballgames and horseraces, Vegas and Puerto Rico. A little warning bell went off in my head. I listened as they talked and kidded with each other. Their words seemed familiar and so did the subtle change in their tone and energy. Gamblers. I had a flash of déjà vu. An uh-oh, here-we-go-again feeling. And I wondered if Bernie loved gambling the way my father had.

Of course, the minute the topic changed, Ruby was winking up a storm at me again.

"Honey, let's go," I whispered to Bernie at the first opportunity.

We went to our table and ordered a bottle of champagne to celebrate Bernie's forty-first birthday. When the waiter brought the tall ice bucket to the table, he said, "That gentleman would like to buy you a drink."

Bernie craned his neck. His face lit up with recognition and he waved to a well-dressed man in tinted glasses, who was toasting him from a booth against the wall. Then he said, "Excuse me, baby. I've got to go say hello to someone. I haven't seen these guys in years. They're from Chicago."

Bernie went over to the booth and I watched him pumping the man's hand. Then he was introduced to the others at the table. He was wearing his best grin, every one of those perfect white teeth on parade as he chatted with the aging boys from Chicago. I was fine. I wasn't bored at all. It was my first night at the Copa and there was plenty for me to gape and gawk at. Then I heard, "Sandy, come here. I want you to meet someone," and he signaled for me to join him.

"This is Rocco Fischetti, and his brother, Charlie. And you might know this guy over here."

Frank Sinatra stood up. He took my hand and kissed it.

"Oh, my God," I said.

"She'll never wash it again," Bernie teased.

We sat with Sinatra and the Fischetti brothers for a couple of minutes. It turned out that in some circles Rocco and Charles were as famous as Frankie. They'd made names for themselves in Chicago serving the legendary "Scarface" Al Capone. Now they ran the town. Of course, that night, when I asked Bernie who they were and what they did, he said, "They're in the fish business."

Someone had told Rocco that it was Bernie's birthday and they bought us a round of drinks. I took just a sip or two. I couldn't drink. I could barely breathe. I excused myself and ran to the phone to call my mother. "Guess who I'm with?" I said.

"Why, you left the old one, the *alter kocker*?" she asked dryly.

"Frank Sinatra!"

There was a silence on the line.

"Ma?"

"Which Frank Sinatra?" she said. Then she laughed.

In the back of the limo, riding up Madison Avenue at dawn, Bernie kissed me. "Did you have a good time, *mamela*?" he asked.

"The greatest."

"You think this was good, wait till your birthday," he promised. "I don't know what we'll do yet but, guaranteed, it'll be something special."

It was. I never cried so much in my life.

On June 13, the night before my birthday, I woke up to the sound of Bernie wheezing and gasping. He could barely lift his head off the pillow. "What is it?" I asked, frightened.

His hair was soaked, his face was beaded with sweat. The bed was drenched. He couldn't catch his breath. I was petrified, paralyzed. I didn't know what to do—whether to pound his back, dry him with a towel, put ice on his burning forehead.

"Bernie, should I call Red? What should I do?" I asked frantically. "Oh, Bernie, I love you. Help me. Tell me."

He couldn't speak. He signaled for me to give him a pencil and paper and, still coughing and wheezing, he wrote down his doctor's name and phone number.

By the time Dr. Sealy arrived, Bernie's fever had reached 103. I was rubbing his shivering body with washcloths soaked in cold water and alcohol. And I was very relieved when the doctor asked me to wait in the living room while he examined Bernie. The tears I'd held back flowed down my cheeks as I chain-smoked and paced. Every ashtray in the place was filled by the time Dr. Sealy came out to talk to me. You could hardly see the red carpet for the Kleenex.

"Are you his daughter?" Sealy asked.

I was embarrassed. "No, I'm his . . . friend?" I suggested.

The doctor sighed. "Well, I hope you're aware of his condition. Bernie is a very sick man. He had rheumatic fever as a child and developed a heart condition. He's got to be very careful about colds. He's prone to pneumonia and that's very, very dangerous for him."

"Is he going to die?" I was twisting a tissue in my hands trying to make them stop shaking.

Dr. Sealy noticed and frowned. He took my hands in his. "He'll be fine tonight. I gave him a shot. I'm going to write a prescription for penicillin. I want you to get it filled in the morning. I'll call later and we'll see how he's doing. I may want to hospitalize him tomorrow."

I smoked and cried till the sun came up, and then I turned twenty.

It was too early to call in sick at work. Too early to get the prescription filled. Bernie was sleeping. He still sounded terrible to me. He was still wheezing, but it was much better than the coughing fit, and he wasn't gasping for breath anymore. I got dressed and looked in my wallet. I had about eight dollars. I went to the dresser where Bernie kept his spare change. There was a couple of hundred dollars in the drawer. I took a twenty and Bernie's keys and went to the little gourmet deli that was open all night on Madison Avenue.

I bought Campbell's chicken noodle soup and Jell-O and Wonderbread for toast. I bought ginger ale and Lipton's tea and a little jar of honey that, on Madison Avenue, cost half a day's salary. I bought whatever I could find that my mother gave me when I was sick. The only thing I left out were coloring books and Crayolas.

Bernie was still asleep. He still felt very hot. I sponged him down with alcohol and changed the pillow cases. He was very pale and his breathing was so noisy it was frightening. I busied myself around the apartment for a while, cleaning up. I opened a can of soup and put it in a pan on the stove and waited, thinking he'd get up. I read the Jell-O instructions and, finally, pessimistically, tried my hand at making a bowl. And every time I walked back into the alcove and saw him struggling to breathe, I'd break down and start crying all over again. I had known him less than two months. I was afraid I was going to lose him forever.

I called work and then I called my friend Judy at her boyfriend's beauty salon.

"He's so sick," I said. "He really looks bad, Judy. He looks like an old man. Like that movie where Ronald Colman takes the girl out of Shangri-la and suddenly she turns two million years old."

"Don't cry, honey. He'll be all right. That doctor said so, didn't he? So what are you crying for? What's the worst that could happen?"

"Oh, Judy," I said, "what if he dies before I get a chance to marry him?"

Dr. Sealy stopped by that afternoon. Bernie was just barely awake. He hadn't eaten all day. He'd had a couple of sips of tea and honey to wash down the penicillin tablets, that was all. And, in spite of my sponging him down with alcohol every twenty minutes or so, his fever was still pretty high.

"I'm going to put him in," Sealy decided. He called Cabrini Hospital on Nineteenth Street and made the arrangements, then gave me the address and left.

I'd called Hot Dog Red for Bernie earlier in the day. Red was going to take care of some business for him uptown and then, he said, he'd come by the apartment to help me out. He arrived shortly after Dr. Sealy left. I'd been holding it together for Bernie. I'd managed not to cry for about fifteen whole minutes. But as soon as Red rang the doorbell, I fell apart again.

"Take it easy, kid. The Dog is here," Red announced, laughing, trying to cheer me up. "You just go in there and get BB dressed and I'll drive you down to the hospital."

In the front seat of Red's caddy, Bernie rested his head on my shoulder. "You sorry you got involved with an old man?" he teased.

"She told *me* she was," Red said.

I wanted to kill him. Bernie started to laugh and had another coughing fit.

I checked him into the hospital. They put him in a wheelchair. It really scared me. He looked so weak. And it reminded me of what my mother had said about riding him around his club in a wheelchair. And now, there he was slumped down in a wheelchair and he did look old and helpless and I felt young and useless. And then, the nurse said, "Are you his daughter, dear?" And, *again*, I started crying.

I stayed at the hospital all day. Finally Dr. Sealy sent me home. "Go on," he said, "Bernie's asleep. There's nothing you can do for him now except get some rest yourself." Before I left, I tiptoed into Bernie's room. He had tubes running into his arms and an oxygen mask over his face. But he looked better than he had when we'd checked in. At least his brow wasn't creased with worry and pain.

Red drove me back uptown. "Bernie said take whatever money you need from the drawer. And if you need more, if you need anything, you just call me."

I thanked him and went inside. I started cleaning things up—I changed the bed linen and hung up Bernie's clothes and threw out the uneaten soup and emptied the ashtrays and picked up the Kleenex. And then I caught a look at myself in the mirror behind the bar. I wasn't wearing any makeup. My hair wasn't even combed. I was wearing a shirt of Bernie's that I'd thrown on when I went shopping at six in the morning.

"Happy birthday, kid," I said to the girl in the mirror. My voice was so hoarse from smoking and crying all day that I sounded just like Bernie. He'd promised me a special birthday, I remembered. Well, I thought, he'd delivered.

The next day, I slept later than usual. I phoned in sick again at work and rushed down to Cabrini Hospital. When I got off the elevator at Bernie's floor, I saw a pretty nurse come giggling out of his room. Then two guys with cigars in their mouths came out. Then a big woman, a candy striper, carrying a stack of magazines. It was like one of those little circus cars out of which comes an endless parade of clowns. He'd been in the hospital less than twenty-four hours, but the room was already filling with flowers, candy, and coffee cups. And Bernie was propped up in bed with the oxygen mask over his nose and a telephone nestled against his ear.

"You're feeling better?" I asked.

He nodded and held up his hand for me to wait. He listened at the receiver for a while, then hung up and pulled off the oxygen mask.

"Bernie, don't!" I protested.

He gave me a great big smile. "Come here, baby, and give me a kiss," he said. He didn't sound as good as he looked, but it was a big improvement over yesterday.

"Who were you talking to?" I asked.

"I wasn't talking. I was listening," he said. "I made a couple of bets."

That was the day after he almost died. By the next day, the traffic in and out of Bernie's private room was unbelievable. If there'd been a turnstile at the door, he could have raked in a fortune. Wise guys in shiny suits took turns squeezing into the space between the bed and the window. Nurses had to nudge past the visitors. The television was on, the ballgame was blaring. There were open Chinese food containers on Bernie's bed tray. The little chest of drawers under the TV set was as well stocked as The Velvet Club's bar. Red was on the phone placing bets for Bernie. And Bernie, in his hospital gown, was sitting up in bed in the middle of all this chaos scribbling in a little notebook.

"My God, what are you doing?" I asked him.

"Keeping track," he said cryptically, and stuck the book under his pillow.

Later that night, when there was a dinner-time lull in the crowd, Bernie took out the notebook again. He was jotting down names. Again, I asked about the book.

"I'm writing down who was here, who came to visit me," he explained, "Who came to give me *koved*."

"Koved?" I'd never heard the word.

"It means respect. Honor. You've got to keep track of these things, of who shows up to pay respect."

The fourth day when I came to visit after work, Bernie threw everyone out of the room. "I feel better," he said, grinning.

"Oh, honey, I'm so glad."

"Lock the door and I'll show you," he said.

I thought he was kidding. I laughed. He wasn't kidding.

We made love in his hospital bed. I was afraid someone would barge in and catch us and throw me out. I was afraid the embarrassment would kill me and the excitement would kill him. I had my eyes squeezed shut the whole time, praying that he wouldn't die, and thinking, this can't be good for a heart condition.

* * *

The week following Bernie's hospitalization, I stayed home from work to take care of him. We were together day and night. I think it was the most time I'd ever spent alone with another human being and it was never boring.

I discovered how much Bernie loved to read. He sent me to the library with lists of books. It was the first time I'd ever really used a library, and I was almost as proud of myself as I was of him. He read Shakespeare's plays aloud to me. We'd act out some of the scenes together. Elizabeth Barrett Browning was his favorite poet. Bernie recited her work from memory. We played cards and board games like kids. And we talked and talked and talked.

I learned more about him that week than I had in the nearly two months we'd been seeing each other.

I lit a cigarette one night while we were playing Monopoly. "Did you know I used to smoke? You want to know how I quit?" he asked, laughing. "When I was in prison. The doctor told me I had to stop smoking, but I didn't. They made me an auxiliary fireman. I had my own room in the firehouse, my own bathroom. And one day this muscle-bound giant, this *bulvon*, knocks on the door. And he says he's been watching me and he likes me and he wants to be my girlfriend. I say, thank you very much, a girlfriend with testicles I don't need; however, I could use a maid. And we cut this deal for cigarettes. He did my laundry, kept the place nice, and I paid him off in cigarettes. That's how I quit smoking."

Another afternoon, Bernie was in bed reading to me. He started coughing and put down the book. "I always liked to read," he said, after he'd caught his breath again. "But in prison, that's where I first had the time. That's also where I found out about this heart condition. In Atlanta. I'd catch a cold and be laid up for weeks. Finally, the prison doctor discovered that one of the valves in my heart was shriveled from the rheumatic fever I had when I was seven. I still remember being sick when I was a kid. My mother laid me out on blocks of ice on the kitchen table to get the fever down. Ice from the ice box. That was before refrigerators. An old man used to come a couple of times a week with the ice and shlep it up the three flights of stairs on his back. He'd have a gunny sack over his shoulder with a three-foot square block of ice lying on top of it. Each block weighed about a ton. I still remember how it felt, laying there on top of the ice."

"What happened," I asked tentatively. "I mean, with prison. Why were you there?"

"I'll show you. Behind the bar, there's a scrapbook. Bring it here."

I did. It was an old-fashioned scrapbook. The black pages were filled with scotch-taped newspaper clippings and snapshots fastened at the corners with little white triangular picture holders. The newsprint on most of the articles was yellowed. The stories were headlined: *Teamster Official Indicted. Mobster Convicted. Union Boss Charged with Racketeering.* We sat on the bed and looked through the pages together. But to this day, I don't remember the specifics of Bernie's case, only that it had to do with crooked union activities, and once he'd been convicted and sent away, he couldn't be reinstated. And that was that, as he put it, for his short career as a rising labor leader.

The scrapbook included lots of pictures of friends, from his days on the Lower East Side to his bid in Atlanta. "I used to sit with the old man," he said, meaning New York City's Boss of all Bosses, Vito Genovese, who was serving time on a narcotics rap in the same prison. "Ziggy Schwartz was there, too. And a Jewish guy, a swindler called Tiny who must've been twelve feet tall," Bernie reminisced.

That started us kidding around about the difference between the Cosa Nostra and the Kosher Nostra. "Sure, everyone thinks, the Jews are the brains and the ginzos are the brawn," Bernie said. "Well, *mamela*, it ain't necessarily so." And he rattled off the names of Jewish mobsters as famous for their muscle as their minds—Legs Diamond, Dutch Shultz, Monk Eastman, Big Jack Zelig, Lefty Louis Rosenzweig, Waxy Gordon, Bugsy Siegel, and even Meyer Lansky, the most famous business head in the mob. He had stories about them all.

I'd listen, with my mouth hanging open, seeing the crowded, shadowy streets of the Lower East Side as he talked, and the bootlegging trucks and the *shtarkes*, the strong-arm men, making their weekly collections from the shopkeepers or fighting with baseball bats and blackjacks, one day on the side of labor, the next with management.

One of my favorites from that time, from the week Bernie was recuperating, was his story of how "racketeering" got its name. "Did you ever hear of Dopey Benny Fein?" Bernie asked me. "He had droopy eyelids, that's why they called him 'Dopey.' Started out as a pickpocket, a little street hustler selling 'protection' to the neighborhood greenhorns . . . This guy practically started labor racketeering single-handed. In fact, the whole thing with 'rackets'—the word 'racketeer' started when Dopey Benny Fein used to hustle money from little Jewish shopkeepers on Grand Street by muscling them to buy tickets to a dance. In those days, dances were called 'rackets.' And, believe me, Benny made a fistful of money on the 'rackets.' "

That was how Benny got started, Bernie told me. Then, as the Jewish labor movement began to grow, "the Dope," he said, hired himself out as a head-basher to any union local that needed help during a strike. From the butchers and bakers to the rag pickers and umbrella makers, nobody crossed the picket lines while Dopey Benny Fein's gangs patrolled them. And no workers voted against the leadership if the leaders had hired Dopey. He even put together a gang of women who used umbrellas weighted with lead to convince nonunion women workers to join the movement.

I remember I asked Bernie if he still saw Dopey. He gave me such a look, and then he laughed. "I'm not that old, baby," he said. Dopey Benny Fein's time was around the turn of the century. Bernie hadn't known him; he'd heard stories and he'd read about the original racketeer. But the way Bernie Barton told a story, not only would you have sworn he was there, you felt like you were right there with him.

Our time together during that week after he got out of the hospital brought us closer than ever. When he told me he was going away for about six weeks to a spa in Connecticut, it was all I could do not to cry. He left for Bill Hahn's and I went back to work. But I still spent a couple of nights a week at his apartment. I'd take the long, luxurious bubble baths I loved and listen to the stereo. And I'd sleep in Bernie's T-shirts, sniffing the cool white cotton, trying to catch a trace of his aftershave around the collar, hoping for a scent of him.

We talked on the phone almost every night. He sounded better and better. Finally, near the end of July, he said he was feeling great and he thought he'd be back in a week.

The next day, he called me at the showroom. "I'm home," he announced. It was maybe two o'clock in the afternoon. I threw my dress on over the little light satin modeling slip we wore and tore out of Midwest Couture.

Bernie was sitting at the white tufted-leather bar having a drink.

He looked up at me as I came through the door. He had a spectacular tan, and his eyes seemed twice as blue as I remembered them. His face was relaxed and his body back to its youthful strength. "What are you waiting for?" he asked, as I stood, suddenly speechless and awkward, in the entry hall staring at him. "Did you miss your daddy, baby? Are you my girl?"

At the end of that summer, he asked the question again. "Are you my girl?"

We'd spent most of August together. Almost every night, I'd meet Bernie at the club and we'd have a late supper and go uptown to his place. Once in a while, he'd be busy or have to go somewhere on business, and he'd send me home to Brooklyn in the limo.

One night in August, Carmine Lombardozzi, who was very connected with the Gambino family and very married, came in with a tall, gorgeous platinum blonde.

Carmine, a warm, darkly handsome man in his mid-forties, had fallen in love with a wise guy's twenty-three-year-old kid. She was about five-eight in her stiletto heels, with a body that could stop a B59, and was wrapped skin tight in a teeny-weeny, thigh-high dress. Her name was Rosemary. She was as sweet as could be and crazy about Carmine. And Carmine couldn't keep his hands off her. Bernie kept asking him to quit it. "What're you feeling her up in my place for?" he said. "Come on, Carmine, does this look like the backseat of your car?"

Bernie introduced Carmine Lombardozzi to me as "The Doctor," but some people called Carmine "the King of Wall Street" because of the stranglehold he was supposed to have—through loansharking, gambling, and stolen securities—on some of the stock exchange's biggest traders.

"Why do you call him the doctor?" I asked Bernie.

"Because he's an operator," Bernie said.

But Ziggy or Moishe Pickles or maybe it was Red had another explanation. "Because he puts people in the hospital," one of them said.

We went to the Copa a couple of times with Carmine and Rosemary. We spent a weekend at a dude ranch in New Jersey, The Sakasooner Ranch, with friends of mine, and a weekend at the Concord Hotel in the Catskills with friends of Bernie's. All summer long I'd met more of the club—the racket club, as some of the wives used to call it.

And on Labor Day, Bernie said to me: "So, are you my girl?"

I said, "Of course I am."

"Okay," he said. "Then go home and pack. You're going to live with me."

CHAPTER FOUR

Playing House

It was like a Jewish joke—a bad Jewish joke. It was like being caught up in a melodrama from the Yiddish Theatre on Second Avenue or suddenly turning the television on to a bizarre sitcom in which the Goldbergs enter the Twilight Zone.

It was the best of times. It was the worst of times. It was the day I packed my bags and left Brooklyn.

"*Er zol ligen in drerd!* He should rot in hell!" my mother shouted. Rage lifted her onto her tiptoes, wrath hauled her arm up, forefinger pointed to heaven, God as her witness. "In *drerd!*" she screamed as I dumped the contents of my two dresser drawers into shopping bags.

"I love him, Ma," I shouted back. "And he loves me!"

"Pah!" she spat. "This is love?! What do you know about it? This is a gangster, a hoodlum, a man capable of God knows what kind of *mishegas*, what kind of insanity and lies! This man loves you? *Vi a lokh in kop*—like a hole in the head! What did I raise? What kind of moron? If a man loves you, he marries you!" She paced and spun and shouted behind me in the crowded kitchen while my little sister cowered on her daybed, holding her ears and crying.

"Don't worry, Ma. I'll still pay the bills," I hollered.

She gasped. "This is what you think I'm talking about? Money?!" and she gave such a bloodcurdling scream that I whirled around. She was tearing her hair.

"Ma, don't! Stop it, please!" I begged her. I put my arms around Marlene. "Don't look at her. She's crazy," I said.

"Sandy, don't go. Please," my little sister sobbed.

"I love him, Marlene. You don't understand. Mom will be all right after a while. She's just crazy now. She'll be okay and I'll still pay the rent and there'll be enough money for you, for your clothes, for whatever you want, baby. But I've got to get out of here. I'm leaving this mad house. There hasn't been a minute's peace between Mom and me since Daddy left. You get along with her. It won't be bad once I'm gone, Marlene."

"You'll see! You'll see," my mother raged. "You think he loves you? You think he's going to marry you, Mrs. Wise Guy? No man buys a cow when milk is cheap!"

I slammed shut my little suitcase. I stuffed the last sweater into the shopping bag. "What do you know," I said. "What do you know?" But I saw the pain cross her face, as if she'd read my mind, and I bit my lip and didn't finish the thought: You're so smart you're alone!

I grabbed whatever I could carry and ran for the door. But she let out a wail that stopped me in my tracks. "Nooo!" she screamed. And I watched, in stunned silence, as my mother threw herself onto the floor! She threw herself onto the green floral kitchen linoleum and started to flail like a dying fish. She banged her head against the floor. She screamed and prayed and flopped around. *"Got in himmel, Gotenyu, Vey isz mir, Gevalt!"*

I was beyond feeling now. I flew out the door and ran down the hall to the elevator. All the way down to the ground floor, I could hear her.

The driver Bernie had sent was leaning against the front fender of the car, reading a newspaper. He saw me shoot out of the apartment building. God knows what I must have looked like, but he threw down the paper, grabbed my suitcase, and yanked open the car door for me. Then he jumped into the front seat and we sped off into the night—just like in a gangster movie.

The first couple of months we lived together, I was Barbie, Bernie was Ken, and the brownstone on Seventy-ninth Street was our doll house. Or so it seemed to me. Ponytail swinging, high heels clacking, I went to work every day in the Garment Center, no longer a subway shlepper from Brooklyn but a real New Yorker now. The spacious apartment in one of Manhattan's best neighborhoods, the silk-stocking district as it was known, was where I really lived, where I slept and woke every single day. And I adored coming home to it. The man I loved was strong, handsome, rich, and if not famous at least well-known and liked among a select circle of celebrities.

Most evenings, we'd have dinner at the club. But if Bernie said, "Baby, don't come down tonight. Relax at home and I'll call you later," it was no problem—because I loved being in that apartment alone. Bernie had shown me the secret hiding places: the dresser drawer where a couple of hundreds were always stashed; the white Moroccan leather hassock in the living room with the false lid on it in which Bernie kept thick envelopes of money, private papers, a gun, jewelry, and God knows what else. I even had a set of keys to Bernie's big green Cadillac with the swept-back tail fins that sat parked right outside our building day and night. Bernie rarely used it. He preferred taxi cabs or hired cars. And, of course, I never drove it. I didn't know how to drive. I didn't know how to cook. I didn't know how to iron. And these were some of the things that almost brought the doll house tumbling down.

At first, Bernie thought it was cute that I didn't know how to boil an egg. I didn't even know how to boil water. Literally. He bought me a glass pot and actually had to show me that when the water bubbled, that meant it was "boiling hot."

Rock Hudson's butcher, at Schaffer's on Madison Avenue, where customers waited in chairs for their meat to be trimmed, was not as thorough a teacher as Bernie. Don't get me wrong: He sold me a fabulous filet mignon, thick and beautifully marbled. A steak for a king, he kidded me, after I told him I wanted to fix a perfect dinner for my boyfriend. I asked him the best way to cook it, and he said, just put it under the broiler.

Bernie came home from the club early that Thursday. I showed him the steak and he was very proud of me. "That's a gorgeous cut of beef," he said. "How much did it cost?"

I told him and he gave me one of his are-you-out-of-your-mind looks.

"Why, is that a lot?" I asked innocently.

"Naw," he said sarcastically. "Not if you got the rest of the steer cooling in the fridge."

My feelings were hurt and I huffed away. He shook his head and walked off to the bar and made himself a drink while I turned on the broiler.

The butcher never told me to turn the steak over. And every time I looked into the stove and lifted the piece of meat up, it looked ter-

ribly raw on the bottom. So I let it broil and broil and, finally, when
it was nice and brown and there was no blood oozing from underneath it, I put it on a plate and carried it in to Bernie.

He went crazy. He looked at this little curled black knob of steak
I'd brought him and you could practically hear the whistle tooting
and see smoke shoot from his ears. That was my personal introduc-
tion to the highly touted Barton temper. Moishe Pickles hadn't lied.

He threw the plate across the room with all his might. The steak
flew like a hockey puck. The plate shattered. The baked potato,
half raw, cold, and hard as a rock inside its tepid skin, landed with
a thud, then skittered across the bar, bowling over a couple of
glasses and an ashtray. And before all that registered, Bernie's
mouth went off.

I had never in my entire twenty years ever heard such language
used, let alone directed at me. I was not just frightened, I was embarrassed by the words. "Stupid bitch. Cunt," he screamed. And
"dumb douche bag."

I couldn't believe it. This was my Prince Charming, my Ken
doll? I stared at him, incredulous, as he leapt up from the chair and
went from pounding the table to pounding the walls. I watched
dumbfounded. I trembled in fear and stood still and said nothing as
Bernie, biting his fist, ran past me out the front door.

It was obvious that I had a lot to learn. And despite that frightening explosive temper, Bernie was a terrific teacher. Like my father,
he enjoyed taking me shopping. We'd go to Lily Rubin or Wilma's
on Fifty-seventh Street and he'd sit on the little gilt chairs or Victo-
rian settees as I modeled tailored suits and flowing fitted evening
gowns for him. With a nod or a shake of his head, he'd make the final decision on every item. Bernie had an opinion on everything I
wore, the way my hair was done, the kind of makeup that was right
for me. Sometimes he liked me looking sophisticated; sometimes
innocent and young.

He liked me in elbow-length gloves and elegant hats—the same
big-brimmed picture hats that I'd admired as a kid on the ultimate
gangster's moll, Virginia Hill. I had a dozen of them in a rainbow
of colors in velvet, felt, and straw.

Poor Jimmy Doyle, Johnny Dio's uncle, went to his grave with a
scar on his skull from one of my picture hats. Bernie and I had
lunch with him in a restaurant one Mother's Day and, as we were
leaving, I bent to kiss him goodbye. I was wearing a stiff-brimmed
straw picture hat, red, I remember. And as I straightened up, the

brim ripped a hole in his forehead. Blood started gushing out. Everyone at the table stared in shock. A couple of guys tried to mop Jimmy up with linen napkins dipped in ice water. I just stood there, white as a sheet, stunned and horrified, as they rushed him out of the restaurant to an emergency room where it took three butterfly stitches to stop the bleeding.

Of course, at Bernie's, clothes in plain brown bags would appear from out of nowhere. Coats and sweaters. Suits and gowns. Shopping bags would show up in the living room. Hat boxes and shoeboxes and garment bags that were left like orphaned babies.

There were a couple of brothers from Little Italy, Tony and Charlie North, who'd come by from time to time, always together, with suitcases full of designer gowns. Ceil Chapman was a big label in those days and, unbeknownst to her I'm sure, Tony and Charlie were her best customers. They were short and stocky. They looked and dressed alike in dark shirts and shiny suits. A couple of wise guys Walt Disney could have created, they were so ugly they were cute. Fences and loansharks for most of their lives, they'd been in and out of jail countless times. Bernie knew one of them from prison.

In addition to handling some of the most beautiful and elegant evening gowns I'd ever seen, the North brothers helped me understand one of Bernie's strangest habits. He talked in his sleep. He didn't just talk. He fought, cursed, and yelled. "You bastard, I'll kill you!" "Back off, fucker!" "You're a dead man! I'm going to get you!" I'd awaken with a start, my heart pounding violently, only to find Bernie sound asleep, fighting some invisible dream demon.

It wasn't until I heard Tony North teasing Charlie about the same kind of nightmares, the same loud, violent conversations in his sleep, that I began to realize that Bernie's bizarre and frightening outbursts were common among men who'd spent time in prison. Later, other women, girlfriends and wives of guys who'd been inside, told me they had the same experience.

As furs and clothing seemed to appear at the apartment out of thin air, so, one day, did Raven with her magic pink cosmetic box. Raven was one of the stars of Club 82, a mob-controlled nightspot in Greenwich Village with a floor show that featured men dressed and made-up as women. They were so good at it that customers always gasped at the end of the show when the wigs came off and the sexy girls they'd been drooling over all night turned out to be boys in drag. Of course, the tuxedoed, crew-cut waiters at Club 82 were women—women every bit as tough and stocky as the North brothers.

Raven was a make-up artist, a thin boy with reddish black hair, a pointy face, and a beak that left no doubt where he'd gotten his stage name. He was a sad-looking unattractive guy. In drag, he became a sad-looking unattractive girl. But he was a wizard with cosmetics and, at Bernie's request, he taught me all his favorite make-up tricks. Talking a mile a minute, Raven would drape a towel around my neck and, hands fluttering, open his prized pink leather cosmetic case.

"So you're gawn to the Concord? So what'ya wearin'? Black? Wha'four? Y'need a little color, Sandy. Ooooh!" he'd scream when I'd show him the dress or gown or suit du jour. "Oooooh, my Gawd, gorgeous! Like Rita Hayworth, Sandy! With that hair of yours and those long kid gloves. I can't stand it! Just like Rita in *Gilda*. You could drive Glenn Ford wild. So—" He'd swoop down on a lipstick brush, a compact of Pan-Cake, a lightening sponge. "We'll give you that Gilda look! The luscious lips. The flashing eyes!" Raven could build bones and sink cheeks and create what he liked to call gypsy-goddess-eyes-to-die-for.

There was so much Bernie wanted to show me, so much about life he got a kick out of and wanted to share with me. He was at home everywhere. And wherever he was, he picked up the pulse, the accents, the style of his surroundings. At The Velvet Club, he was genial, the best host in the world, nodding and waving and shaking hands, taking care of business with that big Chiclet smile of his. At the Copa he was stylish, generous, bright. With the North brothers, he was strictly street. With guys from the old neighborhood, his conversation was suddenly spiced with Yiddish words and humor. And up in Harlem, where he took me one crisp and sunny fall afternoon, he was as loose and alive as I'd ever seen him anywhere.

I'd never been uptown before. I don't remember why we went, but sitting beside Bernie in the green Caddy, I was dressed to the nines in a stylish new blue suit with a navy blue picture hat. The car radio was on. The windows were open. The big Caddy made a U-turn on 125th Street and pulled right into a perfect parking spot just waiting in front of a storefront with a Chicken Take Out sign hanging over its door. Bernie said, "Just sit there, baby. I'll come around and open your door." He got out on the street side of the car and by the time he walked around the front grill, guys were drifting toward us, coming from across the street and out of the chicken shack.

Men were calling out, "Hey, mah man." "BB." "Mr. B, where you been?"

And Bernie started grinning from ear to ear like he was home. "Hey, man," he'd say. "How you? How you been?" He acted just the same as everyone else. There was no mockery or mimicry about the change that came over him. He was in Harlem, behaving like he'd been born there, looking proud and pleased and welcome. He opened my side of the door and gave me his hand. I stepped out, high heels and nylons first.

"How'do?" men mumbled. Some tipped their hats. "Look what Mr. B's got." They smiled and nodded approvingly. Bernie helped me up onto the front fender of the Caddy. I sat there, fishing in my purse for a cigarette. The minute I found my cigarette case and drew one out, a match appeared under it. "Light?" one of Bernie's friends offered. "It's BB's princess," I heard.

"Who's that?"

"It's BB's princess."

Big eyed, I watched as Bernie talked to people outside the Chicken Take Out. I felt so proud of him. Everywhere we went, he had friends, people liked him, trusted him, slapped him on the back or hand, grinned and joked with him. And every other guy would sneak a peek at me, and touch his cap and say, "How'do?"

Bernie had friends in Harlem. He also had business in Harlem. As we made the rounds that first day, conversations that began with laughs would turn suddenly serious and hushed. Even as I sat on the fender of the Caddy, I noticed a tall black man touch Bernie's elbow and the two of them kind of faded back over toward the Chicken Take Out storefront. Bernie's smile changed just a little. He was listening to the man, nodding his head. The smile was still on his lips, but you could tell it was his ears and eyes that were doing the real work now—alert, at attention, all business. And then, of course, the thick white envelope in which by now I could nearly smell the cash was passed. Bernie tucked it into his breast pocket, clapped the guy on the shoulder, and we were off again.

We drove around and Bernie pointed out the sights to me. That was where the old Cotton Club used to be. A bootlegger named Owney Madden controlled the place. Lucky Luciano was supposed to have had a piece of it. So had a white political boss named Arnold Rothstein. And a black numbers banker named Bumpy Johnson. Did I know that *shvartzas*, colored people, were not even allowed inside the Cotton Club back in its heyday? Only the stars among them—the rich, famous, and dangerous.

I met Bumpy Johnson at an afterhours club uptown a few months later. He was dark and clean, immaculately well dressed with processed straight hair. An elegant-looking man who spoke in a quiet, refined way and never used the popular language of jazz or the streets. Bernie introduced him to me as though he was an elder statesman, with great respect and pride. He had balls. He was honorable. He'd organized unions in Harlem. He'd bankrolled everything from numbers operations to neighborhood bars. And back when black folks couldn't get in the front door of the Cotton Club, Bumpy Johnson could and did. And back when black folks were supposed to take a backseat to the wise guys from downtown, Bumpy Johnson sat where he pleased.

We continued our tour of Harlem and pulled up outside Sugar Ray's, the bar owned by boxing champ Sugar Ray Robinson. Purple was Robinson's favorite color. His big purple Cadillac was often parked right outside the bar, which was, of course, decorated in purple from its lilac and lavender walls to its deep purple leather bar stools and tufted banquettes. That day, my first in Harlem, the champ's car wasn't outside the bar, but Cokey's Cadillac was.

Cokey was one of Bernie's favorite uptown running mates. Bernie had known Cokey almost as long as he'd known Hot Dog Red, but the two men were very different. Where Red was mellow and easy-going, Cokey was quick and electric. He was a wiry, light-skinned black man who owned some chicken and ribs places in Harlem and had a string of prize fighters. What else Cokey was into only God, Bernie, and the D.A.'s office knew for sure. But I had my suspicions about his nickname. We picked Cokey up at Sugar Ray's and the three of us went over to the gym where some of Cokey's fighters were training.

Bernie was wild about boxing. He also owned a fighter or two. But he was a lot more successful betting on fights than owning fighters. The gym on the second floor of a rickety corner building was steamy, loud, and exciting. Both Cokey and Bernie quickly got caught up in watching the training bouts. Again, I was surprised at how many people knew Bernie and came by to say hi. Some ribbed him about one of his fighters who'd taken a terrific licking at Sunnyside Gardens a couple of weeks earlier.

The kid's name was Carlos. Bernie had been excited about taking me to the fights, especially when one of his boys was on the bill. It was yet another world he was eager to introduce me to. But Carlos, the fighter whose food, rent, and training bills Bernie paid, had put in a short and miserable performance before getting knocked down in the second round and Bernie went nuts! He actually pushed up to the ring and started pounding the mat with his fist, screaming, "Get up, you bum. I feed you, I dress you. How can you do this to me?! Get up or I'll kill you!"

The kid tried, I'll give him that. He looked at Bernie pleadingly through his one good eye. The other was swollen shut. "Please, Mr. B," he managed.

"Get up!" Bernie roared.

Carlos tried, made it to one knee, then collapsed.

Bernie bellowed like a wounded bull: "Noooo! You bum, you dog, you dirt bag bastard! Where's your balls? Where's your pride?! How can you do this to me?! Get up!" He started scrambling into the ring. It took a couple of security guards to stop him from crawling under the ropes. I don't know if he was going to fulfill his threat and go after Carlos or if he intended to show the kid how to fight by taking on the winner. I was just glad somebody stopped him.

Despite his threat to kill the kid, Bernie eventually got Carlos, who clearly didn't have what it took to stay alive in the ring, a job in the Garment Center.

None of Bernie's fighters amounted to anything. His judgment in this arena was a joke. One time, Cokey tried to interest him in a new young guy up at the gym. Bernie looked the kid over. "Nah," he said, instantly. "He's too big, too awkward. No way. He'll never make it."

Cokey said, "You're wrong. The kid's got the goods. He can go the whole way."

"Too gawky, too big," Bernie insisted. "What's his name?"

"Cassius Clay," said Cokey.

"Forget him," Bernie said.

A few years later, the kid took a new name: Muhammad Ali.

Bernie loved Harlem. He knew its ins and outs, from neighborhood bars and little chicken and rib joints where thousands of dollars in numbers money changed hands to the celebrity spots, jazz clubs, and luxurious afterhours places where gambling, smoke, and coke were openly indulged in from midnight through the wee small hours. After a night's work at The Velvet Club, he'd go uptown to unwind at places like Reefer May's, a town house in Harlem's classiest section, Sugar Hill.

Reefer May's was like a decadent Disneyland, a sprawling adult theme park for urban vampires. One never arrived before midnight. After the witching hour, the place began to fill with wise guys, slumming socialites, jazz musicians, and the occasional rich, adventuresome college kid. People came in every color and many of them came with guns. Weapons were like accessories, as important as cufflinks or tie pins, no more. Women floated through the rooms in every stunning style of dress. Models in sequined gowns dragging floor-length furs behind them. Square girls in blonde pageboys and ankle-length taffeta skirts. Actresses, dancers, entertainers still in their stage makeup, their heads covered in Audrey Hepburn-type scarves. Older women in good jewels and dark glasses.

And, of course, there was Reefer May herself. She was an enormous and beautiful middle-aged black woman, who wore floor-length caftans and her thick, still-dark hair pulled back tightly in a large, neat bun. She was extremely sweet-faced with flawless, shiny cocoa skin. According to Red, she'd been a breathtakingly handsome girl, the mistress of a white numbers banker. An Irish or Italian guy, a nice man, Red said, who'd been wildly in love with her. Reefer had put away the money she'd gotten from him and with it, after he died, she'd bought her place.

There were at least eight huge rooms at Reefer May's and each was decorated differently. You would wander from the purple, red, and gold-cushioned Arabian Nights room into the brass, mahogany, and red velvet decor of a turn-of-the-century bordello; from a jungle setting of tropical plants and tigerskins to the elegant, pleated fabric walls of the gambling casino. In one room musicians would be jamming, passing joints, getting up to chat or take a break, and their seats would immediately be filled by new musicians, whose girls would sway against the wall or carry fresh glasses of scotch, bourbon, vodka, or cognac over to them. If the jam didn't smell of marijuana smoke it smelled of Gitanes or Gauloise, the musky French cigarettes so many of the jazzmen had gotten used to in Paris. At the bar, people would knock powdered lines of cocaine onto the backs of their hands and snort them up or offer them around in the ritual way one might suck on a lemon after a shot of tequila.

* * *

I continued working in the Garment Center, but it was hard showing up early in the morning after spending time either with or waiting for Bernie. His schedule, his way of life, was never going to be conventional, I realized, but I did the best I could to keep up with it. Sometimes, he'd come home at six in the evening, with a little bag of food for me from the club. He'd have a drink and unwind while I ate dinner. We'd talk, cuddle, catch up, and he'd leave again at ten to go back to work. And he might not come back until three or four in the morning. Some days, he was walking in the door as I was walking out. Some nights, he wanted me to be with him when he visited an afterhours club in Harlem or a gambling joint downtown. All in all we spent more time together than most couples I knew back then. It was great for our relationship, but deadly for my career. In late October, I got fired.

CHAPTER FIVE

Easy Come, Easy Go

My nose was running and my eyes were red from crying when Bernie came home that night. "Baby, what's the matter, are you sick?" he asked.

I was in bed, surrounded by tissues. "No. I got fired."

"Thank God," he said.

"What do you mean, thank God? How am I going to support my family. They need my help. My mother makes *bubkes* at that dumb cleaning store. Marlene's too young to go to work, even part-time. She's only twelve. She's got to study to get decent grades. How can you say, 'thank God'?"

"Thank God it's your job, not your health," he said, and sat down next to me on the bed. "Look," he said, taking my hand. "You got fired. You'll collect unemployment. You'll send Tillie your unemployment check and I'll make up the difference. It's nothing. It's just money, baby."

He was as good as his word. My mother despised him and he knew it. But he never took it personally. "Why should I," he'd ask. "She's never even met me. When she meets me and hates me, *then* I'll start worrying."

He gave me cash every two weeks to send home to Brooklyn. And, for a long time, I didn't tell my mother where the money was coming from. I didn't want to worry her about my losing my job. I knew how awful she'd feel about it. How afraid she'd be of my total reliance on Bernie, a man in whose love for me she had no faith at all.

It took me a little while to get used to depending on Bernie for money. I felt very uncomfortable asking for cash, although he never made a big deal about it. "Go to the drawer," he'd say. That was it. He never said, take five dollars or take five hundred. Just "Go to the drawer. Get what you need."

There were always a couple of hundreds in that magical drawer. Even during sports seasons, when Bernie's betting fever really took off. That's when both TVs and the radio would be blasting off and there'd be hot and cold running bookmakers in the apartment all day long. A guy would walk in with an envelope of money and hand it to Bernie. Fifteen minutes later, another guy would walk out with two envelopes. And Bernie wouldn't blink one way or another. He'd just grab the phone and lay the next bet, shushing me, shushing Red, running from one room to the other checking the game scores, from the NFL on ABC to the NHL on CBS.

A few weeks after I lost my job, and the maple trees lining Seventy-ninth Street shed the last of their leaves, I looked out the window one morning and saw that the green Caddy was gone. "Bernie," I called, rushing back to the bedroom where he was still asleep. "The car's missing."

"It's okay," he mumbled.

"What do you mean, 'it's okay'? You lent it to someone?"

"No. I *gave* it to someone."

"I don't understand."

"I owed the guy. I gave him the car. Now you understand?"

It was Hot Dog Red, that afternoon, who explained that the guy Bernie had given the car to was a bookmaker and the Cadillac was payment for a gambling debt.

A week later, the Caddy was back.

A couple of weeks before Christmas, a white-haired old man showed up in our livingroom. His name was Sonny, not Santa. And he didn't have a beard. Outside of that, the resemblance was uncanny. Bernie had been caught up in football action for a while and there seemed to be more fat envelopes leaving the house with bookmakers or their runners than coming in. So I was surprised when he suggested that I do some holiday shopping. "Go with Sonny. Get whatever you want for yourself, for Marlene and your mother. Buy stuff for everybody. Go. Sonny'll take you."

"Okay, fine," I said, and got ready to go out. "How much money should I take?"

"No, babe. You don't need money," Bernie said. "Sonny'll handle it."

We went to Saks Fifth Avenue. Sonny was a sweetheart. He was very patient. He'd lean against a pillar or when there was a chair available, he'd sit and wait with the growing pile of boxes and shopping bags while I examined each new item. "Is this worth it?" I'd ask him. Or, "I don't know, do you think it's too expensive?"

And Sonny would always encourage me. "It's beautiful. Buy it. Don't worry. Bernie'll pay for it." So I bought gifts for my mother, my sister, my cousins, my friends and, of course, for Bernie. I bought cashmere sweaters, suede belts, leather pocketbooks, silk scarves, magnificent shawls, shirts, jewelry, perfume. "Beautiful," Sonny would say. "Buy it. It's a bargain. Don't worry about it." And Sonny charged everything.

We took a cab back to the brownstone. It took Sonny two trips up the stairs to get all that I'd bought into the apartment. It added up to several thousand dollars' worth of gifts. Sonny had a drink with us. "Okay," Bernie said to him. "So what's the damage?"

Sweet as ever, smiling kindly, Sonny held up the fingers of his right hand.

"Five," Bernie said, peeling off the bills.

Five thousand dollars. Oh, my God, I thought. I didn't know I'd spent that much! But Bernie didn't blink.

"Five hundred," he said, slapping the last bill into Sonny's outstretched hand. "Thanks, man."

"Take care," Sonny said, draining the drink. "Sandy, you've got wonderful taste, honey. It's a pleasure going shopping with you."

I waited until Sonny was gone. Then I said, "Bernie, I added up the sales receipts. I know it comes to much more than five hundred dollars."

"Forget it. It's nothing. It's a credit card thing, a fugazy." Then he stopped and reconsidered. "Don't worry about it," he said evenly. "You're better off not knowing. Anytime you want to go shopping, just let me know and I'll call Sonny, okay?"

"Okay," I said. But later, on the phone with Toni, a friend of mine who was also seeing a wise guy, I said, "Did you ever hear the word 'fugazy'?"

"Sure," she said. "It means phoney. Phoney. Fugazy. It's just another word for it."

In January, Bernie and I were having steak at the Hickory House and one of the bookmakers I'd met a couple of times came in.

Bernie asked him to join us. What does he want to drink? How's the family? They're just sitting there shooting the breeze and, casually, Bernie pulled a pink piece of paper out of his wallet, signed it, and handed it over to the guy. Then he took a couple of keys off his key ring, handed those over, too. The bookmaker smiled, nodded, put the pink slip and the keys in his jacket pocket. Then he finished the drink Bernie had bought him, and got up with an "Okay, Bernie. So long, Sandy. You're looking great. Prettier every day." And off he went.

Before I could say, "What was that?" Bernie said, "I just signed over the car." He was cutting his steak. He didn't even look up. "You've got cash for a cab, right, baby?"

The money came. The money went. Two weeks after he gave up the car, Bernie was flush again. He decided to take me out to a new French restaurant he'd been hearing about, a small, romantic, elegant place on the Upper East Side. It held no more than sixty people and, at nine, when we got there, it was already packed. We had a drink at the bar, which sported gleaming brass and etched-glass fixtures and huge bouquets of fresh flowers.

I wore a beautiful pantsuit, a sort of silk pajama outfit with a tunic top and gorgeously tailored loose-fitting trousers. The silky fabric moved wonderfully and Bernie thought it was not just chic but sexy as hell. He couldn't have been happier when the maitre d' led us to a secluded table at the back of the restaurant.

Bernie ordered a bottle of wine. We were on our second glass, teasing each other, fooling around under the table like kids. It must have been ten or ten-thirty when two men at a table near the front stood up suddenly, pulled out guns, and announced, "This is a stick up."

Immediately, Bernie started to get up. I put my hand on his thigh and he stayed put, but his fist closed dangerously around the table knife. "They've got guns, baby. Don't," I whispered.

Some of the diners had their hands up in the air, others were shaking visibly. At the table next to ours, a good-looking, gray-haired woman was crying. Her husband was trying to comfort her in a frightened whisper. "Shhh, Belle, it's all right, darling."

The well-dressed gunmen quickly locked the front door. One of them, a guy with a blond crewcut, started barking out orders: "Empty your wallets. Cash on the table. Take off your jewelry."

The second man, dark-haired and tall, emptied the register, then stayed at the front of the restaurant as the blond went from table to table throwing the cash and jewelry into what looked like a pillow-case.

"A square joint," Bernie was muttering. "This is what happens when you go to a square joint. You don't get robbed in a wise guy's place. Okay," he said to me. "Take off all your jewelry like he said. But under the table. Very carefully. Put your hands under the table. Here," he said. He slipped me a stack of money. "It's about a grand. That top you're wearing is nice and loose. Put the money in your pants, okay? And the jewelry, too. The blouse'll cover it. Just leave the earrings on the table. I've got about five hundred in my other pocket. Let that bastard have it."

I did exactly as Bernie told me. Very, very carefully, with my hands under the table, I pulled off the rings, my watch, and gold bracelets. And put them into my panties, along with the thousand dollars he'd handed me. Then I began to take off my earrings, with big, exaggerated gestures, trying to show the blond guy with the sack that I was doing what he'd said to do.

"Shit," Bernie grumbled as the crew cut headed directly for us. "I think the guy at the door must've seen you and signaled the other one."

No sooner were the words out of Bernie's mouth than the blond banged a fist on the table. "You think you're smart, right? You think you're being a very clever fellow. Get up!" he ordered me. "I'm taking the broad into the ladies' room, smart guy. And I'm making her strip, and if I have to I'm going to shake her and everything can fall out of her cunt. I don't care."

"You son of a bitch," Bernie said.

The guy had a gun pointed at us. "Bernie, please, don't," I said. "It's okay. I'll go. Don't say anything, please."

But Bernie was half out of his mind. He talked very softly, more like a growl than language, and I knew he was hanging on to that temper of his by a cuticle. "You don't know who I am, buddy, and you're better off not knowing right now. But you're dead, fucker. You hear me?" A scary, soft growl.

The guy got nervous. He started waving the gun under Bernie's nose. "This is what I know, asshole. This. You see this. Now shut up. You," he said to me, "stand up. Move."

And thank God Bernie controlled himself. His fingers were white from how hard he was pressing them against the tablecloth. His face had drained of color. But he let us go.

In the ladies' room, the guy was all business. He pointed the gun at my face and said, "Take your pants off." The waistband of the slacks was elastic, so I just pulled them down with my underwear, and everything I'd hidden inside the pants went clattering to the floor: rings and watches and money and bracelets. It was incredibly noisy. Things were bouncing on the tiles and Bernie's money fanned out all over the place. The gunman swept the stuff up and put it into the pillowcase and walked me back to the table.

The police showed up about ten minutes after the thieves left. Everyone was questioned about what had been taken. Bernie played it very, very square with the cops. He told them exactly what had happened, including how he had told me to hide the jewelry and some cash in my pants. He had to tell the truth because other people had already told the police about the man taking me into the bathroom, which had scared most of them to death because they hadn't heard the exchange between Bernie and the gunman and had no idea why he'd singled me out. In fact, the gray-haired lady from the next table put her arm around me and said, "You were very brave." I was touched. I told her that she had been, too. And we hugged.

All the way home, Bernie couldn't stop ranting about how this would never have happened if he hadn't decided to try a square restaurant. Nobody would've walked into a mob-run joint and pulled a couple of guns, he said, unless they were prepared to use them—and quick!

In the apartment, he was on the phone before he had his coat off. "You hear anybody pulled off a heist like that, you get back to me right away," he said. He described the guys. Then, "WASPs," I heard him say. "They looked like WASPs, but I feel it in my gut they were guineas. Yeah, the blond prick, too. Italian."

He hung up. "I'm sorry, kid," he said to me. I was sitting in a heap on the sofa. I'd thrown water on my face to try to calm down. My mascara had run and I didn't care, so I was collapsed on the couch with big black smudges running down my cheeks. Bernie sat on the arm of the sofa. He pulled out his handkerchief and wet a corner of it in his mouth and, almost absentmindedly, started to wipe the mascara off my face. "It's not so much what they took," he said. "It's what they did to you. You don't know how it felt sitting there. I had all kinds of fantasies. I should have killed the bastard."

So word went out on the street. Two weeks later Bernie got a phone call from someone who said, okay, all the jewelry and the thousand in cash were going to be returned. But Bernie wanted a piece of the guys. The middleman on the telephone said, "Look, we don't want to give these guys up. They know who you are now, but they didn't know in the restaurant. They're sorry, Bernie. They know you now."

"Okay," Bernie said. "Fine. You don't want to give them up. That's up to you. But if I ever see them walking the streets, I'm going to put a couple of shots into them." He sounded as cold and deadly serious as I'd ever heard him.

But when he got off the phone, he shrugged his shoulders and said, "Hey, at least we played it square for the night, didn't we?" It was as if the whole thing were a Halloween prank and we'd been costumed as normal people for an evening. Looking down the barrel of a gun was just part of the everyday trick-or-treat setup squares had to live with.

Tough guys lived by different rules. And at an engagement party one Sunday afternoon at Ben Maksis's Town and Country Club on Ocean Parkway, Bernie decided it was time for me to learn a couple of the basics. The Town and Country was to Brooklyn what The Copa was to Manhattan—a supper club setting for the borough's rich and famous, which included politicians and crooks. I can't remember whose daughter had gotten engaged at the black-tie party, a councilman's or a consigliere's, or if the band, after a run of mambos, lindys, and fox-trots, finished up with a hora or tarantella. I don't remember whether the solid-gold *chais* and diamond-chip-trimmed Stars of David outnumbered the Florentined holy medals and jewel-encrusted crucifixes.

I just remember that the band was good and that I wanted to dance. I sat, searching the room for Bernie, at a big, round table with people I didn't know. All of them were much older than I. Most of them were heavyset women in pastel chiffon and bright hair, whose husbands were making the rounds, drinks in hand, cigars lit, breast pockets bulging with gift envelopes of cash for the father of the betrothed. I had on a new black beaded cocktail dress that had arrived in the traditional shopping bag and was wearing my Breath-of-Spring mink stole, of course. Bernie was bent out of shape about being in a tux on a Sunday afternoon.

When finally he returned to our table, I said, "Honey, dance with me. The music is terrific." It was a slow dance. Bernie sighed and gave me a look. "What?" I said. "I just asked you to dance with me, that's all."

"Okay. One," he said.

He wasn't a terrific dancer, but it felt good being in his arms. I liked the thought of how nice we looked together. I imagined other people watching us, thinking, what a handsome couple—Bernie with his rugged good looks and pale blue eyes, me in my glamorous black beaded dress, auburn hair piled high on my head twisted in a fashionable French knot. The music was slow and sexy.

Then the song ended and Bernie started walking me back to the table. "Wait," I said. "Maybe they'll play another slow one."

He shook his head and kept on going. I stopped and held on to his hand. "Come on, honey. Just one more."

"Sandra," he said. He'd used that name, that warning tone, only a couple of times before. I rolled my eyes waiting for the lecture. "I don't dance," he said. "You get it? I danced with you once because you asked me to. And I told you just once, I'd do it. And I did. And that's it."

I'd had a couple of screwdrivers. I felt a little playful. I hurried after him as he walked away. "And that's it," I repeated, mimicking him. "What's it? What's 'that's it'?"

We were off the dance floor now. Bernie pulled me along to a quiet corner just outside the banquet room. "I'm going to set you straight now," he said with strained patience, like a teacher talking to a dull child. "Tough guys don't dance, you understand?"

I was embarrassed by the way he was speaking to me. "Oh, yeah," I said with bravado. "Tough guys don't cry. They don't go down on broads—they don't eat anything unless it's on a platter. And they definitely don't dance."

"You got it," Bernie said and walked away.

The band played a drum roll. The lights dimmed. And a dozen waiters sailed out of the kitchen carrying trays of flaming cherries jubilee.

I'd left Brooklyn at the end of August. In early February, Bernie went to Florida on business. My mother and I hadn't exactly resumed "normal relations"—we'd been fighting since I was thirteen—but we did speak regularly now on the telephone. And Bernie, with his Jewish sense of family, never missed an opportunity to promote peace between us.

When George Raft came into The Velvet Room one night with a couple of wise guys, it was Bernie who suggested my mother might get a kick out of hearing about it. "Oh, Mr. Raft," I'd gushed, "I've loved you since I was a little girl." Everyone at the table laughed. It took me a while to realize I'd implied he was old. "Thanks a lot, kid," he'd said. From then on he always called me kid. And it was Bernie who said, "Go call your mother, tell her you just met George Raft. Let her *kvell* a little."

If he bought me something new that I loved, he'd say, "Why don't you give Tillie a call? Tell her what I got you. Make her happy." He'd always remind me to buy Marlene a birthday gift or send my mother a couple of extra dollars for whatever special occasion was coming up.

In February, before he left for Florida, Bernie left me extra money and suggested that I invite my mother to come into the city and stay with me for the couple of days he'd be gone. "Make sure she takes a taxi," he said, tossing the extra cash into the drawer. He wanted her to see where and how I was living. He wanted her to know that I was safe and being well cared for.

Much to my surprise, my mother accepted. "He's not going to be there?" she asked three times.

"No, Ma. He's going to Florida."

"But not with you."

"It's business, Ma."

"Business? What kind of business does a man like that have? Monkey business, maybe. But you, you're sure it's business."

"What are you saying, he's lying to me? He's going for pleasure?"

"Excuse me. Did I say pleasure? For his *health*, maybe. A man his age—I thought maybe he's got rheumatism, maybe arthritis like the other *alter kockers* and he's going to take the waters in Miami Beach."

"Take a cab, Ma. I'll pay for it when you get here."

The apartment was spotless. But I spent the morning compulsively straightening things anyway, fluffing the pillows on the black sofa, picking lint from the red velvet side chairs and red carpeting, blowing ashes off the gold-flecked glass coffee table top and imaginary dust off the ornate mirrors and brass and crystal lamps with their towering pleated shades. Between chores, I paced and smoked and peered out the tall livingroom windows, watching for my mother's taxi.

My mother was a short woman, blonde, stylish, and neat. It hadn't been that long since I'd seen her, but she looked smaller than I remembered as she stepped out of the cab in her good wool coat and leather gloves. Standing there with her pocketbook tucked under one arm and her little overnight bag in her hands, she looked tiny, vulnerable, and lost. And I found myself thrilled and close to tears at the sight of her.

I knocked on the window for her to tell the driver to wait. I waved the money Bernie had left for the cab and signaled that I'd be right down. I saw her joy at the sight of me—for just an instant she let it show. Then she made an annoyed face and waved me away. By the time I ran downstairs to the front door, she was snapping shut her change purse and the taxi was pulling away from the curb.

She allowed me to kiss her cheeks. "Why'd you pay him, Ma? I have the money. I told you I was going to take care of it."

"Seven dollars and fifty cents with the tip. You'll send it with the unemployment money, all right?"

I wrestled her suitcase out of her hand and took her arm and we walked inside together. "You look great, Ma."

"You're too skinny," she said.

"Isn't this a gorgeous building? Look, Ma," I said, leading her upstairs, toward our apartment door. "Isn't this pretty, wallpaper in the hallway, carpeted stairs, and everything. Wait until you see the apartment."

"Very nice, very nice," she acquiesced. The hallway was neutral turf.

I threw open the apartment door. "And this is our place."

She sighed and walked inside. "Oh, my God," was the first thing she said, and that only when she was standing in the middle of the black, white, and red livingroom. She turned slowly. There was a little grin on her face and she was fighting it all the way. "*Oy, oy, oy.* Look at this. Like Ali Baba and the Forty Thieves!"

I cracked up. I don't know why, but instead of being hurt or angry I thought it was the funniest thing I'd ever heard. It was clever, sarcastic, and awestruck—just like my mother. And I'd really missed her. Not just for the couple of months since I'd moved to Manhattan, but for all the years we'd fought and grieved. I just started laughing. She did, too. From that moment on the weekend was just us, a couple of girls laughing and being sarcastic and clever and, once in a while, annoyed with each other, and awestruck, too.

I took her on a tour of the house. She was not impressed by the tiny kitchen. She stared at the half-fridge and shook her head in disbelief. "Such a rich man can't afford a real refrigerator?" She clicked her tongue over the mirrored bedroom walls and ceiling. "Whoever saw mirrors like this? What for? He likes to look at himself in bed?" The telephone in the bathroom floored her. "Why?

Very nice. It's very nice. But for what?" I couldn't tell her Bernie didn't like to be too far from his bookmaker.

I took her to Stark's on Madison Avenue for lunch. And then we went shopping, stopping in at all the beautiful shops on Madison and Fifth Avenue. We walked over to Rockefeller Center. As we watched the ice skaters in the rink below, I said, "I'm going to take you to Bernie's club for dinner. I can't wait for you to see The Velvet Room." My mother shook her head.

"But why, Ma?" I was so eager for her to see it, to see me in it and how well I was treated and how many famous people came there. But she flat refused.

"Don't ask me why, Sandy. I don't know. When he marries you, then I'll go there. Until then, it's like asking me to eat *trayf*."

So we went to dinner in Little Italy at a place a friend of Bernie's owned. We had a bottle of wine and ordered lavishly, and I saw her flush when the check came and I laid a hundred dollar bill on top of it. But the owner came over quickly and stopped the waiter from taking the money. "Sandy, what's the matter with you," he said sadly. "You know your money's no good here, kid. Here, let me buy you and your beautiful sister here a Sambuca. Did you have enough of everything? You liked the fish? Tommy," he called to the waiter, "pack up a couple of cannolis for the girls to take home."

We slept together in the king-sized bed. We were both a little high and very, very happy and it was like a kids' pajama party. Then, in the middle of the night my mother's screams woke me up.

"What?! Ma, what's the matter? What happened?"

She was cowering under the covers. "Ma," I started whispering, afraid there was someone in the house. "Ma, what happened? What scared you? Is someone here?" I was afraid to put on the light.

"I saw someone looking at me," she said.

"Who? Where?"

There was a moment's silence. Then, sheepishly, she stuck her head out from under the covers. Pointing at the ceiling, embarrassed and still shaken, "There," she yelled. "In that *meshuggene* mirror, where else?!"

My mother had to go back to work on Monday. Sunday evening, we kissed and hugged and she said, "Thank you for a wonderful weekend."

"You know, Ma. You could call Bernie sometime and tell him thanks, too," I said. "It was really his idea. It's his money, his apartment."

"When he marries you," she said. Then she stroked my cheek and got into the cab. I waited outside until the car was out of sight.

That night, when Bernie called me from Florida, he asked how the weekend had gone.

"Great," I said and sighed.

"So why do you sound like you're dying?"

"It's nothing. We had a great time."

"Sandra . . . What's going on?"

"Baby," I said, "when are we going to get married?"

CHAPTER SIX

Mrs. Wise Guy

We were in bed the night Bernie came home from Florida.

"Did you miss me?" I asked, snuggling up against him.

He had just showered. His dark hair was slicked back and damp. He looked tan, clean, healthy, and very sexy. He moved up against me and, laughing, said, "You have to ask?"

Against my better judgment, I wriggled closer. I could feel my resolve melting. I tried again. "Do you love me?"

He put his arms around me. "Yes, baby. Of course I love you. Can't you feel how I love you? How I missed you? What do you think is going on here?"

"Then why can't we get married?"

"Sandra!" he hollered. "What the hell's the matter with you? I just got home. It's my first night back. What are you trying to ruin it for?"

"I want to get married, Bernie."

"Good," he said. He threw back the covers. "Great!" He got out of bed. "Go, get married. Good luck to you."

"I want to marry *you*!" I screamed after him as he stormed into the bathroom and slammed the door.

I was crying when he finally came back out. "Now, listen, kid," he said. He sat down at the edge of the bed and hugged me. "You know I love you. You're my baby. You're my girl, aren't you? But this isn't a good time for me. I'll tell you the truth, *mamela*, business is lousy. I may have to give up the club. I've been losing on the games. I need some peace around here. I need, well, you know, baby. I'm a man. You know what I need. Come on, Sandy, don't go nuts on me here. You love your daddy, don't you, baby?"

I fell apart. I loved him so much. I felt so sorry for him. I wanted to be his good little girl, his stand-up broad, the one he could count on. "Yes," I said.

We made love.

"Bernie," I said the next day. "I want to get married."

He was coming out of the bathroom rubbing his hair with a towel. He stopped. He tilted his head and looked at me as though he was unsure he'd heard right.

"Seriously," I said.

He walked back into the bathroom and shut the door.

A couple of nights later when we were in bed and I began *hocking* him, nagging him about marriage again, he rolled away from me and reached over to his night table. He pulled open the night table drawer. For a split second, I wondered if he was going to pull out a gun and shoot me. Instead, he pulled out two wads of cotton and made a big show of putting them in his ears. Then he rolled back over to me and picked up where he'd left off.

But I was a woman with a mission now. And Bernie had been a better teacher than he thought. Along with the lessons he constantly gave me on everything from elocution, manners, and morality to makeup, hairdos, and homemaking, Bernie had taught me more than he knew about persistence, stubbornness, fighting for what you want, standing up to an adversary, hanging in against the odds. Everything I'd heard him say and watched him do I tried now. And I was getting good at it, too.

I even enlisted my mother in the cause. My sister Marlene had told me how impressed she'd been with her weekend in the city. "The minute she got back to Brooklyn," Marlene said, "she got right on the horn and called up all her friends. 'Such a gorgeous apartment.' 'Such a fine neighborhood.' 'A phone in the bathroom yet!' " So when Bernie suggested that I invite my mother to join us on New Year's Eve, I did it with more urgency than usual.

"Ma, you've got to come," I insisted. "I need you. You want him to marry me, you've got to get to know him and he's got to meet you. Let's start the new year right. Let's be together. I need your help, Ma."

It was an amazing evening. Bernie handed me his tuxedo and told me to get it pressed. I had no idea he meant professionally. I assumed he wanted me to iron it. So I did. And handed it back to him about twenty minutes before my mother was due at the apartment. He took one look at the shiny, crooked creases I'd ironed into the trousers and hit the roof.

"What the hell is wrong with you? Where do you come from, Mars?" He picked up a bedside book and hurled it at the bathroom door. He flipped a big glass ashtray off the dresser, and when it stopped bouncing and rolling he jumped on it with two feet. "You never heard of a dry cleaner? Your mother works at a cleaning store! What do you do, sit on your fucking brains all day?" He slammed his fist into the wall and God was with him—or with me—because the spot turned out to be plasterboard, not concrete, and his fist went right through it. "God damn New Year's Eve and I'm going to wear pleated fucking trousers to the fucking club tonight?! What the hell is the matter with you?!"

I was still getting dressed when my mother arrived. Bernie, with an ice pack on his knuckles, answered the door. They had spoken a couple of times on the phone. They had bantered back and forth, Bernie perhaps a little more good-naturedly than Tillie. Now, five minutes into their first face-to-face meeting, he said to her: "Tillie, didn't you teach that kid of yours anything? She can't cook. She can't iron—"

My mother cut him off. "I didn't raise her to be a cook or a laundress," she said icily. "She only has to be good in one room."

Bernie couldn't believe his ears. He broke up laughing. "Well, there you did a gem of a job," he said.

Boy, was he wrong. I was pretty naive about sex when I met Bernie. But even more naive about birth control. It wasn't long before I became pregnant. I was frightened and frantic and I didn't dare tell Bernie. I knew the last thing he wanted right then was a baby. And I didn't want one. I was too young and I wasn't married.

And as far as abortions went, not only were they not legal but, well, I had seen how Kirk Douglas responded to the news that Eleanor Parker had had an abortion in *Detective Story*. He'd said he wished he could rip his brain out of his head and hold it under cold water to wash it clean of the thought of her.

I called Judy at the beauty salon and sobbed the bad news to her over the phone.

"Now, darlin'," she soothed, "you just come right on down here and we'll think of something."

You'd think two heads were better than one. Not when they belonged to Judy and me. I was filled with fear and she was filled with folklore.

"Okay, I borrowed a car," she said when I burst into her apartment over the shop on East Fifty-fourth Street.

"Good. Where are we going?"

"You want to get rid of it, don't you?"

"Yes," I said. "But where are we going?"

"For a ride," Judy said with an air of cunning.

I had no idea what she was talking about. "Okay. Good. But what about, you know, Judy, my being pregnant?"

She was gathering up her purse and keys and getting into her coat. "Sandy, that's why I borrowed the car, for christsake. We're going to ride over every bump and pothole in New York City until we get rid of it."

"You're kidding."

"Let's go."

True to her daffy Southern-accented word, Judy started up the little black two-seater sports car she'd borrowed from her boyfriend and, with me tearfully riding shotgun, she pulled away from the curb. She was a bad driver at best. Now here she was grinding gears and practically whooping out rebel yells as we sped, bumping and bouncing, over the worst ruts in the city. I was white-knuckled with fear. Only the fact that the car was a convertible kept my skull from being shattered as we hurtled along.

"What if this doesn't work?" I managed to holler through clenched teeth.

"It'll work. Don't worry. Trust me, honey."

We went to Jilly's for a drink after the ride. I was sick to my stomach. It was clear that all we had gotten rid of was my lunch.

"Do you remember Hattie Prince from the beauty shop?" Judy asked.

With prompting, I recalled a very tough lady with short, curly, bleached blue-white hair and big black eyes whom I'd seen at Judy's salon a couple of times. I remembered a throaty liquor voice, a blinding jewelry collection, a commanding, almost masculine manner, and a lot of makeup. Hattie Prince was a *zaftik* little bulldog of a woman. And Judy or someone else at the shop had described her as an ex-madam and a bookmaker.

"I hear she's doing abortions now," Judy said.

"I don't have money for an abortion. Isn't there anything else we can do?"

"Lysol," Judy said, draining her Southern Comfort. "Douching with Lysol."

We wobbled back to her apartment as the sun was setting. "Are you sure?" I asked in the old brass-trimmed elevator heading up to her fifth-floor apartment.

"Well, not one hundred percent. But it can't hurt to try, can it?"

So I douched with Lysol. Which was a little like charbroiling my womb. My insides felt like hamburger meat on fire. I could barely walk to the curb to call a cab. "Well, that should certainly do the trick. Call me when you get home and let me know what happens," Judy urged as she helped me into the taxi.

Nothing happened. I was in great flaming pain for about a week. I developed a vaginal infection. I was still pregnant.

Judy and I called Marilyn and she mentioned my old pharmacist friend Noah from the Garment Center. He suggested Urgatrate, a drug that was supposed to bring on menstrual bleeding. Marilyn and I went down to see him. The pills he gave us were black and big as bullets. I thought if one Urgatrate was good, three would be better. And I got desperately, but bloodlessly, sick.

Bernie was out when I got home. I crawled into bed and curled up, holding my aching stomach. I had the chills and was burning up at the same time. Sweating and shaking, I fell asleep and woke as Bernie got into bed at about four in the morning. He tried to hug me and I groaned and pulled away. "What's the matter?" he asked.

"Nothing. I'm sick."

"From what? Do you have the flu?"

I was too exhausted to get into it. "Yes," I said. "Just let me sleep."

The next day, still queasy, I was leaning against the little Formica kitchen counter waiting for water to boil for a cup of tea, when the doorbell rang. I shuffled to the window and looked down. A slender young guy in a gray overcoat, hatless, his thick dark hair ruffled by the wind, was calling his name through the intercom. Peter something. I'd never seen him before. "Who's that?" I asked Bernie.

"Shit," he said. "It's my P.O. Give me a hand, Sandy. I've got to clear the house quick."

Quick was not in my body's vocabulary that day. I watched as Bernie began to tear around the apartment tossing gold, silver, and crystal ornaments, ashtrays, candlesticks and other valuables into drawers and closets.

"What are you doing? What's a P.O.?"

"P.O.—parole officer. It's the Greek," Bernie said, stuffing a shopping bag full of recently delivered cashmere sweaters under the bed. "He's doing one of his little surprise check-ups and if he sees any of this, I'm screwed. He knows how much I'm supposed to be making to the penny. I can't have expensive stuff like this around."

I was wearing what I'd slept in, one of Bernie's T-shirts. "I'd better change," I said.

"You'd better hide," he said. "Just hang out in the bathroom for a couple of minutes. It won't be long."

"Bernie, I'm sick," I protested.

"Five minutes. I promise."

By the time Peter Knossos, the P.O., entered the apartment, it was stripped to essentials. Never mind that even in its bare state it looked like Liberace's guest room, at least the real high-ticket items were out of sight.

"Hiya, come in, how're you doing, Peter?" Bernie greeted the probation officer like an old friend. "Can I get you a drink? Cigar? What brings you to the neighborhood?"

Either Knossos was soft-spoken or Bernie was effusively loud, but I only heard mumbled replies. Sick as a dog, clutching my belly, I still couldn't resist sneaking a peek at the guy. After a couple of minutes, I opened the bathroom door a crack and peered out. Just in time to see Bernie taking this dark-haired kid's arm, leading him toward the door. "Here," he said, stuffing a wad of bills into the guy's gloved hand. "Buy your kids something nice, Peter. I'll see you next Wednesday."

I waited until the front door closed, then I came out of the bathroom. Bernie came flying into the bedroom. He was wearing just the white undershirt and shorts he'd had on under his scarlet silk Sulka robe when the P.O. had first rung the bell.

"What the hell was wrong with you? I asked you to help me clear the place out and you were just standing there staring at me." Bernie reached under the bed and pulled out the robe which he'd balled up and tossed there a minute before he'd let Peter Knossos into the apartment. "Do you understand this guy could put me away again?" He put on the robe and tied the tasseled silk sash. "Sandy, when I need you, you've got to be there, baby. You're either a stand-up broad or you're not. Now what's going on?"

"I'm sick," I shouted back at him.

"You're not that sick."

"I'm sicker than sick, Bernie. I'm fucking pregnant." That stopped us both; I was as shocked by what I'd said as he was.

"You're what? You're pregnant? How?!"

"What're you, crazy? What do you mean, 'How'?! How does someone get pregnant?"

"I'll tell you how," he yelled, pacing the bedroom like a caged tiger. "By not taking care of themselves, Sandra. That's how. I trusted you. I thought you took care of that."

"I did!" I hollered. "I was using rhythm!"

Bernie screeched to a halt. "Rhythm? What the hell is rhythm?! I'm talking prevention here, precautions. I'm not talking about the goddamn rhumba!"

"It's what the Catholics do!"

"Did you ever notice that Catholics have twenty kids apiece?"

"Stop yelling!" I screamed at the top of my lungs.

"It's fucking hot in here," Bernie said, opening his robe. "It's hot here, right? I'm burning up."

I sat down on the bed, my head in my hands.

He sat down beside me. "Don't cry, baby. I'm sorry I'm yelling. I'm just hot."

"I'm not crying," I said, looking him right in the eye. "I have a headache from all your screaming. We'll have to get married."

He leapt up from the bed. "Impossible. Are you out of your mind? I'm not ready. Not like this." He took off his robe and hurled it into a corner. "It's hot in here. Listen, Sandy, sweetheart, listen to me. Now is not the time to do this—not like this. We're not getting married because you're pregnant. It's not right."

"Oh, and it's more right for me to be pregnant and not married?"

"First we'll take care of one thing, then we'll talk about the other," he said, going suddenly and conveniently philosophical. "I've got a friend, an excellent, competent woman who also happens to be a close personal friend who does abortions. She's got a dozen places all over the city. Clean places with good doctors."

"Bernie, I'm afraid," I said honestly. In my mind abortions meant dirty old men in bloody smocks squinting at you through cigarette smoke. Butchers who used coat hangers and knitting needles. I had heard showgirls in Las Vegas talking about the pain and horrors they'd gone through and how friends of theirs had actually died as the result of botched abortions. I thought about girls who'd wound up infected, who'd been deathly ill for months after or, worse, could now never have a baby. I was very scared.

"It's nothing. Don't worry about it. I'll give Hattie a call—"

"Hattie Prince with the blue poodle cut?"

Bernie's eyes narrowed suspiciously. "How do you know Hattie?"

"She used to get her hair done at Judy's." I narrowed *my* eyes suspiciously. "And what kind of 'close personal friend' is Hattie Prince to you?"

"We went out a couple of times. No big deal. Anyway, I hear she's got a great operation now. I'll call her."

"Is that supposed to make me feel better—an ex-girlfriend of yours is going to kill our baby?"

Bernie was actually sweating now. He tugged at his undershirt collar. "Sandy, baby. I really love you. You've got to believe me. We can live together forever if you want. But now is not the time to get married and you can't have a baby unmarried. It would be a disgrace, a *shande*. So that's it. That's all we can do now. Goddamn it," he cried suddenly, and ripped off his undershirt. "Why does this always happen to me?"

"What?!" I said.

"I can't look at a woman without her getting pregnant! If you knew how many times I've been through this!"

"You bastard!" I said.

"Yeah, yeah, you're right."

"You son of a bitch!"

"I'm sorry, baby."

"You prick!"

"You having fun?" he asked.

Bernie put in the call. Within half an hour, the ubiquitous Hattie Prince phoned us back. It turned out that one of her "clinics" was conveniently located just two blocks away, in a townhouse on Madison Avenue and Eighty-first Street. She was so pleased to hear from Bernie, he made the mistake of telling me later, that she said she'd do the abortion free of charge. Normally her fee was $1,000.

I got back into bed when he told me that and I stayed there, crying and shaking with fear, anger, shame, and despair. A couple of days later, Bernie took me over to Hattie's. It was a freezing cold day in March. The sky was sunless, overcast with threatening gray clouds that echoed my own cheerlessness. Even Bernie had run out of jokes and wisecracks. The two of us bundled together against the wind and walked the two blocks to the townhouse in silent, sad resolve.

Bernie kissed me, mumbled, "I'll make this up to you, kid. I swear," and left me at the door.

I took the small elevator up to the designated apartment. A girl in a white nurse's uniform let me in. The place was much bigger than I'd imagined it from the outside, and far more luxurious than the cold, green-walled institution I'd expected. I was led into a spacious livingroom with big, plush sofas covered in bright chintz on which some girls were resting. Two of them were asleep. One was curled up, holding her belly. It looked like a terribly homey hospital recovery room. There were bowls of fruit and pitchers of orange juice on a mahogany sideboard that looked every bit as attractive as the rich still-life oil paintings ornately framed on the walls.

A second nurse came in and introduced herself as Mary. She took me to a small examining room off a carpeted corridor. She told me to undress and lie down and she draped a white sheet over me. The room was clean and very professional-looking, but as I waited alone for the doctor my fear returned. My heart began thumping again so loudly, I was sure others could hear it and, when the door opened and the doctor came in, I thought he was going to ask me to please be quiet, that my heartbeat was disturbing the other patients.

The doctor was a woman. A short, stocky woman in a white uniform complete with sterile cap and mask. She was perfectly silent as she made her preparations. Pulse pounding, I watched her closely, but her large black eyes never made contact with mine. Then I noticed that distinctive bluish-white hair peeking out from under her cap.

"Hattie, is that you?" I said, my voice quavering with fear.

"Relax, kid," Hattie Prince said. "I can give an abortion better than any of these Park Avenue quacks. And I'm doing you personally."

I was not reassured. That she could drink and swear like a man I never doubted. That she was a financial whiz who owned at least one full-length chinchilla coat was impressive. That she had run a big bookmaking operation and had been a successful madam when she was just a few years older than I was now—none of these things, which Judy had told me about Hattie Prince, qualified her as a competent physician.

"Here." Hattie handed me two pills. "Take these, they'll relax you."

I didn't argue. I gulped them down. After a while, two women entered the room. One of them was Mary, who took my hand and said kindly, "You just squeeze if you need to. I'll be right here." The second nurse laid a cold compress over my eyes and then it was Hattie, I guess, who moved my feet into the stirrups. I remember feeling a searing, stabbing pain, a sudden churning of my insides. Then Hattie said, "It's over, kid. Mary'll help you get dressed and into the other room. You just lie down there and relax with the other girls for a while. We'll get you some hot soup."

I was too groggy to focus on anything, to feel anything. "It's over?" I remember asking Mary as she helped me off the operating table. "Is that it? Is that all? Did I have a baby?"

She was brusque but not unkind. "You're fine," was all she said. "You need to rest." There was a lot of blood. I felt terribly weak. Finally, I stopped asking questions and just let her clean me up and dress me and walk me into the room with the big, soft, floral couches. There were still a few women lying there; a couple of them were moaning. I wanted to lie down. I was exhausted and now my feelings were coming back, waking up slowly in my bruised, churning belly.

"Just lie down now," Mary said, and left me.

A girl moaned. Another one was crying and clutching her stomach.

Suddenly I was afraid to lie down, afraid to close my eyes in this room full of sick, deathly pale strangers. A wave of nausea swept over me. I needed to rest, but not there. Bernie was supposed to pick me up in an hour or so, but I couldn't wait for him. I had to get out of there. I found my coat and it was hard to just lift my arms and slip them into the sleeves. The motion, every movement, felt connected to my womb, tugged nauseatingly at my insides. But I had to get home. I figured I could make it the few blocks on my own.

On Madison Avenue, the icy wind bit through my coat. I hunched against it, walking nearly doubled over. Despite the freezing cold, my insides were boiling. I stopped at a little delicatessen and bought an ice-cream pop, but it didn't cool the burning sensation, it didn't stop the sweat from pouring off me. By the time I reached our building on Seventy-ninth, I was pretty sure I was going to die. I rang our apartment bell and Bernie buzzed me in.

The single flight of stairs to the second floor seemed higher than Mount Everest. Bernie was standing at the top. He looked down at me and I knew how bad I looked by the stunned, scared expression on his face. "What the hell are you doing here?" he shouted. "Are you crazy?"

I held on to the bannister with all my strength and looked up at him. Then I passed out.

Hours later, I woke up in bed. Bernie was sitting beside me holding a bowl of chicken soup. I remember thinking how sweet it was

of him, how Jewish and sweet and typically Bernie. And the fact
that it was Campbell's Chicken Noodle Soup instead of homemade
somehow made it even sweeter. If it had been homemade, it would
have meant he'd bought it somewhere. With Campbell's I knew
he'd had to open the can and add the water and cook it himself.

"Hiya, kid," he said very gently. "You hungry, baby?"

I shook my head.

"Sandy, I'm sorry," he said. "About the baby. About what you
went through." Suddenly, there were tears in his eyes. The tough
guy was crying. I wanted to reach up and wipe away the tears, but
I could barely move my arm. I managed to take his hand. He
brought it to his lips and kissed it. "It's just that the time wasn't
right, baby. But I promise you, I'll give you what you want,
Sandy—everything, love, marriage, a home. We'll have kids, baby.
Just be patient."

It turned out that Hattie's high opinion of her skills was not mis-
placed. She knew her business. She gave Bernie antibiotics for me.
I took them and, about a week later, saw an excellent gynecologist
and told him the entire story. After examining me, he said I was a
lucky girl, that whoever had performed the abortion had done an
excellent job, and that I was perfectly healthy for a young lady who
had gotten off the operating table and walked home in subfreezing
weather.

Easter Sunday the air was crisp, the sun was shining, the city
was thawing out of winter. The ice had melted in Central Park and
from every little patch of urban earth in which a tree or tulip had
been planted, from window boxes to brownstone gardens to
squares cut in the concrete streets, the smell of wet earth signaled
spring. It was a perfect day, Bernie assured me as we drove north
through the park, to see the Easter Parade in Harlem.

In the big new Oldsmobile he'd showed up with a couple of
weeks after he bet the Caddy and lost, we pulled up in front of the
bar and grill Cokey owned on the corner of Seventh Avenue and
125th Street. Folding chairs and barstools had been set up outside
in the sunshine. It was early, not yet noon, but Hot Dog Red was already there smoking his Luckys and looking like spring in a
powder-blue suit and vest, with a tan straw hat on his head, spotless
new white 'gators on his feet, and a frosty mimosa, a tall glass of
orange juice and champagne, in his hand.

"What's shakin', sis?" he said, standing to buzz me on the
cheek. He shook hands with Bernie. "Lookin' fine, Mr. B," he

teased. Red was family. When he called Bernie Mr. B, it was almost a parody of the deferential way others used the term.

"Mr. Dog," Bernie kidded him back.

Cokey came out of the bar to greet us. With him were two locals I'd met before. Red Dillon, tall, skinny, light-skinned, who'd been a mob power around Harlem almost as long as Bumpy Johnson had and was almost as well known. But where Bumpy was a figure of awe and respect, famous and venerated, Red Dillon was notorious and feared. "He'll shoot you first and ask questions later," I'd heard Bernie say of him. The second man with Cokey was a numbers runner named "Parks," a very amiable, very black man who was always bowing and who, Hot Dog had hinted, did a little dealing on the side.

"Miss Sandy," Parks said, touching his cap to me. "You are a vision in red today. You do your man proud."

I was wearing a red linen dress with a white collar and navy-blue piping. And, of course, I had on one of my floppy straw hats, navy blue with a navy and white polka-dot ribbon round the crown. I used to get these terrific headaches from the hat pins. Also, the brims were so wide that I often had to tilt my head back to see. Now I peered out at Parks and thanked him for the compliment.

Cokey, Bernie, and Red Dillon had a little business to discuss inside. "Let them nappy-haired niggers go," Hot Dog said as the men went into the bar. I was used to Red's outrageous mouth by now, but it still jolted me to hear him say "nigger." And he knew it. Grinning, he winked at me and patted the folding chair next to his for me to sit down. A waitress brought me a mimosa. And for the next hour or so, I watched the parade, which was an informal procession of men, women, and children dressed in their spring finery on their way to or from church to celebrate the resurrection of Christ.

Pastels were the order of the day. The women, in magnificent hats garlanded with artificial flowers, fruit, ribbons, and feathers, strolled by in high-heeled shoes dyed lavender, lime, pink, or yellow to match their Easter suits and dresses. Many of them wore square-shouldered fur jackets or stoles from another era, pearly gray Persian lamb and red and silver fox or, draped over their shoulders, a rope of needle-nosed, beady-eyed furry creatures biting each other's tails.

Gloved hands clutched a rainbow of bibles, red, black, royal blue and white; or held the gloved hands or squeaky-clean collars of beautifully dressed, immaculate children. Some of the women, sometimes three generations of them, walked along with their arms linked. Men walked in family groups or lagged behind in twos and threes, in snap-brimmed summer hats and pale patent leather shoes.

So many different faces, so many colors—black, brown, beige and creamy white—walking in the sunlight of Seventh Avenue. Here and there music could be heard, a little school band would appear. Children in rich purple or white satin uniforms with gold braid trim played hymns and marched under the solemn watchfulness of adult chaperones. A group of women in black choral robes, their brightly colored high-heeled shoes visible beneath the hemlines, walked and clapped and sang spirituals.

In time, Bumpy Johnson showed up, as conservatively dressed and elegant as ever. "Here comes the Exterminator," Hot Dog said. I thought he was referring to Bumpy's dark past and tried to shush him, but it turned out that Bumpy Johnson had actually gone into the bug extermination business up in Harlem and was doing quite well at it. Of course those, like Hot Dog, who'd known him as a powerful mobster were especially struck by the irony of his new title.

Shortly after Bumpy arrived, Iris showed up. She was Cokey's girlfriend, and one of the few other women I could count on seeing when the boys got together. Iris was a tall, thin, gorgeous black woman in her early forties. Her face was all dark and silky skin pulled tight as a drum over these amazing African bones. Iris was a sharp, educated woman, an ex-madam, ex-numbers runner, and current restaurateur, whose fabulous soul food place was right around the corner from Cokey's bar.

The way Bernie loved Harlem, Iris loved the Lower East Side. We went shopping for furniture down there one afternoon and, at Benson's, Iris bought a bedroom set that made Bernie's mirrored alcove look like a nuns' retreat. It was white and gold and I think the headboard lit up. It had inset mirrors and shells and velvet panels and cupids and God knows what. I watched Iris count out and hand over seven grand in cash for that big *ungepotchket* bedroom set, and then she dragged me to the pickle barrels and halvah and herring merchants and finally, to Yonah Shimmel's Knishes, where she bought up half the store to take back to Harlem and freeze.

Cokey walked over while Iris and I were in the middle of a conversation. And then something strange happened. I was talking about my friend Toni's "colored girl." It was what I'd always called the cleaning woman who worked for Toni. Colored. Cokey, who'd been drinking for several hours and doing whatever else he did, shot me a terrible silencing look. I'd never seen him angry before, certainly never at me.

"Don't say colored," he said. He held out his hand. "Is this colored? Is it blue? Green? Purple? I'm not colored," he said. "I'm Negro. You got it? Negro, Sandy. Not colored."

"I'm sorry," I said, flushing with embarrassment.

Cokey walked away. Iris winked at me. "He's loaded, honey," she said. "Don't worry about it."

Hot Dog tried to comfort me. "He don't mean a thing by it," he said. "He just blows hot and cold that way. Probably won't even remember it tomorrow. Nothing you can do about it, Sandy. Times are changing," he said with a philosophical shrug.

Hot Dog had it right. Times were changing—up in Harlem and down South where Martin Luther King, Jr., was sentenced to four months at hard labor for sitting at a Whites-Only lunch counter. Richard Nixon was running for president. He said he had no opinion on King's sentencing. John Kennedy, on the other hand, behaved like a *mensch*. He personally phoned King's wife, Coretta, and offered to help any way he could.

Hot Dog Red, the last person in the world I'd expected to pay attention to politics, suddenly knew all about Kennedy and Nixon and how Martin Luther King's father, a Protestant minister, had announced he was voting for Kennedy, even though he never thought he'd vote for a Catholic president. And John F. Kennedy said, "Imagine that, Martin Luther King, Jr.'s father is prejudiced."

That was what Hot Dog meant when he said times were changing. As for me, this is the way I remember events:

A couple of Bernie's friends were dating girls my age. Milty Heinz, the Teamster official and pal of Johnny Dio's, whom I'd met with Lana Turner's ex-husband, had a twenty-five-year-old girlfriend named Diana. And a guy named Whitey Diamond, whom everyone called by his Jewish name, "Muttel," was going out with a cute kid named Trudy. Both Milty's girl and Muttel's in that election year were campaigning hard for marriage.

King got out of jail. Kennedy won the election. Diana and Trudy won *their* campaigns. It was like the new president said, "The torch has been passed to a new generation." And, as if they were afraid of being left in the dark, Milty and Muttel married into that new generation.

And Bernie came home one afternoon. I was sitting at the bar, smoking, flipping through a magazine. I looked up. "You want to get married?" he said before he'd even taken off his coat.

For months I had been nagging, hollering, praying, and *hocking* him. "Oh, my God. Yes!" I said.

"Okay. That's it. No questions. We're getting married."

I jumped off the barstool and flew into his arms. "You really mean it? Oh, God, I'm so happy. You're not kidding, right? We're really going to get married?"

"Sure," Bernie said, grinning now. "You want to get married, we'll get married." He kissed me. Then, "Go," he said, peeling my arms from around his neck, "call your mother. Tell her."

I did. "Ma, you want to go to a wedding?" I said.

Bernie was at the bar, pouring himself a scotch. He looked over at me on the telephone and shook his head indulgently at my childishness. I started to laugh.

"What?" he said. "What'd she say?"

"She says, 'Thank God,' " I told him. "She wants to know when."

"Of course." Bernie laughed. "Okay, Saturday," he said. "Tell her we're getting married next Saturday night, all right?"

Tears stung my eyes. "He says Saturday, Ma," I told her. It went on that way for a little while. She'd ask me a question. I'd ask Bernie. He'd tell me. I'd tell her.

"She wants to know what happened," I said. "What made you decide?"

"I ran into Muttel on Park Avenue," Bernie said distractedly. He'd picked his coat up from the couch and was searching through the pockets for something.

"He says he ran into Muttel. Whitey Diamond, whose Jewish name is Muttel. He's a friend of Bernie's—"

"He was in a limousine," Bernie continued. "With Trudy. He said, 'We just got married.' I said, 'Okay, that's it. I'm doing it.' "

"What?!" I said, putting my hand over the receiver. "Bernie, are you telling me you decided to get married because Muttel got married?!"

"What?" my mother wanted to know.

"What?" Bernie called to me.

"What are you talking about?!" I asked him.

He hardly heard me. He was at the closet, hanging up his coat. "Tell her it's not going to be anything fancy," he hollered. "I have no money for a big wedding right now. I owe everyone. I'm even thinking about getting out of the club. So it'll just be family. A couple of friends. Who knows, maybe this'll change my luck. We'll go downtown tomorrow and get the blood tests. Then we've got to go see my P.O. I'm still on parole. So we need the Greek's permission—"

I took my hand off the phone for a second. "Hang on a minute, Ma," I said, then slammed my palm back over the receiver and, suddenly breathing hard, tried to make sense of the barrage of information Bernie was casually tossing over his shoulder.

He was broke? That meant *we* were broke; that meant Bernie's betting had taken a bad turn again. So why didn't he say what he always said when the money temporarily dried up—I may be broke but I'm not poor? I almost bolted for the window to see if the Oldsmobile was still outside. And the club, The Velvet Club? I knew he'd been aggravated about the place for a while, but this was the first I'd heard about him getting out of the business. And now that he'd finally asked me to marry him—never mind that I wanted to kill him because it was a chance encounter with Whitey Diamond that had somehow convinced him to marry me; never mind that I felt like a mother who wanted to say, "And if Muttel jumped off the roof, Bernie, would you jump, too?"—now that I'd gotten what I'd wanted for so long . . . *now* he told me we'd need to get permission from a parole officer! We couldn't even get married unless Peter Knossos said it was all right.

Not for a minute, not for a million bucks, was I going to pass along one word of this information to my mother.

"Got to go. 'Bye, Ma. I love you," I said, "I'll call you later."

Bernie walked back into the living room as I hung up the phone. "So, we're going to get married. How's that make you feel?" he said, grinning at me. "You happy, baby?"

"Yes," I said, and burst into tears.

There was no doubt in my mind that I loved Bernie with all my heart. I had never known anyone as exciting or generous as he was. I had never felt as desired, protected, or cherished as I did with him. I was happy. But I was also suddenly terrified—that he'd change his mind, that he'd get sick again, that the rollercoaster he called life would come unhinged one day and we'd wind up destitute or dead.

I spent the afternoon phoning friends. I called Judy and Marilyn and even Leona, who still lived in Brooklyn. I called Toni, an ex-showgirl like myself, who was being kept by a big mob guy. I called Iris uptown and Bernie's mom downtown, and I did my best to hide my fears from myself as well as from them.

* * *

We were broke but we weren't poor. We still had the big, shiny new Oldsmobile, I reminded myself as we drove downtown the next day to see Peter Knossos, the parole officer.

"Okay, let's go over it again," Bernie said. "Where did we meet?"

"Oh, Bernie, he's never going to believe me."

Bernie shook his head, frustrated at my lack of confidence. "Sandra, don't start with me today, okay? Just let's do it like I told you. We met at a dance at the synagogue."

I burst out laughing. I couldn't *hear* it with a straight face much less say it. Bernie shot me a look.

"Okay, okay, sweetheart," I capitulated. "I'll tell him we met dancing the hora." I took out my compact and checked my face for the tenth time.

"Don't," Bernie warned.

"I'm not putting on makeup. I'm just looking, okay? God, I look ridiculous. Bernie, I look about twelve years old. The ponytail's okay, but do I have to wear a ribbon?!"

Bernie had supervised my dressing that morning. My long hair was slicked back into a high ponytail with a ribbon wrapped around the rubberband: a *pink* ribbon. And I was wearing a little plaid dress with a Peter Pan collar and very plain little black pumps. I'd left all my jewelry at home, except for a simple Star of David on a thin gold chain, which Bernie insisted I wear. All that was missing were the bobby socks and loose-leaf notebook, I thought.

"You look terrific," Bernie said. "What's with you today? All of a sudden you're teaching the teacher?"

It was one of his favorite expressions—teaching the teacher. And it seemed particularly apt today. I felt as if I was on my way to school and it was pop quiz time.

"No, baby. I'm sorry," I said. "I'm just a nervous wreck. It's like going to take a test or something. I was never good at test taking, Bernie."

He patted my thigh affectionately. "I always thought you were, *mamela*. You passed my tests, didn't you? Sandra—" His tone of voice changed abruptly. He became the teacher again. "Where are the gloves? Put on the fucking gloves, will you?"

"Very nice, Bernie. Fucking gloves. Is that the way you're going to talk in front of Peter?" I said, fueled by raw nerves rather than courage. I put on the white gloves he'd insisted I wear. My palms were perspiring and my hands were shaking with nervousness.

We found a lucky parking spot less than a block from the courthouse. "Remember. We met at *shul*," Bernie said. "At a dance, you got it?"

Bernie waited in the outer office while I went in to see Peter. The parole officer, the same man to whom I'd seen Bernie slip cash, was sitting behind his desk looking very cocky. For a start, he had his foot on the handle of his bottom drawer. He didn't stand up to greet me, but simply motioned for me to have a seat in the wooden chair at the side of his desk.

"You're Sandy?" he said.

My gloved hands were toying with the clasp of the purse in my lap. I couldn't find my voice; I just nodded respectfully.

"I'm Peter Knossos," he said. "I'm Bernie's P.O. Do you know what P.O. means?"

I nodded again.

"Parole officer," Knossos said, just to be sure I understood. On his desk was a wooden picture frame in which there was a photograph of an attractive, dark-haired young woman holding a little boy. Beside the picture was a milk glass vase with a single red rose in it. The rest of the green metal desk was covered with papers and folders.

With the toe of his shoe, Knossos pulled open the bottom desk drawer. Staring at me the entire time, he reached down into the drawer and pulled out a thick manila folder and threw it down on the desk where it landed with an impressive thump. The whole thing was pretty dramatic. "You know what that is?" he asked.

I shook my head no.

"It's your future husband's rap sheet. His file," he explained.

"Wow," I blurted out. "It's pretty thick."

The P.O. laughed. "It sure is," he said. "It dates back to when he was thirteen years old. Do you have any idea what's in it?"

"Of course," I said, trying to make up for the petty disloyalty of being shocked by the thickness of Bernie's arrest record. "He's told me everything."

"Oh, really? I'm just curious," he said. "Did he ever say whether he'd killed anyone?"

I gripped the clasp on my purse so hard it snapped open. "I asked him that," I answered honestly, almost shouting at the parole officer.

"And?" Knossos said, waiting.

"I said, 'Bernie, you never killed anyone, did you?' and he said, 'Naw, babe.' "

"That's it?"

"Yes."

"Good. That's good," Knossos said, unimpressed. He nodded at the Star of David on its chain around my neck. "You're Jewish?"

"Yes."

"Have you ever been married before?"

So much for looking twelve, I thought. "No."

He asked a few more questions about my background, where I came from, my schooling. I answered honestly and, I hoped, demurely. Then Knossos said, "So how did you meet Bernie?"

"At a Jewish dance," I said. "I met him at a dance at the synagogue."

The parole officer cracked up, busted out laughing. Before I knew it, I was laughing with him. Something snapped in me. All the tension that had held me rigid broke and the two of us cackled and shook with uncontrollable laughter. "That's good. That's really good," Knossos gasped, trying to catch his breath.

Finally, he leaned back in his chair and wiped his eyes. "You know, sweetheart," he said. "You really love this guy, that's obvious. So I guess I'm going to give you permission to marry him. Who knows, maybe you can straighten him out. After all, he's still young," Knossos teased. "Just be sure I get a copy of the marriage license. I want to make sure you aren't lying to me."

We both stood up. To my surprise, Bernie's parole officer pulled the rose out of the vase on his desk and handed it to me. Then he gave me a kiss on the cheek. "Good luck," he said. "You're going to need it."

I thanked him and rushed out to the waiting room and into Bernie's arms. "He said yes," I said, elated. "Come on, we can go now. I passed!"

"See, I told you," Bernie said. "Good girl. I'm proud of you."

We left the building holding hands and walked to the car. As we were about to get in, Bernie snapped his fingers. He turned and looked back up to the building. "I knew it!" he growled. "The son of a bitch is watching us!"

I turned to look and, sure enough, there was Peter Knossos leaning out his window. Without thinking, I waved to him.

"Get in," Bernie said, holding the driver's door open for me.

"You want me to slide over?"

"No. I want you to drive. That's why he's watching. The bastard is trying to set me up. I'm not supposed to own a car, much less drive one."

"What are you, crazy?" I whispered, as if Knossos, three stories up and half a block away, could hear me. "I can't drive, Bernie. I don't know how!"

"Get in," he insisted in a strangled voice. I took one look at him and knew he was on the verge of a temper tantrum. That was all we'd need. For his P.O. to watch him jump up and down screaming and biting his fist. I got into the car and sat staring helplessly at the wheel while Bernie walked around to the passenger side.

"Okay, okay." He was trying to calm down. "There's nothing to it, baby. You'll do fine. Okay, breathe," he said. "You're turning blue."

I breathed. The steering wheel felt huge. The car seemed as big as a bus.

"Turn the key," Bernie said. I did. The motor started. "Good girl. See, you're doing great. Now slowly, Sandra, slowly—put your right foot slowly on the gas pedal."

We lurched forward.

"Stop! Hit the brake. No, the other foot. Slowly!!!"

Step by step, Bernie instructed me on how to move the car out of the parking spot and into street traffic. I was sweating like crazy. Now that I'd found the brake, I pumped it for reassurance every two seconds. As soon as the car moved forward, I'd hit the brake—slowly, slowly, I thought. But no matter how slowly, how gently I tried to step on the brake pedal, we sort of bounced down the street. "Okay, good," Bernie tried through clenched teeth to be encouraging. "Okay, keep going. Just go slow, baby. Good. Okay. You're going two miles an hour, Sandra—leave the brake alone! Okay, good. Stop. Sandra, stop! Stop now!"

I hit the brake. Bernie hit the windshield. "You said to leave the brake alone!" I complained.

"The light was red!"

"Oh."

Finally, Bernie said, "Turn here, then pull over to that pump and stop. Slowly stop."

I tried. We jerked around the corner and kind of bounced over to the curb. I eased my foot onto the brake pedal. Bernie was hanging on to the dashboard this time. "Slowly," he cautioned.

I did it with no more damage than the crunch and squeak of tires scraping the curb. I took my sweating palms off the steering wheel. And I waited—for one complaint, one nasty remark. I was so keyed up that I think I would have slugged him had he said anything but what he did say, which was: "Okay, sweetheart, move over."

With immeasurable relief, I traded places with him and lit a cigarette. Smoking it was like learning to breathe again. I felt like a guppy gasping for air. My head was light; my heart was thudding. After we'd put a few blocks behind us, Bernie reached over and affectionately mussed my hair. "You did good today," he said. "But you've got to learn to drive, kid."

"Marry in beige you'll be in a rage," Judy recited, standing back to admire my hair which she'd just teased and patted into place. "That's how it goes, right, Marilyn?"

The three of us were in the bathroom of the rabbi's apartment on the Upper West Side where, in less than ten minutes, Bernie and I were going to be married. Outside, in the living room, the rest of the wedding party, about eight relatives and friends, waited on folding chairs for the ceremony to begin while the rabbi's children chased each other from room to room.

"Rage? Judy, what are you talking about?" I asked.

"You know, honey. 'Marry in white your life will be bright. Marry in red you'll always be in bed. In blue your love will be true. In beige, you'll be in a rage.' That's how it goes."

"Gee," Marilyn said, impressed, "I never heard that. But it's a pretty suit, Sandy. You really look gorgeous . . . even if it is beige."

Bernie had given me $100 two days before the wedding and I'd rushed over to Ohrbach's and picked up a beige shantung knockoff of a Jackie Kennedy suit and some lacy new underwear. At Bakers I got beige shoes and a purse to match. Now I saw myself in the mirror, a vision in beige.

"It's a good thing I'm not superstitious," I said, managing a laugh. But I was. And the only thing I had on that wasn't beige was the *royta bendle*, the red ribbon I had tied to my bra for good luck. So Judy's little poem did nothing to quiet my wedding-day jitters.

Bernie had made all the arrangements. Because of how broke we were, he hadn't told many people that we were getting married. Still, the few friends who knew had wanted to make us a big reception. Bernie wouldn't hear of it. His tremendous pride dictated that we wouldn't accept cash presents or a party he himself couldn't afford to throw. It was ironic given all the fat envelopes, the hundreds of dollars, I'd seen him press into the hands of brides or stuff into "bridal pillowcases" at the weddings we'd been to. I didn't care, though. I was getting my wish. It wasn't the big fancy wedding I'd dreamed of, it was being married to Bernie. My only regret at that moment, big deal, was the color of my suit.

The rabbi's wife knocked at the door. "All right, missus. It's time."

Judy squeezed my hand. "You look jes beautiful, honey," she said, suddenly close to tears. Marilyn kissed me on the cheek, then quickly wiped away a trace of her bright red lipstick. "Oh, Sandy. I love you," she called, grabbing Judy and rushing out. Judy blew me a kiss for luck.

The rabbi's wife was not much older than I, but was short and stout with dimpled arms that looked like they'd already spent a lifetime bathing children and kneading dough. She was wearing an apron over her print housecoat. "Come," she beckoned. She untied the apron and hung it on the back of the bathroom door. "Your man is waiting."

And he was. In a handsome three-piece blue suit with a carnation in his lapel and a white satin yarmulka on his head, my man was standing in front of the rabbi, practically tapping his foot with impatience. The rabbi's wife managed to grab a couple of the running children on our way into the living room. Those heavy hands of hers were faster than they looked. The rabbi himself silenced the rest of the kids with an ominous, dark look. He began the ceremony with the same angry intensity. When it was over, Bernie and I kissed and then he looked around for the glass.

Traditionally, the groom is supposed to step on a glass and that signals the end of the ceremony. Some people said the number of pieces the glass broke into would show you the number of years you'd live in health and happiness together. Some people said stepping on the glass was a way to commemorate the destruction of the temple—to remember at the height of your joy the sadness of your people. Whatever its true meaning, it is tradition at a Jewish wedding for the groom to break the glass and have everyone yell, "Mazel-tov!"

So Bernie said to the rabbi, "Where's the glass?"

The rabbi's wife held up her dimpled arms. "No, no. We can't do it," she said, and started explaining how it would ruin her carpeting. And the rabbi said, "Don't worry, it's only tradition."

"It's supposed to keep away evil," Bernie said. "You know, you shatter the evil spirits."

"No, no. Don't worry, you won't have evil spirits," the rabbi insisted. "Here, we'll have wine and sponge cake and that's it."

Between the beige/rage couplet and not stepping on the glass, the two of us were off to a great start, I thought. I could see that Bernie was annoyed about it, too. "Leave it to Muttel to recommend a rabbi who cares more about his goddamn carpeting than about Jewish tradition," he grumbled, as my mother, Marlene, and I piled into the car after the wedding.

But if the ceremony didn't end traditionally, at least the night did. After a lovely wedding supper with friends and family, Bernie and I picked up the Sunday papers, the *News* and the *Mirror*, and walked home with our arms around each other. It was what we did almost every Saturday night, only this Saturday night, April 15, 1960, we were married.

CHAPTER SEVEN

Changes

The boys were coming over. In the middle of the afternoon, Bernie would come home with a bag full of deli—pastrami, corned beef, chopped liver, pickled red peppers, potato salad, the works. "Listen, babe, just put this out on serving platters. Fill the ice bucket. Make sure there are plenty of ashtrays around. And then, why don't you call Judy or Toni or your mother. Go for a walk. Read a book. You know."

I knew. Bernie had always liked to use the apartment as his club house. He loved having friends over. The "boys"—Hot Dog Red, a rich young Jewish lawyer named Josh, and Uncle Vinny, a dapper Italian about Bernie's age—would put their feet up on the furniture, light cigars that smelled like burnt rope, aim the ashes at the nearest glass or plate, dribble chopped liver onto the carpeting, and put all the big events of the world to bed.

Before we were married, when the boys stopped by, I'd set out the drinks and deli and then, at a high sign from Bernie, discreetly disappear. Now I resented being sent off to bed like a child. It wasn't Bernie's apartment anymore, it was my home. And I found myself wanting to hang out with the grown-ups. Especially when they'd start talking about someone called Lido.

They'd have a couple of drinks, a hit or two of grass. They'd settle the space race, offer their two cents on Kennedy, Khrushchev, and Castro, and on who was in and out of prison and politics—Joey Gallo was in, Carmine DeSapio was out. And then they'd start:

"How can you believe Lido's crap, B?" Hot Dog would say.

Bernie'd laugh. "You think Lido's full of shit? How come you won't look him in the eye, Dog?"

"Just 'cause he's full of shit don't mean the nigger can't give you the evil eye."

Vinny, who was called "uncle" because of his mania for straightening magazines and organizing activities—more like a maiden aunt than an uncle—heart-of-gold Vinny, who owned a couple of little bars and was mostly supported by women, would shake his head and say, "Calls himself a priest? It's a fuckin' sacrilege!"

"Afro-Cuban priest, Vinny. Lido's a Santoro. It's not a Catholic thing."

"Santoro, shmantoro." Josh the lawyer, who idolized Bernie, would shrug skeptically. He was from a very rich family, good people from the Garment Center who'd struck it rich and gotten into the movie business. His cousin was a big Hollywood producer. With his relatives and his law degree Josh could have lived easy in the straight life, but he was nuts about gangsters, especially Bernie, whom he looked up to like a father or an older brother.

"Nigger's a coke machine, that's all," Hot Dog Red declared. "You give him enough toot, he'll tell you whatever you want to hear."

"Who's Lido?" I'd ask Bernie, exchanging a clean ashtray for one filled with Red's ground-down Lucky Strike butts.

"Nothing. None of your business." He'd signal with his eyes, dart his baby blues toward the bedroom. "Go, Sandy. Go read."

"What does Santoro mean?" I'd ask, sweeping a crushed red pepper off the coffee table into my palm.

"Sandra!" Bernie'd give me his best dismissive glare.

But now that I was Sadie-Sadie-Married-Lady, my knees didn't buckle instantly at his every angry glance. I didn't scurry to the bedroom on command. I'd find excuses to hang around and listen.

I knew that Bernie was superstitious. If he won at the track, he'd wear the same shirt the next five times he placed a bet. He made a big deal of kissing the *mezuzah* when he walked out the door. He lit green "money candles" in the house. And I suspected that he was a lot more upset than he'd let on about not breaking the glass at our wedding.

I was superstitious, too. The red ribbon I'd worn on our wedding day was just one of the *royta bendles* in my life—I had red bits of fabric hidden in every closet and cupboard of the apartment. On my birthday, June 13, Saint Anthony's Day, I'd go to church with

Uncle Vinny and make a novena to the patron saint of the poor and the foolish. I believed in the power of those novenas and prayers. I believed in the evil eye, fortune-tellers, gifted people, astrology, good vibrations, men with mustaches. I was always waiting for a miracle, waiting for someone to wave a hand, mumble "shmay-dray," make all the bad disappear.

I'd never discussed any of this with Bernie. But I was determined to find out more about Lido. And the more Bernie put me off, the more determined I became.

In bed, after I'd vacuumed the chopped liver out of the carpeting and wiped the last trace of pickle juice from the coffee table, I'd curl up against him and begin:

"Honey, who's Lido?"

"Come on, Sandy. I'm tired, baby. Aren't you tired?"

"No. Bernie, why did Red say that about the evil eye? Is he really afraid to look at this Lido?"

"You know Red, he's superstitious."

"Are you?"

"Sandra, are you going to knock it off already?"

"Yes, baby. But are you? I mean, do you believe in séances? You know, my mother used to go to séances. She believes in all that stuff—fortune-tellers, curses, the works."

"Tillie?" He laughed. "No kidding."

"And my cousin Francine, the one I lived with in Beverly Hills when I was a kid, she used to do automatic writing, you know, like when a spirit speaks through you, guides your hand."

"And what about you?" Bernie asked cautiously. "Do you believe in that stuff?"

"Some of it, sure." I shrugged. "Do you?" It felt very strange talking about this aloud. It was almost embarrassing, more intimate than sex.

"Yeah. Some," he confessed, sounding as sheepish as I felt.

"What's Santoro?"

"A priest in an Afro-Cuban religion—a kind of voodoo called Santeria, very powerful. And very interesting," he said, backing away from it, getting objective.

"And Lido is a priest in this religion?"

"Yeah, I guess, something like that."

"Bernie, can I go with you sometime?"

"What, are you crazy?"

"Why, is it just for men?"

"No. But it's . . . Take my word for it, baby. It's not for you."

* * *

It took about two months. It was in June, on the anniversary of
Bernie's father's death. Two months after we were married, Bernie
put on a yarmulka, lit a memorial candle for his father, recited the
Kaddish, the ritual Jewish prayer for the dead, then turned to me
and said, "Okay, I'm going uptown tonight to Lido's. You want to,
you can come with me."

I had to work very hard at acting cool as we drove up to Spanish
Harlem. There were a million questions I wanted to ask Bernie, but
I was afraid that he'd get annoyed with me and change his mind
about taking me along. So I sat silently beside him in my black turtleneck and slacks, smoking, and trying to distract myself by looking out the car window at the men sitting on milk boxes, playing
dominoes, women leaning on pillows, watching the street from
their kitchen windows, guys washing cars with water from opened
fire hydrants. Along with the sounds of people and traffic, Latin
music blared from parked car radios and stereo speakers set up in
doorways.

Maybe it was the prospect of meeting Lido, at last, that took me
back. Maybe it was the swarming neighborhood we'd passed
through or the grandmotherly woman I'd noticed moving through
the crowd, a black babushka on her head, an urgent mission in her
rolling, hurried gait. But, as Bernie pulled into a parking space on
108th Street, I found myself remembering something that had happened when I was just a little kid.

My mother had taken me with her to see a rabbi's wife who was
supposed to have psychic powers. The *rebetsn* was going to read
the cards for my mother. I was about eight years old. I remember
having to reach up to hold my mother's hand. Normally, it made
me feel more grown up to walk at a distance from her and pretend
I was on my own, a big girl walking along alone. But that day I
held her hand with no argument because the neighborhood was
strange, a bustling unfamiliar place.

My mother and the rabbi's wife sat at the dining-room table,
which was covered by a lace cloth. There were silver candlesticks
on the table. And there was a bowl of fruit and a dish of hard can-
dies on the sideboard next to the straight-backed chair that I was
sitting on, separate from them, watching from a distance. The
rebetsn laid out the cards for my mother and was studying them. I
waited expectantly, straining to hear before she'd even said a word.

Suddenly the rabbi's wife jumped back from the cards. *"Oy, oy, oy,"* she screamed. "I have to run to the *shul*. Someone is dead."

We all three rushed from the apartment and separated on the street. The rabbi's wife, moving like the elderly woman in Spanish Harlem, hurried toward the synagogue. My mother and I tore away in the other direction, to the subway that would take us home. When I asked my mother about it days later, she shook her head sadly. *"Oy, nebech,"* she said. "She was right. The rabbi had a heart attack and died in the *shul*."

So I was probably thinking of the rabbi's wife as Bernie led me across the street and down three steps into the ground floor of Lido's East Harlem brownstone. I had no clear image of him in my mind before he opened the door to greet us. I just felt spooked and spiritual and eager to meet the man I'd heard so much about, the gifted Afro-Cuban priest whom Bernie regarded with the same awe and reverence my mother had felt for the rabbi's wife.

"Lido," Bernie said, "this is my lady, Sandy."

He looked like Little Richard. He had pale brown skin, pomaded hair, a pencil mustache, and more show-stopping jewelry than the entire orchestra section of a Hadassah matinee.

"Sandy," he said, clasping my hand. I could barely tear my eyes from the diamond in his pinky ring, which had to be about seven carats in a gold gypsy setting that made it look even bigger. Not that this stone needed any help. It was the size of a grape.

"Come in, B." He was all in black, from his velvet slippers and flowing trousers to his wide-sleeved satin shirt. Jangling gold necklaces and bracelets, Lido led the way into a pretty normal-looking living room. Against his black shirt, on top of about ten other necklaces, lay a huge, diamond-studded cross on a thick gold link chain. Fingering that cross after a few minutes of gossipy small talk, Lido said, "What have you brought me, B?" His neatly manicured nails were long; his pinky nail longest of all, and he soon put it to use.

Bernie pulled a small cellophane packet out of his back pocket and clapped it into Lido's hand. And Lido's long pinky nail dipped into the packet and came out carrying a heap of white powder, which he promptly tossed into his nose and snorted with gusto.

Cocaine. I remembered what Hot Dog had said about Lido. Lido was a coke head. It helped him reach his "outer vibrations," he claimed. What vibrations Bernie was reaching for I have no idea, but the two of them were making short work of that packet. Finally, Lido said, "What's bothering you, B? What's the problem?"

And Bernie, who'd forgotten I was even in the room by then, said, "I'm thinking of selling the club. I need cash. My partners'll buy me out. I don't know—it's just not working anymore, Lido."

Lido hadn't forgotten me. He gave me his hand and pulled me to my feet. "We'll look into the bowl," he said to Bernie, leading me to a door at the far end of the living room. "We'll look into the bowl, then we'll see."

The door led to a linoleum-covered basement. There were coins scattered all over the floor—pennies, dimes, nickels, quarters, half-dollars. There were four or five big pillows on the floor, pushed up against the walls. Lido signaled for us to sit down on them. Between the pillows, and in wall alcoves as well, stood brightly painted plaster statues of Saints and Indians. And before the statues were little dishes of food, cigars, money, and leaves, herbs I guess.

"Give me eight cents for the Blessed Mother," Lido said to me. "It's got to be a nickel and three pennies," he insisted, as I rummaged in my purse for the money. When I found the right change, Lido put it into a tin cup, then put the cup at the base of one of the statues.

I remember that he and Bernie talked for a while. I was still enthralled with Lido's jewelry. A couple of the chains around his neck had diamonds running through them, and every time he moved they sparkled. At some point my attention wandered to the change on the floor of the basement. I began counting it, and the process became hypnotic. There were coins everywhere, heaped in corners and thicker around the feet of some of the painted saints. The next thing I knew, Bernie was getting up. Lido, again, helped me to my feet. He led us both to the middle of the room and had us kneel down together. I noticed that there was African music playing. I guess it was African—voices chanting over a quiet, repetitious drum beat.

Lido set down a bowl and wooden spoon in front of us. Talking the entire time, he tossed a handful of what looked like leaves and dirt into the bowl. I can't remember what he was saying, nothing terribly spiritual or hard to understand, but it was like a shower of sounds.

At some point, he left us, Bernie and me, kneeling in that basement room and returned carrying a live chicken. It happened so fast, I didn't have time to know that I knew what was going to happen next. Chanting, Lido laid the chicken on the linoleum in front of us and chopped off its head with a machete knife. I gasped. Lido held the flailing headless carcass upside down and let it bleed into the bowl, then he tossed it away.

He was busy throwing more leaves and dirt into the bowl and seemed not to notice the headless chicken flapping around the room. But I noticed it! I screamed and tried, because we were still on our knees, to roll out of its way. I half rolled, half crawled, and finally scrambled to my feet and started dodging the poor doomed bird as best I could. Bernie and Lido paid no attention to this at all. Not to me. Not to the bird. They were concentrating on the voodoo stew Lido was brewing. He dipped his fingers into the mess and smeared some on Bernie's forehead.

Bernie looked over his shoulder at me cowering in the corner next to the painted Indian. "Sandy, come here, baby," he said very calmly.

Lido lowered his head and looked at me as if he were peering over the rims of a pair of eyeglasses. Was this the famous evil eye Red had talked about? Shaken to the bone by the chicken, I shuddered violently. Lido smiled, then signaled for me to kneel down again next to Bernie. And, of course, I did. And, of course, he smeared my forehead with the same bloody mud.

I don't know what was in the bowl, besides fresh chicken blood, of course. I don't know what blessings or curses the boys were trying to conjure. I know that the blood should have been hot, but it felt incredibly cool on my forehead and that, as repulsive as the mixture was, it worked like a Valium. My fluttering heart quieted down. I took Bernie's hand. And I felt safe.

Despite my upset about the chicken, Bernie was very proud of me. I think he'd half-expected me to tell him he was crazy to put any faith in Lido's mumbo jumbo but, while I had my doubts about the man, I was too superstitious to put him down.

As we were leaving the brownstone that first night, we ran into a couple of heavy hitters from Little Italy going in to see Lido. It was a funny scene. The first jolt of recognition. The guys and Bernie smiling, shaking hands, saying, "Hey, how you been? What're you doing up here?" Then the sudden embarrassment. They were very flustered, all three of them, like kids caught with their fingers in the cookie jar. These were tough guys. Mobsters. The Italians were killers—literally. A couple of connected, respected, street-wise hit men. And here they were bringing drugs or diamonds or bundles of money to a chicken killer who looked like Little Richard and needed cocaine to jump-start his psychic powers.

We went to see Lido a number of times and eventually, at least in part because of the flamboyant Santoro's advice, Bernie did sell his piece of The Velvet Room to his partners. With the exception of that first night, there were always other people around, limousines double-parked outside or cars with bodyguards waiting in them. Bernie saw nothing strange about saying Jewish prayers in the morning and kneeling in front of Lido at night. And, apparently, neither did half of New York's most notorious mobsters and madams. These might be people who thought anyone who read Jeane Dixon's astrology column in the newspapers was soft in the head or square. But Lido who, for a couple of hundred dollars and a spoon or two of coke, would call down curses on an ex-lover or an enemy, they considered a smart investment. I think for Bernie and his friends to feel comfortable, even their psychics had to be crooked.

Bernie had been bugging me to learn how to drive since the day I almost killed us both getting away from Peter Knossos's office.

"You're not working now. You've got nothing to do. If you wanted to, you could take a drive to Brooklyn, see your mother or Leona. You get your license, it'll give you a little freedom. Plus," he added as if it were an afterthought, "you never know when I'll need you to run an errand for me or drive me somewhere."

What else was he going to say? The truth was that Bernie hated to drive, wasn't legally supposed to, and having a licensed chauffeur handy at home couldn't hurt. So I went to driving school and did very well.

The day before I was scheduled to take my driving test, he decided the master should see if the school was giving him his money's worth. And, of course, if I fell short, he was prepared as always to teach me what I needed to know.

Whenever Bernie had taught me anything in the past, I'd always been a willing pupil, as eager as a puppy to earn his praise. I had also always been terrified by his temper. So the instruction process was definitely a carrot-and-stick affair. The carrot was earning a pat on the head from Bernie. The stick was that temper, and I'd do almost anything to avoid its being loosed on me. But now that we were married, even that began to change.

Over my weak objection that it was almost dark out and that my learner's permit was for day-time driving only, Bernie drove the Olds over to Sutton Place. The neighborhood was less than a mile from where we lived, but it was so rich, quiet, and exclusive that it had its own police force. It was a low traffic area with streets wide enough for me to practice U-turns. Which was what Bernie wanted me to do.

We traded seats. I got behind the wheel. "Okay, let's see you do it," he said. And I did, exactly the way my instructor had shown me—looking both ways even though it was a one-way street, double-checking in the mirror as I pulled out, looking over my shoulder, being extremely cautious . . .

"Come on already," Bernie grumbled. "There's nothing coming. It's a one-way street. Hit the gas and go!"

I did but with a bit of my confidence chipped away.

"Watch out for the station wagon. You almost clipped it."

"I saw it, Bernie. I had plenty of room."

"You think so, huh? Okay. Again. Try it in one motion instead of turning, then backing up."

"The instructor told me to back up first."

"Sandra, don't start. I'm telling you to try it this way, okay? In real life you've got to be able to maneuver fast. Come on, try it again."

I tried to do it the way Bernie wanted, but I turned too wide and had to back up again. I wanted to look over my shoulder to be sure I could see everything behind me, but I thought that would annoy him, so I just used the mirror and started backing up.

"Stop, stop, stop!" he shouted. "What are you, a moron? You've got to look over your shoulder or they'll nail you."

"Bernie, you're making me nervous," I said softly between clenched teeth.

"Park," he barked.

"Where?!"

"What the hell's the matter with you? Where? In a parking space, that's where. Go. Over there."

"There's a hydrant there. It's illegal."

He sighed. Actually, it was more a snort of disgust than a sigh. "We're not leaving the car there overnight, Sandra. You're just practicing parking."

"Okay, okay. Stop yelling already. Please!" I pulled parallel to the car in front of the space, checked the mirror, turned the wheel sharply, and began backing up. I was afraid I was moving too slowly—not for me, but for him—so I accelerated.

Bernie had a vein on the side of his neck that used to start jumping when he was really losing it. Out of habit, I glanced over at him to see how far gone he was. The vein was doing the Cha-Cha-Cha even before the Olds jumped the curb and rammed into the fire plug. The car was like a tank. The pump broke. Water shot out of the hydrant. Bernie whirled around, saw what had happened and started cursing at me.

"Shut up!" I heard myself scream. "*You* made me do that, you shmuck! If you hadn't been yelling at me the whole time, it never would have happened. It's your fault. *You're* the moron! *You're* the dumb cunt! *You're* the stupid bitch! Not *me*, Bernie! So just shut up!"

"Are you out of your fucking mind?!" was the gentlest part of his response—and just the beginning.

I put my hands over my ears. "Yeah, yeah, yeah!" I screamed. "I must be out of my fucking mind. I married you, didn't I?"

I was wild. I was gone. I had never opened a mouth like this to anyone ever in my entire life. But something had snapped inside me and suddenly I was a force to be reckoned with. I was a mad woman! I jumped out of the car and slammed the door with all my might. He screamed at me first from his side of the car, then he slid over to the driver's seat to curse me closer up. I think the only thing that prevented his getting out of the car and coming after me was the water shooting out of the busted pump, soaking everything. Dripping wet, I started jumping up and down, hammering on the hood of the Olds.

"Stop it, you bitch, or I'll get out of this car and brain you," he threatened.

I tried to tear the antenna off the Olds to defend myself.

"You didn't do enough damage?! Leave it alone! You touch that again, I'll rip out the steering wheel and wrap it around your fucking neck!"

Sutton Place had never heard anything like this. Suddenly there were sirens and flashing lights added to the melee. Someone had called the cops, the private police patrol. They arrested us. They threw us into the cruiser, put me in the front seat and Bernie in the back like a drowned cat and a rabid dog collected by the ASPCA.

At the Sixty-ninth Precinct we were charged with disturbing the peace and held for about half an hour until we quieted down and the desk sergeant heard our story and discharged us. A domestic quarrel, they called it.

The next day my driving instructor picked me up and I took the test in the driving school's car. When it was over, the inspector told me that I had passed. I returned home in vengeful triumph. "You see," I announced, sweeping past Bernie into the livingroom. "I do know how to drive! I passed the test on my first try!"

I was prepared for all hell to break loose again. Chin out, hands on my hips, I whirled around to face him.

He was smiling. "I knew you'd do it, baby," he said with pride and affection. "I even got you a present." He gave me a hug, a kiss, and a beautiful little diamond bracelet. And, the next day, he gave me a hundred dollars and told me to drive out to Brooklyn and take my mother and sister to lunch.

The Olds was a mess. A couple of weeks after I got my license, a sleek, brown Caddy replaced it. It was a beautiful car that looked like a big chocolate candy bar with caramel leather seats and a burled wood dash. It was Bernie's baby, his new toy, and it sat gleaming and gorgeous in the parking space in front of our building.

Bernie was both proud of me and dismayed by my new policy of talking back. Sometimes it drove him crazy. And now I had another ace in the hole. One he'd delivered on a silver platter—a driver's license and the freedom he'd promised it would bring. One night that first summer we were married, after a quarrel that escalated to name-calling again, I picked up the car keys, waved them in his face, and literally ran out the door. Only the fact that Bernie was in his shorts stopped him from scrambling down the steps into the street after me.

"Get back in here!" he yelled from our window as I started up the car. "Sandy, I'm not kidding! Get up here! This minute!"

I gave him the finger and drove away.

I had no place to go. It was a hot night. I rolled down the windows, turned on the radio, and cruised into Central Park. The breeze was wonderful, the smell of jasmine filled the air. I had just about forgotten Bernie when police sirens went off behind me. I pulled over to get out of the way of the cop car. But it was me they were after. Two officers came over to the car. One of them had his hand on his holster, which really freaked me out. "Let's see some identification, lady," the other one said.

I showed them my driver's license.

"I'd like to see the registration," he said.

"What's going on?" I asked.

"You're driving a stolen vehicle, lady," the itchy trigger finger announced.

My heart started pounding. My hands shook as I searched the glove compartment for the car registration. Of course, I thought. Where else would Bernie get a car like this? I couldn't begin to figure out the consequences of my being arrested or even questioned about how I happened to be driving a stolen car. Between Bernie and the cops, suicide seemed like the best bet. I handed the registration papers over to the police.

The cop looked from my driver's license to the registration. "And you're Sandra Barton, right?"

"Yes, Officer," I said, close to tears.

"Well," the first cop said to his partner, "it's registered in her name. Who called in the complaint?"

"Excuse me," I said. "What complaint?"

"This car was just reported stolen."

I knew who called in the complaint! "But it's registered in my name and here's the insurance card," I said, on the offensive now. They apologized and drove off. Shaken, I headed home, knowing that Bernie had called the cops on me. He'd reported the car stolen but forgotten that he'd had it registered in my name and, of course, he'd never bothered mentioning anything to me about where he'd gotten the Caddy or in whose name it was registered.

He was standing at the window, waiting for me, when I returned. He was standing there, grinning, with his arms folded across his chest.

I walked into the house. "You happy now?" he said, smirking, satisfied that he'd given me enough trouble to call it even.

"Shmuck," I said, brushing past him. And we never mentioned the incident again.

Lido's chicken didn't die for nothing. By August, Bernie was out of The Velvet Room and we'd moved from Bernie's bachelor pad to a spacious, one-bedroom apartment, with a terrace overlooking the river, in a new luxury building on East Seventy-fourth Street.

We had a real home, at last. And I was having a ball fixing it up. With my mother, Marilyn, or Iris I shopped the Lower East Side for furniture, carpeting, curtains, beautiful new sheets and pillowcases and, the pride and joy of my new powder-blue bedroom, a white, custom-made, trapunto-stitched bedspread.

I had gone downtown with Iris one hot August afternoon to buy some pillow shams. I'd taken a swatch of white quilted fabric with me to Benson's so that the ruffled shams I was searching for would perfectly match the bedspread. Hot and tired, I came home loaded down with pillows, sheets, white, blue, and mauve shams, and a new dust ruffle for the bed. It was about five o'clock. All the way up in the elevator all I could think about was the cool shower I was going to take and the big glass of iced tea I was going to fix for myself before Bernie got home.

The minute I turned the key in the door, I knew there was something strange going on inside. And that was *before* I saw the shotgun in the foyer. I heard noises in the bedroom. My arms were filled with packages. I remember seeing the gun resting against the coat closet door. I remember wondering if Bernie had taken up hunting. I'd seen guns around the apartment before, but never a rifle. And then there were these weird grunts and moaning noises.

Bernie called out, "Sandy, is that you?"

"Of course," I said, annoyed, wondering who was groaning in the bedroom with Bernie. "Who were you expecting?"

"Come in here, quick. I'm glad you're here. I need help," he called.

I threw the bags onto the sofa, hurried into the bedroom, and gasped.

A stranger in an undershirt and dark pants was bleeding to death on my new bedspread. A bright red stain was spreading out from his shoulder. His thin gray hair was matted with blood. One side of his face was smeared with it and he was sweating like crazy. There was blood seeping down the side of the bedspread, pooling onto the powder blue carpeting.

"Oh my God, oh my God, oh my God," I chanted, taking a step back, wanting to run from the room but paralyzed with fright.

The man's eyes had been closed. At the sound of my voice, he opened them and tried to look at me. He was so far gone he couldn't focus. His eyes were out of control, rolling wildly. The part of his face that wasn't covered with blood was ashen, slick with sweat, practically paler than the bedspread.

Bernie was standing next to the bed holding a bloody rag that turned out to be the guy's shirt. "Listen to me," he said. "I need your help. I've got to get the bullet out."

"What bullet? What happened? Who is he?"

"Never mind who is he. Get me some water. Towels. The sharpest steak knife you can find—"

"No. No. No." I was shaking my head. I was afraid to look at Bernie. I was afraid to look at the stranger in the bed. I just watched the stain on the carpeting grow. "No, Bernie. We've got to get him to a hospital, call an ambulance, get help. He's bleeding, Bernie. He's dying."

"Sandy. Not now. Don't go nuts on me now. Just do what I ask, okay?" He was eerily calm and serious. "He's been shot. We can't take him to a hospital. It's out of the question. I'm going to take care of him. Now, get me the knife."

"Who is he? Who shot him? Is that his gun out there?"

"Why, is it bothering you, the gun? Don't touch it. Leave it exactly where it is. Don't touch the gun. Don't question me. Just do what I told you and do it right now, Sandy."

I raced to the kitchen, crying and shaken. Fumbling in the kitchen drawer looking for the sharpest knife I could find, I began ranting aloud. "He's going to die," I said bitterly, "on my side of the bed! Bernie killed him and laid him out on my side? Why didn't he put him on his own side of the bed!"

"Sandy, hurry up!"

I was a crazy person, a lunatic. But Bernie's voice cut through the insanity. I grabbed a knife, filled a big pot with hot water from the sink. Put another pot of water up to boil. Grabbed a couple of clean dishtowels and ran back to the bedroom.

"Okay. Hold the water. Just stand there," Bernie said. He took the knife and bent over the guy on the bed and started to cut into him like a surgeon. The bleeding man screamed bloody murder. I closed my eyes and started trembling so hard that water washed over the top of the big pot, splashing my blouse and skirt and shoes. When the screaming stopped, I opened my eyes and saw that the guy had passed out.

Bernie was still hunched over him, digging into his shoulder. I remember thinking how calm, almost professional, Bernie seemed. The nerve in his neck was absolutely still. Then a wave of nausea nearly knocked me to my knees.

Bernie said, "Got it." And started mopping the guy up. He took the bullet into the bathroom and flushed it, I think. I was still standing there, paralyzed, holding the pot of water with the bloody towels in it.

"You look a little green," Bernie said when he came back into the room. "You did great, babe. Go ahead, get out of here. I'll finish up. Make me a cream cheese and onion on a bagel."

I had two cigarettes going and a scotch in my hand when Bernie came into the kitchen. I'd left a cigarette in the living room next to the couch where I'd sat with my head between my knees for five minutes after leaving the bedroom. Bernie brought the lit cigarette into the kitchen with him. When he saw that I had another one going in my mouth, he frowned at me, shook his head, and doused the first one under the tap.

I handed him the plate with his favorite supper on it—toasted ba-

gel, cream cheese, tomato, and red onion. If he had a lecture prepared on leaving lit cigarettes around the house, he never got a
chance to deliver it.

"Who is that man?" I asked. "Bernie, I have a right to know.
What if he dies here? What if the police come? What am I supposed to say? I live here. I'm your wife. You want me to make believe a guy I never saw before in my life isn't lying in there
bleeding to death on my side of the bed? Who shot him? How did
he get here?"

"Don't ask me about my business, Sandy," he said.

Terrific, I thought. Standard wise guy answer. I was all set to
start in on him again. My nerves were as raw as the red onion on his
plate when, suddenly, Bernie did what Bernie did best—a
180-degree turn. "Listen, baby," he said, in a suddenly exhausted
voice. "I'm really glad you showed up. I needed your help. You did
a good job. You're a stand-up broad, Sandy. I'm proud of you."

He walked out of the kitchen with the sandwich.

I knew Bernie's don't-ask-me-about-my-business spiel by heart.
I knew, also, that for the most part it was to protect me, to keep me
ignorant of anything that could get *me* in trouble as well as him.
And, for the most part, I did try to stay out of his business. I wanted
to be a good "racket club" wife. And that meant, no questions.

But I was also a Jewish wife. And that meant, no secrets.

Bernie had the same problem. He was a wise guy, he lived a
tough life by a tight code. He was supposed to be careful whom he
trusted, careful whom he talked to. There were certain things he
wasn't supposed to tell me—for my own good, for his safety, for
the sake of preserving the rules and rituals of a certain way of life.

But he was Jewish, too. And he wanted a real wife, not just an
armpiece; not just a kid who looked up to him, but a partner he
could respect and trust. I wanted so much to be that person. I knew
he was training me to be that person. But it was a slow, cautious
process and in an emergency, like the one we faced that night, neither of us was sure I was ready.

Although I hadn't stopped asking questions or demanding answers since I'd laid eyes on the bleeding man, when all was said
and done, I wasn't sure I really wanted to hear the truth, the whole
truth and nothing but . . . I was very scared. All I wanted was for
Bernie to reassure me that we were safe.

It could have been him in that bed, I thought. It could even have
been me.

Later that evening while Pinky, which was what the wounded

man's name turned out to be, slept in our bed, Bernie and I camped out in the living room—and talked.

"Is he going to live?"

"Yeah. He'll be fine. I'll get him out of here in the morning."

"Good," I said. "Could you move the gun at least? Get it out of the foyer, get it out of my sight?"

"Leave it. It's not bothering you."

We'd had a couple of drinks by then. Bernie had smoked a little grass. We had a long L-shaped couch in the new apartment and I was lying down on the loveseat part of it and Bernie had the four-cushion side. "What happened to him?" I asked again.

"He's a jerk. He tried to hit Red Dillon."

"Red Dillon from uptown?" I remembered the tall, thin, light-skinned gangster I'd met at Cokey's bar. I remembered being told he was quick and dangerous. "The one you always say would shoot you first and ask questions later?"

"Red owed Pinky money. Pinky decided to collect. He knew Red would be at this garage uptown. Pinky is all balls, no brains. He pulled a rifle on Red Dillon in bright daylight in the middle of Harlem. Dumb bastard threatens Red. Red's bodyguard put a hole in him."

The telephone rang. Bernie said, "Only if it's Hot Dog or Vinny. Otherwise, I'm not in." The phone always rang a lot—it was Bernie's lifeline to the world; to business, betting, breathing. That night, it rang more than usual. And each time, I'd answer it and say the caller's name aloud. "Oh, hiya, Carmine," I'd say. And Bernie would shake his head no. "Sorry, he's not here," I'd say. "I'll tell him to call you."

"Are the cops going to come, Bernie?" I asked him.

"I hope not."

"Is anybody else going to come here?"

He shrugged. "I don't think so. If they do, you don't know Pinky. You don't know Red Dillon. You never heard these names."

"How did he get here?"

"He was in trouble. He called me."

"Everyone calls you when they're in trouble," I said. "Everyone comes to you. You're too good. You'll get in trouble."

"Nah," Bernie said. "It doesn't matter, anyway. As long as I do the right thing."

We must have talked until five in the morning. Every fifteen minutes, Bernie would get up and check on his patient. He did a hell of a job. Pinky walked out on his own steam about noon the next day. I never saw him again.

Bernie made a phone call in the morning, then he got Pinky a clean shirt and a raincoat. I think they wrapped the shotgun in the raincoat. I think they must have gone down to the basement garage and that a car—sent by whoever Bernie had spoken to that morning—was waiting there to whisk Pinky away, because Bernie returned to the apartment alone less than fifteen minutes later.

In the short time he'd been away, I'd peeked into the bedroom, seen the blood again and broken down sobbing uncontrollably. I was making a pot of coffee when he returned. He saw that I'd been crying. He put his arms around me.

"I can't live this way, Bernie. It's too scary. This isn't the life I want," I blurted out, almost ashamed to admit it, as though I were letting him down.

"I know, baby. It's okay," he said, as my tears spilled onto his shoulder. "You're right. It's no way to live. Sandy," he said, "it'll never happen again. I swear to you. I'm going to give you the life you want and deserve. Just be patient, baby."

"Really?" I said, stepping back and studying his face. "Really, Bernie, you'll go straight? We'll live like normal people?"

"I swear it to you, Sandy. I promise," he said.

CHAPTER EIGHT

Roman Holiday

I reminded Bernie of that promise every chance I got. But to be honest about it, I didn't always hate the crazy life we were living. It took me places and taught me things "normal" people never experienced. And while danger was the downside—coming home to find guys bleeding in your bed, hearing that a friend you hadn't seen for a while was turning up in pieces around the city, keeping secrets, telling lies, being constantly careful of what you said to whom—it was almost always mixed with a sense of excitement and adventure that was elating and addictive.

For the most part, Bernie kept me out of his business. I was the one who'd ask too many questions and catch him half-asleep or trick him during a fight into telling me more than he wanted me to know. As much as I wanted a decent normal life for us, I also wanted the fun, excitement, and privileges of life in the fast lane.

Of course, I didn't admit that to myself as a twenty-two-year-old newlywed. And if I didn't have absolute faith in Bernie's commitment to reform, at least I had hope. After all, he had said we'd be married one day, and we were. How much more nagging could it take for him to make good on this new promise? My fantasies of living a normal life blossomed.

So, of course, when Bernie came home all excited one afternoon in early September and announced that we were going to Rome, Italy, I jumped on him with gratitude and joy.

"Oh, honey, we're going to have a belated honeymoon!" I cried, like any upstanding citizen of Picket Fence, Suburbia. "I'm so excited. When are we going?"

"Tomorrow," he said.

"Oh, my God, so soon? I can't. I don't have clothes. I've got to shop, pack. And what about passports? Don't we have to get passports?"

"Not necessarily," Bernie said. He was carrying a leather briefcase. He put it down on a barstool, opened it, and pulled out two passports. "Hot Dog's bringing over your wig in a half-hour—"

"Wig?" I asked cautiously. I could feel those fantasies withering on the vine.

"I want you to put on some makeup," Bernie continued, tossing one of the passports to me. "A lot of makeup, baby. And the wig. Then the Dog'll take you to get the photo made and we'll put it on your passport."

I opened the passport book. "Who's Sally Mason?" I asked.

"That's you."

"Bernie, why do we need this? Why can't we just go like normal people?"

" 'Cause we're not doing something normal, baby. This is a very special trip. Listen, I've got to run out for an hour. Don't let that bag out of your sight, okay? And don't let anyone in here but Red. And, Sandy, you can't tell anyone we're going, you understand? Not even your mother. Now, move, sweetheart. *Shmear* on that makeup. I'll be back soon."

I stared at the door as it slammed shut after him. Then I looked at the briefcase sitting on the barstool.

Okay, don't ask questions. Just do what he told you to do. Go into the bedroom, sit down at your dressing table, and turn yourself into Sally Mason, said my mob-wife mind. But my Jewish feet made a beeline for that briefcase. What I saw inside confused me. Paper. Not money but certificates of some kind, in denominations ranging from $5,000 to $50,000. I was a kid. I'd never even heard of bearer bonds, but that's what they were. Payment notes entitling the bearer to hard cash—to the tune of hundreds of thousands of dollars.

I closed the briefcase and carried it with me into the bedroom.

Forget it, I told myself as I attacked my makeup with trembling hands. Who knows what they really are or why he's got them. Maybe he's holding them for a friend, maybe they have nothing to do with this trip. My mind and heart raced as I pencilled on thick black doe eyes, and pasted false eyelashes big as spiders onto my aquamarine shadowed lids.

Hot Dog Red rang the bell about five minutes before Bernie returned. He handed me a hat box in which was a long, trashy, platinum-blond wig.

"So you're going off to meet the Pope," he said, chuckling, as I pinned up my hair to try on the wig.

"We're going to Rome. I've never been to Europe, Red. This is my first trip ever. I'm so excited," I said honestly. "There's so much I want to see! I want to go to all the museums. And see the fountain where you throw in coins and make wishes like in the movies. And shopping!"

To tell the truth, I was even excited about stealing towels and bringing home soap from the best hotels. I thought about being pinched on the street by men who looked like Marcello Mastroianni and about kneeling before the Pope wearing a black lace handkerchief on my head like Jacqueline Kennedy.

"Who knows, maybe we *will* have an audience with the Pope," I kidded Red back. But in my extravagant daydreams, even that was possible.

When Bernie walked in, I said, "Do they let Jewish people meet the Pope? Do you think we could do that?"

He winked at Red. "Well, baby," he said. "I don't know about the Pope, but you might get to meet a couple of friends of his."

I could barely sleep that night.

"I can't wait to see Rome," I said, snuggling against him in bed. "It'll be so romantic."

On the plane the next day, my head was itching like mad from the blond wig. I had to go into the bathroom every fifteen minutes to scratch my scalp. Grabbing every headrest en route for balance, I tottered up the aisle of the plane in the dark glasses, five-inch heels, and tight skirt Bernie had me wearing. He thought it made me look like a typical American tourist. I thought I looked like Bimbo the Wonder Whore.

"Do I have to wear this wig and stuff the whole time we're in Rome?" I asked.

"You can take it off when we get to the hotel," he promised.

We were staying at the Hassler, which was next to a beautiful church at the top of the Spanish Steps. Our room was comfortable and clean, not the presidential suite, but with a breathtaking view of Rome.

As soon as we were alone, I took off the wig and threw it onto the bed. "Oh, God, I want to take a shower and then I want to go for a walk. Did you see the city? It's gorgeous. So many fountains and statues and bridges and scooters!"

"We're not going out today," Bernie said.

"But it's still early. Why not?"

"We're here for business, not pleasure," he said. "Tomorrow morning, you'll put on that little black dress I got you. And the wig and the sunglasses. And then we're going to the Vatican—"

"The Vatican? That's the first place you want to see? What's wrong with you?"

"We're not going there sightseeing, Sandra. I told you, it's strictly business."

"In the Vatican? We're Jewish. What kind of business?"

"I've got to pick up some money," Bernie said.

I waited. I thought he was going to say: I've got to pick up some money *and then* we're going over to the Vatican and . . . But no, apparently it was a complete sentence. I didn't get it. "What's that got to do with the Vatican?" I asked.

We'd both had a couple of drinks on the plane. Now Bernie pulled out a joint he'd had stashed and lit up. "You looked in the briefcase," he said, with a little grin. It wasn't a question. He knew me. "You saw the bonds."

"That's what they are? Bonds?"

"Go shut the curtains, Sandy."

"I want to see the city. It's bad enough I can't go outside. Can't I at least *look* at Rome?"

"Not this trip, baby."

"I know, I know." I sighed and drew the curtains shut. "Strictly business, right?"

"Right. Go ahead, now. Count the bonds."

"I don't feel like it." I threw myself onto the bed and started pulling out the bobbypins that had held my real hair up inside the wig. "Anyway, I know there are a lot of them. So what does the Vatican have to do with it?"

"The Vatican has its own bank. You didn't know that, did you?"

He was teaching me again. And I was in no mood now. Still, what he was saying was news to me. "They have a bank?"

Bernie nodded. "They've got one of the richest portfolios in the world."

"So what are we going to do there, cash in the bonds?" I was being sarcastic.

That little grin widened. "You got it," he said.

"I don't believe it. You're kidding," I insisted. And even when Bernie shook his head at my naiveté I was still dumbfounded, I still thought he had to be joking. "We're taking the bonds to the *Vatican*, Bernie? We're going to cash them there?"

He took another toke of pot, then knocked off the ash on the bottom of his shoe. "First thing tomorrow morning," he said. "We go get the money. We're back in the room. One-two-zipola, then we're out of here. We never were here. Strictly business." Bernie dove onto the bed next to me. He was in a terrific mood. "It's a lot of money, baby. More than you've ever seen."

"Is it yours?"

"Not all of it."

"So who does it belong to, the racket club?"

"The racket club?"

"You know, the organization, the outfit—"

Bernie started to laugh. "That's what you call the boys, 'the racket club'?" He couldn't stop laughing.

"You're stoned," I said.

"You think so?" he said, brushing the bobby pins off the bed. "Come here. You know, you don't look half bad as a blonde. Maybe you ought to put that wig back on."

I did, the next morning. I wore the wig, the black dress, the sunglasses and, at Bernie's suggestion, I stuck two sticks of chewing gum into my mouth, the consummate tourist.

A car was waiting for us outside the hotel. The driver was a young Italian who looked more like a peasant than a jet-set Roman. His face was brown and lined from the sun. He was wearing a cap, baggy pants, and a black vest over shirtsleeves. He drove us to Saint Peter's Square, right through the wrought-iron gates into Vatican City. The car stopped in front of a beautiful church.

Bernie had a gold charm he always wore around his neck on a long gold rope. It had a Jewish star on one side and a Saint Christopher's medal on the other. The minute the car stopped in front of the church, he took off the necklace and turned it around.

"What are you doing?" I asked.

"Putting the Saint Christopher's medal face out. It's wrong for a Jewish God to walk into another God's house," he said.

I hadn't thought about it, but now I agreed with him. And, suddenly, I felt like it was wrong for a Jewish human to walk into another God's house, too—chewing gum, no less. Worrying and half-waiting for one God or another to show up and strike me dead,

I held Bernie's hand and entered a magnificent chapel filled with gold ornaments, marble statues, and beautiful paintings.

There were worshippers in the church, kneeling at dark polished wooden pews. And there were a number of priests dressed in plain black cassocks. While I stared open-mouthed at the stained-glass windows and beautiful arched ceiling, Bernie stopped one of the priests and spoke to him in English. The priest signaled for Bernie to wait. And then he brought a younger priest over to us. The second man spoke English with a lovely Italian accent. Bernie mentioned a name to him and the young priest nodded and said, "Come with me, please."

He led us through the side door of the chapel down a long corridor, then showed us into a study. It was a big, high-ceilinged room with a large wooden desk that had a huge, velvet-covered armchair behind it and two highbacked wooden chairs in front of it. I sat in one of them. Bernie stood. The priest asked if we'd like some coffee and I said yes. And he left us.

All this time, Bernie was clutching the briefcase under one arm. The priest returned with a tray of coffee for me. A second priest entered. Bernie said, "Baby, I'll be right back," and he left with both of them.

I was terribly nervous. I sat there sipping the espresso, I guess it was, and looking at the brocade hangings and the beautiful red patterned rug and the oil paintings of saints and churchmen, cardinals, maybe—what did I know about Vatican rank?—and thinking the most ridiculous thoughts. I wondered, did Jews do the same thing? Did they have their own bank or was it just the *goyim*? I wasn't sure about the bonds, either. Was Bernie doing someone a legitimate favor or were the boys involved? There'd been a Wall Street heist in the papers a couple of months back, a really big one, and there'd been a lot of talk about mob involvement in it. Were these the stolen bonds? Was this a mission for the mob? Then I started wondering if cops would bust in suddenly. And I was very nervous and staring at the door and then I thought, well, maybe the Pope will walk in instead. By mistake, even. That would be interesting.

When the door finally did open, it was Bernie with the young priest. He was holding the case in front of him. He patted it and winked at me and I knew he had gotten the money.

The same driver was waiting for us just outside the church. In the car, Bernie signaled me not to say anything and we rode back to the hotel in silence. The briefcase on his lap seemed almost spotlit to me, so hot it was practically smoking. He hugged it to his chest as we entered the hotel, rode up the elevator, and finally returned to our room.

In the car on the way back it began to hit me about this business trip. Bernie had taken a briefcase full of bearer bonds into the Vatican and come back out again with cash. Though I hadn't seen the money yet, I was sure of it. I wondered again whether the bonds belonged to "the boys." And if they had, did that mean the Vatican was fencing for the mob?

Yes, and they'd been doing it for years, was what Bernie said back at the hotel.

"Where did the bonds come from?" I asked him, tearing the wig off again and throwing it onto the bed.

"You don't need to know," he said.

"Is it from the heist that was in the papers?"

"You don't need to know. You don't want to know. Case closed, baby."

"Okay. So *now* can we go out?" I said, I think just to irritate him.

"No."

"Isn't there a safe in the hotel where you can leave it?"

"No." Bernie set the briefcase down on the bed. "It stays here and we stay here." He drew the shades again.

I'd been edgy all morning. I'd become almost desperate to do something normal, walk around without the goddamn wig, see the city, be a real tourist. Anything to get rid of the nervousness, the fear, I guess, the sense of danger that had walked into the Vatican with me. Now I knew absolutely that I wasn't going anywhere but home tomorrow, that I was really stuck in the hotel room. I was annoyed, angry, frustrated. "Great," I griped. "Join the mob and see the world!"

"Don't say I never took you anywhere," Bernie teased me the next morning on the plane.

"When can we come back and do it for real?" I asked. We were sitting side by side, holding hands.

"It's not over yet," he said. "Now, listen. When we get home, don't talk on the phone. If anyone asks where you were, where we were, we were in and out. Anyone tried to reach us, we were just around. You don't tell anyone about Rome. Tillie you can tell. Your mother's okay. But not on the phone, Sandy. The phone is your worst enemy. The phone is a weapon."

"Again with the teaching?" I said.

"You think I'm going to be around forever? What're you going to do when I'm gone?" Bernie said. "You've got to be smart. You've got to learn. I don't want anyone taking advantage of you."

I didn't want to hear it. I didn't want to know it. Sure, Bernie was more than twenty years older than I. Sure, he was a sick man with a dangerous heart condition and a life-style to match. But death wasn't what I wanted to think about right then, right there.

I pulled away from him and stared gloomily out the window at the field of clouds we were plowing through—a field that suddenly took on the sinister look of heaven.

"I thought you said we were going to live like normal people," I grumbled. "You promised me. So what good will all this information do me, knowing stuff like 'the phone is a weapon'?"

He gave me a look. Then he shook his head and sighed. "Normal?" he said. "Sandy, for me, this *is* normal, baby."

CHAPTER NINE

The Gold Coast

A couple of weeks after our Roman holiday, Bernie was restless and ready for action again. It was late September. The weather was lousy. He'd been hanging around the house a lot. He'd caught a cold, which made him irritable and demanding. And also meant that Dr. Sealy practically moved in with us.

Autumn in New York was no picnic for Bernie. And Bernie, hanging around the house, restless, irritable and demanding, was no picnic for me. Bored, he was like a tiger in a cage. Bored *and sick* he was like a tiger with a toothache—snarling, growling, pacing, unpredictable, dangerous. When I wasn't shopping for him, cooking for him, running errands for him, answering the phone for him, delivering messages for him, giving him his medication and making coffee, drinks, and putting out ashtrays, pastrami, and pickles for the condolence callers, and cleaning up afterwards, I gave him plenty of distance.

About a minute before that first sneeze laid him low, Bernie had been talking about going to Miami for the winter. And boy was I thrilled when Dr. Sealy gave him the go-ahead. I'd never been to Florida. And if Bernie's descriptions of broad white beaches, palm tree-lined avenues, palatial hotels, kidney-shaped swimming pools, and endless sunshine had enticed me before he got sick, after three weeks locked up in the house with him, I was ready to take off on my own.

Late October, we packed up the car, let the street dirt and dying leaves whirl away behind us, and drove South leisurely, in great spirits. Bernie was very relaxed and feeling good. The trip took five days. And as he drove, Bernie pointed out the sights, and talked about Florida, what we'd do and who we'd see.

"You'll get to meet Farvel," he promised. "And who knows, maybe even Meyer." Bernie loved Farvel, whose real name was Philly Kovolick, his mentor from the Lower East Side ghetto decades ago. Farvel was Meyer Lansky's wall, Bernie said. Thick, dependable, hard as stone. You had to go through him to get to Meyer.

Bernie loved Farvel, but he revered Meyer. He called him "the old man." The old man, he said, had been a postwar pioneer, practically single-handedly transforming Florida into "the Gold Coast." Everyone who was anyone had followed Meyer Lansky south in the late forties and early fifties—from Cleveland, Philadelphia, Boston, New York, the *gantse mishpocheh*, the whole family, had bought homes and real estate there and wintered in splendor near where their money was invested.

Meyer had left them for Cuba. If the old man had made Florida "the Gold Coast," he'd turned Havana into a diamond mine, Bernie said. But Fidel Castro's revolution had defeated Lansky's partner, the Cuban president, and closed the lavish clubs and casinos. The "syndicate" had been forced to leave everything.

Now Meyer was back in Florida, living with his second wife, Teddy, whom he'd met while she was a manicurist in a mob-run hotel. Bernie had never met Teddy. He'd never really socialized with Meyer Lansky. He knew of her only through Farvel. But you never could tell, he said, maybe we'd get a chance to meet her this trip.

I can still remember my first palm tree. Bernie pointed it out to me somewhere above Palm Beach. And then, farther south, we began to see the hotels along the ocean. We drove down Collins Avenue past the Thunderbird and the Castaways, down toward the soaring, sprawling hotels of Miami Beach. In the waterway across the road from the Fontainbleau was a huge, gaudy, Chinese-style houseboat.

"Guess who owns that?" Bernie asked. It turned out to be the loveboat our friendly neighborhood abortionist Hattie Prince had built for a well-known New York saloon keeper she was keeping. And next to Hattie's junk was a yacht called *Ocean's Eleven*, named for the recent movie that had starred Frank Sinatra and his "rat pack" pals.

From Collins Avenue, we drove into a beautiful street aptly

named Pine Tree Drive and there, at the end of a circular driveway, was the house Bernie had rented for us.

"Oh, my God, is it really ours? It's gorgeous, Bernie!" I cried. And when I say "I cried," I mean it literally. As he led me from room to room through the spacious, airy house, my eyes misted. I was utterly overwhelmed. Not only were the rooms twice the size of those in our New York apartment, but there was a full dining room, a pantry, a laundry room and a "Florida Room" with a pink and gray terrazzo-tiled floor and three walls of jalousied windows that opened onto a big backyard with palm trees and exquisite hibiscus plants and a blue, kidney-shaped swimming pool.

Our first weeks in Florida were spent seeing the town. We had steaks at the Epicure, overstuffed sandwiches at Wolfies, blintzes at Pumperniks. We ate ribs and chicken at the piano bar in the Barnfire, bet bundles at the dog track, the race track, the trotters, and Jai Lai, caught the shows at the Fontainbleau and Eden Roc, had drinks at the Racket Club and watched, through a plate glass window at the bar, people swimming underwater at the Castaways.

But as we began to settle in, Bernie would disappear for hours during the day. Sometimes he'd have to go back to New York for business. I was left by myself for long stretches of time in a strange place where I knew no one. Or else Bernie and I were constantly together for days on end and that could drive me crazy, too. I had no friends of my own in Florida. I didn't know how to get around. It wasn't like New York, a place where you could walk practically anywhere and take a bus or subway everywhere else. So when Bernie took the car I was stranded, and when Bernie was home I had to depend on him to take me places. Weeks became months and I became as bored, restless, and irritable as he'd been before we left New York.

"Do something with yourself. Get a hobby. Learn something," advised Mr. Self-Improvement.

"Like what?"

"Like what would you like to do? What do you wish you could do?"

"Play the guitar," I decided.

"Okay," Bernie said.

"Well, I don't have a guitar. And I don't know how to play, so I guess I'd need lessons."

"Fine," he said.

Bernie being Bernie, two days later the equipment came rolling in: a metallic-red electric guitar, speakers, an amplifier, what looked to me like enough electrical equipment to short-circuit the East Coast. And the day after that, a guitar instructor showed up. A very nice, very serious young man who meant well and had tremendous patience.

I was very attentive. I worked hard at it. The instructor said I had to cut my fingernails if I wanted to play. With tears and trepidation, I cut my fingernails. I practiced chords. I strained to hear if the guitar was out of tune. I tried to learn how to tune it. I had no aptitude whatsoever. Two weeks and thousands of dollars later, the only thing I could play was "My Dog Has Fleas."

"What counts is you tried," Bernie consoled me. "Take off that halter top, it's too low-cut." He had an appointment with Farvel up at the Castaways. I was going to do a little shopping in Surfside, then pick him up after the meeting.

"I'm going to be in the car the whole time, right? I'm just dropping you off."

"Like that, you are. Get dressed. Put on a nice blouse. Maybe I'll introduce you."

I hadn't met Farvel yet. I hadn't met any of the real players, just a couple of nightclub owners, numbers guys, bar flies, and track touts. I changed into a pretty white piqué blouse with candy-striped pink and white Toreadors and high-heeled sandals. I put on a pair of hoop earrings, tied a pink bandana around my head, and teased the hair behind it until I looked like a real Miami Beach lioness.

"That's better," Bernie approved. "Now I'm proud to show you off."

"I feel bad about the money we wasted on the guitar lessons," I said as we drove up Collins Avenue. "But I've been thinking about what you said. About learning things, improving myself."

Bernie laughed. "I can feel the pain in my wallet now. How much is it going to cost me this time?"

"I want to sing."

"I'll shut off the radio."

"Stop it. You know what I mean. I want to take singing lessons. I think I could really do it, Bernie. I'm young, I'm pretty. How hard can it be to sing?"

"We'll talk about it later," he said, as we pulled up to the Castaways. "Right now, I've got to meet Farvel for lunch and a *shvitz*. Pick me up in an hour."

It was just like in New York. Bernie used to go down to the Luxor Baths to talk business in the steam room with guys who'd come in from out of town. Jewish guys from the midwest, New England, Las Vegas, and Florida steaming together like *kreplach* in soup. The *shvitz*, they called it. The sweat box. They'd sit with cigars clamped in their teeth, towels wrapped around their bellies, sweat pouring off them, attendants dousing them with cold water, while they caught up with world and local events. And then, pink and shiny, they'd waddle into the restaurant at the Baths and load up on pickled herring, borscht, and chopped egg salad.

The Castaways in North Miami Beach looked nothing like the Luxor Baths, however. It was a big, luxurious, sprawling hotel that had its own yacht basin and was designed to resemble a shipwrecked pirate's palace. The Teamsters owned it. And when I drove up to get Bernie, he was standing outside talking to someone I figured was a union official from up north. His skin was so white that I assumed he was just down for business. No one who lived in Florida could be that pale, I thought.

Bernie waved me over and I got out of the car and walked toward them. The union guy barely looked at me. He was about B's height and thickly built—like a wall—which should have given me a clue. The man was several years older than Bernie, but his hair was still thick and dark. He had thick Edward G. Robinson lips, which were wrapped around a forgotten cigar that waggled as he talked with Bernie.

"Farvel," Bernie said, "this is my little girl, my baby."

Farvel the Stick shook his head from side to side. "This is some baby," he said, grinning approvingly. I nodded at him. I *was* a baby, a twenty-two-year-old kid who, if you said hello to me, would be stuck for an answer. Especially in front of a man I'd been hearing about for years.

Bernie was beaming at me.

"Nice to meet you," I managed.

"Come on." Farvel took my arm and said to Bernie, "He's right inside. He should meet her." He led me into the hotel lobby.

Two men, deep in conversation, were walking toward us. One was tall, slender, and elegant-looking. The other was very short and tan, wearing moccasins with a cabana suit of beige shorts and a matching jacket. He had a lined face and long nose and looked like a mild-mannered accountant who'd spent a hard-earned vacation day sunbathing beside a pool.

"Meyer," Farvel said to him, "this is the kid's wife. Ain't she a cutie?"

Meyer Lansky nodded his head at me. "A pleasure to meet you," he said. "Bernie says you're going to be a singer."

Bernie and Farvel laughed. The tall, lean man extended his hand to me. "Good luck," he said.

"Sandy, this is Jimmy." Bernie introduced me to Jimmy Blue Eyes, one of Meyer's Italian associates.

I'm sure I blushed. "How do you do?" I said.

"Okay, kid," Farvel said to Bernie, deftly steering us toward the lobby doors again. "Good to see you. Sandy, don't be a stranger." Without taking the cigar out of his mouth, he leaned forward and buzzed my cheek. "You need something, call my Minnie. What the hell's she got to do all day anyhow?"

Bernie was very proud of me. He was also proud that I'd seen him with Meyer Lansky and Farvel and Jimmy Blue Eyes, men he idolized but rarely saw. He was in a terrific mood, full of gossip and inside information, as we drove back home. I could see how thrilled he was to have spent the afternoon with the old man. "Oh, does he hate Castro," I remember Bernie saying. I remember it because it was hard for me to believe that a little, slight man like that could hate anyone. He seemed too peaceful to be that passionate.

"I can't believe you told Meyer Lansky that I was going to be a singer," I said.

"Why not? You are, aren't you?"

Of course, within a week, I was taking singing lessons. Some mornings my voice coach would come to our house; some mornings I'd meet him for my hour's lesson at the club where he sang nights and played the piano. I thought I was coming along fine. But I was probably so busy belting my heart out that I never saw him wincing.

One morning, as I was getting ready to go out for a voice lesson, I heard men's voices in the kitchen and the sound of things being scraped along the floor. I walked into the kitchen just as the men were leaving and saw three crates that looked like coffins piled one on top of another in the corner of the kitchen.

"What's going on?" I asked Bernie, who was hurrying past me on his way to the bedroom.

"I'm going out of town for a couple of days and I want you to stay in the house and not leave."

"What do you mean, 'not leave'?" I said, following him. "I've got a singing lesson in fifteen minutes."

He was tossing clothes into a small suitcase. "I mean not leave today, tomorrow, the next day. I need you to watch those boxes for me. I mean do not set foot outside this house until I get back."

"What's in them?"

"None of your business," he replied predictably.

I thought about it for a minute. "Okay, then, I'll ask Barry to come here for my lessons."

"Over my dead body. You don't talk to Barry or anyone but me. You don't let in anyone but me. You don't go out for anything until I get back. You need food, order it over the telephone. And I'm going to be calling to make sure you're here, Sandy, so don't fool around, okay? If anyone else calls looking for me, I'm out fishing. I'm sleeping. I'm at the track—just don't make conversation."

"Yeah, I know. The phone is my worst enemy. The phone is a weapon," I recited sarcastically.

He raised an eyebrow at me. I checked his neck for vein movement. I thought I could see a little twitch getting started. I left the bedroom.

The first day and night went by. I watched TV, I practiced singing in the mirror. I started to get claustrophobic. The next day, I left the kitchen and sat outside on the patio, I went swimming, I tossed coconuts around the backyard and cut flowers. The third day, I thought about just taking a walk around the block. But by then I knew I couldn't. Bernie was phoning me about ten times a day to make sure I was home.

The miracle was that it took three whole days before I broke into the crates. I found some tools in the garage and, standing on a kitchen chair, I pried open the top box. My worst fear was that there might be a body inside. No, maybe my worst fear was that there'd be *parts* of a body inside. I never even considered what was actually in the crates—guns. There were enough guns inside those coffin-sized boxes to start a new revolution in Cuba.

"Shit," I said aloud to myself. "I'm baby-sitting guns!" Then, "Shit," I said, staring at the splintered top of the crate, "he'll see that I looked in and he'll get all excited." I ran back out to the garage, and got a hammer and nails and repaired the top as best I could. Bernie kept phoning. I kept my vigil. I walked in circles around the pool like a guy exercising in a prison yard. And as I walked, my imagination went wild. I thought of how Meyer hated Castro and how Bernie loved Meyer and I wondered if, indeed, the guns were destined for Havana.

I know that Bernie did occasionally do favors for Meyer, personal favors. I remember in New York a few years later, he got a telephone call in the middle of the night and ran out of the house with a raincoat on over his pajamas to get Meyer's daughter, whose name was also Sandy, out of a jam she'd gotten into at the Copa.

I never found out about the guns, though. Within an hour of Bernie's return, the crates disappeared from the kitchen. He was in a great mood and I was relieved that he was back and that he hadn't noticed the boxes had been tampered with.

"I've got a surprise for you, baby," he said. I'd been *hocking* him about singing in public, about launching my career. "I spoke to Moey," he said, mentioning a friend of his who owned a disco in Hallendale. "And you're going to open at his place. It's all arranged."

My singing teacher wasn't sure I was ready. Finally, he capitulated, saying that I'd probably make up in enthusiasm for what I lacked in skill. He worked out arrangements for me and instrumentals for the little backup group we'd hired. Bernie helped me pick out a stunning full-length gown. He bought out the disco for the night and packed it with every local character he could find. He didn't invite Meyer or Farvel, thank God. But there were enough people sitting out front when I peeked before the show to drive me to drink.

The champagne Bernie had bought me was already open in the dressing room. I sipped and paced and sipped and touched up my makeup and refilled the glass and sipped and stared at the blurring words to the songs I'd taped onto the mirror. I was so scared that my hands started shaking as I poured and sipped another glass of champagne.

By the time the M.C. announced, "And here, making her singing debut, is the lovely Miss Sandy Barton!" I was totally bombed. In my showstopping evening gown, I stumbled on stage and stood clutching the microphone, swaying, petrified. The band played the opening bars. I opened my mouth. Nothing came out. The group started over. Still nothing. My heart started thudding. My eyes blurred. The last thing I saw was Bernie sitting ringside, all dressed up in his tuxedo.

"God, let the earth open up and swallow me," I prayed. Then I passed out cold.

I came to in the dressing room and started crying. But Bernie took me in his arms and soothed me. "Don't worry, sweetheart. It's okay," he whispered, smoothing back my hair, patting my cheek. "Everything's okay, *mamela*. Don't cry."

* * *

Bernie knew how lonely and bored I'd been. He'd gone along with my wild schemes, he'd given me guitar lessons, tried to help me launch a singing career, and even flew Marlene and my mother down to Miami and entertained them royally, all so that I might be happy in Florida. But what I needed were friends and a social life of my own. Even this, Bernie tried to arrange for me.

He came home one day all excited. "We've been invited to lunch on Davey Yaras's yacht," he said, about a month after my singing career was nipped in the bud at Moey's disco. "Farvel and Minnie are going to be there. And Davey's wife, Blanche, who's like this," Bernie crossed his fingers, "with Teddy Lansky."

He was really pleased—for both us. Yaras was a heavy hitter from Chicago, a colleague of Meyer's, and a good friend of Farvel's. Socializing with Davey Yaras was a big step up from the run-of-the-mill Miami characters we'd been seeing.

Again, Bernie supervised my dressing. No shorts, no halter top. You didn't go to show off your legs on Davey Yaras's yacht. For slumming around at the dogtrack with the girlfriends and mistresses of low-level wise guys, shorts were occasionally permissible. But we were in the big time now. I was going to meet The Wives.

Yaras's yacht was docked at a boat basin somewhere between Fort Lauderdale and Hollywood. The first sight of it took my breath away. It was gleaming white and big as a ship, and carried its own full-sized speedboat aboard. A uniformed captain greeted us.

At the top of the steps was Farvel, white as the yacht and wearing a straw porkpie hat against the sun. An unlit cigar was clamped in his teeth. The only time I ever saw Farvel without a cigar was at his daughter's wedding, and only for the short time it took him to walk her down the aisle.

"It's the kid and his Mrs.," Farvel hollered, extending his hand and practically yanking Bernie onto the boat. "Minnie, come here. What the hell's the matter with you? Come say hello."

So the first of the Florida wives I met was the motherly Minnie Kovolicks, Farvel's heavyset, comfortable, long-suffering partner. *Hamisch* was the word for Minnie. Her expressions, the raised eyebrows, the shoulder shrug, the thin smile, ran a narrow gamut from accepting to tolerant. Decades of Farvel's good-humored Jewish abrasiveness had rounded off any edges Minnie might have had. "Look, a baby," she said of me. "Very pretty, Bernie. You got yourself a sweet little girl. And you," she confided, "you got some prize here."

As plain and soft-spoken as Minnie Kovolicks was, that's how extraordinary, outspoken, and fabulous Blanche Yaras seemed to me. She was a beautiful blonde, twenty years older than I and twice as glamorous. She was dressed in an exquisitely tailored, spotless linen pantsuit. Her brilliant blonde hair was rolled in a perfect soft page-boy. When she spoke, everyone listened. When she moved, a constellation of diamonds caught the sun. When Minnie walked me over to her, it was like being introduced to a spotlight.

"Blanche," Minnie began.

"What Blanche?" Farvel hollered. "Call her by her real name, her Jewish name. Bleema, Bleema we call this beauty. Am I right, Bleemela?"

Blanche Yaras smiled fully and graciously. "Of course, Farvel, darling," she said, laughing. "And you're Sandy? Oh, my God, Bernie, you robbed a cradle." Blanche patted my teased auburn hair and chucked me gently under the chin. "A beautiful little cradle. Davey!" Blanche commanded her husband before whom grown men and investigating senators quavered. "Get this gorgeous little girl of Barton's a drink."

I felt like a child, an awkward, starstruck kid. The minute I met Blanche Yaras I wanted to be her. She intimidated me and I remember watching her that day and thinking I want to grow up to intimidate a kid like me someday.

There was another couple on the yacht as well. The eight of us sat down to a beautiful luncheon around a handsomely set table on the forward deck. There were fresh flowers on the table, linen napkins in tortoise shell rings, crystal goblets for Farvel and Davey's seltzer, silver salt and pepper shakers, and a silver bread tray. And plenty of wine and laughter. Davey Yaras was a very good-looking man, tall and implacable. Every now and then he'd shake his head at Blanche's irrepressible comments and pronouncements, but it was clear that she was her own woman, brash, beautiful, and commanding.

When I admired a pin she was wearing, she said, "I'll give you my jeweler's name. Make him get you one." She tossed her head at Bernie. She didn't lower her voice, either. "Get him to spend that money on you, honey. Get it before it's gone. And wear it."

Teddy Lansky gave me the same advice.

* * *

I don't know if it was Blanche Yaras's doing or Farvel's, but about a week after we spent the day on the Yarases' yacht, we were invited to dinner at the old man's house.

"What old man?" I asked Bernie, who'd come crashing through the hibiscus bushes and palmetto leaves with the happy news. I was sitting at the edge of the pool, swinging my legs in the water. He came around from the garage, beaming his big toothy smile at me.

"What old man?" He laughed. "Meyer," he said. "Meyer!"

I scrambled to my feet as if Meyer Lansky, himself, had entered the backyard with Bernie. "What do I wear? How am I supposed to look?"

I wasn't surprised when Bernie had the answer already. "Nothing low-cut. Nothing showy." But his teaching tone ended right there. "What am I going to bring him?" he wondered aloud, sounding almost as awestruck and uncertain as I felt. "Flowers, dessert, booze? What can you bring to a man like that?" And I was surprised to discover that this was Bernie's first invitation to Meyer's home, too.

For years, he'd been one of the boys, "the kid," a well-liked character but a floater, a loner, a rebel. Now that he was married, he was respectable. Like Farvel, like Meyer, he was a family man again. I'd become an asset he hadn't counted on. I was a sweet kid, a good girl—not a hooker, not a sharp broad—a wife.

I decided on a turquoise linen sheath and heels. I wrapped a turquoise bandana around my hair and pulled back the front and teased the back into an auburn explosion. Very chic, very "swinging," very sixties. Bernie decided to send flowers to Meyer's home, which I thought was a very sophisticated thing to do.

Meyer and Teddy were living then in a handsome, surprisingly unpretentious house up in Lauderdale, I think it was. The neighborhood was quiet and suburban, not one of the elegant gate-guard communities. And the house was spacious but very simple. A nice Florida home. Not a mansion.

Because of what I'd seen of the Yarases' life-style, I think I expected a servant to answer the Lanskys' door. I certainly didn't expect Farvel. But there he was, all spruced up in a loose-fitting dark suit and tie. Even his cigar seemed better dressed than usual. It wasn't the cold chewed stub he traditionally held in his teeth, but a full, freshly lit Havana.

"It's the kid," Farvel announced, leading Bernie and me into the Lanskys' ornately furnished, plushly carpeted livingroom where several couples were having cocktails and hors d'oeuvres. At

Meyer Lansky's house this didn't mean champagne and caviar.
Cocktails meant scotch and hors d'oeuvres meant chopped liver,
which Minnie Kovolicks had prepared according to the old neighborhood recipe and shlepped over to the dinner party in a
Tupperware bowl inside a brown paper bag. Minnie's *gehakte
leber* was served in a cut crystal, silver-trimmed chalice with a silver bread basket full of cocktail rye.

Farvel walked us over to where Blanche Yaras was in the middle
of telling a joke to Georgie Gordon. Georgie, who ran casinos for
Meyer in Las Vegas, was called Geo and that was how, after she
got to the punch line, Blanche introduced him to me. Bernie already knew Geo. While they did their "Hey, how you been? You
look great," Blanche took my arm and walked me around, intro-
ducing me to some of the other women.

"Meyer's with Davey in the Florida room, they'll be back in a
minute," she said. "Have you met Meyer yet?"

"Just once. Just to say hello," I admitted.

Blanche took my breath away all over again. She was larger than
life—with jewelry to match. She patted my hand and said, "You
look adorable. Smile, *mamela*. Don't be nervous. You're among
friends here. Wait'll you meet Teddy." And, on cue, this incredible
little doll came toward us from the dining room.

Blanche had beauty, a stunning figure, and great flair, but you
could still think of her as a basic Jewish broad. Minnie looked like
a Jewish Mother. But Teddy Lansky was a porcelain doll, a perfect
blonde-on-blonde miniature. She was bone-thin and perfectly pro-
portioned with fine features, a tiny nose, pale eyes, and a ready
smile. Even in the high heels she wore under her floor-length brocade caftan and with her platinum hair piled on her head in a high
French knot, she was tiny. Maybe four feet ten inches tall to my
hulking five foot eight.

"So you're Sandy, Bernie Barton's wife," Teddy said. "Well,
isn't he a lucky guy? Such a pretty girl. Isn't she, Blanche? I'm
glad you could make it tonight," she said. "And thanks for the
flowers. It was very thoughtful of you to send them."

"Oh, that was Bernie's idea," I said, then started blushing.

Teddy Lansky laughed. Then someone caught her eye and she
patted my hand and excused herself. "Would you like a drink?
Blanche knows where the bar is."

"Blindfolded," said Blanche.

I followed Blanche around that evening. I was excited but lost,
definitely out of my element. A shy, smiling silence was the best I

could do to hide the way I felt about myself, which was uncomfortable, tongue-tied, dull, dumb, and unattractive. The women around me were all older, all married to men of power. They'd raided their safety deposit boxes for dinner at Meyer's.

"This is Neddie from Boston. Yetta from Cincinnati. Ruchel from Detroit. Malka from New Jersey," Blanche would introduce them. I'd totter from one incredibly bejeweled wife to the next and, grand and glowing, they'd coo over me like pigeons in peacock's clothing.

"So young . . . So pretty . . . I'd kill for that skin!" they cooed.

It didn't matter what they said to me. They treated me kindly, protectively, like a little girl. But it was all I could do to walk with them, sit down to dinner with them. I wanted to learn how to be like them. And they tried to teach me.

"How cute," said one of the midwest wives, viewing the pearl and gold ring that had been Bernie's first gift to me. The hand that lifted mine to examine the ring was weighted down with about $50,000 worth of blindingly "cute" equipment. "You've got to meet Alan Pincus, my jeweler down here, Sandy. He's got a pair of diamond and pearl earrings that would be perfect with that ring. And don't tell me about 'can't afford it,' " she said, waving away my unspoken objection. "If that *mamzer* of yours won't give you the money, you'll stick your hand in his change pocket while he's sleeping and take what you need."

I was shocked. "Oh, I couldn't do that." I practically gulped.

Blanche winked at me. "You're young yet, sweetheart. You'll learn."

Meyer appeared just before dinner. He came in from the Florida room with Davey Yaras. He was wearing a very handsome double-breasted blue blazer with a silk tie and well-tailored navy linen trousers. He was only in his fifties then, but he looked like a really old man to me, small and frail. He appeared to be almost shuffling as he entered the room with Davey. Then I noticed that with his elegant outfit, he was wearing bedroom slippers and white socks!

Teddy, who was in her forties, was like the fountain of youth to Meyer. His whole appearance changed when he was around her. He was only five-four and, soaking wet, weighed maybe one thirty-five but standing next to Teddy he looked toweringly robust. You could tell he really adored her. His face changed when he looked at her, his tone of voice changed. He called her "darling" and "dear." It sounded so loving to me, so tender and sophisticated.

I couldn't help comparing Meyer and Teddy with Blanche and

Davey or Bernie and me, who were the more commonplace "baby" and "sweetheart" kind of couples. And we were a touch of class compared to Farvel, whose terms of endearment to Minnie ran more to "What are you, crazy? What're you, deaf? What're you, stupid?"

We sat down to dinner at a long, handsomely set table in the dining room. Meyer was at one end and Teddy at the other. Beside Meyer's plate was a dinner bell, which he rang as soon as we were all seated. Two servants, a man and a woman, came in from the kitchen with a tureen of matzo ball soup. Everyone talked and tore pieces of bread and challah from the silver baskets while the soup was ladled out. Then there was a lot of laughter and slurping of soup and Farvel calling everyone by their Jewish names. I was down near Teddy's end of the table and she was extremely hospitable to me, asking me questions and smiling and generally trying to put me at ease.

All of a sudden I heard this bell ringing. Then clanging. No one stopped eating or speaking. No one seemed to have heard anything but me. I looked down at Meyer's end of the table and there he was ringing that dinner bell with all his might. "Where the hell are they?" he shouted. "What the hell's wrong with them. Clear away the goddamn soup already! *Zolst ligen in drerd, genavisha mamzers!*" he cursed the servants in Yiddish. And no one stopped eating for a minute but me. People were reaching across one another for the bowls of sauerkraut and pickled tomatoes, or passing bottles of seltzer with silver siphons or refilling their wine glasses.

Between every course, between the brisket and noodle pudding, the chicken and potatonick, there was Meyer in his handsome jacket with the jaunty handkerchief in his pocket, turning red and ringing the bell and letting loose a stream of Yiddish curses that would make a borscht belt comic blush.

Meyer was not really a typical loudmouth gangster. For the most part, he was conservative, quiet, and commanding. His Yiddish cursing was much funnier than it was frightening. And just as Meyer could lapse into a peculiar crudeness, so Farvel had a streak of gentility in him. He extended his love for Bernie to include me. And when he came up to New York, he often invited me to go shopping with him. Of course, I never said no.

We'd stroll the streets of the Lower East Side where Farvel had grown up with Meyer. Many of the merchants they'd known from their boyhood were still in business there. And Farvel, who always wore a hat in New York, a battered fedora that was as recognizable as his trademark cigar, would walk briskly through the narrow streets receiving greetings and nodding hello like royalty visiting a far-flung empire. I had to hurry to keep up with him. We'd stop into one shop after another along Rivington or Allen Street and Farvel would shmooze and bargain.

"What're you getting for seltzer now?" he'd ask a shopkeeper.

"For you, Mr. Kovolicks," most of them responded, "don't worry."

Farvel would smile his thick-lipped smile and order cases of seltzer, tuna fish, herring, jars of pickles and sauerkraut, cartons of toilet paper.

"Okay. Put it away. I'll have someone pick it up later," he'd say, and off we'd go to the next store. "How much do you pay for ketchup?" he'd ask me.

"Gee, Farvel, I don't know."

"Tuna fish—what're they getting up here for a can of tuna fish these days?"

"I don't know, Farvel. I just go to the supermarket and get what I need."

He couldn't believe it. "What kind of housewife are you?" he'd demand. I'd hang on to his arm, scurrying alongside him as fast as I could while he grumbled affectionately about me, about Bernie. "What's wrong with him? You're married to a kid who doesn't know how to save two cents. He spends crazy. Five-hundred-dollar suits?! Feh. The kid doesn't know the meaning of money!"

Both his hands would be stuck in the pockets of his blue double-breasted coat. The battered hat was pulled down low over his eyes, the cold cigar waggled as he spoke. "You know, I put these guys in business years ago," he'd say, tossing his head at a two-by-four jewelry shop or clothing store with Hebrew lettering in the windows. Or "I got his brother-in-law out of a jam." Or "This one owes me a favor from World War II yet!"

On one of these outings Farvel dragged me into Robbins Handbags and asked me to help him choose a pocketbook for Minnie and two for his daughters. I did. Each bag cost over a hundred dollars. And Farvel said, "All right. Now you. Pick out what you like for yourself."

"Oh, no," I protested. "I can't. Really, Farvel, I don't need a new bag."

"Come on, come on. What's the matter with you. You don't refuse a gift. It's an insult. So which one you like?" After I chose one for myself he insisted that I pick out one for my mother.

When I got home, I showed Bernie the bags and praised Farvel's generosity.

"He doesn't pay for them," Bernie said. "The food and toilet paper and clothes. He gets them for free. He shakes down the shopkeepers. They don't charge him for that stuff. He picks it out and then, when he's ready to go back to Florida, he'll send two guys with a U-haul downtown with a list. They drive from store to store picking up the crap he ordered. It sits in his garage in Florida. Wait. Next time we go down, I'll show you. We'll go over to Farvel's house and you'll see."

Sure enough, a month later when Bernie and I went to Florida for our second season, we drove over to Farvel's up in Hollywood. Like Meyer's house, Farvel's was big and attractive but not what you'd imagine from a man with the kind of power and money he commanded. Very low key. The most ostentatious thing about the house was the sweeping circular driveway and the four cars parked in it that belonged to Farvel, Minnie, and their daughters. There was no room in their huge garage for cars. It was stacked floor to ceiling with cartons of tunafish, pickle jars and cases of seltzer and Dr. Brown's Cream Soda and Celery Tonic.

These men were full of contradictions. Meyer Lansky's estimated personal wealth was around three hundred million dollars. But everything about his home and life-style, at least everything I saw firsthand, was simple, unassuming, and very Jewish. One of the richest men in the world wore bedroom slippers at an elegant dinner party, spoke softly and lovingly to his wife, and then, during dinner, rang a bell for servants and, when they didn't show up instantly, cursed them like a punk from Pinsk.

And Farvel, whose cheapness was legendary, threw a wedding for his daughter of mind-boggling extravagance. To begin with, he paid the airfare and hotel bills for all the guests who flew in for the affair. And, oh, that flight from New York to Florida. "If this plane went down," Bernie said, "there'd be no one to run the underworld." Everyone was aboard. Ruby Stein and Uncle Jimmy Doyle, Milty Heinz from the Teamsters, Jimmy Blue Eyes, and there were Gambinos, Giordanos, Gallinas.

Farvel had put together an incredible guest list and it looked like no one had rsvp'd regrets. Even Cab Calloway and his wife were there. The tables were assigned with the wisdom of Solomon.

Great care and thought had been given to who sat where and with whom. At every table were the brands of cigarettes the guests at that table smoked and the right bottles of booze. Farvel circulated collecting *koved* and envelopes of cash. The guys teased him, called out to him, "Hey, Farvel, you going to give the kids the right shake?" Envelopes poured in from around the country. Men who couldn't be there or hadn't been invited sent their tribute with others. Geo must have brought ten stuffed envelopes with him from Las Vegas. At one point, Farvel was carrying around a cigar box filled with envelopes. Every ten minutes he'd rush off to the safe and return with the empty box again.

Bernie had bought me a dress in New York which I just hated. To this day, I have no idea what B-movie he was making in his mind when he envisioned me in this sleeveless Empire aqua chiffon extravaganza with elbow-length satin gloves. I felt as though I'd shown up at the wedding of the decade in my nightgown. I spent half the evening trying not to run into Blanche, who was wearing a sexy, skin-tight beaded gown with about an acre of well-tanned cleavage showing, or Teddy Lansky, who took the prize for dazzling class in a bronze sequined gown under a matching Chanel jacket with sable cuffs.

For me, the most beautiful part of the evening came when the band played "Hava Nagila" and, unexpectedly, men wandered over from the tables and the bar to the dance floor. The dinner and partying had gone on for hours. Most of them had their ties loosened by then, a collar button undone. Some had removed their jackets and rolled back their cuffs. Faces were flushed. Here and there a strand of slicked-back hair fell over a warm forehead. And when the *hora* music began, intense conversations ended, raucous laughter faded, the tight little groups loosened and drifted almost automatically onto the dance floor. As if by some magical unspoken agreement, the women and children who'd begun the traditional Jewish dance moved into the background. And only the men, the wise guys, the tough guys who didn't dance, held each other's shoulders in a big circle and began this amazing, hypnotic, slow step-kick that gradually became a glorious half-serious, half-wild *hora*. Some faces were stern with concentration; others were totally open, grinning, glowing. From the sidelines, squashed between the wives and children clapping time at the edge of the circle, I searched for Bernie. My heart leapt with pride when I saw him in the ring of dancers. Laughing aloud, his face and shirt soaked with perspiration, he was moving with a joy, grace, and pride I'd never seen before.

The party lasted for a whole weekend. Farvel put everyone up at The Hollywood Beach Hotel. The place was like Gangster Heaven. From the snack bar to the spa, everywhere you went you ran into heavy hitters. Bernie got telephone calls from men he hadn't seen in years. They met for a swim, a *shvitz*, a card game, an afternoon at the track. He was like a kid with every invitation. These were the major players he was running with, not the pimps, pushers, numbers runners, and everyday *pishers* he dealt with in the city. And Bernie's being there, being invited, meant that Meyer had given the okay. Again, it was confirmation that he was no longer regarded as a renegade kid.

While he *shvitzed*, I shopped.

"You going to buy it or not?" I was in the hotel boutique admiring a very expensive pearl-trimmed cashmere sweater when I heard the booming voice behind me. I turned and there was Blanche Yaras grinning at me. Laughing beside her, pert and beautiful, was a radiant Teddy Lansky.

"I don't know," I said, thrilled to see them but instantly intimidated by the dynamic duo. "It's a lot of money."

"What do you care?" Teddy asked. "Buy it! Spend it. If he doesn't spend it on you, he'll gamble it away."

"Are you alone here?" Blanche asked, taking my arm. "Come on, Sandy. We'll shop later. Join us for lunch."

The three of us sat out at a table under an umbrella near the pool. It was a terrific lunch. We laughed and gossiped, just me and my idols, a trio of girls with nothing to do but shop and spend their husbands' money. It was Cinderella Time poolside.

"With most of them," Teddy told me, "the money comes and goes. You've got to get it while they've got it."

"Steal from his pockets or from what he leaves you," Blanche advised. "And always tell him everything costs more. He won't even notice."

"Honey, you're young now, but this life eats you up and sucks you dry. Who's going to take care of you? Him? Get it now, while you can. Because you'll need it later—guaranteed."

I laughed and loved being with them, but I could never do what they said. Steal from Bernie? It was inconceivable to me. "But he's my husband," I said. "It's wrong."

I really wanted to be an honest kid. And I was. I never stole from him.

Looking back on the money that, exactly as Teddy said, came

and went and was gambled away, I'm sorry now that I didn't take their advice. Our little hassock, over the years, probably held huge amounts of cash, jewelry, and other valuables. If there wasn't enough in our "petty cash drawer," the drawer in the night table on my side of the bed, I'd take what I needed from the hassock. But I always wrote down the exact amount on a slip of paper and threw it into the hassock when I took the money out.

Temptation was all around me—in the night table, in the hassock, and there was also Bernie's "pocket money." He would empty his pockets onto the dresser each night and there'd be $2,000 or $3,000 lying around. If I'd taken $100, would he have missed it? If I'd put a couple of grand into a safety deposit box, I would have had it instead of the track touts and bookies from New York to Puerto Rico—and, oh yes, the croupiers at the Desert Inn.

I'd already seen Bernie hand over the keys to our car to pay off a debt. Not too long after Teddy and Blanche tried talking sense to me, Bernie made a bundle of money and bought me a magnificent diamond ring. It was close to fourteen carats. "You see," I told myself. "Good things come to good people. I didn't have to steal from him. Look at this gorgeous ring." To tell the truth, I couldn't wait to go down to Florida that year and show it off to Blanche and Teddy.

I never got the chance. We flew out to Vegas about a week after I got the ring. Bernie hit the crap tables. "Stay with me, baby," he said. "I need you for luck." I stayed. I watched him betting big. I heard people all around us start yelling, "High roller! High roller!" Bernie started losing. My heart started thudding against my rib cage. He broke out in a cold sweat. The little vein at the side of his neck was jumping. Beads of perspiration poured down his face. In eighteen minutes flat, he blew $18,000. His voice was raw. He said, "Eighteen grand. That's it. I quit," and I fainted.

I woke up in Geo's private office at the Desert Inn. The first thing I noticed was that my beautiful, brand-new, fourteen-carat, emerald-cut diamond ring was gone. "I've been robbed, I've been robbed," I screamed.

Geo's bodyguards were just outside the door. They quieted me down. One of them went to get Bernie. "Oh, God, thank God you're here," I cried, and fell into his arms. "Bernie, my ring's been stolen. Oh, God, what are we going to do?"

"No, no," he said, trying to comfort me. "It isn't stolen, baby. Don't worry. I took it off your finger while you were out and gave it to Geo for the money I lost."

Needless to say, I never mentioned the ring to Teddy Lansky,

Blanche Yaras, Minnie Kovolicks, or the other Jewish racket club
wives who had tried to wise me up. And if, in my twenties, I'd
thought they were cynical or callous about their husbands, if I'd
felt shocked and scandalized by their advice, they were Pollyannas
compared to the Italian mob wives I ran into later.

Mostly, I met them at weddings. It was strange, but I actually felt
more at ease with the Italian wives than I did with the Jewish. I
think it was because I so idolized women like Teddy and Blanche,
that it was nearly impossible for me to feel equal to them. But I was
a good mimic. I learned how to look like them, and that, I thought,
gave me an edge among the older, and to me less glamorous, Italian
veterans.

It wasn't that the Italian mob wives didn't have the diamonds.
They'd hit the vaults before the weddings, too, and truck out their
best—knuckle rocks, they had. Enormous rings and diamond, ruby
and emerald necklaces and bracelets and gem-encrusted gold
charms marking every occasion in their lives from their mother's
first communion to the high school graduation of their fifth grandchild. And tiaras! These women owned diamond tiaras.

At the wedding supper, the bride would shlep around a bag the
size of a pillowcase, which was made of the same satin or silk fabric as her gown. This enormous sack they called the *busta*, or "the
wedding purse." And couples would walk up to the dais and drop
in the envelopes.

What was amazing to me was that you'd be sitting at the tables
and all of a sudden the men would start asking one another, "Hey,
what are you giving?" "You think six bills is good?" "His mother
is my sister's aunt's god-daughter, so that'll cost me another fiver."

Sometimes, as the discussion went on—and the open bar booze
flowed—men would decide they'd been stingy. They'd take out the
sealed envelopes right at the table and tear them open. Then they'd
dig into their pockets, pull out a bankroll, and peel off another couple of hundred for the bride's wedding purse. "That's enough," I
heard a guy say, "we don't give a penny more than a grand. Who's
kid is this anyway?"

I once asked Bernie, "How much money could kids like this
get?"

"Oh, maybe fifty, sixty thousand dollars," he answered.

"My God, what a place for a robbery."

Bernie laughed. "Look around. You see those guys in tuxedoes
stationed along the walls? They've got guns, Sandy. There aren't a
lot of stick-ups at mob weddings."

At one wedding, the father of the bride had an adding machine sitting next to his dessert plate on the dais.

And just as I'd seen happen at Farvel's daughter's wedding, I noticed that a lot of envelopes would come in from out of town. Men would pull out six or seven envelopes from their pockets and drop them into the wedding purse. The money was a token of respect. It was never really spoken of as giving cash; it was "giving respect." Of course all the money in the envelopes was cash. Although you could tally up the price of the suits and boots and pinky rings, the gowns and furs and tiaras into tens of thousands of dollars, most of the wedding guests didn't know what a checking account looked like. Checks could be traced. Questions of income could be raised. Checks were an invitation for the FBI and IRS to climb into bed with the newlyweds.

There were no more Gene Kellys or Fred Astaires among the Italian mobsters than among their Jewish counterparts. Oh, maybe you'd see a grandfather twirling a little girl or once in a while a father dancing with his daughter or daughter-in-law, but for the most part "tough guys don't dance" was a nonsectarian slogan.

What was different about the Italian mob weddings was that the women danced together. The first time I saw this, I was really surprised. The first time an Italian mob wife asked me to dance, I was speechless. I finally shook my head and said, "No, thanks." And then I got crazy with guilt thinking I'd hurt her feelings.

After the last food course, just as the coffee was being served, the men would leave the tables and head over to the bar or gather in little groups to discuss business. And then the wives would get going.

"Thank God, they're gone so we can have coffee in peace," someone would always say.

"I'll have another drink now. He's not watching me," I heard more than once.

The women were nervous wrecks. Each one had her own tic, eccentric mannerism, or nervous habit. Angie, whose father had been a lieutenant in the Bonanno family and whose husband ran a couple of afterhours spots downtown, wore her jet-black hair pulled back tightly into a high chignon. She had long fingernails, polished translucent white, with which she constantly dug into her scalp, prying loose and twirling one thick strand of hair after another. Another woman, Tina, the wife of a Brooklyn mob boss, had a solid gold Dunhill lighter which she tapped compulsively on the table.

Still another endlessly drummed her long, thick fingernails. They scratched. They twitched. They cursed their husbands.

"Let them stay away," they said. "Let them talk forever!"

Their husbands were lousy lovers, they said. They cackled and called them "The Minute Men."

Angie said, "If he stinks at home, you think he's going to do better for that pig he's got over on East Eighty-fifth Street?" That was another thing that surprised the hell out of me. These women all knew the addresses and telephone numbers of their husbands' mistresses. If they were pushed too far, they called. It was because Italian men, they said, were stupid, careless, or just plain didn't give a damn. They left the addresses and telephone numbers in the pockets of shirts they gave their wives to launder; on the dressers where they left their money at night; on matchbook covers and pieces of torn menus from nightclubs.

"When the FBI comes looking for him, they come to *my* house," said a tall, dark, attractive woman I'd never met before. "My children get involved. They have to hear this. They never bother his girlfriend. It's my house they go through."

A woman sitting across the table at a wedding took a seat next to me after our husbands had gone off to the bar together. "How old do you think I am?" she asked out of the blue. "I'm forty-two." She looked ninety-two. "You see me," she said. "I've got a bleeding ulcer from him. You can't take what they say to heart. It'll kill you."

"I was happier when he was in prison." Boy, oh, boy, did I hear that a lot. And that particular line was not exclusive to the Italian wives.

If Farvel's was the most extravagant wedding I'd ever been to, Freddy the Greek's was indisputably the strangest. Freddy was a very well-respected guy among his peers. He'd pulled off some of the most ingenious and well-known heists of his day. Among them was one of the biggest jewel thefts in New York. On a Sunday, exactly as planned, Freddy snatched several million dollars' worth of uncut diamonds from a midtown exchange. He had a car waiting on Forty-seventh Street and a truck with a ramp ready around the corner. He drove to the truck, backed the car up into it, stowed the ramp, closed the backdoors of the truck, and went tear-assing up Eighth Avenue, a street of potholes to rival the Grand Canyon. As he bumped and banged along Eighth Avenue, the backdoors of the truck were jarred opened and the car, carrying the diamonds, rolled out.

Needless to say, police showed up and Freddy was arrested.

While he was doing time in jail, a nun from his old neighborhood would visit him with messages from his friends. She came once or twice a week and after she delivered the messages, she stayed to talk and they got to know one another. In time, they fell in love.

Freddy was probably in his fifties. The nun, whose name I think was Agnes, was close to forty and had spent her entire life in the service of God. Convent-educated from girlhood, she was from a devout Irish Catholic family teeming with nuns, priests, and cops. But she and Freddy were in love and there was nothing to do about it but make it legit. So here she was, married to God and engaged to a gangster.

The wedding was planned for the day after Freddy the Greek got home from jail. And it went off better than Freddy's last heist had. The ex-con and his virgin bride were married in a huge midtown church just off Ninth Avenue. I remember walking into the chapel at high noon on a Saturday and being absolutely staggered by the crowd. There must have been more than three hundred people packed into the pews and lining the aisles. And of the three hundred at least a third of them were in uniform. There were priests, bishops, a cardinal, nuns, novices, and police brass. At the reception after the ceremony, the guests sat at segregated tables. At some tables were members of the clergy, at others members of the police force, members of the bride's family, members of the groom's family, and then there were tables of members of the five families—the top echelon gangsters who ran New York City at that time.

The strangest thing about this very strange wedding was that everyone had a terrific time. The nuns were thrilled for their "Little Sister." They teased her and laughed and were full of fun and happiness. The priests and the cops got on fine with the mobsters. Many of them had nodding acquaintances before the wedding. Everywhere I went I heard guys saying things like, "I went to school with that red-headed cop," or, "There's Father Joseph, from St. Mary's where my kid goes," or "Isn't that Fat Tony Salerno's bodyguard who did a bid at Dannemora?" And Freddy and Agnes practically needed his truck again, just to haul away the wedding purse.

Not all the marriages I witnessed ended as grandly as they'd begun. Farvel's daughter's marriage to her "plain guy" didn't last. That's what everyone called him because he wasn't mob blood. You'd ask, "Whose son is he?" and someone would say, "No one's. He's a plain guy." Anyway, they wound up divorced. The daughter of a major Jewish mob boss married the extraordinarily handsome son of the owner of one of New York's renowned Jewish dairy restaurants. Her father stopped by their house one afternoon and found his son-in-law in bed with another man and, with remarkable restraint, had the marriage, not the groom, dissolved. And only a couple of years after his wedding, poor Freddy was gunned down in the streets.

CHAPTER TEN

The House of Yenom

Our second season in Florida, Bernie got sick and had to be hospitalized. As soon as he was well enough, we returned to New York. We weren't back in town a day before our apartment became the convalescent clubhouse again. Both telephones were in constant use. Gifts arrived. Guys arrived. Ashtrays filled. Scotch bottles emptied. And I couldn't wait for him to get on his feet again and out into the world.

Bernie always had something going. Even while The Velvet Club was hot, he and Red were partners in a string of Harlem numbers joints. He had a piece of half a dozen different bars. With Cokey he owned a couple of fighters. He was always looking for action. Sometimes he'd fall into wild schemes and quick money. And sometimes the ship he was waiting for sank before it sighted land. Some of his ventures were inspired and some were plain pipe dreams. One of them was both. It began a week after we got back to town. Bernie was sitting around with Cokey one night, passing a joint and watching TV.

The famous evangelist Billy Graham was big then. He'd recently held a rally in Yankee Stadium and was all over the news. "How much you think he rakes in at one of those tent shows?" Cokey asked.

"Plenty. And he doesn't pay taxes, either. Some gig, right?"

"Unreal," Cokey marveled.

"You know, that's what we ought to do. We ought to go into the preacher business," Bernie said. "Get that non-profit license and run it semi-legit."

They talked about it for a while, had a few laughs, kicked around ideas about how it could be done. A couple of days later, Cokey called all excited and said, "Tell B I found our boy. I'm bringing him by tonight."

His name was Tito and he was gorgeous. Dazzling might be more like it because there was something about him, a glow, a warmth, that lit up the room the minute he walked in. With a smile that was shy and seductive at the same time, he looked like a cross between Billie Dee Williams and Jesse Jackson. "Pleasure to meet you, ma'am," he said with this incredible soft Southern accent.

Bernie started grinning the minute he saw him. "Where did you find this kid?" he asked Cokey in the kitchen. Tito was making himself at home on the L-shaped sofa, cleaning some pot and expertly rolling up a couple of joints.

"I know his family. He's up from Alabama. He's got some kind of preaching certificate. Says he got ordained somewhere down South. He's our boy, B."

"Kid's a hustler," Bernie said, "*and* a pothead."

"Yeah, but he's a preacher, too. We could do this, B. We could make this happen."

And they did. Josh, the lawyer who yearned to be a hood, researched the non-profit status for them. A couple of days after Tito showed up, Josh came by and dumped a thick pile of papers on the coffee table for Bernie to read. And Bernie did. He studied the requirements. He made phone calls. He put out the word that he was looking for space uptown. By the time he was well enough to leave the house again, mutual friends had tipped him and Cokey to a beautiful deal on Lenox Avenue.

There was a "superette" that had gone out of business on Lenox and 123rd Street. It was a space smaller than a supermarket but bigger than a large grocery store. Bernie called the landlord and they picked up the lease on it for practically nothing. If the rent was maybe three, three-fifty a month it was a lot. It was a big, raw storefront and the challenge was to turn it into a church.

They had the preacher. They had the place. They needed the name. Bernie and Cokey went back and forth on it for days. We were surveying the boarded-up superette, stepping carefully over broken glass and busted shelves and warped linoleum, when Bernie hit on a winner.

"The House of Yenom," he decided.

"Solid," Cokey said. "Where'd you pull that one from?"

"The House of Yenom," I repeated. It sounded nice, exotic yet solemn. Then I got it and I cracked up.

"What?!" Cokey asked.

And Bernie explained that in Yiddish *yenom* means "Joe Shmoe's, the other guy's, not ours." And in English yenom is money spelled backwards. Perfect. So that was the name of the church, The House of Yenom.

When it was time to renovate the building, Bernie's union connections got them the best skilled labor working off-hours at bargain rates. Guys sent by friends from the Plumbing Union, the Carpenters Union, painters, plasterers, kids who wanted to get into the Teamsters. In the blink of an eye, the place started humming. Some afternoons I'd go uptown to see how the job was coming. It was like walking onto the set of an old MGM movie, the kind where Mickey Rooney says to Judy Garland, "Hey, I've got a great idea—let's build a house of worship in Harlem!"

Everybody got involved, excited, carried away. We'd sit around at night, after the workmen left, Bernie, Tillie, me and Cokey, and sometimes Iris or Josh or Hot Dog Red, and we'd have coffee and talk and laugh and come up with wild new ideas.

Personally supervising every detail of the renovation, Bernie was like a great big kid, a cross between Mickey Rooney, Michelangelo, and, when it came to decor, Father Divine. He ordered black floors and blond wood panelling, ornate prayer benches with royal purple pew cushions, gold wall sconces in the shape of cupids dripping crystal beads, and on the starry sky-blue ceiling he installed colored spotlights focused on a big, step-up pulpit. An arched chapel-style entrance with stained-glass panels replaced the store windows, and then they shlepped in a huge white pipe organ that looked like someone had ripped it off from Ringling Brothers.

In the back, behind the altar area, Bernie had two offices built and an oversized kitchen. He felt that it would be a good gesture for the church to feed some of the neighborhood people once or twice a week at a small soup kitchen. So, in addition to all the glitter up front, big stoves and refrigerators and other appliances were installed.

Bernie wasn't satisfied with just turning the storefront into a religious wet dream; next he went to work on Father Tito, which is what the kid started calling himself—Father Tito or Preacher Tito.

They got him these gorgeous white robes with gold and purple trim. And Bernie laid down the law to him.

"A preacher is always on call," he told the kid who had an apartment a couple of blocks from the storefront. "During the day you look like a business man. Shirt and tie, all the way." He took Father Tito up to Lester's, one of the legendary uptown tailors favored by the Harlem mob boys, and ordered him half a dozen suits and bought him a closet full of shirts and ties and a few fancy pairs of alligator shoes. "And you don't get high during the day," he told him. "If you want to get high, just get high a little bit. But you've got to be straight most of the time."

Father Tito got caught up in the thing fast. He felt he had a true calling. He thought he should have a choir. So a couple of neighborhood kids were recruited, street kids, and they decked them out in beautiful robes, too. Then Cokey got hold of some of the local talent—hookers. High-class, gorgeous call girl hookers, but hookers. And they were going to work Sunday nights, wearing white gowns and these big imitation gold crosses. They were stunning girls and they were going to be called "The Virgins of Father Tito" or "Father Tito's Princesses."

Bernie and Cokey were careful to set everything up legally, to get the proper permits and registrations so The House of Yenom would have tax-exempt status. And though the permits and renovation and choir robes and, finally, even the meat, milk, fruit, and vegetables that he bought through his wholesale connections, all came to a pretty penny, Bernie believed it was worth it. "You have to invest money," he kept saying. "You've got to speculate to accumulate."

The week The House of Yenom was set to open, Bernie had fliers printed and neighborhood kids were hired to stick them into mail boxes, on lampposts, on the sides of buildings, under the doors of apartments, and handfuls were left with local merchants to be given out to customers. They were everywhere, and they announced the Sunday opening, "a mass at high noon," followed by a breakfast.

It was late spring, a beautiful morning. We arrived at the "chapel" at about ten o'clock. A huge banner hung above the entrance and a red carpet had been rolled out over the sidewalk. Spotlights were set up, even though it was a sunny morning. They lit the carpeted sidewalk in front of the arched entrance where a choir of beautifully robed children swayed and clapped and sang hymns. With the spotlights and red carpet, with the choir rocking and singing, when people started showing up, started actually *thronging* into the place, done up in their Sunday best—the furs and flowered hats, the starched shirts and suits pressed to a blinding shine—it looked like a Hollywood premiere.

The house was packed. The organ was playing. And, finally, Father Tito appeared and he was a sight to behold. Robed in white and gold, he walked along a path of rainbow lights followed by his "princesses," eight breathtaking hookers, a rainbow of colors themselves, from ivory to ebony, decked out in flowing white satin gowns. People gasped. "Praise the Lord," you could hear one or two call out. It was astounding.

I looked at Bernie and I started to laugh—out of sheer excitement, out of awe, I think. If I hadn't laughed I would have cried. Father Tito looked so impressive and the whole church was so beautiful. Seeing it filled, seeing people's faces all lit up with pleasure, with joy, it really was like a religious experience. It was almost as if we had succeeded in creating a real church.

Tito was a powerful preacher. Cokey was right about the kid's ability to rock out a crowd. It seemed clear that he really did have a calling. And Bernie was right, too, because it was equally clear that Father Tito was a terrific pothead and he had certainly turned on before he hit the pulpit. People stood and swayed and shouted out to him. They cried "Amen!" whenever he said something they really agreed with, or they shouted, "Preach!" or "Yes, tell it!"

Tillie was having a ball. "It's not so different," she said to me. "Look." She jutted her chin toward a standing man who was rocking back and forth as Tito spoke. "Like *davening*," she said, meaning the swaying prayer stance of Jewish men.

The sermon was a great success. The little black collection boxes were brimming with donations. And after the service, a beautiful brunch was served—ham and scrambled eggs, lox, cream cheese and bagels, and there were even collard greens and black-eyed peas and fabulous soul food because Iris had gotten a couple of terrific bar chefs to come down and do the cooking.

At the end of the day, we went into the office and tallied up the collections. We had a couple of thousand dollars' worth of coins and bills—ranging from pennies and singles to the hundred-dollar bills some of the Harlem wise guys who'd showed up for the opening had tossed in. I counted the money as Bernie had taught me, all the bills facing the same way, presidents up, ranging from low to high denominations.

"Okay," I said, writing down the amount of coins I had to cash in for bills at the bank the next day, "now that we have this money and we're officially open, I'll have to keep records of how much we take in and how much we're spending. I'll need receipts for what everything costs, even if you're paying cash for the food or booze or the coffee. Whatever you do here, you've got to know what you're laying out so you can be reimbursed. Whatever you spend I need to know—the food, toilet paper, washing the robes, everything."

Bernie was crouched in front of the old-fashioned four-legged safe he'd bought. Only he, Cokey, and I knew the combination. His mouth fell open. "What're you out of your mind?" He shot me a look. "Since when did you become a fucking bookkeeper and such a business woman?"

"Well, somebody's got to do it," I said. "Even if it's tax exempt, you have to keep books. You need a record of what comes in and what goes out. It's just common sense."

Little did I know then that what came in and what went out was sometimes a load of television sets or stereos or other fast-moving merchandise that eventually turned the backroom of that little store of God into a Grand Central Station of hot items. After getting Bernie's usual response to questions about what was going on, I learned how to close my eyes to the traffic. And, apparently, so did the neighborhood cops who had to be blind not to notice trucks pulling up to the side entrance and racks of clothing, and huge, sealed cartons being wheeled in and out every half hour.

But that first day I argued forcefully enough to be made the official bookkeeper. And, oh, did I take that job seriously. I was so proud of myself. I felt like a real take-charge kind of business woman, like the controller of a big corporation. I loved it. Controller of The House of Yenom. I could make myself believe that it was a real business; that we were legit, at last. Well, ninety-nine percent legit.

I was up at the church three days a week working on the books. It was impossible, of course, since Bernie and Cokey were used to accounting systems that were a little looser than what I was trying to do. Bernie would hand me a fistful of money and tell me to stash it in the safe. I'd say, "Okay, what does it go under? I've got to record it before I put it in."

"Never mind, just stash it," he'd say. Or "Charge it to sausages, for God's sake!"

I definitely got carried away with myself. But nothing like the way Father Tito started getting carried away.

* * *

Tito was good, no two ways about it. But he was only self-ordained. And after that first day, when we were all sitting around after the chapel was swept and the dishes cleaned and the food and money put away, Tito started talking about television. How we could probably do a deal to have the services televised. And maybe open up other Houses of Yenom in different parts of New York. Make a whole chain of them. Like McDonald's. The kid had lit up the minute the doors were locked and he was ripped. But high as he was on grass, he was higher on himself. Success was like a drug to him—he'd gotten a taste and right away he wanted more.

The House of Yenom was a going concern, a quiet little gold mine that gave the neighborhood people much of what they wanted from it—a place to meet and pray and sit down together for community breakfasts with their families, friends, and neighbors. Things ran pretty smoothly for months. After a while I gave up trying to keep the books straight. But it wasn't the merchandise in the backroom or financial crisis that brought down the House. Ultimately, it was Father Tito's success.

The kid got a lot of attention. Not just through word of mouth, but an uptown newspaper had covered the opening and gave him a great review. The more good things that happened to him, the more he began to believe his own press. He started thinking that he was a real preacher. He began performing wedding ceremonies.

Bernie didn't know anything about this until, one day, two kids whom Tito had married started having trouble. They wanted to get divorced. They'd come to the church to see Tito about it and, when Bernie walked in, Tito tried to shush the kids, get them to make up fast, get them into the other office. Bernie followed them and asked what was wrong. And that was it!

"That son of a bitch is marrying people!" he roared at me. "There are children that are going to be walking around as bastards. And what happens when a couple wants to get a divorce? Do you know the heat that could bring down on me? I'm doing *business* out of that place. I don't know how many marriages he's performed. Sandy, there are people living together who are not married in the eyes of God, and that is one thing I won't go for!"

Bernie tried talking to the kid, tried to set him straight. But Tito had really gone 'round the bend on this thing. He started screaming at Bernie, that he had a divine right to perform weddings, that God had given him the go-ahead. He was screaming and preaching. Bernie got crazy and decked him. Father Tito flew over the desk, out for the count. Within a week, Bernie shut the place down. And that was it, a sweet deal gone sour. Or, as Josh the lawyer used to call it, "the fall of The House of Yenom."

I was sorry to see it go. It was a scam, a hustle, a front for fencing stolen goods maybe. But it was also as close to going straight as we'd gotten, which made it close to heaven for me. After Yenom, when I'd ask, "When are you going to give up the rackets, baby? Aren't we ever going to try to go legit?" more and more, Bernie would just shake his head.

"What do you want me to do, babe? Open up a candy store on the Lower East Side and sell two cents plain, and you can help me stuff the newspapers on Saturday night? No, baby," he'd say with this sad little smile, "I only know one way. Putting my back against the wall. Whatever I make, I can call it my blood money. If I have to pay or do time, that's okay. 'Do the crime, pay the time,' that's the saying. And I accept that."

An exciting idea, a scheme that worked, a pipe dream that came true, The House of Yenom had been hatched while Bernie was home recuperating. It was one of the few good things that ever came out of his sickness. And he was sick now at least twice a year. Because of his heart condition, he'd catch a cold, it would turn into pneumonia and, the next thing you knew, he'd be fighting for his life.

It wasn't something you could get used to. He got weaker after each bout. It took longer for him to get well again. And, when he struggled for breath, so did I. Watching him rigged up to an oxygen tank, seeing the color and life drained from his face, it got so that I could hardly breathe, I was that scared of losing him.

I was angry a lot, too. Because when he was sick, Bernie could become incredibly impatient and demanding. Here was a man who prided himself on never asking for help. But, when he was hospitalized, he had to depend on doctors, medicine, and machines to keep him breathing. And, when he came home, he had to depend on me for everything else. He hated it. It made him crazy. And I was the one he took his frustration out on. He wanted me to learn and do everything in five minutes and get back in time to empty the ashtrays and put up fresh coffee for his friends.

Sometimes I hated him. Sometimes I felt sorry for myself. Sometimes I'd watch him struggling for breath in his sleep or just breathing quietly and peacefully, and I'd be overwhelmed with love for him. I'd want to wake him up with kisses, wake him up just to tell him how much I loved him.

He did what business he could from home during these times. He spoke to Hot Dog Red on the phone five times a day and saw him at least two. "All right, listen. I need you to go to the bank and rent a safety deposit box," he said to me after Red stopped by early one morning and dropped off a brown paper grocery bag.

"I don't know how," I said, which of course was not his favorite response.

"It's simple. I'll tell you how." He was sitting up in bed with his legs crossed like a snake charmer's. "You just walk in and you say you want to rent a safety deposit box, and when they ask what your name is you make up a name. They'll give you a card to sign," he said, dumping the contents of Red's paper bag out onto the bed. Dollar bills rained down onto his crossed legs. "You tell them the box is for you and your husband and you bring home the card for my signature, too."

"It's all legal, right?"

"What the hell do you care what it is? Just do it. Just make up a name—"

"Like what?"

"Like Henny Penny. Like Desdemona Finkelstein. A name, Sandra. Any name but Barton, okay?"

When I'd showered and dressed, Bernie handed me three envelopes. One was full of money—the cash Red had dropped off. The other two were fat and taped shut. I stuck them into my handbag and all the way to the bank, I was racking my brain for just the right name. Opening the box was as simple as Bernie had said. No one asked for identification. No one mentioned a social security number. When they asked my name, I blurted out, "Sadie Green."

I brought the signature card home for Bernie to sign. He shook his head and looked at me as though I were crazy. "Sadie Green? Where did you come up with that?"

"I don't know. It's a name, isn't it? You said make one up. That's it."

He laughed and signed "Hymie Green."

Over the years, I opened five different safety deposit boxes at Bernie's instruction, four under different names—all of them Jewish. We were Anne and Ben Fine. Sara and Abe Weissman. Miriam and Meyer Katz. Only one box belonged to Sandra and Bernie Barton. The safety deposit boxes were our hassocks-away-from-home and worked the same way. Envelopes in; envelopes out. Take a thou, leave a note. But it was my job to keep tabs on what went into which box. I wrote it all on a slip of paper, including the names and numbers of the boxes, and stuck it away in a safe hiding place.

My cousin Francine had moved to New York from L.A. and lived not too far from us now. "Give the keys to Francine," Bernie said. "I don't want them around the house if I'm ever arrested or the place is searched. I don't want the FBI or anyone else finding safety deposit box keys here." So when I needed to make a deposit or withdrawal from the boxes, I just stopped by Francine's first.

I'd been uptown with Bernie to the numbers joint Red ran for him. It was not an impressive setup. The apartment was a fifth-floor walkup on Pleasant Avenue and 116th Street. It was a threadbare railroad flat with a bathtub in the kitchen and a toilet in a closet so small your knees hit the door if you tried to sit down. In the middle room was a long piece of plywood laid across a couple of sawhorses. On top of that makeshift desk were three or four telephones which never stopped ringing, a bunch of adding machines and notebooks in which the bets were recorded. Hot Dog's contribution was the clock on the wall. It was his idea to write down the time a bet came in and he'd go crazy if anyone forgot to do it.

The first time I was there, I just helped myself to a cup of coffee from the percolator on top of the stove and sat quietly on a chair until Bernie and Red had finished talking business. Now Bernie sent me back to the place to pick up a bag from Red, who he said was short-handed and couldn't deliver it himself. I went. I drove up to Harlem alone and shlepped up the five rickety flights of stairs and knocked on the door. Red let me in. The place was jumping. The phones were ringing off the hook. The guys at the plywood table were writing down numbers as fast as they could, and checking the clock. But every one of them took the time to tilt his head or tip his hat in my direction and say, "Afternoon, princess." "Mrs. B. How you doing?" "Miss Sandy, how's BB today? You tell him Sonny says hello."

"You want a soda or a cup of coffee?" Red offered.

"No thanks. Gee, it's busy here."

"Here, sit down, baby," Red said, sliding back a chair in front of one of the phones at the desk. "Let me show you how this works." He slid over an opened notebook and handed me a pencil. "When it rings, you just say, 'Yeah?' and the guy'll give you a number and an amount. You say them back aloud to be sure you got it right, then just write them down right here, look at the clock and jot down the time, and that's it."

The phone in front of me rang. "Go on," Red nodded.

"Yeah?" I said.

The voice at the other end said, "Gimme a dollar on 592." There was a racket behind him. It sounded like he was calling from the subway or a pipe factory. I repeated the number, repeated the amount, his name, wrote them down. Red was grinning, nodding encouragingly at me.

I took a couple more calls. One was from a numbers runner. He reeled off about twenty different combos. "A dollar on 295, two bucks on 826, a fiver on 007, a dollar on 721 . . ." and on and on.

"You did great," Red said when I'd hung up. Then he explained how the winning number was chosen. In the back of the newspapers, in the sports sections, there was a daily tally of "the mutuel handle," or how much money a given racetrack had taken in for the day. In the winter, when the northern tracks were closed, they used the totals at Gulfstream or Hialeah. If a track took in $2,150,657 for the day's races, the last three numbers, 657, in any of six possible combinations, were the winning numbers for that day. That was how they figured "the Brooklyn number." There was a more complicated recipe for what was called "the New York number," which involved the amount of money laid down on the one, two, and three horses in the first race at a particular track. To work that one out you practically had to be a CPA.

"But these people are betting *bubkes*," I said. "A dollar here, a big two bucks there. How can you make a living on that?"

"It adds up," Red assured me and, just to prove it, handed me a sack full of money to take back to Bernie.

I decided that I wouldn't say anything to Bernie about working the phones or learning about how the winning numbers were picked. I knew how he hated to have me nosing around his business, and I didn't want to get Red in trouble. But the minute I walked in the door, Bernie was already grinning, already waiting. "So, how do you like taking bets? Think you got a career in the numbers?"

He'd wanted me to learn. He'd told Red to sit me down and stick a phone in my hand and see how I did. He wanted the boys uptown to get to know me, to get to know that I was him when I showed up, I represented him. Later that night, after I'd thought about it a little,

I felt awful. I realized, or thought anyway, that Bernie was getting me ready to be without him. To know who to go see and what to do. To collect what was due him when he couldn't go anymore. It scared me. I couldn't fall asleep. I locked myself in the bathroom and cried.

CHAPTER ELEVEN

A Stand-Up Broad

All this activity, my learning how his businesses worked, and how to stand in for him, opening the safety deposit boxes, handling the money, all this was rewarded with the ultimate compliment: "Baby, you're a stand-up broad." Being a stand-up broad had almost as many rules as being a tough guy. Stand-up broads didn't ask questions, didn't look at other men. And if her guy looked at other girls, a stand-up broad looked the other way. Stand-up broads made no scenes, no demands, no waves. A stand-up broad stood by her man.

I'd do almost anything to earn that praise, to get that little pat on the head. I almost gave my life for it.

Among his other businesses, Bernie had a piece of an afterhours club in Harlem. It was as classy as the Copa and as wild as Reefer May's. The place was done up like a nightclub from a thirties movie, and on opening night a lot of the patrons dressed that way, in dinner jackets and full-length gowns. The club would start filling up after midnight. The crowd was mixed: politicians, high-priced lawyers, the show biz crowd, sightseers and sights to be seen, underworld characters in assorted colors and affiliations.

For me it was the best thing since The Velvet Room. Bernie and I had our favorite spot—a cozy corner at the crook of the sweeping L-shaped bar. From it we could watch the players and the games. In keeping with the 1930s look of the place, the bar top was deep blue glass and it was as often laced with lines of cocaine as it was ringed with drink coasters. Beyond the bar was a huge gambling room with baize-covered tables for blackjack, craps, and high-stakes poker. The dealers and croupiers all wore dark suits and ties. At four in the morning, the limos would be parked three deep outside.

In the early winter of '63, the place had been open and doing a booming business for a couple of months. It was close to four in the morning. Bernie and I were kibitzing, shooting the breeze, with Uncle Vinny and Hot Dog Red at the bar. We were wedged into our favorite corner. I don't remember what I had for breakfast this morning, but I remember exactly what I was wearing that memorable night. It was a gray peplum suit, nipped in at the waist and, as my old friend Raven would have said, very, very Rita Hayworth.

I was feeling pretty Rita Hayworth, too—sitting there, looking sultry with my long legs crossed, a cognac in my hand, surrounded by the guys I loved best in the world—when the unthinkable happened. Six men walked into the place, a place owned, operated, and usually jammed with some very connected characters. The guys were very well dressed. They looked like any other patrons and they would have blended perfectly into the crowd except for the ski masks they were wearing and the guns they held.

"Oh, God, here we go again," I said, grabbing Bernie's arm.

He froze. His eyes, blue ice, followed them as they went around shoving people, ordering them to the floor, yelling, "Give it up. Empty that wallet. Take off the jewelry. Throw it here, throw it here!" The guys were everywhere at once. The guns were like extensions of their hands, pointing, gesturing, jabbing. A couple of the guys were holding tommy guns, automatic weapons, crooked in their arms like television gangsters'. Some of them hit the gambling room. The rest fanned out near the bar.

We'd been sitting perfectly still, but I could see Bernie's rage building. That telltale little vein in his neck was throbbing. The tops of his ears were red. And then I got the one unmistakable clue. He started muttering. "What're you out of your motherfucking minds you pricks coming in here the fuck you think you are shit for brains bastards you're dead assholes cold meat motherfuckers out of the game . . ."

Mumbling, grumbling, muttering. I couldn't believe it. Neither could the guy with the gun working his way down the bar toward us.

"Shut the fuck up," he said to Bernie. "Shut your fucking mouth right now, dickhead or I'll—"

Let me be honest. I had knocked back a few Remys. And I was

scared for Bernie. How else can I explain why I jumped off the bar-stool, arm raised, finger pointing at the ceiling, and yelled, "Don't you talk to my husband that way!" The gunman was almost as star-tled as I was. He shot me.

"Oooo, Bernie," I said. I reached inside my peplum jacket and found the wetness that turned out to be blood.

It was a small gun. I don't even remember hearing the noise, but it must have shook everybody up because the guy who shot me took off fast. "Let's go, let's go, it's done, let's split, it's over!" he hollered to his pals, and they pounded out of the place.

Suddenly, I was surrounded by people. Everyone was shouting. Bernie had one arm around my waist, the other was pulling my jacket off my injured shoulder. "Hang on, sweetheart. Hang on. Uncle Vinny's getting the car. You'll be okay, baby. Here, drink this. Go on, baby."

He was pouring scotch down my throat. The bartender was pop-ping open bottles right and left, spilling the alcohol onto handker-chiefs that people were handing over. Red and Bernie took turns putting these compresses on the wound, mopping up the blood. Ev-erything hurt. Everything stung. Everything felt and tasted and smelled like alcohol.

Uncle Vinny drove us to a doctor in the neighborhood, a nice Italian guy he knew named Dr. Milardi or Moretti. Anyway, he said it was a flesh wound. In and out. No muscle or nerve damage. He just scooped the little sucker out, and cleaned up the wound.

It was daylight by the time we got home. When I woke the next afternoon, Bernie was on the phone in the living room. I could hear him laughing. "I'm not kidding, that's what she said, 'You can't talk to my man that way,' " he was telling someone. "Oh, yeah," he added, after a pause. "Sandy's a stand-up broad. Always was."

Please. A moron was what I was.

It took me months to stop shaking. Every time a door slammed or I'd be around a crowd of noisy people, my heart would start slamming against my chest and my shoulder would throb an aching little reminder of how close I'd come to death. I don't even know what made me do it, what I was thinking of, or whether I was thinking at all. But my reputation was made in the stand-up ranks. I was a heroine. It became known in high places that BB had some wife. Look how much she loved him, that she took a chance on get-ting herself shot just to defend him. What a gutsy girl. What an id-iot! I was a complete fool to do that. But stand-up broad sounds better than sucker.

"Tell Chalky what happened," Bernie said. "When you send him the *pesach* basket, in the note, write about how you got shot." Chalky Lefkowitz was a childhood friend of Bernie's who was doing ten-to-twenty in Trenton for armed robbery. We'd send him holiday gift baskets and cards, and Bernie always insisted that I write the notes to Chalky. "Wait till you meet him, Sandy. When this guy gets out, we're going to take over the town. There's nothing Chalky and I couldn't do together. This man is closer to me than my own brother. I've known him since we were two years old. White hair, he had, like chalk, he was so blond. Our mothers used to wheel us in carriages together. Write to Chalky, baby. Let him know what a stand-up broad I got."

I did, of course, I wrote to Chalky Lefkowitz and, at Bernie's bidding, I told the shooting story to Johnny Dio's uncle Jimmy Doyle, to Hot Dog's wife, Thelma, to Iris over drinks at Cokey's bar, to Farvel on the phone and Milty Heinz at a birthday party and Billy Daniels in Atlantic City. Bernie even made me tell the story to Della Reese, whose boyfriend, a bald black man who wore a wall-to-wall rug, he knew from uptown.

Even Lido, the Santeria high priest, got into the act. He sent word that we should light the same candles for me as he'd advised for Bernie's recuperations: a white candle for light and good spirits; a green candle for money; and a red candle for well-being. Bernie lit the candles. He put pieces of fruit near them, and a lump of sugar and a white handkerchief and he chanted the prayers that Lido recommended.

Bernie always believed deeply in Lido's power and prescriptions. In fact, when we were about to get involved in a deal that could make us legitimate millionaires overnight, a deal that would actually take us to Africa, Bernie insisted that we go up to Spanish Harlem first for Lido's blessing.

Through Hot Dog Red, Bernie met two black diplomats from Abidjan, the capital of the Ivory Coast, which turned out to be wedged between Ghana and Liberia. The men, who spoke with beautiful clipped English accents and dressed as elegantly as British lords, were very connected in their country, all the way up to the prime minister and the minister of commerce. The way they told it the Ivory Coast was very rich in certain commodities, but lacking in some pretty basic others like baby food, soda pop, laundry detergent, paper products, and even underwear.

Bernie started romancing these guys in order to go into business with them. He wanted to be the purchasing agent for dry goods, appliances, clothing, and other items for their country. Of course, Bernie had great connections for getting hot merchandise, the kind that fell off trucks and into mob hands every day. But the more he researched the project, the more convinced he became that he could do the job on a semi-legit basis and make it pay big. So he and Red were all over the guys, as they used to say, like white on rice.

They wined them, dined them, got them the best smoke in town and the sexiest hookers. And while the boys from Abidjan were getting laid and loaded, Bernie was running to fruit companies, paper products manufacturers, freight outfits, Garment Center connections, guys who ran the docks, and he was busy comparing prices and compiling lists and checking out every aspect of the deal. He'd met the diplomats in June of '64. In August, he came home and said, "Baby, get the passports in order, we're going to the Ivory Coast."

But first, Lido.

It was a steamy night at the end of August. As directed, we arrived at Lido's East Harlem townhouse at midnight. After his traditional greeting, the warm handshake followed by the outstretched open palm waiting for cash and cocaine, Lido snorted up a couple of lines of inspiration and led us down into the basement. He asked about my shoulder. It had been about half a year since the shooting. He asked B whether he'd lit the candles and laid out the fruit and sugar according to directions. Then he checked my wound and nodded, pleased with the healing process.

Bernie and I knelt in the center of the floor as Lido went around the room lighting candles and mumbling prayers. When several candles were lit, dozens of white candles, in every corner of the basement, he shut the overhead light and returned to us carrying a wide white candle. He set it down before us and laid his hands on our heads.

The drumming, thudding, conga music began. Lido's face was dark and shadowy, his white silk sleeves billowing. His huge rings, the gold and diamond chains, the big diamond-encrusted cross, sparkled and shimmered in front of our eyes. Lido chanted a prayer, then cut off a piece of my hair and a piece of Bernie's and put the locks into a bowl. He threw in some dried herbs, added various colored waters, and while he mixed up the potion, he had us close our eyes and recite some special words. Everything was very,

very dark except for the candles which were all white; white candles everywhere.

He stirred and we recited. He mixed new ingredients and gave us new words to say. This went on for several minutes, fifteen, twenty. Then, out came the chicken. Lido wrung its neck. Then he held the poor limp bird by its legs and spun it around our heads. He had the chicken in one hand and these sort of makeshift maracas in the other, rattles and feathers and beads and whatnot hanging off them. And he was shaking them and throwing himself around and screaming and carrying on and singing and talking loudly in a language I couldn't understand. Twenty minutes he carried on like a maniac and then it was all over.

He stuffed the dead chicken into a bag and told us to throw it into water. And that was it.

"How much did you give him?" I asked as we left the town-house with this chicken in a brown paper bag. It smelled awful in the car, sitting on the seat between us.

"Don't ask," Bernie said.

"What, a lot? A hundred? Two?"

"Sandra!"

We left the car with our doorman and walked over to the East River. "What's the big secret? Why can't you tell me?"

It was two, three o'clock in the morning. Dark and hot out. Not a breath of air, not a soul in sight. According to Lido's instructions, we each had to have one hand on the bag. We'd been staying even with one another, but Bernie didn't want to talk to me about the money, so he started to speed up and I was huffing and puffing alongside him, trying to hang on to my end of the chicken.

"A lot, okay?" he grumbled.

"More than five hundred?"

"Yeah."

"You're kidding. Was it a thousand—or more?"

"More. Now stop."

"Holy shit," I said, as we reached the guard rail that ran alongside the river. "This better be good."

"Enough, Sandra," Bernie warned. "Just shut up and read the words, okay?" Lido had written down some prayers for us. He'd written them phonetically and we recited them several times as he'd instructed. And then we heave-hoed the chicken right into the river. According to Lido, we were now spiritually prepared to make a killing on the Ivory Coast.

* * *

Hot Dog Red was going with us. He was Bernie's partner in the deal. The three of us had been invited to stay at the prime minister's palace in Abidjan. While the boys shopped for gifts to shmear the officials and their wives with, I went to Abercrombie and Fitch and bought myself an authentic-looking safari outfit. I mean, what did I know about Africa? Nothing that I hadn't seen in the movies, and that meant snakes and lions in the daytime and mosquito netting and drums at night. In Bermuda shorts and a pith helmet, I was ready for the jungle. It never occurred to me that Abidjan might be a bustling city. I thought Bernie was crazy when he told me to pack a couple of good dresses and high-heeled shoes. But, of course, I did it. And, of course, Bernie booked us all first class.

The tickets cost a fortune. It was the most expensive and longest plane ride I ever took in my life. But, what the hell, we weren't going to Miami, we were going halfway around the world to become millionaires. We started off happy, excited, raring to go, three amigos shlepping a ton of luggage, most of it filled with gifts for the Ivory Coast bigwigs, pens and pencils from Tiffany's, jewelry which B had gotten from friends in the business, silk scarves, gorgeous sweaters, perfume, booze, all beautifully gift-wrapped. But the flight seemed to take nine hundred hours. I think it was actually twenty—twenty hours in the air. And hour by hour, we lost our enthusiasm, got bored and quiet, and drank more and more.

When I say *we* got quiet, I mean Bernie and I. Red became a maniac on fire. When he got drunk, he got very hyper. For a little while, Bernie tried going through some papers with Red, going over prices and contracts and agreements that Josh had drawn up. Then he saw that Hot Dog was getting wilder by the minute, that he was too loaded to focus on business. I remember Bernie, finally, giving up and saying, "Okay, now listen. When we get there, you're going to give very little to the conversation, Red, you got me? All you've got to do is stand there and look black and listen and nod, okay?"

By this time Red had at least two cocktails and half a bottle of wine in him and who knew what else he'd thrown into the mix. A drink at a time, he had turned into a crazed cartoon of himself— louder, faster, blacker, more frantic and friendly than I'd ever seen him before. He was all over the place, laughing, chatting, jiving up a storm with anyone who'd look at him.

Bernie went to sleep. After a while, I conked out, too. But from the way he looked when we finally landed, I'm sure Red kept up his insanity for the rest of the flight. His wavy, processed red hair was sticking up all over the place. His pale brown skin was ashy, almost green. His eyes were bloodshot, the bags under them looked like they weighed as much as our luggage. He reeked of alcohol, smelled like it was oozing out of every pore; fumes curling up out of the tangerine and green racetrack-patterned shirt he was wearing and his shiny forest-green pants and even his pride-and-joy, pointy-toed beige 'gators.

We landed late at night, about ten o'clock, I guess. The diplomats Bernie and Red had befriended in New York had gotten in touch with their superiors, who had insisted on meeting the men who were going to be their purchasing agents in the U.S. A big limousine had been sent to the airport for us accompanied by another car, which was full of uniformed soldiers. They whisked us off the plane, piled our bags into the limo, and off we sped to the prime minister's palace. An assistant was waiting for us inside. He apologized for the prime minister's not being there to greet us personally, but he'd been called away to another part of the country on business and would be back the next day. The assistant showed us to our rooms, which were spacious and beautiful. Bernie and I had our own bedroom and sitting room. Red had the same set up next door. "Man, this is living," he kept saying. "Down here, the rich are rich and the poor are poor. These niggers know how to live."

There was food waiting, fruit and native dishes in beautiful covered platters, vegetable pies and tea. We ate and showered and slept until noon the next day and woke to find the sun streaming in through our windows. We were served an American breakfast in our rooms—bacon, eggs, coffee, and toast—and told that the prime minister was back and waiting for us.

The gifts Bernie had brought were very well received. The prime minister, the minister of commerce, secretaries, assistants, military men, everyone and their wives and children were lined up to meet us. And they oohed and aahed over the gifts Bernie handed out. Then we were escorted to a big terrace out back, a huge patio area where we sat and sipped tea and chatted like old friends. Only a few of the women and none of the children sat with us. Most waited at the edge of the lawn, staring and smiling shyly at us. The women were wearing beautiful bright turbans and long gowns. And, as I returned their quiet smiles, I couldn't help noticing that the entire backyard was ringed with military men, soldiers with guns. Lots of guns.

The minister of commerce, a dignified, gracious man, told Bernie that he didn't want to discuss business on the first day. "Tomorrow is soon enough," he said. "Perhaps you'd care to see a bit of our country today. And tonight we'll welcome you officially with a feast." So off we went to explore the countryside, again escorted by a car full of uniformed, gun-toting soldiers. As for the feast, I was very glad that Bernie had made me pack some dressy clothes. Everyone was done up to the nines for this extraordinary little dinner party the prime minister threw for us. Some of the men wore suits and ties, but most were in fabulous long robes with turbans and lots of gold bracelets and rings. The women looked exquisite in their tribal gowns. The food, native vegetable and fish dishes, was absolutely delicious and, of course, the booze flowed. They served Dom Pérignon and brandy and French wines with dinner. Hot Dog was in seventh heaven. "Man," he kept saying, "these niggers do live right."

"Shush, Red," I said more than once that night. "You can't talk that way. You're going to get us in trouble."

But he was buzzing. His eyes, glistening with pleasure, darted everywhere at once. "Um-hum," he said, smacking his lips. "We have fallen into the old honey pot this time, girl."

If I didn't know better, I thought to myself, I'd say Red was ripped on cocaine. He was speeding, drinking like booze was going out of style, and he could not stop talking.

Bernie had packed boxes of the best American cigars. The men enjoyed an after-dinner smoke. Conversation was pleasant, light, and friendly. The women were quiet, shy, almost subservient. They covered their mouths when they giggled. We had a terrific evening and went back to our rooms tired, happy, and full of optimism.

The next day, we were scheduled to meet with the prime minister after breakfast. We were shown into his office, which was big, sunny, and serious-looking. Aside from the ceiling fans and tall louvered doors, it could have belonged to the chairman of AT&T. Flanked by his minister of commerce and two aides, the prime minister waited in a tall mahogany leather chair behind a big polished desk. Bernie, Red, and I sat down opposite him.

Everything started out fine. Everyone was smiling. Bernie began to explain his business plan, telling them how he had access through his contacts to many kinds of goods. Hot Dog was beautiful, grinning, hadn't said a word, just backing Bernie up with nods and grins. And then Bernie pulled out some of the papers that Josh had drawn up. He passed them over to the prime minister, who gave them to the minister of commerce, as Bernie started to explain the financial arrangements. He sounded so legit, so calm and businesslike, I was very proud of him. Then he said, "For obvious reasons, of course, we've got to handle the whole deal in cash."

The minister of commerce looked up from the papers. He kind of cocked his head like the RCA dog but didn't say anything, just waited and listened. And Bernie went on about how it had to be cash.

I don't know what happened. From the question of cash it started to move very quickly into other problem areas and, finally, the minister of commerce said, "I believe there's a misunderstanding about the question of your fee." He tapped the contract Bernie had given him and showed it to the prime minister and things heated up a little.

Then all of a sudden the prime minister said something to Bernie that Red didn't like. He sort of called him a crook. Bernie didn't like it, either, of course, but he kept cool. The next thing I knew, Red jumped up and started waggling his finger in the prime minister's face, yelling, "You nappy-haired nigger, what are you trying to do, lay some jive on us?"

I could feel the blood drain from my face. I could see it leave Bernie's. We're sitting there, whiter than white, shaking, and all of a sudden, I notice that the prime minister's got a jumping jugular vein that makes Bernie's look laid back. Bim, bam, boom, the minister of commerce calls Bernie a thief or something to that effect. The prime minister rears up, points to the door, and says, "You are to leave my country immediately. Get out!"

Red is already standing, already leaning across the PM's desk, and talking to the head of the Ivory Coast like he's some two-bit uptown numbers runner who's holding out on him. Red really gets into it, waving his hands and shaking his shoulders and really carrying on, when suddenly the door to the office bangs open and soldiers come running into the room with their guns pointed right at us.

Oh, my God, I'm a young girl. I haven't even lived yet. Now I'm going to die in Africa, I thought. My poor mother! No kidding, this is what I thought. I was crazy with fear. Half a dozen uniformed soldiers were standing there, nervous, angry, pointing rifles at us and you could see their hands shaking on the triggers.

From there, it got wilder. We were marched out of the office and made to sit in a small waiting room. Someone said our bags were being packed for us. The soldiers watching us never lowered their rifles. While they stood staring at us, holding guns on us, Bernie and Red started to argue. Bernie said out of the side of his mouth,

"Listen, I know what he was accusing me of and I could have handled it. You and your stupid mouth. I told you to keep quiet."

Red was still revved up. "You were going to let some jive-assed nigger fuck up the sweetest scam I ever saw. You think I'm going to sit there like a dummy watching this nappy-headed sucker steal my deal?"

"Please stop," I begged them. "They're watching us. They're going to shoot us soon. Please stop yelling."

"Look what you did," Bernie growled at Red. "You see how you set us up? You couldn't listen to me. You couldn't keep your mouth shut. I told you, give nothing to the conversation. But you had to carry on! Now we'll either be shot or arrested. You don't listen! You don't learn!"

Within a matter of minutes, our luggage was brought down. The prime minister came in, followed by more soldiers. "You are going to be driven to the airport and you are to get on the plane, which will be here in two hours," he announced in that cool, clipped voice. "The plane will return you to your country. If you aren't on that plane, you will be shot."

I thought I would die. But Bernie wanted to try to talk to him, charm him, change his mind. He started his spiel and the prime minister cut him off. "I don't do business with white trash," he said. I don't know where he learned that expression, but he said it with an ice-cold British accent.

Bernie's eyes narrowed and *his* vein started popping. "*You're* calling *me* white trash?!" He took a step toward the prime minister. And all you could hear in the room were guns clicking into place.

We were driven to the airport in the same limousine that had picked us up, followed again by a car full of soldiers. All during the ride, Red and Bernie were going at it. Then Red said, "Aw, the hell with this. I'm going to light up a joint." He pulled out some pot.

Bernie's eyes almost fell out of his head. "You traveled through Customs with pot?! What are you, crazy?"

"Why, you think I'd come to a hole like this without a stash? I got smoke, I got coke, I got what it takes. Yeah, that's right, you heard me, B. I got some toot here, too!" Red shouted back.

I thought Bernie would kill him. Instead, he got quiet and just shook his head. "You're really out of your fucking mind, you know? I was a fool to get involved with you, to bring you here. I should have known better." He was really stunned. It didn't stop him from taking a toke when Red passed the joint, though.

Red just shrugged at Bernie and rolled his eyes. He passed the joint around and the three of us got high in the back of the limo. It didn't take long before the driver got into the act. "What's that smell?" he asked. Red offered him the joint, told him it was a special tobacco grown in New York. So, the driver got loaded, too. By the time we got to the airport, the four of us were totally tilted.

The soldiers marched us through the place into a private room and we waited for the plane under guard. Instead of two hours, it took almost three for the plane to arrive. The entire time, except for brief smoke breaks when Red lit up another joint, Bernie and Red were at each other's throats. In the end, even I got into it.

"Look, it was a mistake, it wasn't meant to be, okay? What's the big deal?"

"Who asked you?" Bernie yelled at me. "Who the fuck asked for your brilliant opinion on this?"

"Brilliant? Sure, like throwing a chicken into the fucking East River is going to make us millionaires, right? Now, *that's* brilliant."

"Shut up, Sandra."

"Yeah, when you get back to New York and get your money back from Lido, I'll shut up."

"Stop, Sandra. Now!"

It was World War III. The soldiers were staring at us with their mouths open. They'd had three hours of Bernie pacing and grumbling at Red and at me, and me changing chairs trying to get comfortable and yelling at him, and Red just ranting non-stop, calling everybody names. They were nervous wrecks from being locked up with us and ready to put us out of our misery—or shut us up permanently to end theirs. Red's parting shot to the soldiers when the plane finally did arrive was: "When you get back, you tell your main man that I'm going home to Harlem and I'm getting my main man and we're going to come down here with mortars and machine guns and do you right!"

On the plane ride home we were so exhausted that we slept for almost the entire twenty hours. And, of course, once we got back to the United States, Bernie made me shut off the phones. He wouldn't take calls from anybody. He gave Red strict instructions to stay off the streets and not answer his phone and not show his face anywhere. Bernie was terrifically embarrassed at having been thrown out of the country. But after a day or two went by, he started to see the humor in the situation. And, the next thing you knew, he was telling everyone about it, cracking people up with his account of the *gantze megillah*, the whole deal. He was a great storyteller and, really, people used to fall off their chairs when he told this one.

By fall, when Farvel came up to New York, the Ivory Coast adventure had become such a classic that he insisted Bernie tell the story over dinner at Molly's on Rivington Street. It was a command performance—and what an audience! Once or twice a year, the heavy hitters would come into New York. Usually, Bernie would get a call from Farvel, from Florida, heralding the gathering. Within a week, they'd arrive from all over the States—from Boston, Minneapolis, California. There'd be Davey from Chicago, Geo from Las Vegas, Moe from Cleveland, old-timers like Red Levine and Farvel, who'd come up together on the Lower East Side, and younger guys who were learning the business.

Bernie would run down to the Luxor Baths to meet them. Sometimes he'd be away for a day or two. He'd stay over at the baths, spend the days steaming and talking business and eating in the restaurant down there. And then I'd get a call saying, "Okay, babe, get dolled up tonight. I want you to look gorgeous for me. We're going to Molly's," and I'd know that business had been concluded and the unwinding was about to begin.

The guys would put on their expensive suits and diamond tie pins and huge gold pinky rings. They'd be perfectly polished, barbered, manicured, and each of them would have a woman on his arm, an accessory as glittering and valuable as a cuff link. Oddly enough, most of the women these men brought to Molly's were wives. They just weren't married to the men they were with. Their husbands were straight guys; their boyfriends were gangsters.

My age—I was in my twenties, about ten years younger than the rest of the girls—and the fact that Bernie always called me his "lady," never his wife, made me a sort of honorary mistress. But the women I met at Molly's were fun-loving, sweet, *haimisha* girls and they always treated me very nicely, like a little sister or a favorite doll. And did they get *fahpitzed* to spend a night with their fellas? For a little middle-of-the-week dinner at Molly's, out would come the furs, the sequined sweaters, and low-cut, tight black dresses, the pointy-toed shoes with rhinestones stuck in the stiletto heels, the teased hair adding two to twelve inches to their height.

If the customers looked like a million, Molly's didn't. It was just a Jewish restaurant on Rivington Street on the Lower East Side. But when the boys from out of town wanted a place to unwind, to eat the food their mothers had fed them, to hear the songs and voices of their childhood, to take strength from their Jewish roots again, it beat the Copa by a mile.

Molly's was nothing to look at. Two steps down from the street, it was a narrow space with high ceilings and white walls. Behind the cash register was a Jewish calender and a framed photograph of Chaim Weizmann, the first president of the State of Israel. The tables were covered with plain white cloths. The blond wood chairs were scarred, darkened by time and grime, with inset leather seats and backrests. Very plain. And on the table would be bottles of seltzer, the old-fashioned kind that could double as a fire extinguisher, and bowls full of briny pickles and red peppers. There were no bread baskets, just white plates piled high with sliced rye. Hot tea was served in glasses. The sugar containers were tall cannisters with built-in metal funnels. And the white-aproned, singing waiters, who could pour chicken soup from thick metal cups into shallow bowls without losing a *lokshin* or spilling a drop, were wise-cracking, sour-faced veterans. There was a square stand-up bar near the entrance that dispensed everything from Mogen David to Moët.

Molly, herself, was a big-mouthed, bleached blonde made of the same stern stuff and loose flesh as Sophie Tucker. Her breasts bulged over the plunging necklines she wore. Her makeup was as abundant. She was crude, loud, and loving, knew every customer's preferences and peculiarities and those of his father before him. Molly was the original stand-up Jewish broad. And to add a touch of class to her place, she insisted that the musicians who played the whiny, joyous Jewish numbers her customers loved, the cigarette smoker hunched over the upright piano, the sad accordion player and the pasty-white violinist, all wore tuxedos.

"Sandela, *shayna*, how are you? You look so pretty tonight," Farvel would shout out, as we approached the big round table against the wall where the gang was gathered. "The kid's treating you good?"

"Very good, sweetheart," I'd say, kissing the cheek he extended to me. Sometimes he'd remember and take the cigar out of his mouth first; sometimes not.

"You know everyone, right?"

By this Farvel meant the men. The women would introduce themselves. "Hi, honey. Bea Spizer, we met last year when Harry was in town."

That night, that September after the Ivory Coast fiasco, Red Levine—whose last name was pronounced to rhyme with divine—

was sitting across from Farvel. What they had in common, aside from their ever-present cigars, was Meyer. They were his, they'd grown up in the shadows of the same tenements; they'd served him. They were, as the newspapers and television programs called them, his "lieutenants," his "trusted aides."

Red still had the full, if thinning, head of wavy reddish-blond hair that had won him his nickname. He was about my height, no more, and very thin. And sitting beside him was Sylvia, the good-looking woman who'd gotten drunk at another of Molly's dinners and whom I'd had to escort home to a very impressive apartment on Second Avenue. Red was in his late fifties, early sixties then and looked like a kindly Jewish uncle, a nice guy, a sweetheart—which he always was to me. It was hard for me to believe that this was the same man who supposedly carried out one of the most notorious hits in gangland history, the man Meyer assigned to direct the squad of Jewish gunmen who murdered Salvatore Maranzano. After Maranzano's death—four bullets and six knife wounds after—Meyer and his boyhood friend, Lucky Luciano, were supposed to have organized the new mafia, The Syndicate or The Outfit as it was called. The syndicate was run by five "families" rather than one "boss of all bosses"—which was the title Maranzano had reserved for himself.

When Bernie first introduced me to Red Levine, you could always find him hanging out at the bocci courts over at First Street and Avenue A. He'd just be standing there, talking to old friends, patting neighborhood kids on the head. A sweet man. A *ziskite*. And, years later, when Bernie was gone and Red was really an old man, I drove down to the Lower East Side with Jeffrey in the car. Jeffrey was a baby then. We were in the car together and something went wrong. The car started rolling. I couldn't stop it. I screamed for help. And Red Levine, who had to have been in his seventies, ran down the street, threw open the driver's door, and forced the brake down until the car finally stopped. If it hadn't, I'm convinced Red would have done something else, even if it meant hanging on to the bumper until his shoes left skidmarks on the street.

Red knew Bernie from the old days, from when Bernie was an eleven-year-old kid working at—and, as Red never failed to remind him, stealing hats from—the best haberdashery on the Lower East Side. He had a real fondness for Bernie. So when Farvel gave Bernie the high sign and said, "Go on, kid. Tell 'em how the *shvartzas* threw you out. Out of Africa, Red! Wait, this you're not going to believe!" Red started grinning right away.

"Still a *mamzer*," he said, affectionately. Still a little bastard.

The guys never talked business at Molly's. They laughed. They drank. And when the little *klezmer* band played the old favorites, "Bei Mir Bist du Schön" or "Orchu Chonya" and, especially, "My Yiddishe Momme," the men's eyes would mist over. "Oy," they'd sigh. "You remember that song, Farvela? *Gedenkt?*" Do you remember? Sometimes they'd cry. And late at night, fueled by memories and J&B, they'd leap to their feet when the band played a *hora* or a handkerchief dance.

And they ate. Boy, did they eat. The waiters would cruise out with course after course of plates piled high with herring and boiled beef, chopped liver, potato latkes, roast chicken, unborn eggs, brains, stuffed derma, *lokshin kugels*—noodle puddings—and a chopped tenderloin cutlet they used to call "mush steak."

"You don't get food like this in Vegas, do you, Geo?" someone would say. Or, "Go try to find a decent stuffed derma in Cleveland."

Everything was washed down with seltzer, bottle after bottle of bubbly, stinging, belch-inducing seltzer. And when the gatherings got a little wild and the guys a little frisky, it was not unknown for them to have seltzer fights, *shpritzing* each other like schoolboys until Molly trundled over, flesh heaving, hammy fists on her hips, to demand: "What the hell is going on here?!"

I loved it. I loved the old songs. I loved the Jewishness. I loved the food. When I knew we were going to Molly's for dinner, I'd starve myself all day and really go to town.

"Look how skinny she is," Red's girl Sylvia would marvel, watching me put away the food. "So, Bernie, when are you going to fatten her up so I don't have to eat my heart out with jealousy? Tell me, *mamela*, when are you going to get pregnant? When are we going to see a belly on you?"

CHAPTER TWELVE

A Birthday Present for Bernie

Sylvia wasn't the only one who asked. Some of the wives would tease me about it. My friend Judy, who'd finally traded in her famous hairdresser for the piano player from Jilly's (not poor Nicky "Fly Me to the Moon" DeFrancis, who'd thrown himself out a window, but a stunning young Latino named Nino) and now had a beautiful little girl, mentioned it every time I visited her. "Sandy, you're so good with the baby," she'd say in her unconquerable Kentucky drawl. "When are you going to have one of your own?" And, of course, my mother never stopped hoping and hinting. "Maybe you should get a nice two bedroom place, sweetheart. Maybe, if there was room for a baby—"

But nobody asked the question more than I did. It was 1964. I was already twenty-five years old. If not now, when? I began to wonder. "Soon, babe," Bernie would always answer. "I promise you, Sandy. Soon."

He didn't seem to be against the idea, I reasoned during my solitary walks along the river, where I'd see women wheeling baby carriages, or when I sat alone on a bench in the sunshine of the little park behind our building watching nannies and mothers chasing toddlers, or in the supermarket when I'd push my cart full of grown-up food past the grinning baby faces on the Gerber and Beechnut jars.

Bernie was doing well at the time. His health seemed to be holding up. He hadn't been hospitalized in nearly a year. He was running around like crazy, busy day and night. The hassock was stuffed with cash. It was one of those rare times when there was more coming in than going out. I'd carry envelopes to the safety deposit boxes a couple of times a month.

And sometimes when I asked myself, "If not now, when?" it wasn't just the baby I meant. It was "If not now, when will we be *normal*?" Having a baby began to seem like the first installment on that dream.

It was summertime. We were all dressed up, on our way to an engagement party or a wedding. It was an afternoon affair, which meant there'd be kids around. "Bernie, I really want to have a baby," I said. "I'm twenty-five already."

"Yeah, I know," he said, eyes on the road, not even looking at me. "I'm thinking of trading you in for a couple of seventeen-year-olds."

I burst into tears.

"What?" he said. "What the hell's going on with you?"

"You're not kidding," I sobbed.

I believed it. I believed that soon I would be too old to be glamorous to him, that he'd take a mistress like the other mob guys—if he didn't already have one! He was away so much. How did I know he wasn't running around on me? It was part of the life. There were always glamour girls who hung out around mob guys. They had more groupies than rock-and-roll stars—gorgeous young girls turned on by the action, money, and power, as attracted to the scene as I'd been. And hadn't I spent evenings with the guys and their girlfriends—at the Copa, at Molly's, at afterhours joints and racetracks, lowlife bars, and pricey restaurants? I even knew and loved some of the girlfriends. My friend Toni was being kept by a big-deal Italian mobster and had been for years. Even Red Levine, who always seemed so *haimish* to me, had his Sylvia. I'd be with the guys and their girlfriends one night, and two nights later, in the same restaurant, I'd be sitting there with them and their wives.

Once I even asked a friend of Bernie's, "Why do you run around? Why do you cheat?"

"For the glamour," he said. "You've got to have a broad by your side and she's got to be the best." He pointed to some of the girls in the nightclub we were in. Most were sitting beside men who were talking to one another or focused entirely on sawing through their sirloin steaks and wolfing down their baked potatoes. The men barely looked at the women sitting next to them, as beautifully made-up and decked out as they were—with jewels sparkling from their earlobes, around their necks, on the fingers that held the cigarettes, or gold lighters or drink stirrers that they toyed with. "You see how they sit, they listen? Not one of them is smart. You tell them where to stand, where to sit, and you tell them how high to jump."

"Very nice," I remember saying sarcastically.

But now the idea that Bernie might view things the same way, might want, or even have, a decorative little girl to tell how high to jump, drove me crazy.

Sometimes tears infuriated Bernie; sometimes he was moved by them. That afternoon in the car, he pulled his handsome Sulka handkerchief out of his breast pocket and handed it to me. "What the hell's wrong with you today? I was teasing you, that's all," he said. "You want a baby? We'll have a baby. I told you we would. Soon. I promised you, didn't I, that I'd give you the life you wanted?"

"You mean it?" I wrapped my arms around his neck and hugged him. "Oh, sweetheart, you really mean it, right?"

"Yeah, yeah. Take it easy." He grinned and pulled himself free of my grip. "I'm driving, baby."

"But you mean it."

"Sure," Bernie said. "Soon."

That was the last day I took the Pill. I didn't say anything to Bernie about it. I just went off birth control and onto sex. I took him at his word. Soon meant soon. Within three months, I knew I was pregnant. But the urine test I took came back negative—three times. "I don't care what that shows," I told Tillie in the luncheonette where we were having coffee. "I know when I'm pregnant, Ma. And I'm pregnant."

"From your mouth to God's ear," she said, clasping her hands together dramatically. "But, *mamela*, this time, if the doctor says no, I mean, this time you took a blood test, right? So, if he says no today, don't worry. You'll just forget about it and you'll keep trying."

"Is it time yet? What time is it, Ma?" I was supposed to call Dr. Truppin at five o'clock to find out the results of the blood test.

"You've got time. It's four-thirty."

"I'm going to call him right now. I'm pregnant, Ma. I just know it."

Truppin was in. "Good news," he said.

"I'm pregnant?!"

"You're pregnant, Sandy. You were right." When he gave me the due date, I whooped with joy.

"What?!" my mother said when I came back to the booth.

"Bingo! I'm having a baby, Ma."

"No!"

"Yes! And you'll never guess the due date. May twenty-eighth, Ma! I'm going to give birth on Bernie's birthday!"

"Mazel-tov! Oh, my God, I'm going to be a grandma!" We both laughed.

"It's a boy," I said. "I know it like I knew I was pregnant even when the tests said no." This was before amnio or sonograms, before it was possible to know the sex of the baby in advance.

"Whatever it is, as long as it's healthy, you'll be happy," my mother assured me. "And, Sandy, wait. Now you'll see. Things'll change."

"What's it like," I asked, as we left the coffee shop together, "having a baby, Ma?"

She squeezed my arm and shook her head. "*Oy*, don't ask," she said. "Better you shouldn't know." But not even that could daunt me. I put Tillie in a cab to Brooklyn and rushed home to Bernie.

It was a beautiful October day. The terrace door was open and he was sitting near it, at the bar, having a drink before he went out for the evening. His hair was slicked back, still wet from the shower he'd taken. The top button on his monogrammed powder-blue shirt was open; his silk tie was unknotted. He looked relaxed, comfortable.

"Do you have to go out tonight?" I asked.

"Why? You want to come along? Come with me, I'm going uptown for a couple of hours, then we'll stop in and see Cokey—"

"No, honey. That's not what I meant. I mean, can't you stay home with me? Bernie, there's something I want to tell you."

He looked at me and sighed and shook his head. "Here we go," he said. "I hate surprises, Sandra. And I can tell you've got a beauty cooking."

"Well, you're right," I blurted out, laughing. "I'm pregnant, Bernie. I'm giving you a son on your birthday!"

He gave me a long, stunned look, then set his drink down on the bar. "You're pregnant?"

The laugh began to stick in my throat. Suddenly, I was ready to cry, ready for him to blow his top. "Yeah, I am," I said, and nodded.

"We're going to have a baby?" he said, and slowly his face broke into a huge smile. "No shit?"

"A boy, Bernie. On your birthday. The doctor said the due date is May twenty-eighth."

He jumped up off the barstool. "How do you know it's a boy?"
I shrugged. "I just know."

"A baby. A son. You think I'm going to have a son?" He was
definitely warming to the idea, getting excited. I nodded and he
gave me a great big hug, then he leapt away from me. "Oh, my
God, did I hurt you? Are you okay?"

"I'm fine."

"This is great. Great, baby! We've got to do something. We've
got to celebrate!" Within fifteen minutes, he'd hit the phone and
told the world that we were expecting, that *he* was expecting an
heir. "This is it," I heard him tell Vinny. "No more fooling around.
I'm going to get my act together." He'd said the same or similar to
at least four other friends he'd called. "I'm going to put aside a little bread, then go legit," he'd told them. "This kid is going to have
a decent life, the best of everything. Come on over, we're going to
celebrate."

Oh, my God, I thought. Tillie was right when she said things
would change. Here was Bernie making promises, not just to me,
but to Vinnie and Josh and Red. He even put in a call to Trenton, to
tell Chalky in prison that night.

The gang assembled and it was party time. After the last guest
had left, and it was probably Hot Dog at three or four in the morning, when we were finally alone in the apartment, Bernie put his
arms around me. "I'm so happy, baby. And I don't want you to
worry about a thing," he said, earnestly. "Everything is going to
work out for us now. I know things have been rough for you. But
it'll be different now, Sandy. This baby is going to change our luck.
And I'm going to take good care of you, both of you. You wait and
see. I'm going to take care of everything."

He meant it. In the next couple of months, Bernie went into high
gear. He became obsessed with getting ready for the baby, but in
his own way, in his own style. A two-bedroom apartment became
available in our own building, a beautiful, sunny place with a terrace overlooking the river. The rent was outrageous, but Bernie
snapped it up immediately. "He's got to have the best, our kid,"
he'd say. "I've got to put the money together now because you
never can tell what'll happen down the road."

We went shopping for baby furniture. And again, of course,
nothing but the best would do. At a very exclusive showroom on
lower Fifth Avenue, which featured British baby furniture and carriages, we chose everything we needed for the nursery and a Royal
Coach baby carriage. It was a huge, extravagant carriage—"The

kind you see British nannies wheeling in Hyde Park," the salesman in the three-piece suit and uptown accent assured us. "It'll take a month to arrive from London, but it's well worth the wait."

"Bernie," I whispered. "It's so expensive."

"I keep telling you, Sandy, this kid's going first class. He's got to start out right, baby."

The bigger I got, the more tenderly Bernie treated me, and the harder he worked. I asked him to slow down, stay home. "First, I want to put together a couple of big scores," he'd say. "You never know. I'm not going to leave you young with a baby to take care of and no money."

He started talking about the future that way more and more. How he had to run and set up this little deal downtown, put out a couple of loans uptown, take a trip here, make a call there . . .

"Because what are you going to do if something happens to me, baby?" . . . "Because I'm not going to be around forever and you're going to need a nest egg to bring my son up right." . . . "Because there's no telling what's in the cards, Sandy, and then where would you live? What would you do?"

"Stop it!" I'd wind up shouting at him. "I don't want to hear it, Bernie!" I was pregnant. I was superstitious. I was in love with him. I couldn't think about living without him. I sure as hell wasn't going to talk about it. The sickness and danger were behind us, I told myself. This was a time of joy. We were having a baby, taking a step toward the good life, the straight life. And that meant Mommy and Daddy and baby makes three, not two.

Like a harbinger of doom, like a bird of prey, slimy Hymie the Sleazeball showed up. Hymie was a cousin of Bernie's from the Lower East Side. He was a nervous, chubby, pear-shaped little *shlemiel*, whom Bernie had helped out of a jam years ago. Hymie, who talked a mile a minute and whose eyes shifted just as fast, had been caught embezzling from the men's clothing store he'd managed. Bernie had paid back the money—$20,000 or $30,000 it was—out of his strong sense of family loyalty and he'd gotten the owner to drop the charges.

Except for their blue eyes, there was no family resemblance at all between Bernie and Hymie. Hymie was older, shorter, paler—he had the pasty white skin of a *yeshiva bucher*. What hair he had left was a washed-out reddish-blond and his balding head was always beaded with sweat. Hot Dog Red couldn't believe they were related by blood. He hated Hymie on sight—which wasn't that hard to do. The guy oozed flattery and deceit.

But he was family. In Bernie's book that made him trustworthy. And the way Bernie was setting up new deals and businesses now, he needed more help than Hot Dog could give him. He'd even started putting out a little shylock money and he assigned Hymie to keep track of the loans and pick up the payments.

"I don't understand it," I'd tell Red. "Bernie knows how sticky this sleazeball's fingers are. How can he trust him? How can he bring him into the business, into our home?"

Hymie's marriage was on the rocks. I'd met his girlfriend, who looked more like a whale than a homewrecker. She towered over him. With a little heave, her breasts, which were enormous, could've rested comfortably on his hunched shoulders. Breasts aside, she looked like a guy in drag.

Because he hated to go home, Sleazeball used to hang around our place. He'd poke around, look in the medicine chest, in the kitchen cabinets, the refrigerator. He'd walk behind the bar and fix himself a nice stiff scotch. He started answering the phone when it rang.

"Hymie, this is my house," I'd say. "You can't answer the phone."

"What's the difference, Bernie's expecting an important telephone call," he'd say in that voice like a chipmunk on speed, "so I picked it up, what's the harm, relax, Sandy." This round-shouldered, pear-shaped, pasty-faced, sweat-soaked loser was suddenly swaggering around my apartment doing gangster imitations. "Relax, Sandy. I'm just trying to help out. Remember, if anything happens to the big guy, you can count on me."

I wanted to kill him. I'd complain to Red or my mother, but I never said anything to Bernie about Sleazeball, which was what I'd taken to calling him. Bernie had enough on his mind. He was running himself ragged. I could see it coming. "You're going to get sick if you keep up this pace, Bernie. You've got to get some rest."

"You're the one who needs the rest, sweetheart. I'm doing fine. Never felt better in my life. Hey, I'm going to be a father, right? A father works hard, gets things set up for his kid, right? So you go lay down, baby. I've got to make a couple more calls. Then Hymie's stopping by and we're going downtown for an hour or so."

* * *

Bernie was doing a lot of things I hadn't seen him do before. Although, in the old days, on East Seventy-ninth Street, he'd sometimes ask me to wait in the bedroom alcove or even in the bathroom while he talked a deal with a couple of visitors, he'd never asked me to leave the house. Now, it was getting to be a habit. A squat, dark-haired Spanish-speaking man would show up from time to time. He'd come in with suitcases and Bernie would ask me to take a walk. I saw this dark-haired guy maybe four or five times in the apartment or I'd pass him in the hallway or the lobby as I was leaving. He spoke no English. He was always shlepping those suitcases. I didn't ask Bernie what was in them. I had a feeling it was drugs, pot maybe, maybe even cocaine. I never asked. And Bernie never offered an explanation.

Of course, *I* also did a couple of things I hadn't done before. We were going out to dinner with Cokey and Iris one Friday. I had a beauty parlor appointment that day. It was supposed to be just for a manicure, but I decided to get my hair cut—short. My hairdresser tried to talk me out of it, but I'd made up my mind. With great reluctance, he gave me what I'd asked for. The shop was in the lobby of our building. I thought I looked great until I got upstairs.

Cokey and Iris were already there. Bernie was at the bar fixing them a drink. I walked in, or waddled—I was close to six months pregnant then—expecting oohs and aahs. Cokey and Iris were kind enough just to go slack-jawed. Bernie was more expressive. "What the hell did you do?" he demanded.

"Why? I like it. I think it's cute," I protested.

"You look like a fat boy!" Bernie said.

"Bastard," I mumbled, biting back the tears.

"I swear, a fat *boy*! Look at her. Tell her. Come on, Cokey. Iris, tell her the truth. Cute, she says!"

"It is cute. I think it's cute," Iris soothed.

I steamed off into the bedroom to change for dinner. "You're late," Bernie called after me. When we were ready to leave, he grabbed my coat and held it up for me to slip into. Instead of sliding an arm into the sleeve, I made a fist and pushed through hard and punched Bernie in the nuts. "Jesus!" he gasped and went down on one knee behind me.

"Oh, honey, I'm so sorry," I said sweetly.

Iris took my arm and hurried me out the door while Cokey waited, trying to keep a straight face, for Bernie to catch his breath again.

* * *

I was having a very healthy pregnancy. I felt good most of the time. But I was gaining weight like crazy. I don't know if I looked like a fat boy but, boy, was I fat! My belly, at five months, stuck out so far I used to rest my arms on it. Which Bernie hated. It made him nervous. "Stop that," he'd beg me. "Look how you're pressing down on your belly. You'll crush the baby's head."

I was in my sixth month when Bernie had another attack. He caught a cold that quickly turned into pneumonia and he went into congestive heart failure. Red and I rushed him to the hospital once again. I was distraught. I was hugely pregnant, super-sensitive, and very scared. I knew how much these bouts with illness took out of Bernie. I knew how much his convalescences took out of me even when I was normal, how much running around I'd have to do. I knew the house would fill up with his friends again, and I was in no condition to trundle around emptying ashtrays and cleaning up after the boys.

I was at the hospital, sitting outside Bernie's room, feeling sorry for myself when Dr. Sealy finished his examination and came out into the hallway.

"How are you, Sandy?" he asked gravely.

"Fat," I said, and laughed. "Other than that, I'm okay. A little tired. A little nervous about Bernie. He's really been running around like mad these past few months, Doctor Sealy. He got himself really run down."

"If you're feeling up to it, come take a walk with me. I want to talk to you." Sealy helped me up out of the chair. He kept a hand on my elbow as we walked along the corridor on the way to his office. "You know, you were right. Bernie has exhausted himself. He's always been a very sick man, Sandy, and he's gotten worse."

He opened the door to his office and we went inside. "I'm sorry, Sandy. I hate to have to tell you this, especially now, at a time like this. This should be a happy time for you. Your first baby. But Bernie is very sick," Dr. Sealy said, once we were seated. "The hole in his heart has gotten too big."

"What does that mean?" I asked, afraid that I already knew. I sat there with my hands crossed on my belly. I'm crushing the baby's head, I thought, as if Bernie were inside my brain, as if I could hold on to him by becoming him, thinking his thoughts instead of mine.

"Sandy, I'm sorry," Dr. Sealy said. "I don't think he'll live out the year."

For a minute, I just sat there. Then I shook my head no.

I kept on shaking my head as if that could change things, as if I could shake out Sealy's words. My head whirled with noise—I was thinking a thousand things at once, feeling a thousand feelings. Fear. Terrible, raw fear gripped me.

No, I kept thinking, this isn't true. How can he do this to me, I thought, as if Bernie's being sick was just some mean thing he was doing to hurt me, to frighten me. I shouldn't have cut my hair, I thought, as if that had something to do with his sickness, as if the hair I'd cut off had held whatever magic it took to keep Bernie healthy. I won't live through this, I thought. I don't know how to live. I couldn't take care of Bernie; how can I take care of a baby? I don't even know how to take care of myself. Who'll tell me what to do? Who'll teach me? And I could hear Bernie saying, "Don't forget, kid. I taught you everything you know. But I didn't teach you everything *I* know."

And underneath the jumble of thoughts and feelings, I heard myself sort of chanting. "He can't die, it's not true, he can't die, it's not true, he can't die."

Finally, I said, "Does Bernie know, Doctor Sealy? Did you tell him what you just told me?"

"No."

"Does anyone else know?"

"No, Sandy. No one knows but you."

"I want to tell my mother," I said, "nobody else."

A nurse was carrying a basket of fruit into Bernie's room when I got back. There were already two or three more bouquets of flowers than when I'd left, and almost an entirely new shift of friends. Hot Dog was gone, but Uncle Vinny had showed up. Bernie was propped up on the pillows. He winked at me. His face creased with pain.

"He looks like shit," Vinny said to me, not bothering to lower his voice.

I walked past him to the side of Bernie's bed. There was a needle in his hand attached to an intravenous tube. I just put his palm onto mine and held his hand for a little while. "Baby, I'm going to call my mother, then I'm going home. I'm very tired. But I'll be back later."

"No. You take it easy. You're carrying precious cargo. Stay home tonight. Give Tillie my love. I'll see you tomorrow."

I kissed his head and went home.

"He's dying, Mama," I said when Tillie came over to our apartment that evening. I'd asked her to spend the night with me. I didn't want to be alone.

while carrying the most terrible secret of my life. And as comforting as Hot Dog and Tillie were, that was how irritating Hymie was. More and more he came to resemble a vulture, a miserable fat bird circling, sniffing around, waiting to make his move.

He sidled up to me in the kitchen one day with half a pastrami sandwich in his hand. Josh and Uncle Vinny and some of the other guys always made sure there was plenty of food around. As soon as one platter started to look depleted, they'd phone out and order more from the deli. So the Sleaze came in carrying this huge, over-stuffed half of a sandwich and, again, he started with his big plans for the future. "Sandy, I just want you to know that if anything happens to Bernie, we'll keep the businesses going, you and me, just like Bernie would want. We'll keep everything in the family and we'll take care of that baby in your belly, because I know you really know a lot about Bernie's businesses."

Although I had a miraculously healthy pregnancy, I was very depressed that day. I hadn't had my home to myself, except for a few hours while we slept, in weeks and weeks. There were always strangers coming and going and friends dropping around. Even when Red or Josh would drive Bernie uptown or to someplace out of the house when he had an appointment, there'd usually be a couple of people hanging around waiting for them to come back. So I'd gone into the kitchen to get away from the tumult for a minute, and here came Hymie, his pasty face oiled with sweat as usual, bringing with him the future that I tried so hard not to think about. I despised him at that moment. But, oddly enough, I didn't let loose on him.

"Thanks, Hymie," I said. "I know I can count on you. But, you never know, life changes from minute to minute. Let's just wait and see what it brings us."

Sleazeball left the kitchen and I was amazed at the way I'd handled myself. Later that day, I told Red what had happened. "You're turning into 'my man,' " he said, and laughed. "You handled that roach exactly the way B would have done it."

As the weather got nicer, Bernie would sometimes sit out on the terrace. He'd take the phone out there with him and make his calls and shmooze for hours. He was physically weak but his mind—and his mouth—were working a mile a minute. My mouth was going, too. Mostly to the kitchen, where I'd nosh on the leftover appetizing and deli and Chinese food. I was eating out of nerves and I was very nervous and very big. I was also always tired. Sometimes Bernie would wake me in the middle of the night and ask me to make him a cup of tea. I wanted to sleep. I needed my sleep. Sometimes, I'd just turn my back on him and say, "No, you go do it yourself. I'm exhausted." Sometimes we'd have screaming fights in the dark over such garbage. And sometimes, I'd just climb out of bed and shuffle into the kitchen half-asleep and put up the water and lean against the refrigerator door with my arms crossed and resting on my huge belly, and wait for the water to boil for his tea.

One afternoon, I remember, I'd gone into the baby's room, probably to find a moment's peace and quiet. The furniture we'd ordered from England hadn't arrived yet but the blue carpeting was in and the pretty wallpaper Tillie and I had picked out. I ran my hand over the teddy bear pattern on the wall and I walked over to the closet and opened the door. The closet was empty, of course. I stepped inside and closed the door behind me. The next thing I knew, I was sitting on the floor of the empty closet in the baby's room, sobbing. I felt like a little girl in a secret hide-away trying to find a place where no one could find me and nothing could hurt me. But all I could think about was how alone I felt and how lonely I was going to be without Bernie.

Halfway through my seventh month, the baby's room was still bare. The fine furniture and fancy carriage we'd ordered had arrived from England, but a dock strike had shut down the New York piers. No one dared cross the stevedores' picket lines. No cargo was being unloaded.

Finally, Bernie made a phone call. "Okay," he said to me, one icy morning in March, "here's the story. You go down to the docks on the West Side, go to Pier #21, and ask for Tommy P."

My belly had outgrown my widest winter coat, but I wore the coat anyway, open, of course, over a couple of layers of sweaters and, in slacks and flats and gloves and a woolen hat pulled over my still short and choppy hair, I caught a cab down to the docks. I waddled onto Pier #21 clutching the piece of paper on which I'd written Bernie's instructions.

Crates were stacked high in front of every ship. The ships were as tall as buildings and the pier seemed endlessly long. With my belly sticking out of the coat, I shlepped the length of three city blocks before I found Tommy P. He was a rough-looking guy in his fifties, with a nose full of broken veins and a full head of salt-and-pepper hair that whipped around in the wind. He was standing outside a little wooden shack. He helped me inside and asked where the baby furniture had come from and the name of the store where we'd bought it. With large, scarred, and callused hands he rifled through endless papers. Then he took my arm and together we shuffled along another mile or so of oil-stained rotting boards until we got to the ship.

There was a man in a pea coat and Navy watch cap standing next to the boxes piled in front of an enormous ship. Tommy P. talked to him. The guy went scurrying up onto the ship and Tommy said to me, "Stay here and don't move. They're going to bring a chair for you, and then we'll get your stuff."

Well, they sat me down, belly and all, right there on the dock amongst the cartons and crates and ropes and dollies and picketing stevedores and sailors gaping down from the ships. They even brought me hot tea. And, for about forty minutes, I sat there, alone, in a chair on the dock, sipping tea in the wind. It was the most luxurious, relaxing time I'd had in weeks.

Tommy came back with six *bulvons*—six of the biggest, strongest, most strapping men I'd ever seen—and while they carried carton after carton of baby furniture off the ship, a truck pulled up and a couple of other *shtarkers* started loading our stuff onto it. "Okay," Tommy said when everything was accounted for and waiting in the truck. "Just give me the address and we'll deliver it."

I gave him our address and then took out the envelope full of cash Bernie had given me. "How much do I owe you?" I asked.

He put up his palm like a traffic cop. "Don't worry about it. It's all been taken care of." Then he put me in a car and I was driven home. The truck arrived moments after I did. Six guys carried in the crates and cartons. They put together every piece of furniture and assembled the magnificent baby carriage for us and, refusing anything but a couple of beers, they left.

We were ready.

About a month before I gave birth, Bernie started to feel better. The color returned to his face. He could breathe normally again. Even his voice seemed stronger. I thought a miracle had happened. But Dr. Sealy warned me against optimism. However wonderful Bernie felt or looked at that moment, nothing had changed inside. The hole in his heart was as dangerous, and inevitably fatal, as ever.

The baby was due on May twenty-eighth, just before the Memorial Day weekend. Dr. Truppin, my obstetrician, had plans to go on vacation. He had me come in for an examination on May twenty-seventh, and he said, "You're ready. We'll deliver you tomorrow."

I was shocked. "What do you mean? How can you tell?" I asked.

"If the water hasn't broken by tomorrow morning, you come into the office and I'll do it for you. Then we'll put you in the hospital."

I went home and, of course, I told Bernie. We had plans to go to the Copa that night, to celebrate his birthday at midnight. It was a Thursday, the night the Copa opened its new acts, and the whole world was there. We ran into Hattie Prince at the bar. "Mazel-tov." She grinned at my belly. "See. I told you you'd be fine, kid, didn't I?" she whispered to me after extending her cheek to Bernie for a kiss. "So when are you due? You look like you're going to have it tonight."

"Tomorrow," Bernie said. "It's my birthday gift."

Uncle Vinny waved us over to a table near the dance floor. He was wearing a three-piece suit and his usual immaculate pin-striped shirt. Vinny believed pin-stripes made him look taller. He was considered a stylish dresser, a bit of a trend setter, because he wore vests before anyone else we knew did. And because, on a gold chain hanging from his vest pocket, he wore his father's watch. And hanging from the chain was a tiny fourteen-carat-gold box with a teeny, tiny gold spoon attached to it. In 1965, this opulent little coke stash was considered terribly cool. The medical establishment had not even begun to talk about cocaine as "the only non-addictive drug." That joke went off half a decade later.

Vinny pulled out a chair for me and, after Bernie introduced me to the other men at the table, I gratefully lowered myself into it. I knew Ruby Stein of the twitching eye, of course. "BB, you look like a million bucks," he said to Bernie. "Jesus, I heard you were dying, and look at you."

I must have flinched, but I laughed along with everyone else. It was one of those times when it was almost impossible to believe Dr. Sealy's dire prediction. Bernie had really had a miraculously good month. He was eating, sleeping, and breathing normally again and, tonight, flushed with excitement about the baby's birth, grinning, shaking hands and kibitzing with the guys, he did look like a million.

Next to Ruby was Gribbs Tremonte, a neat but not dapper gray-haired man who was, Uncle Vinny later confided, "very connected," a lieutenant in Fat Tony Salerno's family.

When the second or third round of drinks came, Vinny toasted

Bernie's birthday. Everyone at the table joined in. "Tonight's your birthday?" someone asked.

"No," Bernie said. "Tomorrow. And guess what my lady's giving me for my birthday—a baby. She's having a baby on my birthday."

Everybody laughed. Someone said, "How do you know it's going to be tomorrow?"

"Hey, she's got an appointment," Bernie answered.

"You're kidding," Ruby said. "What kind of appointment?"

"I never heard of such a thing," someone else commented. "Who ever heard of having an appointment to have a baby?"

"No such thing," another skeptic chimed in.

"Leave it to my girl," Bernie said. "She knows how to do things right. She's having the baby tomorrow morning. On my forty-sixth birthday, she's going to give me a son."

Well, that was too much for them. "A son?! How do you know it's going to be a boy?" Gribbs Tremonte asked.

"Sandy said so, that's how."

"Well, I tell you what," Gribbs said. "You're a sporting man, Bernie. I'll make you a bet. I'll bet you twenty thousand dollars that you have a girl."

A couple of people had been laughing, teasing, shmoozing. They stopped. A hush fell over the table.

"Take it or leave it."

"You got it," Bernie said. "Twenty grand that I have a son."

Gribbs said, "Twenty thousand says it's a girl."

And that was it. The bet was made. I almost fell off my chair.

"You better have a boy," Bernie whispered to me when the chit-chat began again.

"But what if it's a girl? Bernie, this is the craziest! I've seen you take some pretty cockeyed bets, but twenty thousand dollars on the sex of your child?!"

"Baby," he said to me, all blue eyes and big white grinning Chiclets, "tomorrow, on my forty-sixth birthday, I'm going to have a son *and* an extra twenty thousand dollars."

It was a good bet.

The next morning, we went to the hospital. Five hours later, I was the very tired but happy mother of a nine-pound baby boy.

After Tillie's great tales of childbirth, I'd opted for total unconsciousness. And the first thing I saw when I opened my eyes after the delivery was a crowd of men standing in the doorway of my hospital room. They looked like a jury. And the verdict was in. The moment I stirred, they started grinning and laughing and calling out congratulations. "He's beautiful," Josh the lawyer said. "You did great."

"We saw him," Uncle Vinny hollered.

"A bruiser," someone else called out. "Big, he's big."

And Red said, "Wait till Bernie sees him. He'll be here soon, Sandy. He sends his love."

There were twelve or thirteen men crowded around the door but Bernie wasn't among them. "He was sick, Sandy," Red explained after he'd shooed the others out of the place. "He hung in for a couple of hours. We were downstairs waiting for the news, but the doc said it could be hours yet and he told B to go home. Just between us, baby, he's not well. He's looking really bad, Sandy. You think he wouldn't be here right this minute if he was feeling okay?"

It was not what I wanted to hear. Whatever happiness I'd felt when I woke up disappeared at Red's words and a chilling ache set in. Tears welled as he spoke and, from that moment on, they came with baffling ease and suddenness. The private room overlooking Central Park that Bernie had ordered for me was filled with flowers. There were nineteen bouquets and floral arrangements already there when I opened my eyes and more arrived hourly. People sent baskets of fruit and jams, different kinds of salamis and assorted cheeses. There was even a box of grapefruits and oranges from some of the Florida *mishpocheh*. But there was no Bernie.

"Your mother's throwing a little birthday party for him this afternoon," Red said. "Then he'll be by. He'll see you tonight, Sandy. He's so proud of you. And he's so happy, kid. You did great. Have you seen your son yet?"

I shook my head. Bernie was sick again. Too sick to visit me. Too sick to see the son he'd been so excited about.

"So what are you going to name the kid?" Hot Dog asked, trying to cheer me up. "You got something picked out yet?"

"Jeffrey," I said. "We're naming him for Bernie's aunt Jenny, the one who owned the candy store his mother worked in. He loved her so much. She helped raise him. So we're naming him with a 'J' for Jenny. Jeffrey or Jason. I think it'll be Jeffrey. I like that best."

"Yeah. Jeffrey." Red rolled the name around. "Jeffrey Barton. Very slick. Very distinguished. What a kid."

"Jeffrey *Allen* Barton," I said.

"Allen. Nice," Red said. "Like my last name." Though hardly

anyone we knew ever used it, Hot Dog's real name was Harrison Allen.

"Not 'like,' " I said. "We're naming him for you, Red. Allen is for you."

"Sandy. Come on," he said, shaking his head as if I were putting him on.

"Ask Bernie. We already decided on that a long time ago. Jeffrey for Bernie's aunt Jenny. Allen for you."

"For me?" Red's grin nearly split his cheeks. "No shit," he said, and laughed. "You named him for me."

I was dozing when the nurse brought Jeffrey to me for the first time. "Mrs. Barton," she called. "It's feeding time. I brought you a bottle and your baby."

I opened my eyes. Each time I'd opened my eyes since Red had gone I'd felt that breath-sucking blueness, that empty-hearted ache. "I can't," I said, barely looking at her, turning away from the little blanket-wrapped creature in her arms.

"Of course you can, Mommy," she said. She looked like a kid, a little Puerto Rican nurse, with big dark eyes and long pretty hair trailing down the back of her uniform. "Here you go." With the authority of someone twice her age and size, she adjusted my arm and laid Jeffrey down onto it.

And once she did, once I looked at him, it was over. I was in love. I'd never seen or felt anything like it in my life. Here was this absolutely perfect, unblemished child with so much silky black hair that someone had made him bangs and tied back the rest in a bow to keep it out of his eyes. He was big, gorgeous, and clean with not a mark on him. And he went at the bottle like a chip off the old block. My side of the block, not Bernie's. At that point, even after the delivery, I was up to well over 170 pounds.

Jeffrey was an angel from the beginning. Tillie used to say it was like he knew he had to be good, that he knew he'd been born into a time of chaos and crisis and that his job was to give no trouble. He was the most peaceful, placid, loving baby, the blessing in a cursed family. His father met him later that day, at the evening feeding, and was as quickly smitten.

Bernie looked *shvakh*—pale and sickly, washed out, like a limp, wrung-out rag. He walked into the hospital room slowly because his legs were terribly swollen and aching. And he apologized for coming empty-handed, although he'd already sent a magnificent, huge floral arrangement that had arrived earlier in the day. I could see that it was all he could do to get himself to the hospital. But he

apologized for not bringing a gift or flowers—just as during his re-
cuperation before I gave birth he'd begun to apologize for not making love to me. He'd been too weak to walk, then. Too weak to get
himself a drink of water. But he felt he should have made love to
me. Like it was the tenth commandment of the Tough Guys Torah.
I was seven, eight, and nine months pregnant at the time. The doctor had told me my husband was dying. Sex hadn't been a priority
issue for me.

"So how are you, kid?" he asked. "You did good. I just saw him.
What a beauty. He's the biggest one in the nursery. And that hair."

"More than me." I tried to laugh. "What about you? You feeling
lousy?"

Don't, my mother shook her head, signaling me from the door.

"I'm okay. Tillie made me a nice little birthday party. She and
Marlene brought over a cake. It said, 'Happy Birthday, Dad.' It
was terrific."

"I'm glad," I said, swallowing back the tears. I couldn't think of
anything that didn't make me more depressed. Even Bernie's mentioning the birthday party made me think, oh, my God, what if this
is his last birthday? I wasn't there for the party. I'll never celebrate
another birthday with him.

CHAPTER THIRTEEN

———◆———

Life and Death

The Friday we brought Jeffrey home, Bernie was ecstatic and uncharacteristically shy.

We'd hired a baby nurse—you guessed it, nothing but the best. She was good enough for Steve Lawrence and Edie Gorme's children; she was good enough for Bernie Barton's son. And she really was good—a good, competent woman who almost wound up taking care of three patients instead of one. Her name was Ruth. Bernie asked her, would she mind very much if he put Jeffrey into the crib instead of her doing it. He was so happy and eager and heartbreakingly humble with Ruth.

"I don't mean to bother you, but you understand," he kept saying to her. "This is my first child in how many years—twenty-five? I have a twenty-five-year-old daughter. And this is the first boy born in my family in forty-six years. I don't mean to bother you, Ruth, but I want to spend time with him. I don't want to get in your way, Ruth, but I'd like to rock him for a while."

And he did. He took Jeffrey from my arms and put him into the magnificent blue and white canopied cradle. Then he sat because he was very weak. He sat in the white rocking chair and talked to his son through the crib bars. He called him Tiger. He'd say, "Tiger, I'm going to walk you in your carriage in the park and I'm going to sit with you in the playground."

Twice that day, with Ruth's approval, of course, he took Jeffrey out of the crib and fed him. He gave his son his first bottle at home. And he couldn't stop talking to him. It was like, in one afternoon,

Bernie was trying to describe to that little week-old baby the life-time he wanted them to have together. Every time I popped my head into the room, he was talking to Jeffrey: "And wait until you're old enough to play ball . . . And I'm going to read to you. You're going to love Shakespeare, Tiger."

My girlfriend Judy was at the house. By that time, she knew how sick Bernie was. She'd walked into my hospital room when I was crying uncontrollably. I'd been hysterical for hours. It was Judy who'd made the nurses phone Dr. Truppin. He gave me a sedative and stayed with me, holding my hand for forty-five minutes while I spilled out my tears and sorrow. And, of course, Judy heard everything. She became one of my rocks. She came to see me every day and called in between times and she was there when I brought Jeffrey home that first day.

Sleazeball Hymie was waiting for us, too, and my mother, and my sister, Marlene, I think. And, thank God, Red was there. He'd driven us home from the hospital.

But for most of the afternoon, Bernie sat in the baby's room talking to Jeffrey, hanging out with him, like he was one of the boys. Around sunset, we sat down to eat and Bernie said, "I don't feel well."

I asked, "Should I call the doctor?"

"No." He stood up. "I just don't feel well," he said again, and then he collapsed.

My mother stayed with Ruth and the baby while Hot Dog, Hymie, and I got Bernie to the hospital. It was Mount Sinai, the hospital from which we'd brought home his son that morning. Dr. Sealy had been called. He was waiting for us. We checked Bernie in and, four or five hours later, we left. He was alive. He was hooked up to the oxygen tank again with tubes running in and out of him and a mask over his face. He was very weak. It had been a close call. But he was alive.

The next three weeks were so hectic that I was almost too busy to be depressed. I was a new mother, brand new. I had an infant at home. Every morning I'd go marketing, clean the house, then rush over to the hospital to be with Bernie.

"Did you know he was taking amphetamines?" Dr. Sealy asked me one day. "All last month. That remission we saw—he was taking pills."

Red knew about it. He'd tried to stop B. "I said, 'Man, that speed's going to kill you with your bad heart.' I didn't find out about it till the day Jeffrey was born and he was coming by the hospital to see you, Sandy. I said, 'B, you're crazy popping those pills.' But he said he needed that get up and go. He wanted to see his boy, he said. He'd never make it to the hospital without them.''

So he hadn't gotten better. He'd only tried to convince me that he was feeling fine, tried to keep me from worrying about him during the last month of my pregnancy, tried to make life easier for me and for his son. But at a terrible price.

And he didn't seem to have learned a thing.

The day after his collapse, the party was in full swing again. Bernie's hospital room was crowded with friends, flowers, forbidden booze, and food. He was doing business from his sick bed. Now and then, I'd arrive to find his door locked. On those days, he might give me five or ten thousand dollars to take home; some days he'd ask me to bring him that amount. We had no health insurance. Guys like Bernie didn't apply for Blue Cross or Blue Shield. So, often the cash he gave me to take home one day—thousands of dollars stuffed into envelopes—I'd bring back the next to pay the hospital and doctor bills.

The hospital staff was crazy about Bernie. He'd send me out to buy perfume for his favorite nurses; there was always food in his room—not just the fruit and candy baskets friends had sent, but the coffee and fresh rolls, lox and bagels, deli sandwiches, Chinese food, chicken and ribs, and even charbroiled sirloin steaks that his visitors phoned out for or brought to him—and no nurse, orderly, technician, porter, or intern (or their families and pets, for that matter) ever went hungry when Bernie Barton was around. They'd drop into his room for a snack day or night.

Some came to nibble, some came to gawk. The hospital staff was never sure exactly who Bernie was or what he did, but they were awed by both the quantity and quality of his visitors. As usual, an endless parade of characters showed up, dressed in everything from jeans and lumber jackets to tuxedos. And the floor staff had their favorites.

The nurses were wild for Billy Daniels. They'd find excuses to come into the room while he was there and ask for his autograph. One evening, one of them asked Billy to sing "That Old Black Magic," the song he'd made famous. Then all the nurses started begging him to do it. And the wise guys were kidding Billy, and egging the nurses on. Finally, Bernie said, "Go ahead, Billy. Make them happy." Well, if someone had been dying down the hall there'd have been nobody to help him, because everyone on the floor was either squeezed into or lined up outside Bernie's room listening to Billy's little concert.

And that wasn't the only command performance held there. Bing Crosby's brother was in the room next to Bernie's. And one evening, while I was sitting in the lounge, Bing came in and we started talking. He told me how sick his brother was and I told him a little about Bernie and about just having had the baby. The next thing I knew, Bing was dropping into Bernie's room every now and then. And one night, he said something like, "If there's anything I can do for you, just let me know." And Bernie said, "Well, I'd love to hear you sing 'White Christmas.' "

Bing Crosby turned to me. "This is some guy you got here." He laughed. And then, "How can I refuse?" he said. So Bing Crosby sang "White Christmas" in Bernie's room. And, again, the hospital staff gathered 'round to sway and swoon.

Please. By the time George Raft showed up, they were ready to nominate Bernie for President.

One evening, I got off the elevator and everyone at the nursing station was eating Chinese food. I went down the hall to Bernie's room and there were nurses and orderlies and wise guys squeezed into the place among the flowers, fruit baskets, scotch bottles, racing forms, bags of ice, and what seemed like hundreds of white take out food containers.

Bernie had ordered up from Bill Hong's, one of the best and most expensive Chinese restaurants in the city and, naturally, he'd bought enough to feed the entire eighth floor. Just as naturally, no ban on eating the forbidden, heavily salted food was going to stop him from enjoying it. So there he was, sitting up in bed, holding court, laughing and eating Chinese food.

I was in the doorway, about to say, "What are you doing?!" but Dr. Sealy beat me to it. He pushed past me into the room. "What the hell are you doing?" he shouted at Bernie and, without a moment's hesitation, he cut through the crowd, wiped his hand across the hospital tray on Bernie's bed, and sent the containers flying. The walls were covered with Chinese food. Wise guys scattered like scared schoolboys. The nurses practically crawled out the door.

"What the hell is wrong with you, Bernie?" Dr. Sealy demanded. "Are you trying to kill yourself?"

Bernie looked at him. "Come on, Doc," he said, with this lopsided grin, this resigned smile. "Let's stop the bullshit. I'm not going to live much longer. Leave me alone and let me enjoy the time I've got."

The second week of Bernie's hospitalization, Uncle Vinny, who was a devout Catholic, stopped by to give me a lift to the hospital. "I've got an idea," he said. "Let's go to your synagogue first and have a prayer said for Bernie."

So we did. We drove to the *shul* where Bernie used to go for High Holy Day services and to say Kaddish for his father. I spoke to the rabbi and gave him some money and he said they'd make a prayer for Bernie at the temple that night.

"Thanks," I said to Vinny. "I'm glad we did that. Now let's go to the hospital. I want to see Bernie."

"In five minutes," Vinny promised. "Now, I want to go to my church and light a candle for B. What's the difference? Let's have all the gods going for it."

Vinny was so good to me. He was there like my right arm. All of Bernie's friends were. Usually I'd drive to the hospital by myself, but if I didn't feel up to it one of them would always show up to give me a lift. They'd take turns staying with Bernie. Hot Dog and Josh and Uncle Vinny were keeping a sort of tag-team vigil at the hospital. If one of them left the room to run an errand or to bring me to the hospital, another would stay with Bernie until I got there. They never left him alone.

Hymie was hanging around, too. He'd either be at the hospital or at our apartment. In fact, he was at the house a lot while I was out. When I'd come home from visiting Bernie, Ruth would tell me that Hymie had been there using the phone and cleaning out the refrigerator. I didn't like it. I remembered how he'd sniffed and snooped around when the house was crowded with people. I didn't even want to think about the liberties he'd take there on his own.

About this time, Bernie's childhood friend, Chalky, got out of prison. Now, at Bernie's request, I had written letters to Chalky for years and sent him Jewish New Year's cards and birthday gifts. I felt as though I knew the guy. But as fate would have it, I never ran into him at the hospital. I'd leave for twenty minutes to run an errand or I'd show up after dinner and Bernie would say, "Chalky was here. You just missed him, baby. Wait till you meet him, Sandy, you're going to love him."

"If I ever get out of here, Chalky and I are going to tear up this town," he'd say. "You can trust him, Sandy. If you ever need something, he's one of the people you'll be able to count on."

But one day I walked in and, again, Chalky had been there and gone. Only this time, Bernie shook his head. "There's something wrong with him. He's changed," he said. "But what the hell can you expect? A man does twelve consecutive years from the age of thirty-two to forty-four—he's got to come out bent."

Every now and then, Bernie would send everyone home and we'd just sit together in his room and watch TV. It was one of those nights. We were alone together. Out of the blue, Bernie turned to me and said, "You know, babe, I'm going to die. I'm going to be leaving you sooner than I thought—"

I started to protest, but he said, "No, don't say anything. Just listen to me, okay?" So I nodded, but I didn't want to hear anything he said. I couldn't stand the fact that he could mention his death, talk about it calmly, when I couldn't even think about it without being overwhelmed by fear and despair.

"I hope you've learned the things I taught you, Sandy," he said, and rattled off a couple of lessons: Don't get mad at anyone, get even. And be careful of people. You can trust but don't trust that much. And then he said, "When I die, baby, you and Red'll carry on the numbers business as much as you can. Red will look after you. Him you know you can depend on. Hymie's been taking care of a couple of loans I put out. He'll tell you who owes what and where the book is." He said there were a couple of other businesses I could expect money from and there were some that might dry up without him because they might not want to deal with a woman. And then he said, "And, of course, it goes without saying, if you need anything, you can trust Chalky. I hope you get to meet him before I die."

"Stop," I finally said. "You're not dying." But he brushed off my words.

"All of a sudden the pupil is smarter than the teacher? Stop kidding me," he said. "We both know what's what. I just thought we'd have more time, kiddo. I'm sorry."

I was fighting back tears, but I was also relieved that Bernie knew how sick he was and that he didn't seem scared or angry. He was doing what he always did—trying to take care of me. Trying to teach me. Trying to prepare me to take care of myself. And his son.

He was heavily medicated. Sometimes he'd be a little woozy. His thoughts would wander, his conversations would start and stop abruptly.

"I know sometimes you've been unhappy," he'd say, "and I'm sorry, Sandy. I wish I could've done better by us. But this is the way our life is. This life-style. It's almost like being in a maze. You can't find which way is out.

"Maybe I didn't do it right all the time but I did it mȳ way, on my own," he'd say. "Yeah, I'm a member of the mob, a gangster, whatever. I only know one kind of life. But I've never been beholden to anyone; I never took orders. And you know what, baby, it's how I am. I can't help it. What's wrong with me, they can't fix.

"Take good care of my son, Sandy. Maybe from him you'll get what I promised you. A decent life. You'll raise him to be a man, a good man, an honest man."

And he said that when he met me he fell madly in love and that he'd meant it when he promised me all those things—a house, marriage, and a baby carriage. And he said he was sorry now that he'd probably never see his son grow up. He'd never be able to walk in the park with him or talk with him or teach him things. He was sorry that life did this to him and to me.

While I was grateful that he could tell me these things, needless to say, these conversations often left me shaken and depressed. I'd leave the room and hurry down the hall to the lounge to have a cigarette, and I'd wind up either staring at the wall or crying uncontrollably. I was crying one afternoon and there was an elderly lady in the lounge. "What's wrong?" she asked me.

"I have a very sick husband who might die," I said.

And she said, "My husband is definitely dying. It's any day now." She said to me, "Don't cry now. Don't let him see you cry. Don't let anybody see you crying now. When he does die, you'll have all the time in the world to cry."

I never forgot what she said. She was right.

Three weeks. Three weeks was the time Bernie usually stayed in the hospital during a bout of illness. And now that he'd been at Mount Sinai exactly three weeks, he wanted to go home. It was a Friday night. Everyone else had left. Bernie said to me, "I feel all right. I want to get out of here. If I'm going to die, I want to die at home."

"You can't be serious," I said.

"Don't tell me I can't be serious. Who the hell do you think you're talking to. You know better than me all of a sudden? Is that what you're saying? I feel fine. And I'm going home."

We argued a little and then, to placate him, I said, "Well, at least wait until you see Doctor Sealy later on tonight or tomorrow morning and just ask him what he thinks."

"Sure. Okay," Bernie said. The little skirmish had tired him out. Or else, he was pacifying me. But he agreed to check with Dr. Sealy before doing anything.

Saturday morning I was in the kitchen warming the baby's bottle. It was a hot day at the end of June. The terrace door was open. Ruth was in the nursery getting Jeffrey dressed for a stroll in the park behind the house. In the three weeks since I'd brought him home from the hospital I'd had so little time to spend with this beautiful little boy. I was lamenting that fact, looking forward to feeding him his bottle and just sitting with him for a few minutes before rushing back to Bernie, when the doorbell rang. Barefoot, in a housecoat, I shlepped my 170 pounds over to the door, opened it, and almost went into cardiac arrest.

Standing there, in a trenchcoat and bedroom slippers, with nothing else on underneath, was Bernie. He shoved past me into the apartment. "Don't say a word!" he fumed. "I don't want to hear a fucking word out of your mouth about the goddam hospital or what am I doing here. I told you I was coming home. This is my house and if you don't like it, you can get your ass out of here. Not a word, Sandra. I'm warning you."

Typical. He was yelling at me so that I wouldn't yell at him. "All right," I said. "Calm down. Are you naked under that?"

"Don't do it, Sandra." He waved a finger under my nose, cautioning me against laughing at how he looked. "I spoke to Sealy and he said 'no way.' And I told him I've got things to do here. Important things—"

"And you left against his advice? You just walked out?"

"Of course I did. I have a son I don't even know yet—"

"Okay, okay. Stop yelling. You want to scare your son to death?"

"No. I want to see him. Where is he?"

"Put some clothes on first, Bernie. You look like a pervert."

"Don't start!" he hollered, but he went into the bedroom and changed his clothes and then he went right into the baby's room and started buttering up Ruth to let him feed Jeffrey. So twenty minutes after the great escape, there he was sitting in the rocking chair cooing to Jeffrey and giving him his bottle.

I stood in the doorway for a second, watching them, and Bernie saw me. "Can you deny me this?" he asked. "If I'm going to die, first I'm going to spend some time with my child."

After a while, Ruth took the baby out to the park and Bernie, who was clearly exhausted, got into bed and fell asleep.

I didn't know what to do. I was scared stiff. The minute he dozed off, I called Hot Dog and Vinny and Josh and told them what had happened. Then I got on the phone with Dr. Sealy, who by this time, of course, knew that Bernie had bolted. He said, "I don't like it. I told him not to do it, but we've got to deal with it the way it is for now. We'll keep him in the house and see how it goes."

I was shaking. I whispered into the phone. "Doctor Sealy, what if something happens? What if he—"

"I'll be by this afternoon with his medication and I'll have a talk with him. Try not to worry. You've been through a lot in the past month, Sandy. With Bernie. With being a new mother. You've got to take care of yourself, too. You need some rest."

"Doctor Sealy, I don't think I can do it," I said softly. I didn't want Bernie to hear me. I was ashamed. I didn't want anyone to hear me. "I don't think I can take care of him now. I don't have the strength left or the energy or the mentality for it. I'm afraid of what will happen here. I don't want him to die in this house. I know I sound selfish, but I really don't want that. I have a baby here. A newborn son I haven't spent two minutes with. Doctor Sealy, please, I don't want to be selfish, but this apartment is all I have. It's the only place I've had where I could find a little peace and quiet in the past three weeks. And I'm afraid to look at him, Doctor Sealy. I can't live with that feeling of gloom and doom every time I look at Bernie."

"I know," Sealy kept saying. "Just hang on, Sandy. I'll be there as soon as I can. Take it easy. Try to get some rest yourself."

Dr. Sealy arrived about four in the afternoon. He examined Bernie, then read him the riot act. That he was to take it easy. He had to only eat what I gave him and I was to watch his diet. No salt in his food. No excitement. He was supposed to stay in bed and rest, quietly and calmly.

I knew it would never work. Bernie was incapable of being still, of sticking to a diet, of not getting excited. But I didn't say anything. When Dr. Sealy was leaving, he took me aside and said, "The first sign of any difficulty, no matter what it is—if he sneezes too often or goes to the bathroom more than normal, anything—you're to call me right away."

Later that day, Uncle Vinny came by and then Hot Dog and Josh showed up. My mother came over. Only the close friends were there and they kept up my morale and they made Bernie laugh and they fussed over the baby and kept saying how much he looked like his father. Which was true. The resemblance was uncanny then and now.

So Saturday ended quietly.

On Sunday the telephone started to ring. Everyone who'd gone to the hospital to visit Bernie and been surprised to find someone else in his room, or who'd phoned him there and been told the patient was gone, had by Sunday discovered that he was home. Flowers started arriving, baskets of fruit, boxes of candy. The buzzer from the lobby went off every ten minutes to announce another delivery. The doorbell never stopped chiming. The telephones rang so constantly that by ten A.M., I had to take them both off the hook.

Then people started dropping by. Hymie showed up with the enormous woman he'd left his wife and children for, and the wise guys came, the union *machers*, the bookies and numbers runners, the uptown crowd in their snappy clothes and pointy alligator shoes, the boys from Little Italy all dressed for church, the madams and ex-madams, some mistresses, some wives. And out came the cigars, the cigarettes, the grass, the booze. People would come in, look around and head straight for the phones to tell their friends to come by.

Bernie was home. The party was on.

Only the nursery was off-limits. Thank God for Ruth, who stood guard and forbade anyone to enter the baby's room. Other than that, there was no privacy anywhere. It was as if I was on public display. It was only a month since I'd given birth. I was heavy and depressed. I walked around constantly in a housecoat. I hadn't bothered about a manicure or had my hair done since the delivery. And I didn't care. I didn't care how I looked or dressed or behaved. There were some men I had to be polite to and I was. There were medicines I had to give to Bernie at the right times and I did. I had to inject him. I had to prepare his food the way the doctor had ordered it prepared. I did all this mechanically, like a zombie. And I served coffee and cleaned up the drinks and cups and the cake plates.

The party lasted from Sunday through Tuesday. Tillie came as often as possible to help out. And Red and Vinny and Josh were almost always there and there was another friend of Bernie's, Morty, and a couple of other guys I could depend on. They were the only ones I spoke to at all. The others, the ones who came to pay respect or talk business, I hardly acknowledged. At one point, in the kitchen with my mother, I cried. I didn't care who might walk in and find us. I couldn't hold it together anymore. I couldn't even get into my own bathroom to cry in privacy because the door was locked and who knew who might be in there or what might be going on.

I was feeling very sorry for myself. I said, "Ma, I'm coming apart. Why is this happening to me, Mama? I just had a baby. I waited my whole life to have a home and a husband and a baby. Why is this happening now, why to me?"

"It's an old Jewish expression, *mamela*," Tillie said, wiping my tears with a corner of the dishcloth. " 'This is the way God voted the day you were born.' *Vos is geshribed, is geshribed.* What is written, is written."

Wednesday was a bright and sunny day. That morning, the nurse was getting Jeffrey ready to go out. She'd sit with him in the sunshine in the little park behind the house for a couple of hours each day. About eleven o'clock, Bernie said to me, "I want you to be out of here between twelve and two if you can. Red will be here with me, so I'll be okay. I'm expecting some people."

Because of the way I looked and felt, I hadn't left the house in days. But I put on a pair of sunglasses and told Ruth I'd be going downstairs with her and the baby. We were walking toward the elevator. Ruth was wheeling the carriage and I was holding on to the bar like a second child, like a frightened but obedient sister, when I saw the short Spanish-speaking guy with the suitcase coming toward us. He had company this time. A second man with a second suitcase. I just kept walking and the men passed us and, of course, headed right for our apartment.

When we returned a couple of hours later, Bernie called me into the bedroom. He was wearing a white T-shirt and shorts, but there was a pair of trousers lying at the foot of the bed. I could tell he'd gotten up and dressed for his visitors. Now he was stretched out again, propped up on two pillows, looking pretty worn out. There were two wrapped packages next to him. "How's the kid?" he asked.

"An angel. He slept in the sun. Ruth is going to feed him now."

"Good. That's good," Bernie said, but I could see he was distracted. "Sandy, I want you to take these packages to the vault tomorrow. And there's a message in there from me to you, in with the packages. If I die, the message tells you what to do with the contents of these packages, all right?"

"All right," I echoed flatly. I didn't ask questions. Intuition told me what Bernie didn't need to anymore—that I was better off not knowing. I didn't want to ask or argue anything. I did what I'd been doing since Bernie had come home from the hospital—what I knew I had to do, automatically, mechanically, without thought or question. It was the way I'd made it through the past four days and, so far, against my expectations, I was still moving. I hadn't collapsed or broken down in front of anyone but my mother or started screaming—all of which I'd felt like doing almost every waking minute of the four days.

It was a quiet afternoon. For some reason, the house was empty. Maybe Bernie had asked everyone but Red to stay away. Whatever the reason, there were no strangers around that afternoon and, thank God, because shortly after the Spanish guys left Lido paid us a call. And he was dressed up not to be believed—all in white with his biggest and best jewelry sparkling and clanging with every velvet-slippered step he took. The four thousand gold and silver bracelets, neck chains studded with diamonds and emeralds, rings on every finger, diamonds and star sapphires set in platinum and rubies in pink gold. The jewelry, oh, the jewelry!—it crossed my mind to take Bernie's gun down from the closet and hold Lido up. Oh, yes, and he had brought a gift for Jeffrey. He was standing there in all his splendor carrying a floor-to-ceiling teddy bear he'd just bought at F.A.O. Schwarz for the baby.

Anyway, Ruth, whose eyes almost fell out of her head at the sight of this man, took the bear and I ushered Lido into Bernie's bedroom. After a few pleasantries, Lido asked me to make the room dark. He'd brought a tape over with him which he asked me to put on the stereo. It was African music, soft, very, very soothing. While the music was going, Lido chanted and prayed and shook rattles over Bernie's sick bed. The Santoro's eyes rolled and his body was waving back and forth like cattails in the Jersey swamps. After a while, he tied a red ribbon entwined with herbs around my waist and told me to wear it for twenty-four hours. He put *santos*, plaster saints, and pots of incense, and herbs and God only knows what else under Bernie's bed. And he said this would make Bernie well and protect the house from evil. "You will not die," Lido promised. "You will recover at once to full health and take up your lives as before."

Bernie thanked him. Then Lido sat around and chatted and had black coffee laced with brandy and smoked some pot.

After he left, I said, "What did he charge you this time?"

Bernie said, "Absolutely nothing. His showing up here today

was a complete surprise. I never called him. I never said a word to him about being sick. And he wouldn't take a cent from me today."

It had been almost one week since Bernie came home. During that week, Dr. Sealy had come by once a day, sometimes twice to check him. Technicians came to take blood. A young doctor showed up with a portable cardiograph machine. And all in all it seemed that Bernie was holding his own.

"Let's call this a state of remission or a quiet period," Sealy said. "But, Sandy, the slightest show of anything wrong, day or night, you call me."

"Is it possible that he'll be all right?" I asked. "I mean, he's home. He walked out of the hospital. You say he's doing okay. Maybe he'll make it."

Dr. Sealy shook his head. "The tests we did in the hospital show that his heart muscle is deteriorating." He could see that I didn't understand. "His heart isn't pumping right. It's getting weaker. Eventually his kidneys will go and there's no way he can be put on a machine. It just wouldn't work. What will probably get him is encephalitis, or what's commonly called sleeping sickness. When the heart and kidneys are damaged this way, waste matter backs up and causes brain damage. Eventually, he'll go into coma. He's not strong enough to fight this, Sandy. Though God knows he's trying. He's putting up a hell of a fight. But he's not going to make it, Sandy. I'm sorry."

The very next day, Bernie started to cough. By mid-day he was running a high fever. By Saturday night, Sealy rushed over and wanted to put him back in the hospital. Bernie refused, fought him tooth and nail. "No way. You're out of your mind if you think I'm going back there."

"This is serious, Bernie," Sealy said. "You're sicker than you know."

"Come on, come on. You're not getting rid of me that fast," he said, trying to laugh, trying to joke, through the coughing spasm.

I walked Dr. Sealy to the elevator. He said, "I don't care how you do it or what you have to do, Sandy, you get that man back into Mount Sinai. Leave a message on the service and I'll meet you there. He's had a relapse. He's got to be hospitalized."

I went back into the apartment. "Bernie," I said. "Sweetheart, you've got to go back. I can't take care of you here. I'm scared, Bernie. Really, I am. I have the baby to take care of. And I'm so tired, sweetheart. I can't give you what you need now, Bernie. You've got to go back where they have nurses twenty-four hours a day and the right medicine and machines right there. I can't do it."

He went crazy. He began cursing me, accusing me of not caring about him. "No, it's not that you can't take care of me. You don't fucking want to. You're too goddamn lazy. Don't give me that shit about the baby. The baby, you've got nothing to do with him. You've got a nurse. A housekeeper. You've got your mother and Marlene to help out. You've got everything you need. You're trying to get rid of me, that's all. What, am I ruining your fun? You can't stand looking at me? No, when I'm flush, when I got money coming out of my ass, then you'll be happy to hang around, right? You're no damn good. You and that fucking quack, Sealy. You're trying to dump me. Both of you! Well, fuck you. Fuck you both. I'm home. This is my home! You don't want to nurse a sick man, get the fuck out!"

It went on like that for two hours. Screaming. Coughing. His face was bright red. He was having trouble breathing, but he wouldn't stop shouting. Finally, he took a couple of sleeping pills and fell out.

I got on the phone and spoke with Uncle Vinny and Josh the lawyer and I talked to Hot Dog. I called all his close friends and told them what was going on. And they all said, Sandy, you'll just have to do it. "Throw him out," Vinny said.

"How can I throw him out? The man's in bed. He's dying."

"No matter what. No matter how sick he is. Throw him out," Vinny advised.

The next day, he was sicker. The fever was higher. He was coughing more. Dr. Sealy said he'd send an ambulance.

"But he won't go," I tried explaining again. "Doctor Sealy, what do you want me to do? I can't physically lift him and put him in an ambulance. You'll have to take him out with a derrick."

"You'd better do something," Sealy said. "Carry on, scream, rant and rave. Do whatever you have to do to get Bernie out of the house and back into the hospital where he belongs. Or else, Sandy, he's going to die right there in your bed."

Bernie and I fought all that morning. I was out of my mind, crying, begging, screaming and, finally, cursing, too.

"That's it," Bernie shouted suddenly. He threw back the covers and hauled himself out of bed. "Get out of here this minute, or I'll kill you."

I cowered in a corner but I wouldn't leave. I thought he was going to keel over right then and there. He was that weak. Oh, but what a set of lungs on him and oh, the power of his anger. It was like a drug, like speed—it turned him sharp, raw, and fast. He got on the phone to Hot Dog and, staring daggers at me, demanded that Red come over and get him out of the house immediately. He slammed down the phone and started getting dressed and then he ran over to the hassock and took whatever cash was in there.

All the while, he screamed at me. "You want me out, you bitch? I'm out of here. I don't have to listen to you anymore. I'm checking into a hotel." He was opening and closing drawers, throwing things out of them, looking for money. "I'm taking everything. I'm going to clean out the vault. You'll have nothing. You're no damn good, you whore. You cunt." Slamming closet doors. Stuffing cash into his pants pocket though the zipper wasn't even zipped yet. "I'll get even with you for this. You want me out? You want to throw me out in the street when I'm dying? I'll get you! Even if I die, I'll get you for this!"

In the middle of this insanity, Hot Dog showed up. He was sitting on the sofa watching Bernie fly around the place cursing me, grabbing money and shaking his fist. Red winked at me as if to say, Let him talk. Don't worry, I'll get him to the hospital.

"Let's go!" Bernie hollered. And he was out the door, with Red loping along behind him.

A couple of frantic phone calls to Dr. Sealy and a couple of hours later, Hot Dog called.

"Where are you? Is Bernie with you? Is he all right?"

"Oh, Mr. B is fine and dandy. We are in the Presidential Suite of the Plaza Hotel is where we are. Your man says if he's dying, he's going to die in the Presidential Suite no matter what it costs him. You've got to admit, Sandy, our boy has style."

"Should I come over?"

"Not if you value your life. Woman," Red said, in that very emphatic tone of voice, "he says he hates your guts right now and he's going to kill you. And he is just wild enough, Sandy. Do not come, do not call. Give me time alone with him. He brought his medication with him, so he'll be okay. By Monday, I'll have him back in the hospital."

I didn't sleep much Sunday night. My mother came over and she and Ruth and I were up for most of the night talking. We were in the living room having coffee. It was past midnight when something hit me.

"Mom," I said. "I bet he took the vault key and he's going to clean out our box."

"Don't be crazy," Tillie said. "How would he even think of that? The man was angry, crazy, but he's sick, Sandy. You think he's going to stroll into a bank and take all your money?"

"I'm right, Ma. I've got a feeling, an instinct about this." I went into the bedroom to the drawer in which I kept most of our keys. The only vault key we had in the house was the one to the Mr. and Mrs. Barton box. A duplicate of it, along with all the other vault keys, was at my cousin's house. Sure enough, the vault key was missing.

"He's going to clean out the vault. He said he was going to take all the money and, I guess, he meant it."

"Well, he's sick. He's just being a little *meshugge*."

"I know. But when he's back in the hospital and there are bills to pay, what then? He's checked himself into the Plaza. He's living it up. I know this man. He could blow every cent we have in a fit of spite and there'd be nothing left for the hospital and doctors."

"What can you do?"

"What can I do? I can beat him at his own game. I'm going to Francine's to get the key tonight and first thing tomorrow I'm going to the vault."

Tillie laughed. "Look at you, Mrs. Tough Guy."

The next morning, Monday at a quarter to nine, in sunglasses with a kerchief over my unwashed hair, I was waiting outside the bank. The minute the doors opened, I hurried down to the vault and cleared out our safety deposit box. I didn't close the account. I just cleared out all the money and then, as an afterthought, I threw in a single that I had with me. I left one dollar in the box. I didn't want to take the money home, so I told the man I wanted another box under the name of Sandra Barton, alone. I paid for it, signed the signature card, locked the money inside, and left the vault.

I walked up the steps, breathing a sigh of relief and wondering where I'd gotten the nerve to do what I'd just done, where I'd gotten the brains to open a new box and leave the money where it would be safe. I heard voices, footsteps. I looked up. And there was Bernie, all pumped up, with Red on one side of him and a black man I'd never seen before on the other, coming down the stairs. A brass rail separated us.

I kept walking up and they kept coming down. "You!" Bernie screamed. I thought he'd have his final heart attack right there. But I was as angry as he was and as arrogantly pumped up. "You thieving, no-good bitch," he screamed. "Conniving cunt! Did you take the money? It's not enough you want me dead, you want me broke, too?!" Red grabbed his arm.

"Tough shit, tough guy," I hollered back at him. "The early worm wins!" It wasn't till later, in the taxi headed home, that I realized I'd gotten it wrong, that I'd meant the early *bird.* "I was here first!" I shouted, and then I ran out of the bank as fast as my legs could carry me.

Tillie couldn't stop laughing when I told her what had happened. She was holding her belly. Tears were running out of her eyes. And she kept gasping and saying, "God forgive me, I know it's not funny. It's not nice. God forgive me."

I wasn't home ten minutes when Bernie called. I heard the street noises in the background and I knew he was at a payphone. "I'm going to kill you, Sandra," he growled. "I'm not kidding this time. You think you're going to get away with this stunt? You're crazier than I thought. And you're dead, lady. You and your mother and you better get the kid out of the house because I'm going to blow up the whole fucking place!"

With that, Red got on the phone. He was hysterical, laughing. "You should have seen your face. What a look when you saw us. Woman, you were wild. I'll never forget that scene as long as I live!"

"He's going to kill me?" I asked.

"Just keep cool. I'm going to try to get him back into the hospital," Red said.

That afternoon, Bernie collapsed at the Plaza. Red reached Dr. Sealy and they returned Bernie by ambulance to Mount Sinai. I rushed over to the hospital to find out that Bernie had asked Security to bar me from the room.

Red walked me to the lounge and filled me in on what had happened. After his phone call to me, Bernie had gone back to the hotel. "He was steaming," Red said. "You know how he gets, he couldn't shut up. The more he thought about it, talked about it, the wilder he got. He hit the phones and called Vinny and Josh, Cokey, Frank, Muttel, Farvel. He was calling the whole world, telling them how you robbed him and how he's going to get even with you. Sandy, he even tried to put a contract out on you. He called a guy to put a hit on you and then he went crazy because the guy he called wouldn't do it. He'd already heard what went down and refused to get mixed up in the shit. I think that was the last straw," Red said. "He started coughing and spitting up and then he collapsed."

Uncle Vinny came into the lounge. I was crying. "He hates me, Vinny. He tried to put a hit out on me."

"He doesn't hate you," Vinny said, putting an arm around me. "He's just running scared now. He knows it's over, but he doesn't know how to lay down. So he's blaming you. But I'll tell you something, Sandy. He's also proud of you. He said to me, 'Look how her mind works, Vinnie. I taught her too well.' "

"It must be terrible for him to believe I would rob him. I wasn't robbing him, Vinny. I'm going to need the money for the bills, his bills. Do you think I'd hurt him?"

"Of course not. And you did the right thing. I've known this man for years. He had that money, he might've gotten on a plane and gone off to Europe. He could've hit Vegas and lost it all on a throw of the dice. No one thinks you robbed him, Sandy. You did the right thing."

Josh the lawyer drove me home. "He can't believe it. He can't get over how you beat him." Josh laughed. "He says you should have worked for the CIA. So Red says, 'What about the FBI?' And Bernie said, 'Naw, they're too dumb.' "

It only took two days for him to relent. Red walked me into the hospital room. "So how's my son?" Bernie asked.

"Gorgeous and good as gold—what else?" I said.

We never mentioned what happened at the bank.

Bernie was in the hospital for seven weeks. Specialists came from Boston to try to put him on a kidney machine, but just as Dr. Sealy had predicted, it didn't work. I went to Mount Sinai every day. It was like going to a job. I'd get up early, shower, dress, make sure the house was stocked with whatever the nurse and baby needed. Ruth had only been able to stay with us for six weeks before moving on to her next baby, her next commitment.

Jeffrey's new nurse was a wonderful Jamaican woman named Nora who was in her mid-forties and had a son in the Navy. So clean she smelled like fresh laundry. Nora was as gentle and caring to me as she was to the baby. Her good-natured disposition and lilting accent enchanted everyone who met her. So I'd leave Jeffrey in Nora's capable hands and then I'd drive over to the hospital, almost always with cash in my bag to pay the bills, which mounted as he got sicker.

Between the heavy medication and the progression of the illness, Bernie was in and out of consciousness most of the time. People still came up to see him. They'd come and go. Sometimes, he'd be able to talk and kid around. Sometimes, now, he'd want to be alone. Chalky called while I was there one day. I answered the phone. "No," Bernie said. "I don't want him here. I'm not in the mood. He's gone stir-crazy, Sandy. I love that man. I'd do anything for him. But I don't want him hanging around now."

There were many nights when I slept at the hospital. And there were many nights when Red or Vinny stayed over, too. They'd sleep in the lounge. I'd sleep in the room with Bernie, but it was a different sleep he had now. He was in a semi-coma and I'd talk to him. "You've got to hang on," I'd beg him. "You can't die. You can't leave me this way. You promised we'd have a regular life—a house and baby. You promised me, sweetheart. You've got to hang on."

It was weird. I felt so attached to him. I felt that I was dying with him. And I wanted to live, to continue, to have a life. And I believed that it would be over, my life with his, when he died. So I wished he would stay in a coma forever. Because it would give me something to do. I'd have to come to the hospital. I'd talk to him. I'd comb his hair. I'd do anything so that I could still be married to him. I'd realized that once Bernie died, I wouldn't be married anymore. I know how simple, how stupid, that must seem, but it left me breathless with terror. I wouldn't be Bernie's wife. I wouldn't be married. Then what would I do, who would I be? I'd be nothing. Nobody. Alone.

I got into this funny habit. Every night after I left the hospital, before I went to bed—and it could have been one or two in the morning, it didn't matter—I'd have to find out if Bernie was all right. It was too late to call his room. But there was a wonderful old woman who was the floor nurse on duty after midnight. I'd call her. Her name was Mrs. Zimmerman. I'd say, "Mrs. Zimmerman, this is Mrs. Barton. Is my husband still alive?" And she'd say, "Stop that, relax yourself. He's fine." It was unbelievable. I couldn't sleep unless I heard this kind woman's comforting voice.

Bernie slipped into a coma. All his close friends still came to the hospital every day. We'd take turns clapping hands, making noises, to see if he'd respond. I'd play music and talk to him, but it was no good most of the time. Once in a while, though, he'd stir and come awake. Once he said, "Sandy, we had such little time together. I thought we'd have more." Another time, he opened his eyes and I said, "Do you know who I am?" "Yes," he said. "You're the mother of my beautiful son. Take care of him."

It was a Friday night, August 6, 1965. Bernie had been in a coma ninety percent of the time for the past three weeks. But that evening, everybody was there. Hot Dog, Vinny and Josh, of course. But there were many other visitors, as well. In fact, my uncle Meyer, my father's brother who'd kept in touch with us for all those years, showed up at the hospital that night. My mother came with him. It was like one big party again. People were walking in and out of the room. Some of the staff brought us coffee and hung around to chat. Of course, the place was still bright with flowers and gift baskets. And in the middle of everything, Bernie woke up. His blue eyes were clear, alert. He said hello to everybody as if nothing had happened. He looked beautiful. He looked rested, as if he'd just woken from a long sleep.

We were all talking to him. "I heard you were sick," Uncle Meyer said. "But look at you. You look better than me."

"That's not so hard to do," my mother teased. And Bernie actually laughed.

He was chatting with Red and Vinny when I pulled my mother out into the hallway. "Mom, you see, it's a miracle!" I said. "He's going to make it. He'll live to see his son Bar Mitzvahed, yet. I know he will. It's a miracle!"

She shook her head. "No, sweetheart, this won't be. There's an old Jewish superstition, Sandy. When someone is ready to die, God gives them a chance to say goodbye. That's what's happening, *mamela.* He's ready."

I thought she was crazy. I didn't believe her. I couldn't. When we left the hospital that night, my uncle, my mother, Vinny, and I went out for coffee together. I was so happy. "A miracle is taking place," I said. "Something wonderful is happening."

At seven-thirty Saturday morning the hospital called. "You'd better come over," one of our favorite nurses said. "He's bad. I'm sorry. I think you'd better hurry."

By the time I got there, Bernie was dead.

CHAPTER FOURTEEN

My *Gutta Better*

I walked out of the hospital and stared numbly into the sunlight at Central Park across the street. The pills Dr. Sealy had given me were making me light-headed. My eyes felt raw from crying. My throat hurt from screaming, aloud and silently. Hot Dog was at my elbow. Vinny and Josh followed us through the door. I was very tired. I didn't feel like I had the strength to stand. So Red and I sat down on the hospital steps, and Vinny and Josh leaned up against the railing.

"What do I do now?" I asked.

Josh said, "Let's go home."

Vinny nodded. "We'll go home and get some coffee, then you'll make plans."

I didn't want to move. Every step took me farther from Bernie and closer to a terrifying uncertainty. I didn't want to lose sight of the hospital. Sitting on the steps kept me attached to it. To a life that was receding faster than I could think. I'd had my baby and left my husband here. From this building, I'd brought home a new life and lost my old one. I doubled over suddenly, clutching my stomach. The ache was there. The loss. The feeling I'd first known as a girl when my father left. It had grown with me, that yawning emptiness. It was too big now ever to be repaired.

"Come on, Sandy," Red said, standing, offering me his hand. "Let's go home. There's nothing left for us to do here."

The boys took me home and stayed with my mother and me. She was terribly sad, Tillie. She had grown to love Bernie so much and now she grieved for him. But she was also my tower of strength. Nora put up coffee and we all sat down together and stirred the cups listlessly. Red was pacing. Everyone was stunned and sad. But at least we were together.

In less than an hour, the phones started ringing. Josh answered one of the first calls. I heard him say, "Yes, he's dead," so I assumed it was a friend. But Josh's voice was off, he sounded annoyed, snappish. "Yes, I'm sure," he said. Then, "This is Josh Loew. I'm an attorney and a friend of the family. And if you've got a problem, why don't you go over to Riverside Chapel and pry open the coffin!" He slammed down the phone.

Vinny looked up when Josh came back into the room. "FBI?" he said.

Josh said, "How did you know?"

Vinny said, "I thought something was going on. Sandy, when I'd pick you up to drive you over to Mount Sinai, I knew it. I saw the bastards. I didn't want to worry you. They were parked right outside your door for weeks."

"Scum," Josh said. " 'Are you sure he's dead?' the guy kept asking. Scum bastards."

"Did he say why?" Red asked.

Josh looked over at my mother. "Naw," he said. "He didn't say."

I knew he was lying to protect Tillie's feelings and probably mine. Later, Vinny told me that the FBI was setting Bernie up for a drug bust; a conspiracy charge of some kind. They'd had a tap on the house phones and on Bernie's hospital room telephones, too. He said Josh had told him the FBI agent who'd called an hour after Bernie died had sounded almost pissed off that he'd been cheated out of a bust.

After that, the telephone just started ringing. People had heard that Bernie had died. The FBI weren't the only ones who cared or found it hard to believe. After a while, I gathered my strength and changed my clothes, and the boys took me crosstown to Riverside Chapel on Amsterdam Avenue to make the funeral arrangements.

"When do you think you want to have it?" Hot Dog asked on the way over.

"Right away. Sunday," I said. "He's Jewish. I want him buried according to tradition, right away."

"Tomorrow?" Vinny was surprised. "That soon?"

I looked at Josh, who came from a good Jewish family. "That's how it's done," Josh told them. "But Sandy, there'll be a lot of people from out of town who might want to come."

"He was very well-liked," Vinny added. "He had friends every-where. I think he would've wanted them to have a chance to say goodbye."

"I don't care," I said. But by the time we got to the chapel, I'd come up with a compromise.

I picked out a beautiful casket and reserved the largest chapel, which held about two hundred people and, just in case the boys were right, I asked the funeral director for the latest possible time on Sunday, which turned out to be two-thirty in the afternoon, so that anyone who wanted to come in from out of town to pay re-spects to Bernie would have at least twenty-four hours to do it. It was also a Jewish tradition that time be made for people to gather the night before the funeral, and so the last thing I arranged at Riv-erside that morning was for the viewing, as it was called, from seven to ten that night.

The boys brought me back to the apartment and left. My mother, the baby, and my sister were there, but I felt very alone. I wandered from room to room. I tried not to look at anything. Bernie had been right when he'd shouted, "This is my house!" He was dead, but ev-erything in the apartment belonged to him. And everything that caught my eye reminded me that he wasn't coming home—from the portrait of him in the living room to the cuff link tray on the bedroom dresser to the shaving gear in the bathroom to the highball glasses on the kitchen sink drain that Marlene had used for milk but Bernie'd always used for scotch. Everything looked as lonely and abandoned as I felt. So I tried not to look or feel or think.

When finally I did break down, it came out cockeyed—not about the loss of Bernie but about my not having a dress to wear to the viewing. I'd caught a glimpse of myself in the bedroom mirror dur-ing my aimless pacing. And suddenly I was crying uncontrollably. Tillie rushed into the bedroom and put her arms around me.

"I have nothing to wear," I sobbed. "Look how fat I am. Look how terrible, how disgusting I am. I have nothing to wear. I've been wearing maternity clothes." What I'd thought but didn't dare say aloud was that Bernie's casket would be open at the viewing and I kept thinking: He'll see me like this. He always cared so much about the way I looked, he tried so hard to teach me how to take care of myself, how to put on makeup, how to dress. Now, with his casket open, he'll see me and be repulsed. "I want to be beautiful for him, Ma," I tried to explain, in a ragged voice.

I borrowed a black chemise from a girlfriend and someone gave

me a black lace kerchief for my head. And I did the best I could. By
six o'clock, I couldn't wait any more. "Let's go now. I want to be
with him," I told my mother. "I don't want him to be alone."

I wanted to get to the funeral parlor and see his face. I felt as long
as I could look at him, he wouldn't really be dead. I'd have a husband.

So we went to the viewing early. And, God, the sight that greeted
me. There were so many people already there. It was a stifling hot
August night and people came in three-piece suits and ties and
many of the women wore long-sleeved dresses. The casket was
open and draped over it was a *blanket* of red roses. I had never seen
anything like it, hundreds of red roses! And the walls of the room,
the biggest viewing room they had, were lined with flowers. We'd
arrived early and there were at least twenty or thirty extravagant
floral arrangements, from towering bouquets to a horseshoe of
white roses with a gold sash across the middle that said, "Love ya,
Ricky."

"What is that?" I said to Josh. "It looks like something they'd
send to Sea Biscuit for winning the Kentucky Derby. What are all
these flowers doing here? This is a Jewish funeral home. Jewish
people don't send flowers to the chapel. Get them out."

"Don't," Josh whispered to me. "They're obviously from
friends who aren't Jewish and this is how they show their love. So
let it be, Sandy. Bernie would have liked it."

And you know what? The minute Josh said that, I thought, I bet
he does like it. I could just picture Bernie watching the whole affair, checking out the inscribed ribbons and the cards and *kvelling*
at the crowd he'd drawn. He looked beautiful, handsome, and comfortable, as if he were just sleeping, but so much more peacefully
than he'd slept in the past several weeks. And I thought how nice it
must be for him to finally lie back on a satin pillow and be covered
in sweet-smelling roses.

Vinny and Hot Dog took me back to the house and stayed
awhile. The baby had a bad night. He was crying a lot, which was
very, very unusual for him. And, of course, it was the day his father
died. Ten weeks old he was, and fatherless now. Why shouldn't he
cry? "There goes the Jab," Red said that night.

"Jab?"

"Mr. Jeffrey Allen Barton," said Red. "That's J.A.B. The Jab."

Well, Hot Dog went home to Thelma. Vinny stayed over on the
couch in the living room. The poor guy didn't get much rest because the Jab and I cried through most of that night. The sleeping

pills the doctor had given me kept me from getting up and walking around, but they didn't stop the tears. And Nora who, walking and rocking the baby, was Jeffrey's sedative, didn't have much luck, either. The Jab and I cried, each of us in our separate rooms, each of us mourning our separate loss. And then the sun came up—it was a hot and horrible Sunday—and I got ready to bury my husband.

I sat in the little private room in the funeral parlor staring at Bernie, knowing it was going to be the last time I saw him. Again, I had the strange feeling that as long as I could see him, nothing had changed, but that when the coffin lid closed it would be on my life as well as his. "You know this is it, Ma," I'd said that morning. "Today it ends. What do I do after today is over?"

"You'll worry about it tomorrow," she'd said.

"Like Scarlett in 'Gone With the Wind'? What will I do? I'll worry about it tomorrow?"

"Yes," Tillie said firmly. "That's exactly what you'll do."

The rabbi came into the family room. He said a prayer for us and then he cut *schnear*—he made a tear in a little piece of black ribbon—and handed it to me to pin on my dress. It was my mourning badge. I had to wear it for seven days.

I didn't want to be in the room when they closed the casket lid. I took Josh's hand and my mother's and I said, "Come on, I want to see who's here. We'll just take a peek."

I was amazed! The entire chapel was full. The room held two hundred, maybe two hundred and fifty people. And it was standing room only. Every seat was filled and people were lining the aisles. Josh had been right about giving people time to get there. I saw the boys from Vegas, who'd clearly spent the night on the Red Eye and rushed over from the airport still in their white slacks and rumpled jackets, and the Florida crowd in seersucker and patent leather white loafers. I recognized friends of B's from Boston and from Cleveland. Half of Harlem was there. There were some old black women sitting at the back of the chapel, rocking back and forth. I nearly burst into tears! Bernie, I wanted to say, look! Can you see this? Do you know how loved and respected you are?!

Lido was there draped in purple and bright gold with some friends we'd met at his townhouse. There were people done up like they were going to a wedding and people who'd rushed over in jeans. My childhood friend Leona from Brooklyn was sitting next to Judy, who'd been with me the night Bernie and I met. High-ranking members of the five families had all showed up. They were shaking hands, turning slightly this way and that in their seats, to acknowledge one another and their constituents. Their body guards in shiny suits and dark glasses kibitzed among themselves.

Toward the back, a balding, blond-haired man was standing against the wall. He seemed very solitary, very self-contained yet self-conscious, as if he expected attention but was above caring about whether he got it or not. He was about Bernie's age and coldly attractive, dressed to the nines on that sweltering summer day in an immaculate suit with a pale blue shirt and silk tie. "Who's the blond guy in the back?" I asked Josh.

"Oh him? That's Chalky Lefkowitz. Bernie's friend who just got out of Trenton State. I thought you knew him."

"No," I said. "I've only spoken to him on the phone. But Bernie adored the man."

"Yeah, I know." Josh shrugged. "Not my kind of guy," he said cryptically.

Vinny, who'd gone outside for a cigarette, had spotted us peeking through the door. He shouldered his way up the aisle toward us.

"Look at this," I said to him. "Every seat in the house is taken. It's standing room only. Like an opening," I said. "Or a closing."

"Yeah," Vinny said angrily. "They're even crawling around outside, taking license plate numbers."

"The FBI?" Josh asked.

"Unbelievable. Cars are triple-parked outside and these jerks are stepping over bumpers and crouching down to get the numbers. They've got no respect."

I went numb again once the service began. I sat through the eulogy conscious of people crying around me, of murmured agreement with some of the things the rabbi said and even a little relieved laughter every now and then. And then Vinny took my elbow and helped me up and we went outside to the waiting limousines.

There were two limos for the family and close personal friends. The heat outside was awful. The streets looked yellow and were practically steaming in the glaring daylight. I followed my mother into the first car and sat back in a daze. It wasn't until we were on the Long Island Expressway that I turned around and looked back.

"What is that?" I asked Vinny, who was in our car. "I hear music."

"It's Red," he said.

I looked out the back window and there was a procession of seventeen cars following us. And first among them, filled to capacity with mourners, was Hot Dog's white Cadillac convertible. Red had the top down and the tape deck on full blast. He was playing "When the Saints Come Marching In" for Bernie. And he played it, full blast, all the way to the cemetery.

I stood unsteadily in the oppressive heat and watched my husband's casket lowered into the grave. When the rabbi signaled, my mother had to remind me what to do. At her whispered instruction, I tossed a shovel of dirt onto the casket. What a wrenching sound, that sad little hail of earth and pebbles on mahogany wood. Most of the flowers from the funeral home were at the gravesite. When I stepped back into my mother's arms, people began to walk past the grave. They'd throw in bouquets or just take a flower and toss it onto the casket. A couple of men blew kisses as they went by. Then a guy reached into his pocket and pulled out a handful of pot and sprinkled it over the grave. Someone threw in a little cocaine. A woman came up and tossed in perfume. Guys cried. It was an unbelievable procession of people, Bernie's people, which meant rich and poor, young and old, black and white, Jews and gentiles, street and straight.

"He would've loved it," everyone kept saying back at the house. The seven days of sitting shivah, of mourning, began right after the service. People came from the cemetery and crowded into the apartment. Some who hadn't made it out to Farmingdale were already waiting at the house. Platters of food had been delivered. Liquor and champagne were sent up. Some friends had even sent over their housekeeper to help with the serving and cleaning. The wooden boxes on which the family was supposed to sit were set up; the mirrors were covered so that the soul on its journey to heaven wouldn't catch a glimpse of itself and despair. For seven days, the lost loved one was supposed to be remembered, spoken of, wept over, even laughed about; and his bereaved survivors were not supposed to mourn alone.

So the party was on again.

People were coming and going all day and long into the nights. The doormen of the building were in seventh heaven. Every time someone tossed his keys to a doorman or left a limo double-parked he'd tip the building guys extravagantly. The doormen would phone up in voices so happy they were almost laughing and they'd say, "Mr. Gruzetti is on the way up. And I'm watching his car!" They made out like bandits.

And everyone who showed up brought a gift for the baby.

Stuffed animals of every size and species were piled up in his room, silver rattles, cups and spoons, clothing—the wardrobe was not to be believed. It was during this hectic time that I began to learn how to take care of my child.

There were only two places I could find peace during that week when the apartment was constantly filled with people. I'd sit out on the terrace in the evenings, the way Bernie had, and smoke a cigarette and stare out at the city lights or I'd hide in Jeffrey's room and, sometimes, just rock and watch him breathe. I began feeding him his bottles, learning how to change his diapers, how to bathe him, hold him, cool him. From the time I'd brought him home from the hospital, I hadn't had much of a chance to get to know my son. It was strange, but that terrible mourning period brought at least that blessing.

The apartment was crowded most of the time. People came up to me. They kissed me. They patted my hands. They reminded me of things Bernie had said or done. They talked about how honorable he was, how loyal, how funny. "A lovable lunatic," more than one guy called him.

"He was an original," his friend Morty said. "We'd meet the Italian guys downtown. Bernie'd be sitting at the table. A guy would say, 'Who you wit? I'm wit Bonanno. Who you wit?' And Bernie'd say, in the same way as them, 'I'm wit everybody. I don't stand alone. I stand wit everybody.' And you know," Morty said, shaking his head, sighing, "he was, Sandy. He was there for whoever needed him."

"He was always there for me," Josh the lawyer told me. He came and found me out on the terrace. He looked rumpled. His sport shirt was wrinkled, the collar lying kind of cockeyed, one side up, one side down. "He'd say, that shingle of yours is worth everything. He wanted me to do better, to be better. He always said that, Sandy. You can do better than this, barrister, he'd say to me. Make a living off us, but don't become one of us," Josh remembered. He looked so sad.

After a while, he sat down next to me and put his feet up on the railing. And the two of us stared out into space.

God bless Red. That first week after Bernie's death, that week of sitting shivah, a lot of people treated me as though I were very fragile—which I was. To tell the truth, they treated me as though I were crazy—which I also was. I never knew when I'd laugh, when I'd cry, when I'd scream. But Hot Dog treated me as though he had total confidence in me. As if he needed me. Oh, do I remember his slicked-back red hair and pale-coffee skin, his pencil mustache, those little laughing eyes, and that big Cab Calloway grin.

In the middle of mourning, with the house constantly crowded, with people smoking, drinking, eating, laughing, and grieving, Hot Dog would call me into the bedroom or the kitchen, wherever it was momentarily quiet, and we'd go into a huddle. He'd hand me the brown paper bag full of numbers money. He'd start talking to me about the business, about what he'd done and what he thought we ought to do. He'd ask my opinion. And for a couple of minutes each day, I'd have to pull myself together. I'd have to think like a rational human being. And what would I think? I'd think, what would Bernie say in this situation? What would Bernie do?

Hymie was at the apartment every day. He'd even offered to stay over. He was a close relative, he reminded me. It was his duty to be near, to watch out for me. And with him, too, I thought, what would Bernie do? And I tried to be nice to him. "No, sweetheart," I told him. "You must be exhausted, too. Go home. Come back to-morrow, in the day time. Come every day. But I don't want anyone sleeping in the house."

Hot Dog and Vinny, our real family, Bernie's and mine, the ones he truly loved and left to watch out for me, did stay over. They'd fall out on the floor or the living room couch. And, of course, my mother was with me, and Nora and the baby. But not Sleazeball. During the shivah week, the fat little man who'd walked hunched over for most of his life began to strut around the apartment as if he owned the place, trying to hold court, trying to chat up the *machers* and wise guys, playing the big shot.

I would not allow him to spend the night. I would not allow him to answer the phones anymore. For Bernie's sake, I'd start out nicely with, "Hymie, thank you very much, sweetheart, but don't answer the phones for me," but I'd wind up with, "This is my house now. Mine alone, Hymie. Keep away from my phones!"

Hymie wasn't the only one I shouted at. One of Bernie's ex-partners from The Velvet Club, we'll call him Georgie Mahoney, Mahoney the Phoney, had moved down to Florida. He'd come back to New York for the funeral and decided to hang around for a little while.

Georgie was an attractive guy. He had a great tan. He took excellent care of himself—every and any way he could. He paid a shivah call at the apartment one afternoon. After he'd made the rounds, shook hands, shot the breeze with the boys, he came out to the terrace and, carefully hiking up his linen trousers at the knees, sat down next to me to chat.

"What are you going to do after all this is over?" he said to me.

"Georgie, I don't know," I said. "It's one day at a time at this point in my life. I have to get through the mourning period. I have an infant to take care of. Why?"

"Well, you're a young girl yet. You're beautiful. I always said you were beautiful, Sandy. You'll take off all the weight you've put on. And then, you'll meet a man. You'll get married again. A girl like you—you'll have another life. You could have any life you want."

He went on that way for a while. He made me nervous, uncomfortable. I blurted out, "What are you saying, Georgie? Are you propositioning me or proposing?"

"A little of both," he said.

"I'm sitting shivah for one of your friends, Georgie, and you're sitting here making a pitch for me? Georgie," I said, "do you think I was left a lot of money?"

He gave a little wink. "Well," he said, "we know B had tons of money."

I said, "Is that what you think? Who says so? I'm not saying he did or didn't. That's no one's business, Georgie. It's definitely not your fucking business!"

He gave me a look, like how dare I speak to him that way. But before he could come up with the words, I hauled off and smacked him across the face so hard his head shook. Then I started to scream.

I had Georgie put out of the apartment. Vinny came running. A couple of the other *shtarkers* sitting around stuffing their faces dropped everything and ran to help me. I pushed past them into the apartment and ran through the living room shouting, "Get that bastard out of my house!" Then I spun around and looked at everyone who was staring at me. "And if anyone else here thinks Bernie left me money . . . If he did leave me money . . . If he left me a dollar or a million dollars, he put his back up against the wall for it! It's blood money! And it's nobody's business but mine!"

And all these big men, these tough guys, they looked down at their feet. They looked up at the ceiling. They were embarrassed because they knew what I meant. I'd heard them guessing and gossiping. They'd be sitting around the dining room table and their favorite topic of conversation was how much money Bernie might have left me. One would say, "Oh, he was loaded. The guy had millions stashed away." Somebody else would shake his head and say, "Get outta here, the guy didn't have two nickels to rub together. He was a gambler. He lost his shirt." And then I'd hear, "BB knew how to live. He lived big. He left a bundle." They sounded like a bunch of *yentas*.

Bernie's old friend from the Teamsters, Milty Heinz, came by one day. The house was crowded. I was in terrible shape; just moving was an effort. I looked up and there was Milty at the bar. "Sandy," he said. "I need to talk to you, baby. You know B borrowed a nice little piece of change from me a couple of months ago. And I know you're good for it."

"What are you saying, Milty? That I owe you money?"

The big *shlub*, the hot shot who blew money at the Copa like it was dust. "Well, yeah," he says. "Twelve grand to be exact."

"I don't believe you," I said. "Bernie made you one of Jeffrey's godfathers. Doesn't that mean you're supposed to help look after his kid, not try to steal the milk from his mouth. Excuse me, I've got to talk to someone," I said.

I found Josh and dragged him into the bedroom and told him what Milty had said.

"That bastard! He's trying to make a move on you. He's trying to shake you down. Did he show you a piece of paper? Is he holding a note? He's lying, Sandy. Tell him to go fuck himself."

I marched out of the bedroom. "Milty," I asked, "do you have anything with B's signature on it that says he owes you?"

"Hey, we didn't need paper—" He started giving me what good friends they were, trust, favors, all the nice words.

"Milty, you're lying," I yelled. "On the advice of my attorney, go fuck yourself!"

The whole place sucked air for a second. There was this collective gasp. Then tongues clucked and tongues wagged and people came to put their arms around me and some guys tried to make Milty feel better as he headed for the door. Personally, I don't even think he took it hard. He was one of the guys who believed Bernie had left me a fortune. So what would a measly twelve grand mean to me? Hey, no hard feelings was his attitude as he walked out the door.

He was just another *gonif* looking for an easy score.

One of the reasons all the talk about money got to me was that I didn't know myself what Bernie had left us. Certainly there was no will. Other than the cash I'd taken from our joint safety deposit box—most of which had gone to pay medical bills—I had no idea whether I'd have a dollar or a dime to live on. I had the apartment rent to pay and, for those days, it was an expensive place. I had the baby to support. It scared me. Red always said not to worry. But I knew we weren't going to live on a paper bag full of singles and fivers. I tried to push the fear out of my mind, but it would creep back in.

I began sitting shivah on Sunday, as soon as we got back from the cemetery. All day, every day, people came up to pay their respects and they all brought cakes, liquor, casseroles of food, platters of deli, and gifts for the baby. They'd kiss me, they'd say something to the other members of the family, and quite a few of them would make a point of spending some time with my mother, too. It was about Tuesday when Tillie called me into the bedroom.

"Sit down," she said, locking the door behind us. "I've got something to tell you." She opened the closet and pulled out a plastic bag full of envelopes. "From the day of his funeral people have been giving me these envelopes. There's money in them."

"For what?" I asked.

"For you and the baby."

We began to open the envelopes.

"I didn't know what to do," Tillie said, as if she'd done something wrong.

"No, Ma," I said. "It's good. Take it. Because Bernie would have done the same thing for anyone else's widow. You always give widows money."

"Well," said Tillie, not entirely convinced. "I heard about them doing this at Italian funerals, but not at Jewish."

"Maybe it was the Italian guys that gave them to you."

"To tell you truth, I don't know who they were. Men kept coming over to me that Sunday in the funeral parlor, people that were here yesterday. I lost track. I'm sorry. I don't even know who they were. And I'm sorry because they didn't even write their whole names on the envelopes. Look," she said. "Here's initials. Here's first names only. In two days, you got from four different Sals and even more Jimmys. This is it."

There was close to $8,000 in that first batch of envelopes. "Ma," I said, smiling for the first time that day. "If anyone else hands you an envelope, just take it and tell them 'God bless you.' "

She laughed at me. "Sandy, you'll never get to heaven this way," she said.

"Is there really a heaven, Ma?" I asked her later that day. She'd found me out on the terrace and sat down beside me. She looked exhausted. "Do any of us really get to heaven? Do you think Bernie is up there looking at us?"

"Absolutely," she said. "He's up there in heaven and he'll be a *gutta better* for you." She saw that I didn't know what she meant. "A *gutta better* is an angel," she explained. "Someone who has died and gone ahead to look out for your interests. He'll argue and pray for you—and for his son and even for me. He'll talk to God for all his loved ones, that God should take care of them. He'll help to see that it'll be okay."

"A guardian angel," I said.

"Exactly. It's like having the best lawyer money can buy; a defense attorney who pleads your case before God. And with that mind of his, and that mouth, how can we lose?"

About a second later, Josh poked his head outside and said, "Excuse me, Tillie. Sandy, can I see you for a second?"

"Speaking of lawyers," I said. "Stay, Ma. I'll be right back." Josh put his arm around me and we walked through the partying crowd. "I've got good news for you. I was just in touch with one of the FBI agents who was on Bernie's case. They called me. They wanted to let me know that I was on record as Bernie's attorney and that the tap's been taken off your phone, so your phone is clean now."

"Josh, what the hell are you talking about?"

"The FBI had Bernie under surveillance, Sandy. They had a tap on your phones for two months before Bernie went into the hospital. I told you about it the day he died, remember? They thought he was involved with drugs. Well, the tap is off now. Your phone is clean."

"You mean, all the months he was in the hospital, everything I said to anyone on these phones—they were listening?"

"Yeah. They have tapes of everything."

It had not registered before. Now I felt nauseated with humiliation and shame. I remembered the anger and exhaustion, the disgust and hopelessness I'd felt about Bernie during that terrible time. I remembered every rotten thing I'd said about my dying husband to intimate friends, who I knew would understand the stress I was under and not take me too seriously or judge me too harshly. Now I was mortified. To think that strangers had been listening, men who had wanted to bring harm to Bernie had heard his wife bitching about him as he lay dying.

"They were taping conversations?" I asked Josh, sick with shame. I tried to remember whether Hot Dog and I had talked business on the phone. Or the men who'd been here night and day—had they known our phones were tapped?

Josh was saying that he hadn't trusted the agent who'd called him, so he had phoned a friend of his who was with the FBI and that the friend said, yes, the tap had been released, the lines really were clean now.

I realized again, how different our life had been from other people's. It was a very strange way to live. I wondered if I'd ever find a better one.

Smack in the middle of the shivah week, I was sitting with Judy and Nino and I glanced up and saw that Hot Dog had arrived. He was nervous, dancing around in the restless way he had. As soon as I looked up, he signaled for me to come talk. "A couple of the kids got pinched this afternoon," he said. "We've got to bail them out."

"Runners?"

"Yeah. Good kids."

"Okay, let's get Josh," I said.

"No," Red said. "They don't need a lawyer. We just gotta bail them out."

It was about ten at night. There weren't too many people still hanging around. Even Hymie had gone home. I looked for my mother and saw that the door to Jeffrey's room was ajar. "God, Red," I said. "I don't know. I'm sitting shivah. I don't think I can do it."

"Sandy, they might get panicky. Someone's got to go down and bail them out. I can't go on record like that. You've got to do it."

"Okay," I decided. "How much is it going to be?"

"About seven bills. Here," Red said, handing me the nightly brown paper bag.

"All right," I said, as Tillie tiptoed out of the baby's room and carefully pulled the door shut behind her. "Let me just tell my mother. I'll be right back."

I took her into the big bedroom and told her as I changed my clothes. She hit the ceiling. "What are you crazy?!" she hollered at me. "It's a *shande*, a shameful thing! You can't leave a shivah house. You're in mourning!"

"I know. But I've got to do it, Ma," I said, struggling to get my size 18 body into my size 16 jeans, hopping around on one foot, then the other. "Bernie left me this business. And Red needs me. I'm going to bail out a couple of kids who run for us."

"God will punish you," she shouted.

That did it. I zipped up and broke into tears. "God will punish me?" I said. "Why, Ma, you don't think He's punished me enough already, that at twenty-six years old I have to sit shivah for the man I love, the father of your new grandchild?!"

The night air was stale but sweet to me. I hadn't been out of the house in days. I looked up at the sky as Red's convertible carried us downtown to night court and I wondered what my *gutta better* would say to God to square this one for me. She's just doing what I would have done, Your Honor, I thought Bernie might say. She's my stand-up girl and she's doing what I taught her.

Whatever excuses he might have to make for me, I realized that for the first time in weeks, I felt okay. I had a purpose, a mission. People were counting on me—Red, the runners. I even felt that Bernie was counting on me in some weird way and that he'd be proud of me. A man's got to do what a man's got to do, I remember thinking. And then realizing that, for the moment, I was the "man" I was talking about.

Down at night court, I sat on a back bench and spilled hundreds of dollar bills out of the brown paper bag Red had given me. I counted the money the way Bernie had taught me to, presidents up, all facing the same way. I counted out $700 in singles. When I signed the bail form, I was asked about my relationship to the guys. "I'm a friend of theirs," I said. "I know them." I surprised myself with how cool and efficent I was. I did what I had to do and I felt very good about it. I felt, to tell you the truth, guided from above. And I knew I had done what Bernie would have in the same circumstances. If he'd been sitting shivah, he'd have done exactly the same thing.

It was a very temporary respite from the sorrow. Red dropped me off in front of our building and, by the time the elevator got to our floor, I was frightened, lonely, and depressed again.

Shivah ended officially that Sunday, one week after Bernie had been buried. Following another custom, my mother and I and Hymie and other relatives went downstairs and walked around the building from left to right. We made a full circle to ward off the evil spirits. Then everyone went home.

CHAPTER FIFTEEN

Alone

I remember lying in my mother's arms and sobbing.

"Ma, there's a hole in my heart. Will it ever go away? I feel as if I can't breathe."

She said, "I promise you it will. But when I don't know. It will go away, *mamela*. One day at a time. And that's how you'll live your life. Go dry your eyes, wash your face, sweetheart. You'll feel better."

"I can't," I said.

Hot Dog, Vinny, Josh, and big, burly Morty, the guy who'd told me how Bernie used to say "I'm wit everybody," came over in shifts to keep me company. Morty would say, "Get out of that *shmatte*, that rag you're wearing. You'll feel better."

"I can't," I said.

"Sandy, just put a comb through your hair. Put on a little makeup. You'll feel better," Judy urged.

"Come walk with us, your beautiful child and me," Nora would say. "Come down to the park for a little air."

"Eat real food. Stop stuffing yourself with junk."

"Don't lay around in bed so much."

"Of course you can go to the supermarket. You've got yourself and the baby to feed."

"What do you mean, you're afraid to stand in the stall shower alone? It's ninety-five degrees out, Sandy. Take a shower, you'll feel better."

Bernie had been dead for two weeks and my vocabulary seemed to be reduced to two words: "I can't."

For some reason I'd had tremendous physical strength while he was ill. Only days after giving birth I was running to the hospital, shopping, cleaning, cooking, entertaining friends. I'd done whatever needed to be done—not graciously, not without anger, self-pity, and tears, but somehow I'd found the energy. Now, two weeks after his death, I moved like a zombie. I couldn't stop crying. I'd fall to my knees doubled over with a sense of loss and fear so deep it literally stole my breath away. My mother had to teach me how to breathe into a paper bag so that I wouldn't pass out.

Alone was how I felt. Terrified, inadequate, alone.

But I wasn't alone. Each day Vinny would stop by. Hot Dog would deliver the brown paper bag. Morty would clown for me and try to teach me card tricks. Josh would phone daily and visit whenever he could. My little sister Marlene hung around, tried to help. And most of the time, Nora took care of Jeffrey and me as though we were brother and sister. And, of course, Tillie slept over every night and spent as much time during the day with me as she could.

"Just give me a month," I told Red one day, "then I'll come out swinging."

Hymie wanted to talk business. "Not now. Not yet," I said. "Give me a month to mourn."

One day, we gathered up all of Bernie's belongings. There's an old Jewish superstition that says no one should walk in the shoes of a dead man. So we threw all the shoes into the incinerator. The clothing we gave to the doormen and to charity. The jewelry I kept, except for a couple of special pieces that went to those Bernie had loved best, family and friends. It must have been the beginning of the third week. I looked around the apartment and, except for the portrait of him that hung next to mine in the living room, the portraits we'd had painted in Florida, there was nothing left of the man. Even the smell of him was gone from the bedsheets. I used to lie down in bed and I couldn't smell him anymore. The only thing left of Bernie in the house was that little boy lying in the crib.

I wanted to die. I wanted to die so badly that I made a half-assed attempt at slitting my wrists. It was one morning after Tillie had gone to work. Mornings were the hardest, waking up with that thump of fear, that first terrible consciousness, the dread. I heard Nora in the kitchen talking to Jeffrey. I knew she was getting his bottle ready, then they would go out. I knew Jeffrey would be better off without me. I was useless, crazy, incapable of taking care of anyone. I couldn't even brush my teeth anymore. I was standing at the sink holding a razor blade. It was as much of an effort to drag it across my wrist as it had been to drag my 170 pounds out of bed. I cut my wrist very carefully. I stared down at what looked like a little scratch dotted with red droplets and watched the blood begin to ooze out of it. I was crying. And suddenly, I thought: "Hey, what am I doing? This hurts. I'm not strong enough to kill myself. I'm a fucking coward."

It was so weird. I went from this dull, aching, definitely wanting to die feeling to sudden clarity. I wouldn't be able to do it and, what was more, I didn't really want to.

I hadn't done much damage. I cleaned myself up and then I started swabbing the blood in the sink. And I looked in the mirror. I remember taking off my housecoat, the loose-fitting sleeveless cover up, the *shmatte* I'd been wearing. I looked at myself in the mirror, at this fat body, the hanging breasts and flab, and I thought: But the face is young, the girl's face is young. It's still a pretty face.

I thought: You know what, you'd better shape up, baby.

Then I looked up at the ceiling, as if I could see right through it to heaven. And I screamed, "BERNIE!" Oh, how I wanted him. How I wanted to hear his deep, gravelly voice again. I screamed his name at the top of my lungs. And Nora came running into the bathroom. There was still some blood on the sink and she saw it.

"It's all right," I said. "Don't worry about it. Please believe me, I'm all right. Everything is fine." I walked her out of the bathroom. "Nora, it's over," I said. "From here on in, it's got to be up because I've reached the bottom. My mother told me, you can only go so low in life, you can only be so crazy and miserable, and that when you reach the bottom there is only one way to go after that because you have no choice."

I made a promise to myself that day in the bathroom. I reminded myself of what I'd told Red and Hymie and everyone else who was either worried about me or wanted to talk business. I'd said, "Let a month go by and I'll come out swinging." Bernie had died August seventh. It was now September first. That morning with the razor blade, I reminded myself that it was almost time.

"Ma, I'm taking the car and driving out to see Bernie," I said that weekend.

"What are you talking about?"

It had begun to dawn on me that he was really gone, that he hadn't just left for a little while. He was never ever coming back.

The realization was absolutely intolerable. I wanted him. I needed to be near him. "I'm going to the cemetery," I said.

"You can't do that. It's not even a month yet. You don't do that in the Jewish religion until the headstone is put up."

"The hell with the Jewish religion, Ma. I want to see him. I want to be close to him." I put some coffee in a Thermos, I took a sandwich along, and I drove all the way out to the Island. I parked in front of his grave and sat there and ate and spoke to him.

"Why did you leave me?" I asked. I was a little scared and tentative, at first, as if Bernie were really listening to me and, because he'd been sick, because he'd been dead, I didn't want to yell at him about it. I wanted to be nice. But as I spoke, I gathered force. The sadness and loneliness gave way to anger. And, boy, was I mad. I had no idea how pissed off I was until the words came pouring out.

"Shmuck, you couldn't take care of yourself? How many times did Doctor Sealy tell you to lay off the fucking salt, Bernie? How many times? Was it worth it, the goddamn Chinese food and the deli? The cigars and speed? Speed, you took! Jerk! What the hell was the matter with you? Was it worth it to never see your son again? I'm so mad at you," I said. "You could have had it all, if you'd just been straight—with yourself, with Doctor Sealy, with me. You could have enjoyed the good life. Watched Jeffrey grow up. You could have been with me. I miss you so much, you moron! Oh, Bernie, what am I going to do? How am I going to raise our son? I don't know how to do it, baby. I'm scared. What do I do now, Bernie? Tell me!"

All this between bites of a bologna sandwich and sips of coffee from the Thermos cup. I laughed at myself. I cried for Bernie. I expected him to answer my questions, to consider my side of things. I ran my hand over the warm earth and knew he was beneath it. Strange as it seems, it was comforting to know that he was there. He was somewhere real in the world, near enough for me to drive out and talk to. I needed to know he existed, that he had lived and been real and was real still. And, finally, I forgave him. "I'll live," I promised. "And you know what, Bernie, I'm going to make you proud of me." When I drove home in the early evening, I felt much better. I felt that I had been with him.

Later that week, I took off the piece of black ribbon that I'd pinned to my bra every morning, and I put it away in a drawer. And I took out Bernie's necklace, the gold medal with Saint Christopher on one side and the Star of David on the other, and put it on. And that day, Vinny and Red and Morty took me marketing. It was the first time I'd gone shopping since Bernie died. Nora dressed Jeffrey and I put him in his carriage— not the Royal Coach baby carriage, which had turned out to be totally useless; it was so big we could only fit it in the building's freight elevator—but a nice, normal little stroller. And the five of us went to the supermarket.

The five of us went everywhere together that fall, the guys and Jeffrey and me. The boys stayed close. God forbid Jeffrey shouldn't have a male image around. Here came the volunteer squad, the proud godfathers: Red, a reed-thin rainbow in his straw fedora, Hawaiian shirts, and green, orange, or electric blue pants; Vinny, immaculately coiffed, shooting his cuffs, always clean and crisp; and hulking Morty, all six-foot-three of him, wreathed in cigar smoke, dark, wavy hair slicked back, long rambling nose in the air. They came with me to the pediatrician for Jeffrey's checkups. They wheeled him in his stroller in the little park behind our house. They'd sit in the playground for hours and watch over him while he slept in the sunshine. They'd prop him up in the supermarket cart and wheel him along the aisles while I shopped. They had loved Bernie. Now they were taking care of his wife and kid.

I was still breaking into uncontrollable tears a couple of times a day. Knowing that his closets were empty, his side of the medicine chest, his side of the bed, his foods were not in the kitchen cupboards anymore caused a sick ache in my gut. And if, for a minute, I was able to forget him, the next minute I was beating myself up for being so selfish and uncaring. I was very lonely and lost. But I had promised Bernie I'd live. I had promised myself I'd come out swinging. Bills had been piling up. Ready or not, it was time to take care of business.

"We've got to talk, Red," I said when Hot Dog came by to drop off the numbers money.

He grinned. "I've been waiting for you, partner. Let's do it."

We sat down and, for the first time since Bernie's death, we really discussed finances. The business was healthy. Red ran it right. The runners were good neighborhood kids, loyal, honest, competent. So were the guys who manned the phones in the walkup. There'd never been a doubt in Red's mind that he and I were now partners, that I was in for fifty-fifty just as Bernie had been. "But what do I have to do?" I asked.

"Just come down to the place for a while," Red said. "Let people see you around. Let them get to know you're in for Bernie. Let them get to know you're not the boss's old lady, you're the boss."

Did I hear Red's brain ticking? You'll have to get out of that housecoat, woman, he might just as well have said. You won't be able to sit around and mope all day, or break down crying, or feel sorry for yourself.

"So what would I do? Take numbers, make coffee, what?" I asked, warming to the idea.

"Yeah. That. And whatever you want. Just stop up. Kibitz with the boys. Hang out."

The next people I contacted were Shorty and P.D., two of the dozen partners in another of Bernie's businesses, a seedy but profitable neighborhood bar on East Ninety-sixth Street and Second Avenue. We'd driven past the place countless times on our way up to Harlem and stopped in for drinks occasionally. The neighborhood then was Italian and Irish. There'd be grandmothers sitting on the stoops shelling peas, or leaning out the windows on fat feather pillows. Lots of kids around. The old men would sit around the bar watching the ball games and eating the free hardboiled eggs.

Shorty and P.D. had paid a shivah call and been very sweet about telling me that, as far as they were concerned, Bernie's share of the profits now belonged to me. What that meant, I didn't know. So I phoned the bar one afternoon and Shorty was there. He said, "You want to talk? Great. Come over in half an hour, P.D.'ll be here. It'll be a pleasure to see you, honey."

Shorty was, what else? short, and chubby with salt-and-pepper hair that he wore in what they used to call a Caesar cut—which meant that what was left of his hair he combed forward in a little Frank Sinatra-style fringe. P.D. was tall and skinny. What made him unique was his passion for climbing greased poles. He'd talk for hours about the flag-pole shimmying contests he'd been in and the techniques he used to win them. People would run when he got started. P.D. would open with, "First you gotta grease your palms—"

And never mind that this was a connected guy, a gangster talking, half the bar would knock back their drinks in one gulp and disappear.

I got dressed and drove over to the bar. P.D. and Shorty were waiting. "You're in," Shorty said. "You'll get your piece same as like when Bernie was alive."

"Good," I said, even though I still had no idea whether he was talking about $5.00 a week or $500.

"It'll vary," P.D. read my mind. "Depending on the action in the place. Some weeks a hundred. Some weeks three bills—"

"And the action is?"

"Aw, you know, kid. A little numbers biz. A little a this, a little a that. It varies."

"Tell you what," said Shorty. "You come in a couple days a week. Bring the kid. How's that big boy? Bring him with you anytime. Come in, help out around the place a little. Get to know the action. That's the best way."

"It may not look like much," P.D. said, "but this here's a little gold mine, Sandy. And it ain't a half-bad place to hang out."

How can I explain how good it felt, sitting there in a dark booth in a musty old bar that stank of booze and sawdust, talking to a couple of wise guys who were treating me as an equal? Here I was, yesterday a weepy young widow, today a full partner in two of Bernie's businesses.

There was only one other person I had to see—Sleazeball Hymie, who was supposed to be collecting interest and keeping the books on the loans Bernie had put out.

At the end of shivah, when I was giving away some of Bernie's jewelry, I remembered that I'd left my diamond wedding band and a couple of other good pieces of jewelry in the secret hiding place in the hassock. I'd put them there during my pregnancy, when my fingers had gotten too swollen to wear the ring anymore. So the day I was cleaning out Bernie's things, I'd gone to the hassock to get my jewelry. And it was gone. I searched the whole house. I thought I'd gone crazy. I knew I'd put the ring, a diamond-studded gold watch and my good diamond earrings into the hassock. What the hell had happened to them? Who knew about the secret compartment in the hassock besides me and Bernie? No one. Not Hot Dog. Not my mother.

Hymie!, I thought. During that period when Bernie was sick at home and Sleazeball first started running errands for him, Bernie had probably told him about the hassock. He's blood, he used to say. Bernie trusted blood.

I remembered how Hymie had been hanging around the house while I was at the hospital with Bernie. I remembered Ruth, the baby nurse, always telling me that he'd been at the apartment, making phone calls, cleaning out the fridge, and poking into everything.

Well, no sooner did I think Hymie! than I got this full-blown picture of Hymie's full-blown girlfriend showing up at the house the week after the funeral wearing a gorgeous new cocktail ring on her pudgy finger, a ring that cost far more than a haberdashery clerk could afford. Hymie was still working days in a men's clothing store, not the one he'd embezzled from, of course. I'd commented on his girlfriend's new ring, which she immediately said Hymie had given her along with a beautiful diamond pin and a pair of earrings to match. "Very nice," I'd said to the Sleaze that night. "Must have cost you a fortune."

"Oh, um, ah," he went. "I got lucky gambling."

I almost laughed in his face. The man was the worst gambler, the biggest loser, the *shlemiel* of the century. But I was on good behavior with him during that shivah week. I was trying to treat him the way I felt Bernie would have wanted me to.

Now I thought, yeah, Hymie, you got lucky. You're lucky Bernie is dead. I could not shake the notion that Sleazeball had stolen my jewelry. I knew it in my head and I knew it in my gut. But I'd never confronted him. I'd never suggested that I didn't trust him. Now it was time to find out what was going on with the business he was supposed to be taking care of. And now was the time, also, to remember Bernie's advice: Don't get mad. Get even.

I phoned him at the clothing store. "Hymie, it's time," I said. "I'm ready now for us to have our little talk." He was so excited. This was what he'd been waiting for. He felt that he was the rightful heir to Bernie's kingdom. Who was I, what was I? A kid. A girl. Bernie would never turn his business over to a woman. Like everyone else, Hymie had speculated on how much money Bernie had stashed away, how much his schemes and dreams brought in. And like everyone else, Hymie thought the figure was astronomical. He was practically giggling when he said, "Sure, sure, Sandy. Right away. The sooner the better. Tonight's no good? How about tomorrow?"

The next evening, after dinner, Hymie came to the house. I poured the coffee and asked my mother to excuse us, and he and I sat down at the dining room table to talk business.

"Hymie, I don't know exactly what you were doing for Bernie while he was so sick and then after, these past few weeks, well, I really didn't want to know. But now I'm ready, sweetheart. You tell me."

"I'm glad you're feeling better, Sandy. And I'm glad you're asking. You know I wanted to have this talk before, but I respected your feelings. He was my blood. It's been a terrible loss. But life goes on. And all I want is what Bernie would have wanted. For me to help out you and the baby. And you can count on me one hun-

dred percent," Hymie announced, struggling to keep his gaze
steady and sincere, his watery blue eyes focused on me.

"Thanks."

"You know Bernie had a little loan money out on the streets.
Nothing. A couple of bills. It's no big business, believe me. And
whatever little money he lent he asked me to collect the juice, the
vig—you understand vigorish? The interest, Sandy—he wanted
me to collect it and so I did and I'm still doing it."

I knew that near the end, Bernie had gone into loansharking.
He'd lent money at mob rates. I also knew that he'd kept a black
book somewhere because at one point he'd showed it to me and
said, "You see this. This is money, baby. This is a record of who
I've lent money to and how much they owe." I hadn't seen the
book when I'd cleaned out his things, but I knew one existed.
"Hymie, you keep a record, don't you?"

"Of course," he said, a little indignant that I'd question his com-
petence.

"I'm only asking, Hymie. It's a black notebook, right?"

"No. It's not black. But, don't worry, I have every cent written
down. And I even have some money for you tonight—"

"What else did you do for Bernie?" I asked.

"Well, whatever else I did, it's over with. I can't do more about it
unless you get involved."

I had a hunch Hymie had delivered some of those packages from
the Spanish suitcases and that he'd be happy if I knew where we
could get some more. "Good. Then that's over," I said. "Because
whatever else you did for Bernie I'm not getting involved in. Just
the loans, that's all. So what percentage was Bernie giving you,
Hymie?"

"Oh, you know Bernie. He was a generous guy. He'd throw me
some here, throw me there. He took good care of me."

I said, "Hymie, I'll take good care of you. Don't worry about it,
sweetheart. The people Bernie lent the money to, I have no interest
in meeting them. You take care of it. You just continue on with it.
But, Hymie, the rest of Bernie's business, what Bernie had going
with Hot Dog and his other investments—Hymie, that you cannot
touch."

He didn't like it. "Come on, Sandy. This is family talking. I just
want to take care of business the way Bernie would have wanted.
I'm just trying to look out for you. Somebody's got to keep an eye
on Bernie's interests for you and the kid."

I said, "You know what, Hymie, we'll be okay. Don't worry about it. So you said you have some money for me?"

"Yeah." He wasn't happy, but he dug out his wallet and pulled a banded bankroll out of it. "It's what mounted up the past couple of weeks while you were out of commission. I was holding it for you. Friday nights I usually go collecting. I'll bring you the juice."

"Hymie, you'll let me see your records," I said.

His blue eyes blazed for a second. "I don't have them on me now. You worried? I'll bring them to you."

Without Bernie's little black book I was at Hymie's mercy. He'd bring me what he brought me. Whether it was the right amount or not I'd never know. Plus, I was still steaming about the stolen jewelry. For the moment, there was nothing I could do about it. So I smiled and stood up. "Okay, Hymie. Don't worry about it now. I'm very glad we had this talk. I feel much better," I said. I picked up his coffee cup and mine and took them into the kitchen and left him with his mouth hanging open.

So what could I count on? A little money from Red here, a little from the bar there and, from Hymie, as little as he could get away with. It was time to answer the question on everyone's mind: How much did I really have? It was time to hit the vaults.

In the next couple of days, I got the keys from my cousin Francine and the paper telling me what my name was at which bank, and off I went to discover what my future held.

Believe me, the *yentas* would have been disappointed.

Most of the cash had gone to pay doctors and hospital bills. Most, but not all. There was enough left to live on for a while, although it wasn't going to be in the lap of luxury. Still, as my mother said, "It'll buy a lot of milk and diapers for Jeffrey. Plenty of young girls with babies have been left off worse." And there was a surprise. The jewelry that had disappeared from the hassock was not in any of the vaults, but in an envelope I'd thought contained cash, was Bernie's black book—complete with the names and interest rates on every loan on which Hymie was supposed to be collecting juice.

All in all, it wasn't bad.

And then it got better.

At the end of September, I got a phone call from a man named Nathan. "I'm a friend of Meyer's," he said. "I'd like to buy you lunch and—" I was instantly nervous. "Meyer who?" I asked, although of course I knew who he meant.

"Meyer Lansky," said the man. "My name is Nathan and I'd like to discuss something with you. It's good. Don't get upset, it's only good."

"How did you get this number?" I asked. It was an unlisted line.

"Meyer got it from Farvel."

"Oh," I said. "Do you know Farvel?"

"Of course," said Nathan. "I had dinner with him and Minnie last week at—"

"Have you ever been to his house?" I asked.

"Many times."

"You've seen his garage?"

Nathan laughed. "You mean the warehouse?"

That did it. "Okay," I said. "I'm sorry I asked you so many . . . questions."

"Please," he brushed off my apology. "I understand. So you'll meet me for lunch? It's a good surprise. I don't want to talk over the phone."

"Of course," I said. I was still huge, but I worked hard at making myself look decent. I squeezed into a dark dress and high heels. I put on some makeup, did the best I could with my hair, and I drove down to Little Italy to meet Meyer's emissary at the Villa Penza, an Italian restaurant on Grand Street.

Nathan turned out to be a couple of years younger than Meyer and older than Bernie. He was a tall, tanned, heavyset man with a full head of hair that was graying at the temples. Conservatively dressed in a blue blazer and charcoal gray trousers, he stood as the head waiter led me to his table in the backroom.

"Nice to meet you," he said, patting my hand solicitously, "even under these sad circumstances. Sit, please. How's the baby? Such a terrible thing," he said in a *haimisha* way that was nevertheless politely formal. "I knew Bernie from years ago. A lovely man. I always liked him."

We made small talk for a while, ordered lunch. Finally, Nathan said, "I have a present for you, from Meyer himself. It has nothing to do with anybody else. It's a personal thing he's doing on his own. A baby gift."

"But he already gave us—" I began.

"No, no, take it." He laid a plain white envelope onto my palm and closed my fingers over it with his two hands. "So you'll keep it for the Bar Mitzvah. Meyer wants you to have it. Also, he asked me to call up your building management, which I did. Sandy, Meyer liked Bernie very much. Bernie was dear to him. And we know he didn't leave you millions. You're a young woman on your own with a newborn baby to raise. So Meyer sent them a check. So you shouldn't have to worry about that."

"About what?" I asked.

"About your rent, Sandy. Meyer paid your rent for the remainder of this lease and the next. That's three years, I think. So, your rent is paid in advance. Don't worry about it. Meyer owes this to Bernie. We don't want you to think it's charity."

I was overwhelmed. I wasn't sure what I ought to say, how I was supposed to behave. Three years' rent! I thought of the little man I'd seen sitting at the head of his table, ringing the dinner bell and cursing in Yiddish. I thought of him grinning, his thin lips stretched almost ear to ear, his head dipping in a self-deprecating, modest gesture. The long, bony nose. The bright, twinkling eyes. Meyer's class and generosity overwhelmed me. I tried to refuse the gift. "No, no. It's too much," I protested. But Nathan insisted it was money due Bernie, that Meyer would be hurt if I turned it down, that it was already a done deed, the building management had been contacted, the check had probably already cleared.

I remembered how Bernie had always lit up in Meyer's presence, how he respected, *revered*, the man. I wondered if he'd ever realized how much Meyer cared for him. Enough to make this extraordinary gesture, to free his widow and son from worrying about how they'd pay the rent—for the next three years!

"Okay," I said finally. "Please tell Meyer, 'Thank you,' " and Nathan, clearly relieved, winked at me and nodded his head as if to say: good girl, that's better.

The money in the plain white envelope, Meyer Lansky's gift to Bernie's son, turned out to be five thousand dollars.

"Five thousand dollars and three years rent!" I told my mother as soon as I got home. "Can you believe it, Ma?"

"Very nice." She tsked and clucked and shook her head in admiration of Meyer's gift. "Very nice." Then she clasped her hands together. "Oh, my God, I almost forgot. Wait. Wait, Sandy, sweetheart. Come, quick."

She dragged me into the bedroom. "What?" I kept saying, starting to laugh because Tillie was grinning all of a sudden, almost giggling now.

"*Oy-yoi-yoi*, can you believe it, to forget this?" She opened the closet door and, standing on her tip-toes, pulled down two shoe boxes from the shelf.

"The cards from the *t'alainas*," she said. "The Italians. They kept bringing me envelopes and you told me to keep taking—so here they are!"

She took the lids off the boxes. Each of them was stuffed to the brim with envelopes bearing sympathy cards and cash! I spilled the contents onto the bed and kicked off my high heels. Then my mother and I sat down and started ripping open the envelopes. There was money in every single one. As Tillie had told me before, most of the cards were signed with just a first name or initials. The ones I knew how to contact, I did, and they were very, very sweet, almost embarrassed by my thanking them. Forget it, this is what we do, they said. And if you need anything else, we're here for you.

September, October, November—the months rolled by. I started taking care of myself. I went to a doctor, who put me on a diet, and I stayed with it. I was very determined, very gung-ho to get skinny and look gorgeous. And it was working. It was a miracle. It was like watching a real human being begin to take shape out of a great lump of flesh. It wasn't just the weight loss, of course. I was coming back to life. It was visible in my face, my hair, the way I walked and sat and even talked on the telephone.

I started taking care of the baby, spending real time with him. I'd dress Jeffrey up in one of the beautiful little outfits friends had given us—little shorts and T-shirts that made him look like a miniature boxer in training. I'd tuck his silky dark hair under the tiny baseball cap Red had bought him. The Jab was big, bright, good; and goofy-looking when he smiled. And he smiled as soon as he saw me now, he knew me.

I'd take him down to the park and sit there with the other mothers. Not with them exactly, but near them. I didn't really have many single friends or girlfriends to hang out with. Leona worked. Judy had Nino and the baby to take care of. So I remember sitting on the wooden benches in the concrete playground, watching the other mothers and trying to pretend that I was just like them. That I had to go up at four o'clock or five to feed the baby and get dinner started for my husband. I don't know who I was trying to fool, myself or the harried but efficient-looking young women who seemed so normal, whose lives I imagined with envy. I wondered what they talked about to one another. I tried to hear what they said to their children. Sometimes, I'd say the same things to Jeffrey, just to see how it sounded, how it felt. "Okay, time to go upstairs, *tateleh*. Daddy'll be home soon and you've got to have your supper and your bath and you'll be all clean and smell so beautiful when he comes in."

Sometimes, I'd take Jeffrey with me to the bar on East Ninety-sixth. P.D. or Shorty or the other guys would fuss over him and call him "Champ," or "Little B," but no one called him "Tiger." Eventually, I cut Nora down from full- to part-time and, when she was there, I'd sometimes drive up to Harlem and hang out with Red at our numbers place. A couple of evenings a week, I'd work at the bar. I'd serve drinks and sit around and kibitz and laugh with the old Italian and Irish guys and their women. It was good to have somewhere to go and something to do.

My mother would stay over for one week now, then spend the next week at home in Brooklyn. She was a working woman and she'd been doing two big jobs for over a month—her real one on Wall Street and the even more exhausting one of being there with me, for me, while I cried and screamed and mourned. She needed a rest and, boy, had she earned it.

When my mother wasn't around, Hot Dog was. He and his wife, Thelma, stayed close, and took care of me. Thelma was in her forties, a smart, good-natured, light-skinned, top-heavy woman who owned a beauty parlor in Queens. She adored Red, and kept a great home up on the Riverdale/Bronx border. And, working as hard as she did six days a week, she'd invite me and the baby to dinner early every night and lay out a home-cooked feast that came as close to tempting me off my diet as anything ever did. Red and Thelma had no kids of their own. Jeffrey was their delight. My man, my namesake, Mr. Jab, the prince, Hot Dog called him.

So time passed. I tried to keep busy. I took care of business. I lived . . . and I learned.

Every week on Friday night, Hymie used to come over and give me the interest, the vigorish, on Bernie's loans. One week it would be one figure, the next another. He said he'd taken out his piece, the amount he and Bernie had agreed upon. I didn't even try to figure out what his deal had been with Bernie. Fine. I had the book. Most of the names in it belonged to men I didn't know. But the way it worked, many of them would be legitimate businessmen who'd needed money fast and couldn't get it from a bank. Some were people who didn't have any kind of collateral to put up. I wasn't going to call them and ask what they'd given Hymie on Friday. And, although I'd considered it once or twice, I had enough sense not to ask anyone to intervene for me.

First of all, I remembered what Bernie used to say about keeping up a good front. "Never let anyone know you're hurting. Let peo-

ple think you have more than you have. That way they'll never
think you want something from them. And when you do go to
them, they feel that your credit is good." So, I figured if the time
came that I really needed help, I'd ask. For now, I'd save the muscle.

Well, one afternoon I got a phone call from a guy whose name
was in the black book. He was very straightforward. He said that he
owed Bernie money. He knew I was B's wife and that I was well-
connected. So he wanted to let me know that he was going to pay
off the entire loan the following Friday. He'd be giving Hymie
$18,000 and that would complete his loan.

Okay. Fine. I called Hymie and told him what to expect. "When
you meet this man on Friday, Hymie, he's going to give you the full
amount," I said. "Eighteen thousand dollars."

"Terrific. Super. That's great," says the Sleaze.

"And Hymie," I said, "keep two grand for yourself. And sixteen
you bring back to me. Okay?"

"Okay. Very generous of you. Super. Don't worry."

Right. So, Friday night I'm watching the clock. Normally he'd
show about eight. It's nine, ten, eleven. No Hymie. Finally, eleven-
fifteen, they buzz from downstairs to say he's on his way up and I
can hear in the doorman's voice that something's wrong. And in
comes Hymie. His hair is a mess, washed-out, reddish-blond tufts
standing up all over his head. His face is not just pasty and sweating, it's shmeared with dirt that looks like axle grease. There's a little blood on his cheek—something red, anyway. Maybe it's his
girlfriend's nail polish. He's huffing and puffing. His coat is open
so you can see his shirt, which is ripped with a couple of buttons
missing. White, heaving blubber showing through. Not a pretty
sight.

I could have mouthed the words right alongside him: "I've been
robbed!"

Right.

"Eighteen grand!" he hollers. "They took everything. The
week's vig. The payoff. Every cent!"

Poor thing.

"Hymie, calm down, sweetheart," I said aloud. To myself I'm
chanting, You dirty motherfucking lying bastard, this is how you're
going to rob me?!

Well, he was entitled. He hated my guts. He was jealous of
Bernie. He was a low life. Fine. Of course, he'd try to rob me. And,
of course, I thought about calling in a couple of specialists who'd

give Hymie's knee caps a remedial course in debt collecting. Instead, I brought the fat man a drink. I gave him a washcloth soaked in cold water to put on his bruises. And then I went into my bedroom and brought out Bernie's little black book.

"Hymie," I said, making sure he saw the book. "Don't worry about it. You know what, Hymie, you don't have to do this anymore. It's over with."

His fat mouth went slack. I thought he'd throw a blood clot to the brain from all the effort he was making trying to figure out what that would mean to him.

"Hymie, I'm going to call up everyone in this book and tell them, the hell with it, their debts are cancelled. They owe me nothing!"

His wormy lips started working; there were sounds, but no words came out.

"Or better yet, I'll have one of the big guys from downtown, one of Bernie's friends, intervene. Hymie," I said tenderly, "I never want this to happen to you again."

"I can't think. I'm too upset," he said, and left.

The next day, like a good in-law, I called him at home to see how he was feeling. He said, "You know, Sandy, we really shouldn't stop this. Why should people get away with taking Bernie's hardearned money?"

"It's over with," I said. "I'm going downtown this afternoon and putting out the word. I'm giving them the book and telling them to call up everyone who can't pay and tell them that all debts are cancelled. I really don't want to be a part of this anyway," I said. "It's dirty and I really don't want it."

I could hear this bastard gulping, but there really was nothing he could say. In any case, I figured he was sitting on eighteen grand and whatever else he'd managed to embezzle from Bernie's business. So he'd be all right for a while. And I wouldn't have to put up with seeing him on Friday nights and having him try to wheedle and whine his way into any little piece of action he caught wind of. He could keep the bread and good riddance.

Well, a month later, I got a call from a guy who handled junkets to the Desert Inn in Las Vegas. He said that Hymie had called him up and said that he was a close relative of Bernie Barton's and he'd like to go on a junket. This man said, "I'm calling to find out if he's legit. And what do you want me to do?"

"I'll call you back," I said.

I thought about it for a while. All I kept remembering, aside from how angry I was at the fat weasel, was what an unlucky *shlep* Hymie was.

I phoned the man back. "Look," I said. "Yes, he's a relative. But he's also a bastard. I think he ripped me off for close to twenty grand. Put him on the junket, why not? But don't give him credit. Just let him travel free, let him eat, drink, let him stay in a gorgeous room and see the shows, but don't comp him any credit at all, because the guy's a stumble bum. He stole from me."

"In that case, we won't put him on at all."

"No," I said. "Whatever he stole from me, let him go for it. Maybe his luck will turn and he'll win money. Maybe. But if I know Hymie, he's going to lose and lose big. Maybe twenty's worth. Maybe more. No matter what, though, no credit."

"You got it," the guy said.

So Hymie drank Dom Pérignon for breakfast and ate sturgeon for brunch. And he dropped a bundle bigger than his belly. He let it slip like sand through his fingers. He came back from Vegas dry-cleaned.

Revenge was definitely tempered by regret. *Eighteen grand*—I'd let it get away from me. So, six months later, when my friend Lila phoned with a sudden cash-flow problem, I was determined to help her claim what was rightfully hers.

Let me tell you about Lila.

Lila Navarro was stacked. She was a leggy blonde with a pair of doe eyes that made Bambi look like he was squinting. And she was as bubbly and upbeat as she was beautiful. In addition to her physical and temperamental assets—or maybe because of them—Lila had enviable assets in jewelry and hard cash. These she'd collected from a very big wise guy who'd kept her for years, and kept her very well. Duke was a major mob *macher*. So when you said, "Lila, those diamonds are to die for," you weren't that far off the mark.

About half a year after Hymie lost his shirt and my money in Vegas, Lila called me, sounding uncharacteristically blue. "Well, I don't have any more jewelry," she said. "Duke's under investigation, and the lawyers told him to put it all in the vault."

"All of it?" I groaned, thinking of the blinding rocks, the exquisite rings, pins, necklaces, and earrings that kept Lila lit up like Christmas twelve months a year. "But you've got access to the vault, right?"

"No," she said. "But, what the heck. It's just for a couple of weeks. Just in case the FBI busts into my place one night while he's here. Just so they don't find the jewelry or take it. You know how the FBI can be. It's no big deal, Sandy. What's a couple of weeks?"

A lifetime, as it turned out.

While Lila's jewelry was buried in an iron box in the basement of the First National Savings Bank, Duke had a massive heart attack.

I dragged Lila out of her apartment and shlepped her over to the hospital. Duke was trussed up like a turkey ready for the oven, and looked about the same color. He was gray. He had tubes running in and out of him. Lila didn't want to do it, but I made her ask him about the vault. Which one had he put her jewelry in? I didn't feel that great about doing it, either—but she was my friend, lost in grief and fear, a couple of things I knew a little about.

Duke understood. He told us which vault and the name it was under. Lila had the keys to all his safety deposit boxes at her apartment. Then he tried to give her a hard look. "What's the matter," he said. "You worried? You think I'm going to die?"

I was holding Lila's hand. "Yeah," we both blurted out. And he cracked up.

Five weeks later he was dead.

After the funeral, Lila was wild with panic. Duke had supported her for years and years. The gifts he'd given her, her retirement fund—hundreds of thousands of dollars' worth of jewelry, and the fifty or sixty thousand dollars that had been in the house—were now locked away, lost to her forever.

The two of us sat around Lila's place drinking J&B and pondering the mess. Lila was an ex-showgirl. The walk-in closet in her bedroom held a couple of wigs. She was dynamite with makeup. We drank, we wandered around her house. On the chaise in her bedroom lay a suit of Duke's she couldn't bring herself to throw out. I must have passed the suit ten times going to and from the bathroom. Passed the wigs on their wooden stands. Passed the makeup on her dressing table. And I still don't know how it all came together. How we hatched the scheme.

What I do remember is waking up to the alarm one Friday morning and thinking: It's dark out, it's too early—what the hell am I doing up at this hour? And then I thought about what Lila and I were supposed to do that day. I sort of smiled, thinking in that foggy, not-quite-awake way that it was a dream, a joke, right? Then my heart kicked in like a jackhammer. I knew it was real. Lila and I were going to get the diamonds today.

In front of the mirror, at Lila's dressing table, the transformation began. The men's wigs she'd gotten from the theatrical supply house were good. Hers was auburn, mine a darker brown, like mink almost—dark with a couple of lighter strands running through it. It looked prematurely gray and very real.

As she pinned my hair up close to my head, Lila's hands were shaking. And why not? She was lucky her fingers worked at all. She'd spent the better part of two days practicing Duke's signature. The cream-colored carpet was littered with crumpled sheets of paper on which was written—in Duke's childish scrawl—the bank alias he'd confided at the hospital.

The thick hairpins Lila used did a good job of flattening my thick hair. She put a stocking over the top of my head and we both burst into nervous laughter. I looked like Dopey of the Seven Dwarves until she slipped my wig on. I shut my eyes. Lila slopped a coat of gummy glue all over my cheeks, pressed my upper lip, chin, temples. I opened my eyes a minute later—presto!, I had sideburns and a nicely trimmed beard and mustache. Then she thickened my eyebrows. The whole thing looked pretty good, but putting on a pair of shades, these masculine-looking sunglasses she'd picked up, really finished the face trick.

The morning was almost gone by the time she had herself done up. We wrapped bandages around our breasts, flattening them as best we could—two *zaftik* ex-showgirls, better endowed than the Rockefeller Foundation, trying to pass for men. Barrel-chested men. Lila'd bought extra padding from the theatrical place, too, to make us look bigger, fleshing out our shoulders, chests, arms, even our necks. Lila was going to wear a scarf. I had on one of Duke's cashmere turtlenecks.

We put on our suits, hats, dark glasses and studied ourselves in her mirrored closet doors. It was a great look. "A couple of inches taller," I told her, "and I could fall for me." We left Lila's place giddy with self-confidence.

The bank was on West Forty-seventh Street, in the crowded heart of the jewelry district. We got out of the cab and shouldered our way through the lunch-time noise and chaos. The narrow street was filled with rushing people—solid-looking women in fur coats and jackets and pale-skinned orthodox Jews, many of them dressed in long, shiny black coats, with beaver hats and sidecurls tucked behind their ears; but, surprisingly, there were plenty of guys who looked a lot like us. Pale, bearded men of medium height in business suits and hats, walking with their heads down, in a hurry.

Just outside the bank, Lila grabbed me. "I can't do it," she whispered, dragging on my arm. "Let's not do this, Sandy. Forget it."

I wavered for a moment, but then I thought of my own vault adventure and how I'd never have made it without that money. That got my blood pumping. But I spoke very calmly. I didn't want to make a scene in the street. "No way," I said. "We're going for it."

In we went, straight through the bank without another word, and down the stairs to the vault room. Lila gave a nod and a grunt to the officer in charge of the vault. I slapped down the safety deposit box key authoritatively as Lila, gloved hand trembling only slightly, quickly signed, in that cramped, practiced scrawl, the name Duke had given us.

The guy picked up the signature tag, went to check it, and said nothing to us. Next thing we knew, he'd swung open the door to the vault room and we were in like Flynn.

There was about $72,000 in cash in the box—along with all of Lila's jewelry. What a treasure chest. What a sight. It reminded me of the pirate movies I'd seen as a child. I didn't dare look at Lila's face. I was trying with all my might not to burst into gleeful laughter. It was way too soon to relax. I furrowed my brow and played my role straight and did just what we'd planned to do.

We'd brought along handkerchiefs to wrap the jewelry. We put them in the inside breast pockets of our jackets and in our slacks pockets. We divvied up the money and stashed it as evenly as possible so we wouldn't leave the bank bulging lopsidedly, and we sauntered out of the vault.

Back at her apartment, Lila and I poured the treasure trove onto her coffee table and screamed and hugged each other and literally danced with delight. Then we poured ourselves some stiff drinks—in part to celebrate our triumph; in part to numb us against the agony of removing the false beards.

Sitting there, half-plotzed on scotch, I had a sudden sense that Bernie was near, that he'd been with us all along, laughing, approving. Maybe it came from the sweater, the turtleneck I was wearing. The smell of cigars, a pale whiff of aftershave that clung to the fear-dampened cashmere. It was Duke's sweater but it could have been Bernie's. Putting together some wacky plan, risking his neck for a friend, it was something Bernie would have done. I looked at Lila, all flushed with excitement. I thought, Bernie would have been proud of me today.

CHAPTER SIXTEEN

The Merry Widow

Wise guys were my friends. Wise guys were my partners. Wise guys were practically the only men I knew. But I was determined not to be swept off my feet by one ever again. Mahoney the Phoney might have been the first of Bernie's old pals to hit on me, but he certainly wasn't the last. Almost a year after Bernie's death, I was slim and trim again. Now that I could wear high heels, form-fitting dresses, short skirts, and hip-hugger jeans, now that my auburn hair was long and lustrous again, now that laughter didn't feel like a foreign language, the wise guys came out of the woodwork.

If I showed up in a restaurant with Morty or Hot Dog, they'd float over to the table with stars in their eyes. If Vinny took me to a wedding or even a funeral, guys who'd treated me like the invisible woman were suddenly my lost friends and last hope. It wasn't that *I* was so irresistibly attractive. But a slim, pretty, possibly naive, young widow with maybe millions stashed away sure was. And it wasn't just that most of these sudden suitors were *cafones*, jerks, shmucks—though they were. I still wanted what Bernie had promised me but hadn't lived to deliver—a normal, picket-fence life.

I wasn't the only wise guy widow on the block. A girl named Doris, whose husband, Lenny the Dentist, had died half a year before Bernie, called me while I was sitting shivah to extend her condolences. It turned out that she worked for a company that booked gambling junkets. We talked once in a while and, almost a year after Bernie's death, she invited me to join her on a junket to Monte Carlo. Five days, four nights, in the South of France, with everything free except the casino gambling. And, would you believe it, my mother and Red and even Morty had to help convince me to go. As the anniversary of Bernie's death drew near I'd begun to slump again into sadness. "Go," Tillie commanded. "Don't look a gift horse from God in the mouth."

Our very first evening on the glamorous Côte d'Azur, Doris and I, who were sharing a beautiful two-bedroom suite overlooking the yacht-filled harbor of Monte Carlo, shimmied into floor-length basic black and headed over to the legendary casino.

I was bent over a hot craps table, when a European-accented male voice said, "Do it, cupcake."

I had hit a seven and then another seven on the first roll-out, and my third throw had just been an eleven. The casinos in France are much quieter than those in Vegas. The deep, accented voice sounded very loud and forceful. It threw me off. My hand and luck wavered. I threw a point—a five, I think. And then, annoyed, I turned and looked up. And up. And up. And there was the Marlboro Man in a tuxedo, a towering blond god, a six-foot-six Dutchman named Peter Von Shlemme.

I quickly forgave him for blowing my winning streak. We chatted and laughed. He staked me to black jack, craps, champagne, and, within hours of our meeting, a diamond bracelet. Not a big-deal diamond bracelet, just a cute, delicate little one, padded with rubies and lesser stones. He was tall, gorgeous, a gentleman to his well-clipped fingertips *and* he had a yacht parked outside that made Davey Yaras's boat look like a toy. It was three stories tall.

We wound up watching the sun come up from the deck of this ship. Then, Peter escorted me back to the hotel where Doris was frantic, ready to get the police to drag the Mediterranean for the poor, depressed widow she'd talked into coming to France. I thought we'd need her dead husband, Lenny the Dentist, to wire shut her jaw when I introduced her to Peter, who was, as my mother would've said, a gift horse from God.

Peter and I were inseparable for the next few days. We danced, gambled, dined at the best restaurants, drank Dom Pérignon, and saw a lot of dawns from the deck of the yacht. During the day, we'd swim, sunbathe, and listen to music on deck or sleep in one of the countless luxurious cabins below.

On our third day together Peter had to go into town on business. He left me aboard the yacht alone. After a while, I started exploring the rest of the place.

The yacht was amazing. Bedrooms, dining areas, sitting

rooms—all exquisitely put together, very glamorous, with gold fixtures, paintings, antiques, ankle-deep carpeting, and fresh flowers
in huge crystal vases. And as I explored, I kept saying to myself,
"This is how the other half lives—the really rich, one hundred percent legit."

Two flights below deck, I opened a door and there were the
crates. Coffin-shaped. Big. Instantly familiar. I stepped into the
room and flipped up the top on one of the boxes. I didn't have to
pry it open this time, just lifted the lid and there they were. Guns. A
cabin full of them.

I ran upstairs as fast as my feet could carry me, determined to
head straight back to the hotel. Peter was just stepping back aboard.

"Listen," I said, tossing my suntan oil and cigarettes into my
beachbag. "I didn't mean to pry, but I saw the crates downstairs.
The guns. Peter," I said, "are you a gun runner? A dope smug-
gler?"

He laughed. "I'm in munitions, guns, various enterprises. Let's
just say I am an entrepreneur."

But I knew better. I just knew it. "You don't do anything really
legal, do you?" I asked.

Again with the laugh. "What do you know about these things?"

Well, in a couple of choice words, I told him.

He was thrilled, delighted. It was the best news he'd had all
week. At last, someone who could understand. Share his life.
Travel the world with him.

"What is it?" I said, angrily. "Do I have a sign on my back that
says, Wise Guys Apply Here?!"

I scrambled off the yacht and headed back to the hotel full steam
ahead. Two days later, I flew back to the States with Doris. I was
glad I'd met Peter, glad we'd had our fling. I felt more like a
woman than I had in a long time and I was grateful for the fun. But
I didn't need anyone new in my life who wasn't one hundred percent kosher.

I'd had it with wise guys.

During the shivah period, I'd made friends with a couple who
lived down the hall, Margo and Warren Steiner. Margo was as short
as I was tall. She was a bright, personable, stylish girl, no more
than five-foot-two, and every inch a *mensch*. The first time she
spoke to me, we were both carrying bags of garbage to the incinerator at the end of the hall. "I'm sorry about your loss," this lovely
girl said in a voice filled with such sincerity that I almost burst into

tears. "I don't know how you'll manage, with a brand-new baby and everything. If there's anything we can do to help, please come by. Just knock on the door."

She and her husband, Warren, a short, wiry, attractive young stockbroker, had no children. She oohed and aahed over Jeffrey, who gave her a great big drooly grin. And from then on, through the months of mourning, their apartment became my haven. They were bright, successful, and straight. They became my friends.

Two weeks after I got back from France, I threw a great big party for Jeffrey's first birthday. It was Memorial Day weekend. I ordered dozens of bottles of champagne and platters of smoked fish and deli from Zabar's. There were breads and bagels, strudels and cookies, and a great big birthday cake with a huge blue candle in the shape of the number one. Tillie, Marlene, and I, with a little help from Margo down the hall, blew up balloons and strung crepe paper around the place. And we crowned Jeffrey with a little blue party hat.

The birthday boy's proud godfathers were there—Red, Vinny, big Morty. Margo and Warren came over with some of their friends. Shorty, P.D., and a few of the guys from the bar stopped by. Judy and Nino brought their little girl. Thirty or forty people showed up, all of them bearing gifts. The baby's room was piled high with huge stuffed animals, alphabet blocks, Legos, trucks, planes and pull toys, little footballs and baseballs and whiffle ball bats. And, again, some of the guys came up to me or my mother and pressed envelopes filled with birthday cards and cash into our hands.

It was a joyous occasion but it was Bernie's birthday, too, and his friends remembered it. All afternoon, guys would walk up to me and say:

"He would've been forty-seven today, right?"

"Great party. B would've loved it."

"You know, Sandy, I miss him, too."

Toward sunset, I stepped out onto the terrace. The apartment was noisy with talk and laughter. With Thelma at his side, bearing a cotton cloth to wipe Jeffrey's drooling mouth, Red was toting the baby around. Jeffrey had begun speaking early and one of his first words was "hat." He loved Hot Dog's hats and now he was peeking out from under Red's straw fedora as one adoring friend after another took turns tickling him, tossing pretend punches at him, kissing his sweet cheeks and wet chin. And the Jab was giggling and grinning. My mother was talking with Margo and Warren.

Morty was showing Marlene card tricks. I saw all this from the terrace and I remember feeling very blessed and content and proud of the party I'd put together. Then I turned away and looked up at the pink-streaked twilight sky. "Thanks, babe," I said. "Happy birthday."

I'd had my batteries charged in Monte Carlo and I was speeding through everyday life now. A couple of times a week I'd go uptown to help Red out. And at the end of the day, when the two of us ambled along 125th Street on our way to Cokey's bar or one of our other favorite places, I'd feel special again—the way I used to with Bernie. The older guys who'd known him and the new guys who'd gotten to know me would call out, "Hey, princess. How you doin'? How's it going? Lookin' good, woman." And I loved it. I loved being known, feeling safe, walking tall.

I had that same good feeling in the bar on Second Avenue when the wise guys and the squares treated me with respect and deference. No one minded that I couldn't mix a decent drink. It was easy enough to pour straight shots and sit around making small talk. I liked the dank, shady atmosphere, the characters, the gamblers and tough guys, the players and pretenders. It was a world that was totally separate from my life at home, from sitting in the park with Jeffrey or wheeling a shopping cart through the supermarket. And I loved it, too, because it was a world that kept me connected to Bernie. It was a way of keeping him alive for me. At the bar or up in Harlem, ten times a day, I'd catch myself thinking, "What would Bernie say in a case like this? What would Bernie do?" And when I drove, I'd realize that I was checking the rearview mirror because Bernie always said to make sure no one was following me.

Nights I'd spend quietly at home with Jeffrey. My mom or Nora kept me company. Some evenings, I'd take Jeffrey with me to Margo and Warren's apartment and we'd hang out there and he'd fall asleep on their big, soft sofa. Warren was teaching me how to play the stock market. He was very bright and very busy in those boom days. He'd take companies that were shells and build up the value of their stock and get out with bundles of money. I started off with $2,000 and Warren gave me a tip on an over-the-counter stock that all of a sudden started going up and up. I got out, a couple of weeks later, with a terrific profit and an addiction to playing the market. I started reading *The Wall Street Journal*. I'd listen very carefully to Warren's stock conversations and advice.

In that era of Day Trading, when you could buy a stock in the morning and sell it in the afternoon, Margo and I decided to form an informal little corporation, to pool our money and play. A couple of days a week, Warren would send a limo to take us down to the trading floor and we'd buy and sell and go to lunch with friends we'd made at the exchange.

Margo and I might have looked as different from one another as day from night, but we were kindred spirits and became fast friends. She was an Argentinian Jew who'd been raised in Buenos Aires. She'd come to America as a young girl and one of the things we discovered we had in common, even though I was born here, was a feeling of being different and of working hard to fit in. Another thing we discovered about each other, to our mutual delight, was that we both believed in psychic phenomena. In fact, Margo had a Santeria priest she'd go to occasionally who was fresh off the boat from Cuba.

I was in seventh heaven, meeting bright new people, making money hand over fist one week, then throwing it away the next. And I was working hard at improving myself, my vocabulary and diction. I was trying to absorb everything about this new and exciting world. And, best of all, to these people, I was just a rich widow—a *normal* rich widow.

One of the people I met through Warren and Margo was Sybil Burton, who'd recently been divorced from Richard Burton, who'd left her for Elizabeth Taylor. Now she was trying to put together financing for an elegant new kind of club in New York—a discotheque. She'd borrowed $1,000 each from hundreds of people and Warren, Margo, and I became three of them, three of the countless investors in Arthur's, Manhattan's first glamor and glitter, celeb-haunted disco.

And who did I invite to be my escort for opening night? None other than Hot Dog Red, himself. Margo and I in our floor-length gowns, Red and Warren in tuxedos, drove up to the spotlit entrance, where it looked like thousands of wild celebrity stalkers were bunched behind ropes, gawking and screaming at the entering stars. There was a red carpet leading up to the doors and plenty of dark-suited muscle holding back the barricaded fans.

We stepped out of our big, black limo and walked toward the doors and suddenly people were shouting, "Cab Calloway! Cab Calloway!" Red waved graciously to the crowd, then started signing autographs until I dragged him away. Roddy McDowall, Sybil

Burton's main partner in the club, was greeting people at the door. As we walked in, he said, "Hello, Cab." And Red said, "How do!"

I'd begun to feel like I was in control of my life—and that it was a pretty good life. I did what I wanted to do when I wanted to do it. I ran my house that way. I ran the businesses that way. I ran my social life that way. I slept when I wanted to sleep, ate when I wanted to eat, I had no one to answer to except myself, right or wrong. For the first time in my entire life, I was footloose and fancy free.

Morty was not. The poor guy had been busted on a narcotics thing and he knew he couldn't beat the rap. He was destined to do time.

"You know, Sandy," he said during one of our evening card games, "you're doing okay now. But you never know what could happen. When you might need someone to help you out of a jam. A guy with connections. Look at me. Out of the blue, I'm going away for a year. But you know who always asks for you—and he really never met you; only saw you from a distance at the funeral—is Chalky."

"That's strange, Morty," I said, "the man never called me or anything, never showed up at the house when I was sitting shivah. He was supposed to be such a close friend of Bernie's. I know how much Bernie loved him, but I don't know him."

"Well, being that I'm going away and being that Chalky is interested in meeting you, how about one night the three of us get together for dinner? Would you like that?"

I wasn't sure and I said so.

About a week later, Warren was out of town and Morty decided to take Margo and me to dinner at Gatsby's on First Avenue. At that moment in time, Gatsby's was the place to go—a big, beautiful restaurant where you'd always find a couple of wise guys thrown in with the Upper East Side thrill seekers, the big-money garmentos, lawyers, brokers, wealthy college kids, and slumming socialites who mobbed the place on weekends. So I wasn't totally surprised to see Chalky Lefkowitz already there, sitting silently at a table with a glum-looking blonde at his side.

"Hey, there's Chalky," Morty said, trying to make it seem like a stunning coincidence. "Why don't we ask him to join us?"

He was such a bad liar, no wonder he was going to do time. "Join us? Morty, they're sitting alone at a table set for five. Maybe we should join them."

Chalky perked up as we approached his table. It didn't take two minutes for him to invite us to sit down and order drinks. He was a couple of years younger than Bernie and there wasn't much left of the white-blond hair that had given him his nickname. But he was tall, tanned, slim, and fit-looking and, in a crisp pin-striped shirt and an elegant dove gray suit, he was dressed in that squeaky clean, tightly buttoned-up way he'd been at Bernie's funeral. The girl with him was a standard issue mob playmate—attractive, young, nervous, and quiet.

It was a pleasant evening. Chalky was charming. He didn't laugh as much as Morty did. He didn't tell jokes. He wasn't clever. But he was nice and, at Morty's prompting, he started to tell stories about the old days on the Lower East Side with Bernie. I'd heard how their mothers had pushed them side by side in carriages before they could walk, how they'd known each other practically from birth. But Chalky brought me glimpses of Bernie's childhood. They stole together, he said. They were never athletes, Chalky and Bernie. While other kids were playing stickball and stoop ball, they'd be shooting pennies, playing cards, and stealing apples off neighborhood pushcarts.

"And Bernie," Chalky said, "was the best-looking kid in the world. A lot better looking than me," he said. "Even as a kid, he had the *shtik* to get girls. The talk, the style, the balls. I'd tag along with him when I was ten, eleven and he was, what, a big shot of thirteen? We'd get dressed up and go uptown to pick up girls. Our neighborhood was First Street and First Avenue. Uptown to us was Fourteenth Street. Then Bernie found out there was a Forty-second Street and that was that!"

What Chalky didn't say that night was that his own childhood had ended at seventeen when he'd done his first bid at Dannemora. Morty told me that on the way home. He also told me that Chalky was connected, feared, and respected. He was closer to Meyer than Bernie had ever been. And he was tight with the Italians, the old Luciano mob that had been taken over by Vito Genovese. Also, the fact that he'd done time bought him an edge. Hard time, too. He'd fucked up good, but he'd paid his dues.

Chalky had been to prison a couple of times. The last bid he'd done, he and a friend had set out to rob the New Jersey home of a bookmaker reputed to hold millions in his safe. The friend had clocked the comings and goings of the mark, knew when the guy was home, when he was away, knew the family went out to dinner every Thursday night at the same time, and knew exactly how long they'd be gone. Easy pickings.

So one Thursday night, after the family left for dinner, Chalky and his pal broke into the house and were meandering around the ground floor feeling safe and comfy, utterly oblivious to the fact that one of the bookmaker's kids was sick and had stayed home with a maid that night. The little girl surprised them coming down the stairs. The maid called the cops. And the easy pickings turned into a grotesque shootout under the Hudson.

With cop cars in close pursuit, Chalky's friend drove into the Lincoln Tunnel, headed like a bat out of hell for New York. The cops were shooting. Chalky returned some of the heat. Meanwhile, the NYPD had been alerted and the tunnel was sealed on the Manhattan side. So they were ducks in a barrel, and Chalky's partner's face was blown off in the crossfire. Chalky wound up with the guy's blood and brains all over his jacket. And a cop was killed.

They couldn't pin the cop's death on him. With all the bullets flying, nobody knew who'd killed who. But New Jersey definitely had him for armed robbery and a couple of other things. He was sentenced to twenty years in Trenton and had done twelve when he was paroled.

I didn't know any of this at the restaurant, of course. I said, "What puzzles me, I mean, you loved Bernie so much and he was always talking about you— Why didn't you come by the house during shivah? Why didn't you ever get in touch after the funeral?"

He fumbled and bumbled for an answer and then he finally said, "That's in the past. Now, with Morty going away . . . and I know how close he's been to you, a good friend . . . I'd like you to have my phone number and know at all times where you can get in touch with me. Just in case you ever need a favor."

So I filed it—under friend in need. I had no interest in the man romantically. He was respected, he was connected. Maybe he could even do card tricks like Morty. Great. My motto was: No More Mobsters.

Then my girlfriend, Lila, introduced me to Eddie.

One night Lila and I decided to go out dancing. We were at Arthur's, hadn't been in the place ten minutes, when she started tugging me toward a small table off the dance floor where a guy was sitting alone with a bottle of champagne cooling in an ice bucket. "It's Eddie," Lila bubbled. "I've been dying for you to meet him, Sandy. He's gorgeous. He's loaded. He's in the trucking business. And he owns a couple of horses."

She was right about gorgeous. Sitting there was a young Greek god who, as it turned out, was Italian. He was thirty, maybe thirty-one years old, with olive skin, thick dark hair, and the kind of green eyes that look up at you out of a black forest of lashes. He was beautifully dressed and, when Lila introduced us, he extended this cool, brown, manicured hand and tugged me gently toward the seat beside him.

We had a lovely time, talking, laughing, drinking champagne. I asked whether it was true that he owned a couple of racehorses. He said absolutely, and he invited Lila and me to go out to the track with him the next day. Lila said she'd love to. Eddie took my hand and said, "And you—you're mine. You're definitely coming with me."

I was flattered. I loved his looks, I'd enjoyed the conversation and laughter. It was time to leave. I stood up. Then he stood. He came up to my shoulder. In flats, he was maybe only an inch or two shorter than me. In heels, I towered over him.

It didn't seem to bother him, not that night nor the next day at the track. The three of us had a fabulous brunch, lost most of the races we bet on, and then went down to the stables where Eddie, with an iron grip on my hand, kibitzed with and introduced us to everyone from the owners to the stable boys. It was a terrific day and, before it was over, Eddie was in love. And that was okay with me.

We started seeing each other. He had a beautiful light-filled apartment on the Upper East Side and he was as fastidious about it as he was about his clothes, which he changed a couple of times a day. He was a good cook. He enjoyed fixing dinners for us. Jeffrey was small and portable then and it was nice for me, having the three of us together. In fact, one of the quirky things about dating Eddie was that I'd never met any of his friends except for Lila. We'd have dinner with her at a nice restaurant once in a while, but mostly it was just the two of us, or Eddie would cook at home for Jeffrey and me.

Inevitably, I moved away from my friends and associates. I didn't want Eddie connecting me with the racket club. Red understood. "You just go and have a good time," he said. "You deserve it, woman. I'll take care of business and when you can help me out you will." He even arranged to cover for me at the bar.

Six months into the relationship, Eddie took me to dinner at Monsignor, an elegant Italian restaurant off Park Avenue in the Fifties. When the waiter came over, Eddie said, "We'll order drinks now, but we'll wait with dinner." Then he turned to me. "My uncle's going to join us," he explained.

Before I could ask him more about it, in walked a consiglieri of the Gambino family, a tall, graying man of sixty, who in his youth had been a noted mob enforcer. He'd recently finished a bid in Atlanta. Of course, the table he was heading for was ours.

"Sandy, this is my uncle Aneillo." Eddie beamed.

"I know him," I said. "Hello, nice to see you."

"I was sorry to hear about Bernie. He was a good man. I always liked him," the big man said.

"It's been over two years."

"I was away." He shrugged philosophically.

I could hardly look at Eddie through dinner. My head was spinning. I'd prided myself on keeping the past out of this new relationship, and here it was, sitting across the table in gray hair and a neat suit. And Eddie didn't seem the least bit flustered.

"What's going on?" I demanded after we'd said goodnight to the consiglieri. "You didn't act surprised at all that I knew your uncle—or that he knew me! You knew all about me, everything, who my husband was? Talk to me, Eddie. Tell me how, what, where?!"

"Of course I knew," he said. "Sandy, when I met you, after I realized I liked you, I went downtown and asked permission to start seeing you—"

"You got permission to date me?! From who?!" I wanted to know. Later I found out that it was the North brothers he'd gone to, the short, stocky guys who used to show up at Bernie's apartment on East Seventy-ninth Street with suitcases full of Ceil Chapman gowns.

"What's the difference who?" Eddie said. "I told them my intentions were honorable and they are. I'll probably marry you."

"No!" I hollered, scaring the hell out of him, I think. "I mean, I don't know what's going on here. I'm in shock. I can't talk about it now."

Marriage? I had told my friends, "I like this man. He's good to me. He's good to my son. It's nice to have a boyfriend—but I miss Bernie. When I'm in bed with him, I miss Bernie. When I think something's funny and he doesn't get it, I miss Bernie. When I have a problem and I ask his advice, I miss Bernie. He loves me. He takes care of me. But he's not sweet, he's not passionate like Bernie was."

And friends would tell me, "Get that out of your head. Nobody and nothing'll ever be like Bernie was."

Oh no, oh shit, I was thinking all the way uptown in the cab, how did I wind up again with a connected guy, an *Italian* connected guy? Not my life, but all the Italian wives' lives I'd seen, flashed before my eyes: the nervous wrecks watching their macho men strut; the women who drank on the sly and phoned their husbands' mistresses in the middle of the night; the ones who made fun of what selfish bastards their husbands were in bed.

Eddie was selfish in bed. Eddie was a gambler, a big loser, who owed money to everyone. His family was always bailing him out with the shylocks. And he had that macho way about him that sometimes fascinated but more often frustrated me. He had very rigid, old-fashioned Italian ideas of how everyone should behave—especially me. And he had this thing about my being Jewish. He'd say things like, "You know, you're very beautiful, for a Jewish girl," or "You're great, for a Jewish girl."

I could almost hear Bernie asking, "Is this the man you picked to replace me? Is this the kind of 'substantial' man you think is good enough to be a father to my son?"

I knew I'd never marry Eddie. I knew I should stop seeing him, end it. But I didn't know how quickly and terribly fate would do for me what I couldn't do for myself.

A few weeks after the restaurant encounter with his uncle, Eddie and I had plans to go to dinner and the race track. That day I came down with a virus. I ran a high fever, I was practically delirious. I called Eddie and told him I couldn't make it, then I slept for the rest of the day and through the night. At eight the next morning, I got a phone call from Eddie's brother, whom I'd met at the trucking office once or twice. He told me Eddie was dead.

I learned from the newspapers as well as from friends that he'd been shot "gangland style," a bullet hole in the back of the head. His car had been found somewhere out on the Island. It was front-page news. GANGLAND NEPHEW SHOT the headlines read. And there were pictures of Eddie's bloody body on the cover of *The Daily News.*

As the first shock subsided, the realization that I was supposed to be with him that night set in. It could have been me in that car on the front page of *The Daily News*—or, God forbid, Jeffrey—lying dead beside Eddie right on the bloodsoaked seat of the Lincoln we'd ridden in so many times before.

God had to have been watching over me that night, God or my *gutta better.* Because hit men, contract killers, don't spend a lot of time worrying about who's sitting next to their target. If the hit's set, it goes. And if I hadn't come down with a twenty-four-hour flu,

I'd have been sitting right next to Eddie, and Bernie's son would've been an orphan. I was grief-stricken, petrified, and grateful all at the same time. And I kept saying, over and over again, "What is with me? What's wrong with me? Why do I get involved with these men? How do they find me? How do they know?"

Four or five months later, on a beautiful mild day in early fall, I decided, on a whim, to treat myself to lunch at Tavern on the Green. I asked for and was ushered to a quiet table where I could lunch alone, looking out at the garden and the still lush lawns of Central Park. Midway through the meal I noticed a table of three men. I looked at them and said to myself, mafiosi, wise guys having a meeting at a safe place in the afternoon where mostly elderly people or tourists go. Smart, I said to myself, and I went back to minding my own business.

When I'd finished lunch and looked up to signal the waiter, I saw they were gone. "I'm ready," I said to the waiter.

"Your check was picked up by the men at that table," he said, nodding at, what else, the one where the wise guys had been sitting, the table with the cigar butts still smoldering in the ashtray. I laughed to myself. Maybe I even looked up to heaven to ask Bernie to witness my innocence. See, I was just sitting here minding my own business. They find me.

I walked back out into the sunshine, ready to hail a cab. One of the men from the wise guy table was waiting. He took my arm and said, "Did you enjoy your lunch?"

Was he good-looking? Would God with his sense of humor tempt me with anything less than a stunning, tall, dark, and handsome wise guy? He was gorgeous. A cross between Robert De Niro and Vic Damone.

"Do I have to thank you for it?" I asked.

"You do," he said, and started making small talk.

"Excuse me. Here's a cab. Thanks again for lunch," I said.

He held on to my arm. "No, don't. I'll drive you."

I pulled my arm out of his grip, smiling pleasantly. "Very nice of you. No thanks."

"Why not? I don't get it. I've got some time to kill—"

"I said no thanks and I mean it," I interrupted him. "I don't get into cars with strange men."

He laughed. "Okay. Fair enough." He opened the cab door for me. "You take the cab and I'll follow you home."

"Don't be ridiculous," I said, and got into the taxi. He closed the door and gave me a smile and, fifteen minutes later, as I was getting out of the cab at my building, he pulled into the driveway behind us.

His name was Nicky.

"Let me guess," I said. "You're Italian."

"You got it. You like Italian men?"

"I've really got to go. Thanks for lunch."

Ten minutes later, with my phone number scrawled on the back of a matchbook in the pocket of his overcoat, he waved goodbye with a great big smile. And, with my emotions turned on and my brain shut off, I went upstairs to wait for his call.

I liked him. I liked the way he'd come on to me, the way he looked, the sound of his voice. I liked him so much that when he phoned later that night as he'd said he would, I told myself, *really* did I know he was a wise guy? How could I be so sure? Was it just because he was Italian? Had I been jumping to conclusions, making a federal case out of nothing? I told myself a lot of things. Him I told, "Yes, I'd love to have dinner with you."

Friday night, when he picked me up, we fell right into easy conversation, teasing and bantering like old friends. Then five minutes into the ride, he said, "Do you like Italian food?"

"I love it."

"Okay. We'll go downtown for dinner."

"Downtown?" I knew he meant Little Italy. But there were lots of restaurants downtown. I thought, maybe we won't bump into anybody who knows me. I said, "Great," and kept the conversation light and breezy—which was no piece of cake after Nicky parked, took my hand, and started walking me toward a restaurant owned by a guy named Sammy who'd been one of Bernie's best friends.

Okay, here goes, I thought, as we walked through the door. He'll find out who I am and I'll find out who he is. And I clung to the diminishing possibility that Nicky would turn out to be a tourist who just liked the Italian atmosphere downtown.

He'd made reservations and they'd picked out a nice corner table for us at the back of the restaurant, where Nicky immediately took the seat facing the door. "You feel safer with your back up against the wall?" I teased.

He raised an eyebrow at me.

"I read a lot of books and see a lot of old gangster movies," I explained.

"Then we have something in common. I love old gangster movies," he said.

About twenty minutes into the meal, a familiar voice called out, "Well, hello Nicola, how are you?" and I realized that Bernie's friend Sammy, the owner of the restaurant, was on his way over to our table. I got very involved with my veal chop and, while Nicky and Sammy conversed in Italian, I kept my head down and pushed food around on my plate. Finally, I had to look up. Sammy did a double-take.

"Sandy, princess, baby, how are you?" He bent down and kissed me hello.

Nicky's mouth fell open. "How do you know him?" he asked, and I could see the macho storm clouds gathering on his brow. He thought Sammy was an old lover of mine.

"Friend of the family," I said.

Sammy sat down with us and started shmoozing with me—how was I, how'd I been, how was my beautiful son? "If BB was around, he'd be so happy with that kid," Sammy said. "But of course, he is looking down at us from heaven, God bless him." The next thing I knew, Sammy had Nicky joining us in a toast to Bernie who, Sammy let him know, was somebody special, a man of respect.

A few minutes after Sammy left us, Nicky excused himself. By the time he came back to the table he knew everything about Bernie and me that he needed to know. He returned with a smile on his face. He looked at me and said, "You know, kid, you're my kind of broad. You and I are going to get along very, very well," he said. "This could be the beginning of a beautiful friendship."

Yeah, he loved gangster movies. He talked gangster movies. He tried to live gangster movies. But he was a bookie. He was in his early thirties and ran a successful bookmaking operation. That's all he did. It was almost legal, I told myself. And though that pleased me, it sure didn't thrill him. Nicky wanted to be a hot shot, a heavy hitter, a made man. He definitely wanted to be bigger and better connected than I—but he wasn't. Poor man, he wasn't a wise guy, he was only a disappointed hood. And when we had arguments, I'd let him know it.

We argued a lot—for me it was almost recreational. Bernie had enjoyed arguing, disagreeing, battling and, as he loved to say, he'd taught me everything I knew. So shooting off my mouth and standing up for myself had become like a sport for me. And I was good at it. I'd learned from one of the best. For Nicky, it was shocking for a woman to talk back, let alone yell back, stand her ground, or even threaten. He was very macho, very used to women, if you'll pardon the expression, jumping when he said jump and humping when he said hump. And, wildly jealous and possessive as he was, he definitely didn't play by the same rules he laid down.

Which is why it ended badly.

He was always checking up on me. Always giving me grief about where I'd been and what I'd done. If he called and I was out, he was sure I was with another guy. If I met one of Bernie's friends at a club or restaurant, he'd sulk while we spoke and give me the fifth degree the minute the guy left. I was totally loyal to him. It never occurred to me to date more than one man at a time.

So, when Nicky got a little loaded one night in a restaurant and started paying a lot of attention to a girl at the bar, I got annoyed. And when I saw him writing down his number on a matchbook and handing it to her on the sly, I got loud. One thing led to another. A shouting match ensued. I spilled a drink on him. He overturned the table. And as he made a move for me, I growled: "Try it, buddy. You think you're connected? You don't know connections. Try it and you'll get to know a couple of mine!"

I looked into his face and he was really frightened. I turned on my heels and walked away.

No more wise guys. No more wanna-be wise guys. I'd had it. From the gunboat buccaneer, to poor Eddie to Nicky the Weasel, my record for picking the wrong men—or having them find me—was three for three. I was through with romance for a while.

CHAPTER SEVENTEEN

Living Dangerously

Bernie had called me his baby. When I was married to him, that's what I was. After he died, I felt like a frightened, rebellious teenager. It was obvious that I didn't know what I was doing when it came to men. In friendships, too, I tended to go overboard. Like every new kid on the block I had to learn through my mistakes. Most of them were merely embarrassing, but some of them were murder. Almost.

Friends showed up after Bernie's death whom I hadn't seen in years. One of them who paid a shivah call was a guy called Tutti, from my old Brooklyn neighborhood. Tutti was a big bruiser, into the martial arts before they became fashionable in America. He'd been a wrestler. He'd studied kung fu. He looked like a samurai warrior. And he came from a very religious Orthodox Jewish family. He and his two brothers owned small neighborhood bars all over Brooklyn. They were strictly legitimate guys, Wall Street players. When disco fever hit New York in the late '60s and clubs were opening all over town, Tutti and his brothers expanded into the security business. They'd collect the night's money from the clubs and drop them at the appropriate vaults.

Tutti had become a pal. He'd stop by, like Morty had, to play with Jeffrey and sit around and gossip over endless cups of coffee. It was an easy-going, brother-sister kind of thing. We'd talk about who we were seeing. When Tutti found a new girlfriend, he'd always bring her to me for approval. If I shook my head, no, he didn't

see her anymore. Nights when I was restless, I'd ride shotgun with
him as he drove from club to club picking up the day's receipts.

One afternoon he showed up at my house ripping mad. Someone
owed him close to $100,000, he said, pacing back and forth in my
living room. He'd lent the guy the money to go into business and,
sure enough, the business had really started taking off. Now, four
or five times, the guy had promised to give Tutti back the hundred
grand and every time he went to meet him, the guy either didn't
show or showed up with some lame excuse and no bread.

"Tonight," Tutti said, pounding his hammy fist into his palm as
he spoke—a fist that could chop through a pile of bricks. "I'm supposed to meet him again. Only this time, if he screws around with
me, I'm going to fucking kill him."

"What kind of guy is he?"

Tutti knew what I meant. "He's straight. He says he's legitimate.
But he's got a cousin who's supposed to be connected downtown."

"If you want me to, Tutti, I'll find out. You can have a roundtable meeting downtown, see what's been going on with your
money. In fact," I offered, "I'll say it's my money, if you want, and
let's see who his cousin is."

Tutti said, "No. Thanks, anyway. He's supposed to give me fifty
grand tonight and he just better be there with it."

I wanted to calm him down so that he wouldn't get into trouble.
The best I could come up with was: "Listen, you're in a bad mood,
Tutti. Let me go with you. Let me ride shotgun with you. You know
I get a kick out of hanging out with you and I've got nothing else to
do tonight."

He was supposed to meet the guy around eleven o'clock all the
way out in the Red Hook section of Brooklyn. Neither of us knew
the area. Anyway, I conned him into taking me along, then I
changed my clothes. I remember it was early fall. I put on a pair of
jeans, boots, my short leather jacket, a turtleneck, and I wore my
dark glasses pushed up on my head, holding back my hair.

I'm a big girl and Tutti had a little car. It was one of the first foreign cars I'd ever seen—a Porsche or an Alfa Romeo, I don't remember. But it was a little bitty low-slung thing and when I sat in
it, my knees would come up to my throat. We took a nice long ride
to Red Hook with me folded up this way, and all I remember is
endless blocks of row upon row of dark warehouses. About five
minutes away from the meeting place, Tutti says, "Here's my gun.
I don't trust this guy. If anything happens, Sandy, just start shooting. Cover me, baby."

I said, "Are you out of your mind?!"

"No. I don't trust the guy. I've just got a hunch," he said.

We pulled up in front of the address—a warehouse. When Tutti cut the car lights, it was jet black outside. I couldn't see my hand in front of me. I began to get a very bad feeling. Then another car wheeled into the street and a man carrying a suitcase stepped out. Tutti got out of our car. And, with my eyes adjusting to the blackness, squinting through the dark, I could see him going to meet the guy. Then they came over to the car where I was sitting with Tutti's gun in my lap. I grabbed it and quickly lowered my hand so that the gun was hidden between the seat and the door, and I just held it there with my knees knocking up against my chin.

Tutti opened up the suitcase and started counting. The money was all there. He tossed it into the car's trunk, then handed the empty satchel back to the man. The second he closed the trunk, another car pulled up. Three guys jumped out. And Tutti hollered to me through the window, "I'm getting into the car! Start shooting!"

I rolled down the window, picked up the gun, and, as Tutti backed out with tires squealing, I started shooting up into the night sky. Like a bat out of hell, we flew. And I just kept shooting and shooting until Tutti finally yelled, "Okay. We made it. Okay, stop!"

"Oh, my God, what if I hit something?" I screamed. "It was so dark. I don't know what the hell I was shooting at."

"The goddamn *moon*," Tutti said. "If they'd parachuted in, you'd *maybe* have nicked one!"

I was shaking when we got upstairs. "That's it!" I ranted. "You're going to find out who this cousin is and I'm going to set up a roundtable meeting downtown. That bastard still owes you fifty grand. Say it was my money that you gave to him. Say whatever you have to!"

I went into the bathroom and threw up.

The next day, the very next evening, Tutti and I sat down with six elderly men at a bar on Mulberry Street. I had called Shorty at Second Avenue as soon as Tutti found out who the cousin was. Shorty recognized the name and contacted the guy's boss, who in turn called his boss, who among a lot of less public assets owned a couple of restaurants in Little Italy. Everybody agreed to sit down to a roundtable meeting, which was what these problem-solving sessions were called.

We went with the story that it was my money on the line. Apologies were tossed like bouquets. Roses to Tutti, orchids to me.

And, of course, the cousin said, "The guy took this on his own to do. If I would have known about it—" He shrugged, he shook his head. "Never."

I said, "I think you knew. I think you helped him set it up."

The old men looked back at him. He said, "I apologize." Another bouquet landed in my lap. "I'd like to help you. I knew nothing about this until I got the telephone call last night. But I'd like to help because he is my cousin and I feel responsible even though I'm not."

The old men looked at me. I had dressed very carefully and well for this occasion. I was wearing my full-length mink coat and as much jewelry as I could flash without looking flashy. I was decked out as a lady. But the mouth was strictly Bernie Barton's. I might as well have been channeling him at a séance. It even surprised me. I knew just what to say, how far to take it. I was sure the cousin had been in on it from the beginning, and I could tell the others believed that, too, though they couldn't take sides against him in front of me.

Anyway, Tutti walked away from that meeting with the other $50,000 due him—which they thought was mine—and an extra $25,000 for the grief. Real flowers were sent to my home; toys were sent to Jeffrey. Tutti was so grateful that he bought me a color TV and then decided to buy one for my mother, too. Of course, word went out on the street again that Bernie's princess was some ballsy chick; some stand-up broad. And, as much as I enjoyed the accolades, I felt as if it had been Bernie, not me, sitting around that table with the old men. Or that, at the very least, it had been his reckless, rebellious spirit guiding me.

My neighbor Margo's Cuban guru as much as said so.

After Margo and I discovered our shared belief in psychic phenomena, we visited Ormando, the Santeria priest she'd told me about. He was a refugee and spoke only Spanish. Margo had to interpret for me. But the first thing he said when I walked through the door of his little apartment uptown was: "Who is the dead man with the blue eyes who sits on her shoulder?"

Ormando was tall and thin with big black eyes, yellow skin, a bony nose, and stringy, pomaded shoulder-length hair. His small apartment was decorated with the same statues, candles, feathers, and offerings I'd seen at Lido's place, but he was much, much less expensive. He charged only three dollars, I remember. And he didn't need to suck an extra hundred up his nose to get the session going.

Ormando impressed the hell out of me with his question about the blue-eyed man. He also knew that I had a baby son, and he said quite a few other startlingly accurate things about my past. Then he predicted that I was going to get married within two years and described the man I would marry: tall, blondish, good-looking, debonair, macho, rich. Just as I was beginning to feel optimistic, Margo said, "But it's not going to be a good marriage, he says. In fact, he thinks you know him now. Oh, you know him," Margo continued to translate, "but you are . . . *unaware* of him. He's not actually in your life now."

"Sandy," I remember she said later, "maybe it's that fellow Morty wanted you to go out with—what's his name who we had dinner with at Gatsby's?"

"Chalky Lefkowitz?" I said. "No. Ormando said good-looking. Do you think Chalky's good-looking? I'm not attracted to him at all."

With Morty gone, Chalky had begun checking in with me. He was a bit of a *yenta*, a typical mob mouth. He'd always tell me what he heard on the street about me and I'd tell him it was an understatement. If he said, "I hear you're always running around up in Harlem," I'd say, "Twenty-four hours a day." If he said, "Bernie must have left you a bundle. A couple of million," I'd say, "A billion." If he said, "I hear you're seeing three different guys," I'd say, "No, seven. A different one for every day of the week." Whenever he tried to find out anything about me, I deflected it by saying, "You're absolutely right. Only more so."

We developed this rough repartee on the telephone and, gradually, we became buddies. Like Tutti, like Josh and Uncle Vinny, Chalky would stop by once in a while just to shoot the breeze. He'd talk to me about the women he was dating. He was going with two different girls at once.

"You'll get caught and wind up all alone," I warned him.

"Well, one of them is Eurasian. Very quiet, sweet, pretty girl. But she's half-Chinese, so I can't marry her. And the other one's a Jewish girl, sharp as a tack, but she's got a little bit of mileage on her, been around the track once or twice."

"How do you do it? I mean, do you see them on a schedule?"

"Yeah," he said. "Every other day. And one day a week I rest."

Actually, he didn't. I'd run into him once in a while on his days of rest and there'd always be a young cocktail waitress or some other Barbie Doll–type on his arm.

And he'd tease me. "When are you going to get married and make someone happy?" he'd ask.

"I tell you what. You get married first and I'll give you a great wedding gift. And then you give me one twice as nice."

"Nah, I'm too cheap," he'd say. Or, "Okay, whatever you need, I'll get you for your wedding—a blender, an iron, a toaster."

"Yeah, the sky's the limit with you, right, Chalky?"

Sometimes he'd call me up in the middle of the day. "I'm bored. Do you want to go to lunch?"

"Well, I was going to take Jeffrey out for the afternoon."

"Bring him along," Chalky would say. So the three of us would lunch, and go for walks and drives together. And, after a time, Jeffrey started calling him Uncle Chalky which—considering his relationship with Bernie, their mothers having been as close as sisters—Chalky sort of was.

After a while, my girlfriends started asking me about him. Lila would say, "Why don't you try to hook Chalky?"

"Because he's my friend, my brother. I don't think of him in those terms."

Judy thought he was attractive.

"Maybe he is," I'd say, "but he's not my type. He doesn't turn me on at all."

Margo said, "He's never been married. He seems to be crazy about you. And Jeffrey. He'd make a good father for Jeffrey. Don't you ever think of marrying him?"

"Never," I said.

And when my girlfriend Leona encouraged romance, pointing out how much like Bernie Chalky was, I'd tell her, "That's just the point. I don't want to marry a man that much older again and have him get sick and die. And also, he's a wise guy. He's connected. Even more than Bernie was. He's been to jail three times already. He'll either get sick and die or go to jail. And anyway," I'd say to Leona or Judy or Margo or Lila or even my mother, "I want a normal life and a normal man who works normal hours. I want to be Sadie-Sadie, Married Lady. I don't want to be Mrs. Wise Guy anymore."

As a pal, Chalky Lefkowitz was fine. He'd call, he'd visit, he'd pledge his friendship and promise that if I ever needed anything, if I ever got into a jam, he'd be there for me, no questions asked. But he was just one of the guys I hung out with. My main man was still Hot Dog Red.

While I'd been having my flings and things, Hot Dog had been taking care of business. On a beautiful evening in early spring, he came down to meet me and the Jab at the bar on Second Avenue.

"Sandy, you know we had a very good week. We're better than even. We've covered expenses and we're way ahead," Red said. "We've got eleven thousand dollars to play with. What do you want to do with it?"

We were sitting in a back booth. Jeffrey was propped up on the bar and Shorty was playing clap-hands with him. "What do you mean?" I said, distractedly. "Put it away in case next week's a bad week."

"Well," Red said sheepishly. "I've got to tell you something. Someone gave me a tip on a horse and I think we should—"

That got my attention. "Hold it right there," I said. "I used to hang around with a guy who had horses. He got tips all the time—from jockeys, stableboys, bookies, even God. He never won."

"Yeah, but this is a boat race," Hot Dog said. "And I've got a very good feeling about it, Sandy." A boat race is a fixed race. Like a submarine, the competition is going down, taking a dive. Red said, "Saturday afternoon at Belmont Park. I got the name of the horse and she's going off at good odds."

"It's not kosher," I said. "What'll happen if someone hits it big next week and we have to pay off—"

"Don't worry about it," Red insisted. "I'll hock my jewelry if I have to. I'll hock my Cadillac. We'll make it. I've just got a feeling about this."

So that Saturday, a lovely spring day in April, we drove out to the track and sat tight until the boat race. Then, while I waited in the stands chain-smoking, Red put the entire $11,000 on a filly named Pride of Rahemia.

The tip had been good. You could practically see the jockeys on the other horses yawning as Pride of Rahemia sailed past them. Red and I jumped up and down, hugging each other and screaming at the top of our lungs. "We won! We won!"

"It's a sign!" he shouted.

"Of what?" We were jostling through the crowd on our way to collect our money.

"That we ought to buy a boat."

"What are you talking about?" We breezed up to the payoff window.

"I've been reading about boats. There's one I saw. It's over in New Jersey. A thirty-two-footer."

"Stop. Hold it right there!" I tugged the short sleeve of his lime-green shirt. "What do you mean, 'we ought to buy a boat'?"

"It's a sign," Red said again. "We won on a boat race. We've got to buy a boat."

"You're insane."

"Just wait till you see the one I've got in mind. You're going to fall in love with it, too." He stepped up to the teller and turned in our tickets and collected the money—which he counted carefully and then tucked away in his pants pocket. "Come on. We'll drive out to Jersey," he said.

Easy come, easy go. All the way out to the boat yard in New Jersey Red is *hocking* me about this incredible yacht that he's been checking out for months and now we've got to have it. And I'm hollering that he's crazy and what the hell are we going to do with a boat? I can't even swim, let alone drive a boat. And Hot Dog is smiling, smoking, driving, nodding, giving me prices and statistics, reasons and excuses, facts and figures and, less than an hour later, we owned a yacht.

This was early April. The boat, a thirty-two-foot Owens that slept six, and would have a state room, galley, shower, depth finders, sonar, radar, even dishes with a nautical pattern, was made to order and delivered to us two days before my mother's birthday, the weekend of July Fourth.

Red and I had gone to school and gotten our captain's licenses by then. And, through a friend of Bernie's, we'd rented prime space, a gorgeous end-of-the-pier slip at the Seventy-ninth Street Boat Basin, which was a five-minute crosstown drive from my door. We christened the yacht *Pride of Rahemia*, in honor of the boat race that had bought her, and on her maiden voyage up the Hudson, we threw a fabulous, catered birthday party for Tillie.

Now, when I wanted solitude, I'd strap on a life vest, make sure the coast guard radio was on, and take to the river. I never really took the boat more than ten miles up the Hudson in either direction. But once out there on the water, I'd drop anchor and loll in the sunshine. Sometimes I'd pour myself a glass of wine and, holding one of the weighted crystal goblets Red and I had ordered for the boat, just stare out at the Manhattan skyline or the Jersey Palisades.

I loved to be alone on the boat. It made me feel very strong, very powerful. I'd think, look at this, look at me, I've got a captain's license. I own a yacht. Years ago, my mother made us mashed potatoes and chicken fat for dinner. And today, look at me.

It was heaven, that hot summer, having a big, beautiful boat with a telephone and TV aboard, docked right in Manhattan. I took Jeffrey down there every chance I got. The slips on either side of us were empty and we'd hang out with a friend or two in voluptuous, breezy privacy. Then one day, Jeffrey, my girlfriend Judy, and I arrived at the boat basin to find a cabin cruiser bobbing in the slip alongside ours. *Pride of Rahemia* was practically eclipsed by her luxurious new neighbor, the *Chicita*.

There was Latin music blaring from the huge cruiser though it was barely noon. Clearly, there were people partying aboard, but we made ourselves comfortable and were minding our own business, sunbathing on the deck of the *Rahemia*, when a man's voice called out, "Hey Sandy! Is that *chew*, baby? Where you get *Yewish* food around here?"

Judy and I sat bolt upright. "Oh, my God," she said. "It's Spanish Ray!"

"Spanish Ray. The King of Harlem. Oh, no," I groaned. "That's all we need!"

Spanish Ray's father was one of the richest men in Harlem. And Spanish Harlem. He owned grocery stores, apartment buildings, street blocks. And Ray was one of the biggest numbers bankers in town. God only knew what else he dealt and did. But if you owed Ray, you had to pay. He was known to walk into bars and actually shoot off men's fingers over broken promises. A very good-looking Puerto Rican, a mustachioed man of Bernie's age but tall and reedy with thick, slicked-back black hair and a dazzling, dangerous smile, Spanish Ray was notorious and nuts.

He and Bernie had been friendly. Whether they'd ever done business together, I didn't know; nothing that ever came into my home, so I assumed they'd just known one another and hadn't really been close. But here was Spanish Ray looking at Judy and me like he'd found his long lost sisters.

"I didn't know you knew Ray," I said to Judy as we made our way over to the *Chicita*. We shot the breeze boat to boat for a few minutes and then accepted Ray's invitation to come by for a drink and a tour of his yacht.

"He goes with my friend Suki, the ice skater."

"That pretty little Japanese girl?"

"Yeah," Judy said. "He drives her crazy. When they go to bed, he wears socks and a gun strapped to his ankle."

Spanish Ray was constantly bringing food over to *Pride of Rahemia*, and booze, and cartons of cigarettes. If we were both on line to get gasoline, he would have paid for mine before I even pulled my boat in next to the pump. And he threw the most extravagant parties. He'd send out for food—"Yewish" food from Zabar's, Chinese food from the Gold Coin, soul food, Spanish food, steaks, and lobsters.

He had the best wine, the best food, and the wildest assortment of people on his boat. Models, centerfolds, and wanna-be's in Band Aid–sized bathing suits would rub shoulders, and whatever else was handy, with stars of show business, mob business, and, yes, even *Fortune 500* business, who'd drop in to slum in opulence. I met Malcolm Forbes on Spanish Ray's yacht. By five P.M., come rain or shine, hell or high water, there was a party going aboard the *Chicita*.

One morning, when my mother and I were sunbathing on my boat, Ray appeared on the deck of the *Chicita* holding a full-length chinchilla coat. It was brand new. The labels were still on it. "Hey, preencess. You like this? Here," he called, tossing me the coat. "Try it on."

It fit me like a dream. "Keep it," Ray said. "It's a present."

I argued with him a little bit but, despite the fact that it was easily eighty-five degrees out, I didn't take off the coat. "Thank you, thank you, thank you. I love it," I finally said. "It's incredible. It's gorgeous, Ray."

He laughed and waved off my excitement. "Okay," he said. "It looks good on you," and he disappeared back into his boat. Twenty minutes later, he came out again, this time with a mink coat. Same drill. Full-length, exquisite, labels dangling off it. "Hey, mami—" he called to my mother. "You like it?"

What else was she going to say? "Beautiful," she cooed.

"Okay. Here. It's yours," Ray said and threw the mink onto our boat.

"Ma, don't take it off," I whispered. "Wear it." Eighty-five degrees, not a breeze in the boat basin, and my mother's little shoulders were sagging under the weight of the full-length mink coat.

"I love you, mami," Ray called. "Enjoy. Keep it. It's yours. I love you, Sandy. I love the baby. I love your mama. I love the whole wide world!"

About two weeks later, I arrived at the boat basin in time to see

Spanish Ray being led off the *Chicita* in handcuffs by four gun-toting men in dark suits—cheap dark suits. FBI agents. Ray winked at me as they marched him away.

One afternoon in late summer, I ran into Chalky. I hadn't seen him for a while or even spoken with him. We stood on a street corner and played catch up. He was engaged, he said.

"So which one turned out to be the lucky lady?" I asked.

"Both of them. I bought them both identical rings. Three carats each."

"Both of them?!"

"Sure. This way, they both stopped *hocking* me about marriage. I figure I've bought at least a year's time."

I shook my head and laughed. "Listen, why don't you come down and see the boat?" I said.

"What boat?"

"Come down and find out. At the Seventy-ninth Street Boat Basin. Here's the number. Call or just come by."

One September afternoon he showed up unexpectedly, as if he were just in the neighborhood looking for a cup of coffee. I was pleased to see him. A couple of friends were on board. Jeffrey was there, of course. And my mother, I think. The weather was still beautiful. We were in our bathing suits, and Chalky was wearing a starched shirt and long pants. And you could see that he was very surprised, very impressed with the boat, especially when he found out it was mine.

"Where'd you get the money for a boat?" he asked.

"None of your business," I said.

"I'm just asking. What's the harm?"

"Hey, if I tell you everything, you'll be smarter than me. You'll know everything I know and everything you know."

It was one of Bernie's lines. Chalky smiled, recognizing it. "Yeah, right," he said, giving me an appraising look. It wasn't just my mind and mouth he was appraising either. I was at fighting weight, wrapped in a bikini, and tan as a berry. And for one moment, I saw him eating me up with his eyes. Sparks passed between us, but I let it go. I didn't want to start anything. As a pal, Chalky was perfect; as a boyfriend—well, for starters, he was already engaged . . . twice.

He was my brother, my father, my friend. Aside from that brief moment on the boat, I didn't look at Chalky through the eyes of a woman. So it surprised me when, in November, he telephoned and started hemming and hawing.

He had a big affair to go to—a legitimate deal—a union fund-raiser at the Plaza. He didn't want to take his Jewish fiancée. She was too loud, too brassy for this bunch. And he didn't feel like showing up with the Eurasian. So, he was thinking and he was wondering and it had occurred to him and . . . Five minutes it took him to *krechtz* out the big question: Would I go with him to the fund-raiser? I'd have a good time, he assured me. Maybe I'd even meet someone.

"Sure," I said, puzzled over why he'd made such a big deal about it.

My girlfriends had never stopped trying to romanticize my friendship with Chalky. To them, he seemed like the perfect guy for me. They knew how in love with Bernie I'd been. They'd seen me come apart after his death. I was doing okay now but—a woman alone, a woman with a baby to support—for how long, they asked, did I think I could make it on my own in a man's world? And here was Chalky Lefkowitz, an attractive bachelor who seemed to enjoy my company and who just happened to be Bernie's best friend.

"It's like it was written this way," Lila would say. "Like a story. Bernie dies and here, Chalky shows up ten minutes later."

"It's a very odd coincidence," Margo, with her belief in fate and the spirit world, agreed. "That he should appear the way he did, just as Bernie was dying."

But the one whose opinion I valued most was Gloria's.

Right after Bernie died, Josh showed up at my house with her. She was in her thirties, beautiful, bright, and Jewish. And she ran the best high-class call girl operation in town. I trusted Gloria. She was tough. She'd made it on her own. She knew how to navigate in this so-called "man's world." And when I told her how awkward Chalky had sounded on the phone, she decided that it was time I made a move on him.

We were shopping for a dress for me to wear to the gala. I'd picked out a couple of hot numbers, but when I tried on a long beaded gown with a side slit the contest was over. It was outrageously expensive, but I'd never worn anything that felt as luxurious or looked as glamorous. And Gloria was unrelenting, insisting that if I couldn't afford it, she'd buy it for me.

"Think of it as an investment," she urged. "I've got a funny feeling about this, my vibes tell me it's going to be the start of something good. You're either going to meet someone at the affair or Chalky will fall madly in love with you."

I bought the dress and I ticked off the reasons Chalky was out of the question for me. When I got to my biggest and best—I don't want a mob guy again; I don't want a mob life—Gloria said, "Sandy, face facts, baby. Have you ever thought what would happen if you did meet a totally straight guy and he found out all about you? You know," she said, "that could turn a legitimate guy off." Then she countered every other objection I had to Chalky, ending with what was to become her anthem: "I think you ought to go for it."

I have never felt as beautiful as I did that Saturday night. I'd had my hair done. I'd taken great care with my makeup. Gloria had lent me a pair of long diamond earrings and a single diamond bracelet to wear with the long-sleeved, body-hugging, floor-length beaded gown. In my high heels, my legs looked a couple of yards long through the side slit. I threw my mink coat over my shoulder and went down to the lobby to meet Chalky.

He had rented a limo. When he stepped out in his tuxedo, he looked stunning. He was tan and trim. His blond-white hair was slicked back. His blue eyes lit up when he saw me. They traveled over me from head to toe, taking in every sequin, bead, and curve along the way. His eyes sparkled and he gave me a big appreciative grin.

"You're beautiful," he said. "You're going to waste with no man in your life."

"You sound like Gloria," I marveled.

He whispered it again as he took my arm and we walked into the Plaza ballroom together. I knew how proud he was to have me with him. I could feel him standing taller, straighter. I could see it in the eyes of other people, how good we looked together. And I knew he saw it, too.

"Jesus, you look great. What a waste," he kept repeating that night.

At least once, I answered, "Find someone for me, big brother. It's all up to you."

We'd had a couple of drinks by then, in addition to the champagne we'd had in the limo. I knew that I was feeling the buzz. And when he said, "Baby, I'll find you one. Right away, sweetheart," he looked at me the way he had on the boat and the same electricity passed between us.

The ballroom was filled with dazzling people, conversation, and music. At one end, tables for black jack, craps, and roulette had been set up as part of the fund-raising effort. At the other there was a band, a dance floor surrounded by dining tables, and a splendid buffet. We moved through the room together. We gambled awhile. When I leaned over to toss the dice, I looked over my shoulder to wink at Chalky for luck. He was looking around, looking like he would kill anybody he caught staring at my beaded behind. When he saw me watching him, he shrugged and grinned. "I'm not the only one who thinks you look great tonight."

Then I asked him to dance with me.

"Gee, Sandy," he began.

"Yeah, I know." I laughed. "You're going to tell me that tough guys don't dance. Tough guys don't go down on a broad. Tough guys don't do this. Tough guys don't do that—"

He studied me for a second with those evil twinkling eyes. "Come on," he said and grabbed my hand and walked me out to the dance floor.

It was more like swaying than dancing. It was more like grinding than swaying. "Where'd you hear that?" Chalky breathed into my neck.

"Where do you think?" I said.

He laughed. "Yeah, well it's true. Most of it anyway," he said. I reared back to look at him and what a sexy, mischievous grin he had on his face.

"Oh, yeah? Which part isn't true?"

"Maybe someday you'll find out," he said.

One dance. Then, while he went to get us some food, I sat at a table where I'd found some couples I'd known when I was married to Bernie.

Willie Rosen, who owned Gatsby's, was there. By that time, everyone was a little loaded and loose. When Chalky came back to the table, Willie started in on us. "You know the two of you make a gorgeous couple. Look at you, Sandy. You're single. He's single. The two of you look like you love each other, or like each other, or whatever. Why don't you give it a try."

And just as I was wondering: Does Willie Rosen know Gloria? Chalky suddenly said, "Well, I would . . . I think about it with her, but . . . She was with my best friend, almost my brother. It isn't right."

"What are you talking about, it isn't right?" said Willie. "The man is dead three years. You've *shtupped* everything that moves and you're still alone. Those broads you're engaged to, what are they, morons? Feh," Willie said, disgusted. "The two of you really ought to try it. You look like a winning combination."

Go for it, I could hear Gloria urge.

"Remember, Chalky," I said. "You promised you'd find me a guy. You didn't say which guy—but you promised."

He started to laugh. He looked at me with those glinting blue eyes like, "I'll get you for that." And all the while, Willie went on and on about how right we were for one another.

Well, by this time, I was more than a little tilted. I excused myself to go to the ladies' room, but all the way there my booze-fogged brain was ticking: Go for it, go for it, go for it. So Chalky had thought of me as more than a friend. Hmmm. So he thought I was beautiful and going to waste without a man. So suddenly he couldn't take his evil blue eyes off me. And he looked so handsome in a tuxedo. We looked so good together. We felt so good together. Dancing with him, standing still and swaying. Maybe, I thought. What the hell, I thought. Go for it.

And I did.

Instead of going to the ladies' room, I veered to the right and careened up the stairs and out to the waiting limo. I gave Chalky's driver a twenty-dollar bill and dismissed him. "We don't need the car. We're spending the night at the Plaza," I said.

Then I rushed back inside and rented a suite for the evening. When I returned to the ballroom, Chalky was talking to some men. I waited and when we were alone at the bar for a few minutes, I dangled the room key in front of him. "I had this terrific idea," I said. "I rented us a suite upstairs."

"You did what?"

"Well, this party's going to go on and on. I'm having a fabulous time. Why should I go home exhausted when we can go right upstairs and get undressed and sleep here? And in the morning we can have a nice breakfast and go on about our business. It's Sunday," I continued breathlessly. "And unless you have other plans. I mean, I think it's a great way to end the evening. And anyway, I told the limo driver to go home."

He was staring at me as though he was waiting for the English subtitles to appear.

"I thought it was a terrific idea," I repeated, less enthusiastically.

"Okay," he said finally. "Why not?"

Well, about two or three in the morning, we said our goodnights. Chalky told some people what I had done and everyone thought it was a great idea, ending the evening in luxury, spending the night at the Plaza. What fun, everyone said, what a clever girl, what a lucky man, what a stunning couple. On our way out of the ballroom, I picked up two clean glasses and Chalky pulled a fresh bottle of champagne out of an ice bucket, and I led him through the lobby, very gaily, like something out of a Hollywood movie—a romantic farce . . . which is just about what the evening boiled down to.

In the suite, he took off his jacket dramatically. I kicked off my shoes. I turned on the radio. He poured the champagne. We got comfy on the sofa. We drank. We laughed. We started necking. We started rolling around on the couch. We rolled off onto the floor. I landed on top of him. I smothered his face with kisses. "You are so delicious," I said, "I'm going to eat you up all over." "Do it, baby. Oh, do it," he said. I kissed his face, his neck. "Yes, baby, yes," Chalky rasped. That was all she wrote. I passed out cold on top of him.

Next morning, I woke up naked in bed. I walked into the other room. Chalky came out of the shower wrapped in towels. I saw the pillow and blanket on the sofa. "You undressed me?" I said.

"You think I never saw a woman's body before?"

"I'm sorry I passed out."

"I thought you'd dropped dead."

"It was a stupid idea," I said.

"Best time I ever had. I never had so much fun with anyone."

I went into the shower and came out wrapped in towels. We ordered breakfast.

"You're not mad at me?"

"No," he said. "But everything's different now."

"What's different?"

"You. Me. I don't know. I'm confused."

That was November.

In December he left town. He was taking a couple weeks off— spending Christmas with one of his fiancées and New Year's week with the other. "You're a very busy man," I said.

"I'm a very confused man," he countered. "Be a good girl and play a dead hand, as they say in the game."

"What does that mean?" I asked. But I knew. Be quiet. Just sit there. Wait.

CHAPTER EIGHTEEN

Courting Trouble

They say be careful what you wish for, you might get it.

From the time we tussled on the floor of the Plaza suite, from the morning I woke to find that Chalky—like Bernie our first night together—hadn't laid a glove on me, from the breakfast when he said things had changed between us, I started wishing Chalky Lefkowitz would fall for me.

It seemed inevitable that I'd wind up with someone connected. Some girls had the Midas touch; I had the Mob touch. Every guy I got involved with turned out to be a player. Well then, why not Chalky, I started thinking.

Gloria, who claimed to know everything about straight guys, had probably been right about legit types being put off by my past. And there was Jeffrey to consider—he needed a father. But who would love him the way Bernie had? And who would love him without judging his real father, without looking down on who Bernie had been, what he'd done? Where was I going to find a guy like that?

A guy who loved and respected Bernie. A guy who adored Jeffrey. A guy who knew everything about my past that I'd tried to hide from other men . . . and still thought of me as an attractive, bright, successful woman—going to waste without a man.

New Year's Eve at one in the morning Chalky called from Florida to wish Jeffrey and me a healthy and happy New Year. "I'll be back soon," he said. "I can't wait to see you."

"You must be exhausted running from fiancée to fiancée," I teased. "How was Miss Christmas?"

"It's over. I told her she could keep the ring. I'll call you as soon as I get home."

The week he got back, we went to dinner with a crowd of people. He stared at my legs all evening. "What's with you?" one of his friends said. "You haven't taken your eyes off her legs."

"I don't know," Chalky said. "I just never noticed what dynamite legs she has. When I look at them it makes me feel good." Before the evening was over, I had a new nickname. Everyone was calling me "Legs."

That's how it went. Little by little, Chalky began noticing things he liked about me that he hadn't seen the day or week or month before.

And little by little I became aware of how attractive he was; how the tan made up for the lack of hair; how the blue eyes always sparkled, and how sometimes they looked mischievous and sexy, sometimes evil. The impeccable conservative suits I'd teased him about, the ones I'd thought made him look always ready for a wedding or a funeral, began to seem more elegant and distinguished than stodgy or formal. And I began to notice that when we ran into old friends of Bernie's, connected guys, they treated Chalky with respect. Not the affection they'd shown toward Bernie, but respect, equality, sometimes even fear.

And little by little, the idea of the *shiddach*, the romantic match everyone was promoting, shifted from preposterous to possible.

"Be a good girl, Legs," he'd say.

And I'd try to be. I'd find myself waiting patiently at the bar while he talked business. I'd cross my long legs and stir my drink and tune out when certain names were dropped. When we were out to dinner, I stopped putting my two cents into every conversation—particularly when the Italians were at the table. Chalky mingled with the heavy hitters differently than Bernie had. Bernie kidded and kibitzed with them. Chalky watched and waited. Bernie with his easy wit and laughter made them smile. Chalky with his thin smile and dangerous, sparkling eyes made them listen.

Although we'd start out as pals and partners at the beginning of the evening, little by little, I'd find myself shifted off to the side. Bernie had shown me off, gotten a kick out of my big mouth, asked my opinion, laughed at my mistakes. Chalky and the Italians preferred me quiet and smiling.

"Be a good girl," he'd say. And I'd light up a Parliament and watch him make his way across the room to the tables against the wall where the guys in silk suits were sawing through sirloin. And, little by little, I'd find myself sitting in smiling silence, mindlessly tapping the bar or table top with my solid gold cigarette lighter.

Gloria phoned me. "I've got a new fella," she said. "He's a diplomat from Ghana. Do you know anything about Ghana? It's an incredibly poor country. They need appliances, clothes, cars, things we have here and never think twice about. They don't have those things but, honey, they are rolling in gold."

As they say, it was déjà vu all over again.

Believe it or not, Gloria had in mind almost the exact same deal that had gotten Red, Bernie, and me a military escort out of Africa. I tried to talk her out of it. I told her what had happened to us. But Gloria was a hard-headed woman. When it came to business, in a lot of ways she was tougher than Bernie had been. She'd learned early in life to never let her heart get in the way of her head.

"We can do this all very legitimately. But I've got to get the merchandise. I need everything from washing machines to tanks, guns and ammunition. Chalky's got connections, hasn't he?" she said. "You and he can be partners on your end. Ask him."

So Chalky and I had lunch at Tavern on the Green one Sunday afternoon to discuss the possibilities. He was very interested. "This could turn out to be a real score," he said. "It could be set up very legitimately. It can be done on the up-and-up."

I remember staring at him through lunch. Oh, I was talking like a big shot. Laying out the plan. Batting around numbers. Laughing like I had the world by the tail. But another part of my mind was watching Chalky and thinking, I'll be damned, this is it—I've fallen for the guy. Another outlaw old enough to be my father. Another nice Jewish boy who's made the trip from Delancey Street to Dannemora. Another wise guy. And this one's in it even deeper than Bernie was. God help me, I remember thinking, I'm in love with Chalky Lefkowitz.

Instead of making me feel excited, elated, or optimistic, the thought sent a chill through me. The unhealed ache in my gut, the one I'd first felt after my father left, the one that was my constant companion through the days of sitting *shivah* for Bernie and for months after . . . I felt it again. A trembling fear, an aching emptiness. Then it passed.

What did I know about love? What did I know about the men I'd trusted, depended on, and cared most about in my life? That they'd left me. It was unbelievable. Almost as soon as I realized that I was in love with Chalky, I began to dread losing him. I felt it in my gut, in my heart—though I didn't understand it that day or for many years to come.

Chalky was demanding, careful, mistrustful, cold. He was an emotional mine field. I never knew whether or not I was doing the right thing around him. And I'd never really cared before. But, once I fell in love with him, it began to matter more and more.

We became partners. My job was to check out prices on TVs, washers and dryers, irons and toasters. I was in charge of appliances. Chalky was researching the heavier hardware. Gloria was pulling the legal end together. And, in a matter of months, contracts had been signed and we were actually doing a little business.

As part of the terms of his parole, Chalky was living with his mother in a fifth-floor walkup on First Street. And he was on the books as an employee of his sister's business in the Garment Center. Chalky's mother, who'd been Bernie's mother's best friend, was an absolute angel, the living image of the good-hearted *Yiddishe Momme* the out-of-towners wept over at Molly's; the kind of Jewish mother whose son could do no wrong. She had carried home-made chicken soup for him to Sing Sing and Dannemora and shlepped to Trenton State every weekend for twelve years with shopping bags full of delicacies from the old neighborhood—and she'd never lost faith in him.

We became friends. Because Chalky and I were together so much, I got to know his family, and Jeffrey and I would sometimes go down to the Essex Street Market where Sarah had a fish stand. The woman had worked her entire life. Her son tipped doormen more in one shot than she probably earned in a week, but Sarah was the original stand-up broad. She knew about me from Bernie's mother and, from the beginning, she was as sweet to Jeffrey and me as if we were her own. She was rooting for me to win out over Chalky's other girls.

And, for better or worse, it looked like I was.

Chalky and I had gone into business together in February. In early April, Red and I went to see about getting the *Pride of Rahemia* out of dry dock and ready for the coming season. We left the boat yard kind of depressed. It was like a visit to the hospital and the doctor had diagnosed *Rahemia* as weather-beaten and in need of a lot of repairs. About $9,000 worth.

"What do you think?" I asked Red on the drive home. "It's a lot of money. And I've been spending like crazy this year—I've lent to friends, I'm helping out my mother and sister, I've got Nora a couple of times a week and household expenses, and I've gone a little crazy over clothes, too. Nine grand. And that's just to get her back into the water."

"You know, I'm getting old and tired," Hot Dog said. "It's up to you, partner. You're the one who uses it most of the time. It's for you and the Jab and for Tillie. What do you want to do?"

Well, we went back and forth on it and, very reluctantly, we decided to sell her. That day, I talked to Red about my changing relationship with Chalky. He was happy for me. Like everyone else I knew, he hoped I'd marry the guy.

"You never can tell," I teased. "Only one more fiancée to go."

A week later, an offer came in for *Rahemia* and after talking it over with me, Red, in whose name the boat had been registered, sold her. I had dinner with Chalky that night.

"What's the matter with you?" he asked, stopping in the middle of a sentence.

"I sold the boat today," I began. "We didn't get much for it and I'm feeling kind of blue because I really—"

He looked as though I'd slapped him across the face. "You did what?" he said very slowly.

"I sold my boat."

"Are you crazy? Without saying a word to me? How could you do that?" he demanded angrily.

"What are you talking about, Chalky? It was my boat. My money—"

"You know, you've got a really big mouth," he growled.

"Chalky," I said, angry myself now. "It was mine. Don't tell me what to do with my possessions. I don't like it."

"Who do you think you're talking to like that? Who do you think you are to open up a mouth like that to me?"

Like what, I wanted to demand? We're friends. We're equals. We're business partners. You don't talk to your friend and partner that way. You talk to some bimbo you have no respect for at all, I thought. You talk that way to some brainless girlfriend, some beaten-down wife. But I said: "Who died and left you boss?"

"Bernie," Chalky answered. It was the first time he said it. It became his classic answer.

"Well, Bernie never told me that," I said.

It was our first fight. He was appalled that I'd talk back to him. I was confused and upset that he felt I owed him explanations about my personal affairs. But my matchmaking girlfriends took it as a good omen.

"I told you he was crazy about you," Lila said, "I mean, look, he's already acting like what's yours is his."

"I know," I said. "And I don't like it."

Two weeks later, at the end of April, a phone call from Gloria woke me up. "Well, baby," she said, "you got some fresh bread in your pocket, don't you?"

I said, "What are you talking about?"

"Didn't Chalky give you money last night?"

I actually laughed. "Chalky never gives me money for anything. Remember that fund-raiser? Gloria, it cost me a fortune. Fourteen hundred for the dress, another two bills for the Plaza suite. He's an expensive guy to go out with—"

"Forget that. Sandy, you mean he didn't give you anything?"

"What are you talking about? You're starting to make me crazy. I thought you meant maybe he gave me some money to buy myself something—"

"Okay. I've got to tell you this. Yesterday afternoon Chalky was over at my place. You know we shipped a load of tools over to Ghana and we made a little profit. Chalky and I split seventeen thousand dollars. And you're going to get paid on his end because you and he are partners. So, let me see, half of seventeen is eight five. So he's got to give you over four grand. He had the money on him yesterday. I knew you two were having dinner, so I thought—"

"Gloria," I said through clenched teeth. "Look, it's early in the morning and you woke me up. I'm confused. Run that by me again."

She did.

"Gloria, I had dinner with the man last night and he never mentioned a single word about the money."

"Well, then," said Gloria, whose clients and friends were among the bluest of blue bloods, "baby, you'd better straighten that cocksucker out."

I hung up the phone with a sick feeling. I paced and smoked and cursed Chalky. I phoned my mother. I blew my top. "Whatever you're going to do," said Tillie, "you'd better do it very quietly. Go see him today. Very quietly. Don't do it over the phone. Do it in person. You hear me, Sandy—do it quietly."

"You're right," I said. And I pulled myself and my battle plan together. I made a production out of getting dressed. I must have changed about a hundred times. I took time with my makeup. My mother always said, when you're meeting an opponent, no matter who it is, look gorgeous. Look your best. And I did.

I went up to Chalky's sister's place in the Garment Center. I walked into his office and he was so surprised and happy to see my beautiful, smiling face that he made a big fuss over me. There were some men in his office when I arrived, so I walked around and chatted with a few people and waited until we were quietly alone. And then I opened fire:

"Did I buy dinner last night, Chalky? Was that my share of the profits you paid the check with, partner? There's got to be a little change left out of *my* four thousand two hundred and fifty dollars—or did you tip big? Goddamn it, Chalky, where's my money?! Why didn't you give me my end?"

He leaned back in his executive leather swivel chair. "You'll get it. You'll get it," he said, grinning.

"It's not funny! Where's my share?!" I hollered.

He let me rant and rave for a while. Then he said, with that little twinkling smile, "Are you finished?"

I was. I'd absolutely exhausted myself. I fell back onto a chair. I just *plotzed*.

"Do you need money?" he asked.

"Yes," I said.

"Naw, you're worth a fortune."

Suddenly everything had switched around. It wasn't about him *owing* me money, now it was about whether I *needed* it. "Don't tell me what I'm worth. You don't know what I'm worth. But it's not a fortune, Chalky," I said. "And I want my piece. I brought you into this deal. It was me. Now, give me my share of the profits and, I'll tell you what, you do whatever you want from now on. I'm out of this partnership. I don't want to have to fight with you."

"There goes that big mouth again," he said. He was grinning. The evil blues were twinkling. "What's right is right," he said. "I'll tell you what—I'll marry you instead."

It caught me totally off guard. I'd come to do battle. I'd been angry and frustrated. I'd felt cheated and misused. Suddenly, I didn't know what I felt.

"How can you marry me?" I asked. "You're engaged."

"Not anymore," he said. "I broke off with the other one. I'm womanless. It's you and me against the world."

He took a small box out of the drawer and slid it across the desk top at me. "I was going to give you this tonight but, here, take it now."

I opened the box and saw the most gorgeous pair of diamond earrings I'd ever seen in my life.

I was speechless—thank God. Because, right that minute, if I'd opened my mouth, I think I would have said, "Did the diamonds run you forty-two-fifty, or do I get change back from my engagement present?"

"You like them?" he asked, proud and grinning.

"Chalky, they're incredible," I said.

Four months later, on August 12, 1969, we were married in the little *shul* on Rivington Street where Chalky had been Bar mitzvahed. He'd teased me into paying for the license. It was only about five dollars—the costliest bargain of my life.

1969. The whole world was changing. There were riots everywhere. Students against universities. Blacks against whites. Hardhat construction workers against long-haired hippies. Women against traditional values.

Some women. Not me.

"I'm an old-fashioned guy with old-fashioned ideas," Chalky kept telling me during our courtship. "I want a normal life."

It was music to my ears. Normal. Every time he said it, I could see roses growing around the doorman's desk at East Seventy-eighth Street, a white picket fence bordering the circular driveway.

"Whatever business you've got going, whatever you're doing, Sandy, I want it stopped," he announced a couple of months before we were married.

"You mean with Red, and the bar, everything?" I asked.

"Everything," he said. "You're going to be a housewife. You've got a house to take care of, and a child. I'll take care of business and you'll stop running around and you'll be normal."

We were having dinner alone at Oscar's, a seafood place on Third Avenue. Chalky had put away a couple of drinks at the bar and a glass or two of wine. And suddenly, he had a bad edge on.

"Do you know exactly what I do for a living?" he asked.

"Exactly? No. I know you're not kosher, Chalky. You're not straight, but I really don't know what you do."

"And you never will," he said triumphantly. "You might hear

stories about me, you might hear conversations. But as long as you're with me, you will never know exactly what I do for a living."

He said it very slowly. I'd begun to notice that whenever Chalky wanted to make a point, he spoke slowly and softly so that you had to bend toward him to hear. You had to bow to him.

"You can think what you want, Sandy, that's your problem," he continued in that slow, deliberate way. "You'll never be involved in my business. After we're married, all I want you to do is be my wife, take care of my home, take care of your son who'll become our son, and that's it. Stay home and be a good girl."

It was the standard rap—familiar to every mob mate. Stay out of my business. I'm only doing this for your own good. It's better if you don't know what's up.

"Okay," I said cheerfully. I'd heard the same little speech from Bernie, but then he'd kept me close to him and his business. He'd get excited about some venture or scheme, and I'd be part of it, however cockeyed some of them turned out to be—the House of Yenom, the African adventure, banking bonds at the Vatican.

But something told me Chalky meant it. He wouldn't bend the way Bernie had. He'd kept me at a distance from his business associates throughout our relationship; more since we'd become engaged than when we'd been just friends. He seemed to be dead serious about wanting me to be a typical TV wife and mother. Nothing more.

About a week after the you'll-never-be-involved-in-my-business chat, the two of us went to a gala at Gatsby's. The occasion was Ruby Stein's "going away" party. Ruby, who put syndicate money to work at outrageous interest by lending it to lesser loansharks, Ruby, the shylock's shylock and sometime employer of Brooklyn's own head-bashing, debt-collecting Gallo gang, Charles Ruby Stein of the Copa and the eye tic, had been busted and was going away to Danbury to do short time.

But before he went, his friends and colleagues were throwing him an all-star send-off. Gatsby's was crowded with the famous and infamous that night. I don't remember exactly who was in or out at that particular moment in time—in or out of jail, in or out of power—but the joint was jumping with Profacis and Colombos, Gambinos and Luccheses. And, true to his words, Chalky parked me at the bar while he joined a couple of other family men at a table across the room.

I was standing alone at the end of the bar. An elderly gray-haired man with a fat nose, fat knuckles, and a big cigar hanging out of his mouth was standing next to me talking to another man. Suddenly, the guy took the cigar out of his mouth and spit on the floor.

"Ugh! That's disgusting," I said. "Don't you have any manners? I'll have the bartender get you a spittoon," I said to him.

He looked at me through narrowed eyes. "Who are you, girlie? Who're you here with?"

I said, "Number one, I'm not your girlie—"

"Oh, yeah. Now I recognize you!" he said. "I remember you from Bernie. Don't you recognize me? I'm Tony Salerno."

Oh, great, I thought. Fat Tony Salerno was a big boss, a don, head of one of the New York families. A great sense of humor was not one of the things he was famous for. "You know," he said, shaking the cigar in my face, "no one else would ever say that to me."

"Well, I'm sorry, but even if I knew who you were I would have said that's disgusting," I told Fat Tony, who is now doing about a hundred years in prison.

"You know something, sweetheart," he said, dribbling tobacco juice through a sudden grin. "You're okay. You've got moxie. Too bad you weren't born a man. I'd like to have you on my side."

He left and I looked across the room at the table full of dark-suited, serious men sitting with Chalky. He was deep in discussion. I thought, thank God he didn't see me with Fat Tony; thank God he won't ask me what we were talking about. He'd have been mortified, I knew. He'd have read me the riot act for not being a good girl, for shooting off my big mouth. And then I thought, if only Bernie were alive; he'd have laughed his head off at the exchange.

There were a lot of differences between Bernie and Chalky. Bernie was hot; Chalky was cold. Bernie wanted to do what was good; Chalky wanted to do what was right. Bernie took risks; Chalky took care. Bernie thought the world of me. Chalky cared about what the world thought of me.

Never mind that he was forty-eight years old and had never been married. Never mind that he'd spent more than a decade locked away from real life. Chalky had a lot of ideas about what the perfect family should look like, sound like, act like. And I bought it. When we were courting, I loved listening to him paint the picture of our lives together, our little family. I loved it. I wanted to believe it. And in some areas, he definitely had me convinced.

"I'm not going to push you about sex," he said the day after we became engaged. "You know, I spent twelve years in prison and I did a lot of reading. I know all about the anatomy of a woman's body. And how a woman should be made love to." We were having a romantic little dinner at Les Champs. Chalky was cutting his roast chicken into neat, bite-sized pieces. Everything about him was neat, clean, precise, thought-out. Even the discussion of sex.

"So if there's anything you want me to do, just ask for it," he said. "Whatever you want, whatever you like sexually or you don't like, don't be ashamed to tell me. Sex is very important between people."

The man was as good as his word. Twelve years of reading had paid off. Big time. When it came to sex, Chalky knew every trick in the book—literally. The guy could've done testimonials for literacy on the rewards of reading.

His relationship with Jeffrey was also a convincer. When he'd stay at my apartment before we were married, he always made sure that Jeffrey would find him on the couch in the morning and not in my bed. I'd wake some days to find them coloring together on the floor of the baby's room. And Chalky would say to Jeffrey, "Would you mind if I married your mommy?" And Jeffrey, who'd been calling him Uncle Chalky forever, would always say, "No." Chalky would say, "Would you want me to be your daddy?" And Jeffrey would always say, "Yes." And, after a while, Chalky started saying, "Why don't you practice calling me daddy," and Jeffrey did. And I'd think, it's going to work out; we're going to be a real family.

CHAPTER NINETEEN

Sadie, Sadie

A couple of Chalky's friends threw us a wedding reception. Because Willie Rosen was one of them, the party was held at Gatsby's. Because Tom Sullivan was another, the Irish mob was well represented. Between family, friends, and business associates, more than a hundred people showed up. Among the associates, the Italians were in the majority. Again, I noticed how, even at our wedding reception, Chalky chose the company of the heavy hitters over family and friends, who didn't have strong mob connections. And, although he drank and smiled, there was a quiet seriousness to everything he did.

I was wearing a long-sleeved, high-necked, A-line mini-dress of beige and gold brocaded lace with two big patch pockets—very 1969. And very convenient, as it turned out, because while Chalky romanced the *machers*, I wandered through the crowd and men would stop me and put envelopes into those pockets and say, "Here's a present. Spend it nicely, honey, and give me a kiss."

When we got home to my apartment that night, we emptied the envelopes. The gifts came to nearly $20,000.

"How do you like this," Chalky said, pleased. "Look at the respect these people have for me. And everyone did it the right way. No one gave me any envelopes. They gave it to the bride."

Then he really surprised me. "You want to redo the house, so do it," he said, grandly handing me the cash. "Buy whatever you need for the place."

"I can do whatever I want?" I was looking forward to it. The

apartment still reflected Bernie's early-Liberace taste. I wanted the
place to look Hollywood sleek and sharp.

"Whatever you want," Chalky said, "but keep a record of how
much everything costs. Keep receipts. When it comes to money, I
like to know where it's going and what it's going for."

So I hired a decorator and I bought new linens and dishes and a
vacuum cleaner. And, because Chalky never gave me any household expense money, I started buying food and paying other bills
out of that "pocket money," and by and by it was gone. At Chalky's
request, I'd given up my other businesses and there was no extra
bread coming in. So I started using the money Bernie had left me.
And one day, I said to Gloria, "He's been living with me for a couple of months and he hasn't asked if I need money, for groceries,
for a cleaning girl, for whatever. He's seen the receipts. He knows
there's nothing left of the wedding money—"

"Well, you did marry a bachelor," she said. "Maybe you just
have to talk to him. You know, like say, 'You're a married man
now, this is your responsibility.' "

I told Margo, "I don't know what to do. He just comes and goes
and he doesn't ask me if I need anything for the house. I think he's
cheap."

"Oh, he's wonderful," she said. "Why don't you sit down and
tell him and I'm sure he'd give you the world."

Now, Chalky had no casual friends, no civilians. Everyone he
socialized with had either done time or was likely to. The people he
did business with were the only ones he trusted. And they were
wise guys.

He didn't like my friends. "I know you love these people," he'd
say about Warren and Margo, Judy, Leona, even Gloria once their
business together had been concluded. "They're your people,"
he'd say. "You can see them alone, but I don't want to have anything to do with them. They're not my cup of tea." He didn't trust
anyone who wasn't part of the mob.

But this was in the early days when Chalky would agree to go to
dinner with Margo and Warren; when Chalky and Warren were
briefly nuzzling up to one another, trying to find out what business
deals they could cook up. It was a short-lived friendship. But while
it lasted, Chalky played the big shot and always picked up the
check, hundreds of dollars' worth of dinner tabs, while Margo and
Warren just sat there or conveniently looked away. Of course,
Margo thought he was wonderful.

"Let a few weeks pass," she suggested.

"Give him a little time," Gloria said. "Then sit him down and tell him the facts of life. Some men have to be taught. They can be great boyfriends, lay gifts on you and everything, but a husband is a whole different thing."

It sounded like good advice. All right, I said to myself. I'll give the man time to settle in. After all, he's never been married. And he spent so many years in jail, it may take awhile for him to figure out how to behave like a husband.

So I waited. And I watched. I saw him fling fifties at doormen and cocktail waitresses. Every time we went to his sister's for Sunday dinner, all the nieces and nephews lined up and they each got $100 apiece from him. Whenever they needed something, there was Uncle Chalky with ready cash. I gave it a little time. Then I started in.

"Chalky, it's been a couple of months now and I've been paying the bills out of my own money—" I'd begin.

"You mean the money Bernie left you," he'd correct me.

"They're *our* household bills, Chalky. Bernie has nothing to do with this."

"Leave me alone," he'd say. "Stop nagging."

Tell me to stop nagging? Tell a fish to breathe through its mouth. Chalky got to play the big shot and I got to pay the bills? So I kept "nagging." But I did try to be tactful. To be nice. To be a good girl.

Finally, one day he said, "Okay. What are the monthly bills here? What's the rent? How much is the phone?"

And, good girl that I was, I shaved the rates. I told him less on each item, thinking he wouldn't be as mad if our expenses weren't as much. I still had a few bucks put away. I figured I'd make up the difference. So we agreed on a figure he'd give me weekly to pay for everything. I think it was $300. I know it wasn't enough. And Fridays became my pay days. That's what Chalky called the household money—my pay.

Now, Chalky was a clothes horse. The way Norman Bates was a devoted son. When it came to his wardrobe, he was incredibly fastidious. There was a very big walk-in closet in our bedroom. And that closet, which became his, was set up with extreme care. Shirts were hung by color, sleeve length, style, each two inches from the next—*exactly* two inches. Chalky used a tape measure to make sure. Each of his suits, too, about twenty of them, hung exactly two inches apart. There was a chart on the closet wall indicating which shirts, ties, and shoes went with each suit. He had hundreds of ties. And they also were perfectly placed. Suits, pants, shoes, ties, all

color-coordinated, all two inches apart, all lined up like little soldiers. The Lefkowitz Collection, I used to call it.

And in that closet was a little bench that Chalky used when he
put on his shoes and socks. Come Friday morning, he'd be sitting
in the closet on his bench. "Sandy, come here," he'd say. And he'd
count out $300 in the closet. In the dark. He paid me off in a dark
closet so that I couldn't see his bankroll!

Three hundred dollars. I think the rent at that time was four hundred. And I'd squirrel the cash away in little envelopes, like a mi-
ser. I'd put so much in the rent envelope and so much in the food
envelope and so much toward the phone. I was a maniac about it. I
couldn't believe what I was doing. But I did it. And he sent me
flowers.

For the first couple of months of our marriage, he sent flowers
twice a week. Not just bunches of roses or pretty bouquets. No,
these were big floral arrangements—the kind people would send to
a wake. My girlfriends would say, "Oh, look how thoughtful he is.
Oh, Sandy, he really loves you. He's so romantic." It turned out
that the guy who owned the flower shop owed Chalky money and
was paying him off in funeral arrangements.

Mr. Wonderful.

Six, seven, eight hundred on a custom suit, four hundred dollars
for shoes. Never went out wearing less than a couple of grand on
his well-scrubbed back. And I remember one day I said, "The
sheets are torn, they have holes in them. I want to buy some new
ones."

And Chalky said, "Why? No one sees them."

"Yeah, but we sleep on them."

"Aah," he said, "what's the difference?"

"Look, I'll go down to Grand Street, to the Lower East Side. I
won't spend a lot, okay?"

He wouldn't give me the money. Instead, he shlepped all the
way downtown with me to make sure we got the cheapest sheets in
the discount store.

I didn't say anything. It wouldn't have mattered. Chalky had to
have the last word in every discussion. "Sandy, when I'm wrong,
I'm right," he used to say, "and when I'm right, I'm very right. You
can't argue with me about that."

He'd say it into the mirror. "When you're wrong, you're right.
And when you're right, you're very right. No argument. That's it."

* * *

Being right—even when he was wrong—was very important to Chalky. He was new to the husband game. He wanted to do it right. And in the first year of our marriage, right meant making Jeffrey his legal son.

I was thrilled when Chalky said he wanted to adopt Jeffrey. It was a warm, loving, beautiful gesture. And Jeffrey, who at four and a half years old, had never known a real father, was all for it. He was already calling Chalky daddy, and it was clear to everyone that Chalky was crazy about the kid. Why wouldn't he be? Jeffrey was adorable, smart, polite, good-natured.

There was a minor hitch. After examining Chalky's arrest record, the surrogate court law clerk, who made recommendations in adoption proceedings, refused to even put the case before the deciding judge.

"Don't worry," Chalky said, on the way home from court. "We'll get around this shmuck." He chatted with some friends and, a few bucks and a couple of days later, he phoned and said, "Okay, the adoption is in the bag."

"What happened?" I asked.

"I made a donation to the Democratic Party for five thousand dollars and the adoption is going to go through. How much did it cost you to give birth?" he asked.

"I don't know, not a lot. Much less than five thousand dollars."

"Well, just remember, it's costing me more to adopt Jeffrey than it cost Bernie to pay for his being born," said the proud papa-to-be.

Less than a week later, our attorney got a call from the judge's clerk. We went down to surrogate court—Jeffrey, Chalky and me, all dressed up like citizens—and were ushered into the judge's chambers. I'd never seen such a magnificent office in my life. The man sat at a desk as big as my mother's apartment. As we walked through the door he said, "Hi, Chalky, I had dinner the other night at Gatsby's with Tommy Ryan and a couple of your other pals."

Tommy Ryan, whose real name was Tommy Eboli, was a member of the Genovese mob; a major member. I'd met him back in the Bernie days with Ruby Stein and Jiggs Forlano. He was supposed to be Vito Genovese's right-hand man. Apparently, he was the judge's friend, too.

"Yeah, I heard," Chalky said. "I know all about it."

"Come here, young man," the judge called to Jeffrey. "I know you like chocolates. Your daddy told me you like chocolates." The judge pulled a bag of Hershey Kisses out of a drawer and called

Jeffrey over. "Now, let me ask you something, Jeffrey. Do you want Chalky to become your real father?"

Jeffrey looked over at Chalky. He was crazy about him. "He is my real father," he said. "My other daddy died when I was born."

The judge winked at Chalky. "Congratulations, daddy," he said.

We drove to First Street, to Chalky's mother's apartment, to celebrate. Sarah was thrilled. "My new little Lefkowitz," she kept saying, pinching Jeffrey's cheeks, smoothing down his hair. She had a huge, delicious, Jewish lunch waiting—a goulash stew and chicken, and Jeffrey's favorite chicken soup with homemade noodles and matzo balls. She'd even baked a cake which she served with one candle on it, for Jeffrey to blow out for good luck. And she gave him a five-hundred-dollar bond. "For my new little Lefkowitz grandson, who will carry on the name one day, *mine einekle*, my gorgeous grandchild." And every time Jeffrey called her *bubbie*, grandma, her eyes misted. And so did mine.

I looked around the table. It was just the four of us. And Chalky looked so comfortable and happy. Sarah was glowing, *kvelling*. She couldn't stop touching Jeffrey's cheeks, his forehead, running her work-worn hand through his hair. We were all right, I thought. We were a family.

In moments like this, I told myself it'll work out. I have what I wanted. I'm really Sadie-Sadie now.

So what if Chalky didn't kid around with me the way Bernie had or hang around the house to kibitz or invite me to meet him somewhere for a drink or dinner just for the hell of it. So what that he left at eleven each morning and rarely returned before three or four A.M. and that he attended more and more gatherings alone because there would be business done at those places and I was his wife, not his partner. So what that when his friend Tom Sullivan finally went to trial on the armed-robbery charge that had been hanging over his head for months, Chalky had to be there for him, in the courtroom day after day, lending emotional support to Tom's wife but getting more irritable, more irrational at home.

Chalky was very attached to Tom, almost like a Siamese twin, and as the trial began to go badly for Tom, Chalky got crazier and crazier. He'd begun waking me up at two or three in the morning. "Make me blueberry pancakes," I'd hear, struggling out of sleep, knowing that Jeffrey would be up bright and early and that I'd have to make breakfast for him in just a few hours. Or Chalky would show up drunk in the middle of the night after being away from home for a day or two and he'd demand sex. Or bacon and scrambled eggs. Or an explanation for why there was a wrinkle in the left sleeve of his favorite blue shirt. He'd ring the doorbell at four A.M. until I woke and let him in. "Where's your key?" I'd ask. "What do you care?" he'd snarl. "I didn't feel like using it."

When Bernie had come home late, or sometimes if he stayed out all night, I used to toss and turn and worry about him. When Chalky went out my only worry was he'd surprise me by coming home early. At first I'd resented being left alone so much of the time. But after a while, I came to cherish my nights without him. When the doorbell rang, I never knew who'd be waiting for me—the lover or the beast.

Rosh Hashona was early that fall. It fell on a Friday. Chalky was going to be home for the holiday dinner and I was very eager to please him. We'd been married for a little more than a year. Things had gone rapidly downhill after Tom Sullivan was convicted and sentenced to eight years in Atlanta. Not only was Chalky furious over what had happened to his best friend, but he'd taken over Tom's business and was stretched pretty thin, working all the time now. At what, believe me, I didn't ask. He was home less and less. And he was never home for dinner on a Friday. So this dinner, this Jewish holiday, was really a special occasion, one of the rare chances for all of us to be together again, family style.

I shopped and cleaned and cooked for days. I roasted a beautiful chicken. I set the table with crystal and candles. Jeffrey was spotless and all dressed up in a handsome new suit. I had my hair and nails done. Chalky brought home flowers—a beautiful bouquet, not a funeral floral arrangement. I think I was even wearing a little TV Mom-type apron when I brought the food to the table. Everything was just the way I thought Chalky would like it. Everything was right.

Right.

"This chicken is delicious," he said. "It's a kosher chicken, isn't it?"

"No," I said. "There are no kosher butchers around here."

"What the hell are you talking about?" He threw his knife and fork into his plate. "You're telling me this chicken isn't kosher? You can't get a kosher chicken for Rosh Hashona? My mother would walk twenty miles for a kosher chicken! Whatever she had to do, wherever she'd have to go!"

"Chalky, you eat bacon," I reminded him. "When did you become kosher?"

He shoved his plate across the table, knocking over a candle-stick. "Don't you open that big mouth to me! On the holidays! How often do I come home? How often do you cook for me, you dumb bitch?!".

Jeffrey's eyes widened with fear.

Chalky stood up suddenly. "Don't you start with me, you pig, you miserable bitch!" He tore at the tablecloth. Dishes and food went flying. Before everything fell to the floor, he jumped up and upended the dining room table and dumped whatever remained.

Jeffrey screamed and ran for cover.

"Stop it!" I yelled. "What's the matter with you? You're scaring the baby! Stop it!"

But Chalky was already at the bar. He began hurling glasses across the room. He threw them at the mirror above the couch. "Couches, you'll have!" he bellowed, as the glass tore into the up-holstery. "Glasses, you'll have!"

He was throwing things and smashing things. He grabbed the cartons of cigarettes that were in the bar and began ripping them up and throwing them around the room. Then he found a handful of matchbooks. He lit them one, two at a time, the whole books, and began flinging them at the drapes, the sofa, and chairs. The place was a disaster. Jeffrey, the son Chalky adored, was quaking and crying in my arms.

"You bitch, you cunt, you filthy pig," Chalky yelled.

"Why, because I tried to make dinner for you? Because I wanted a normal family dinner? A family like you promised. You're never here. You're never home! You wanted a housewife. I'm a house-wife. Not *your* wife. I'm married to this *house*. This house that you're trying to destroy!"

While Chalky ranted, raved, and threw flaming matchbooks, I grabbed Jeffrey and ran. We spent that night upstairs in my girlfriend's apartment. I was afraid to go home. The next morning I took Jeffrey to the park. And, all afternoon, I tried to figure out what had happened.

Sitting on a bench facing the East River, after running out of "knock-knock" jokes to tell Jeffrey, I reminded myself that Bernie'd had a temper, too. He'd thrown and broken things and cursed and threatened me. But we'd always gone toe-to-toe. We'd taken turns. And when the smoke cleared, we'd have a good laugh over it. Chalky's tantrums were a one-way deal. He got to scream and holler. Then he'd ice you for making him lose his cool.

Also, with Bernie, there'd been no child around. He'd never

have let loose like that in front of his son—or any kid, for that matter. But Chalky, who'd read so many books and had so many ideas about how a family should be, had begun to say and do things in front of Jeffrey that you didn't need a Ph.D. in child psychology to know were frightening and harmful.

Not that Chalky didn't love Jeffrey. He did. He wanted to be the perfect dad. He wanted me to be the perfect wife and mother. And, with Jeffrey, really, he had close to the perfect child. But Chalky was trying to live in two different worlds—a normal one at home; a mob life in the world—and it seemed inevitable that the one he'd lived most would win out over the picket-fence fantasy Jeffrey and I were supposed to deliver.

After the jokes and swing rides in the little playground behind our house, we walked to Central Park, to the Alice in Wonderland statue. On the way, I thought of Bernie's generosity and Chalky's cheapness—of spirit as well as cold cash.

Bernie treasured his friends—whether they were up or down on their luck, in or out of prison, straight or crooked, new or old. Chalky's loyalty was reserved for certain people—for the high-echelon mobsters who were his only friends. I couldn't imagine him going to the Dio brothers to plead for an ex-girlfriend, the way I'd seen Bernie do. Women were nothing to Chalky. He had no sense of loyalty or fairness with them. He'd cheated on his fiancées, played them off against one another and me. He demanded loyalty in a wife, but never trusted me. He always required proof. Receipts! And he definitely cared more about what his friends thought of me than what I thought of them.

Chalky was one of the people Bernie had never allowed anyone to say a word against. "He's done hard time. Twelve years locked away will change a guy. But Chalky's solid. He'll be there for you if you need anything," he used to tell me.

And now, walking through the park, knowing it was not just the chill September air making my son shiver, I remembered an incident I'd worked very hard to forget, to tell myself hadn't really meant anything. It had happened about a month before Chalky and I were married.

Downtown, one night, we ran into a man named Black Sal, a well-connected old wise guy with white hair and thick black eyebrows. He sat down with us and Chalky proudly introduced me. "Sal, this is my future wife. You knew her late husband, Bernie Barton."

The old guy had really been putting away the vino when Chalky excused himself to make a telephone call. It was a little awkward, sitting there with this slightly soused stranger. To make conversation, I said, "So you knew Bernie."

"Yeah, I knew him," he said, squinting at me through his cigar smoke. "Never liked him, your husband, your late husband. He was a junkie, Bernie Barton. He fucked around with cocaine. I heard he sold it, too. That's why he died. That's what killed him."

I was stunned. "How dare you?" I gasped. "Who the hell do you think you are to talk to me that way? To talk about my dead husband? You didn't know Bernie. Not really, or I would've met you before. Who the fuck do you think you are?"

He reared back. "Your future husband knows who I am," he answered, furious. "And when I tell him the kind of mouth you got on you— What's wrong with him that he can't control you, he lets you talk this way?"

Chalky returned right then with a smile on his face. I watched it fade as Black Sal complained to him about me. I saw his eyes narrow into glinting blue knives. It was me he was glaring at, not the man who'd insulted me and his dead best friend.

"Chalky, you should have heard what he said about Bernie," I said. "He doesn't even know me and he tells me these disgusting lies. He's bad-mouthing one of your dearest friends, who you say you love as a brother, my late husband, my son's father—I have no right to defend him?"

Chalky was staring at me coldly.

"Who is this man that you have to pay so much homage to, that you make me feel like nothing, like I have no respect and no rights? Why are you putting the importance of this stranger above me?"

"I'm very sorry, Sal," Chalky said. "Let me buy you a drink."

I stalked out of the restaurant and refused to see him. And he called five times a day, every day, for a week. And he must have sent fifty different bouquets and flower arrangements to pacify me—all of them, I learned later, came from the florist who owed him money. And, finally, by the end of the week, he'd convinced me that I'd misunderstood everything. That Bernie had, indeed, been his best friend and that, of course, he'd never tolerate anyone talking against him.

Toward evening, that High Holy Day, in the darkness of a movie theater on Third Avenue, with Jeffrey exhausted and dozing in the seat next to me, I realized the differences in my marriages were not just between Chalky and Bernie. *I* was different now. With Bernie,

I'd been a child. He'd taught me everything—from what to wear to how to think. And I'd been grateful for it.

After Bernie's death I'd been on my own. And once the unbearable pain of loss had let up, I'd made a pretty good life for myself. I'd had money, friends, and freedom. I'd made some dumb choices when it came to men. But, basically, I'd been on my way to being the kind of woman Bernie would have wanted me to be, and more importantly, the kind of person I wanted to be, and *most* importantly, the kind of mother Jeffrey needed me to be.

Now, suddenly, it seemed as though everything Bernie had loved and nurtured in me—my outspoken honesty, my curiosity and eagerness to learn new things, my sense of humor, my ability to stand up for myself—Chalky hated and was trying to destroy.

It was dark out when we left the movie theatre. With Jeffrey half asleep in my arms, I went home. Only it wasn't our home anymore, Jeffrey's and mine. It wasn't a safe place. The streets had seemed safer.

The apartment was in shambles. Chalky was sitting out on the terrace. He didn't say a word to either of us. I put Jeffrey to bed and then I went to the door of the terrace.

"I want out," I said in a voice so calm I hardly recognized it as my own. "I don't want Jeffrey growing up in a house like this. I don't want to be treated this way anymore—"

He didn't even turn his head. "You're not going anywhere. My ego couldn't take it, Sandy," he said. "You're not leaving. I won't let you. Jeffrey is my son. You're not taking him anywhere. Nobody's leaving. Nobody ever leaves me. When it's time, I'll do the leaving."

"You're wrong, Chalky," I said. "I'm walking."

He glanced at me over his shoulder. His eyes were ice. His thin lips were tight, twisted in a sick smile. "You can't walk without legs," he said.

At least I had Red.

When things were bleak at home, when Chalky drove me crazy, I'd sneak up to Harlem and hang out with Hot Dog. Walking around uptown with that sweet, caramel-colored man, with his skinny little mustache and quick Cab Calloway grin, always restored me, reminded me of the old days when I felt respected and secure.

We didn't talk about Chalky. We'd just shmooze and gossip and have a few laughs. But a couple of months after the Rosh Hashona chicken-hurling, I decided to tell Red what was going on at home. I knew Chalky hadn't been kidding when he said he'd never let me leave him. For the time being, I was trying to make the best of a bad situation. I was trying to get along with Chalky for Jeffrey's sake and my own. Trying to act as though that horrible holiday dinner had never happened. But nothing I did seemed to please him. Or comfort me.

Chalky wanted us to get back to a normal life.

His idea of normal—starring me as the silent, smiling housewife buying kosher chickens, ironing underwear, and toasting bagels at three A.M.—was making a wreck of me. I had to do something. I decided to drive uptown and talk to Red about it. He loved Jeffrey and me. He knew us. He knew me as I used to be—a fun-loving, big-mouthed, happy human being, not the nervous rag I was turning into. I thought I'd ask his advice.

It was a warm day in November. Red bought us both ice-cream cones. I was working up to telling him what was on my mind. We'd wandered over to Spanish Harlem. As usual, with the Dog at my side, I was laughing, my steps were springier, my heart was lighter. He saw a couple of men he knew and walked over to talk to them. I waited, leaning up against a car eating my ice cream. Suddenly, his ice-cream cone splattered onto the sidewalk. He turned, reached out to me, and fell.

Hot Dog Red had a massive heart attack. He died in my arms.

It was like the door to a garden had slammed shut in my face. Nothing but darkness left. My best friend was gone. My heart. My last link to a world where I was strong and everything was possible.

CHAPTER TWENTY

The Long Goodbye

Normal. Once it had been my favorite word, my girlish fantasy, my best hope. With Chalky it had become hazardous to my health.

What did a man who'd spent maybe twenty years of his forty-eight behind bars know about normal? But normal was what he wanted his home life to be. Okay. So what's more normal than a wife doing laundry?

"Lint!" he raved. "You got lint on my socks! You put my socks in the washing machine?! Never. You'll never do that again. You'll wash them by hand from now on!"

"When you were in jail all those years you didn't care if your socks were linty," I reminded him. But this was no ordinary human being I was trying to reason with. This was Chalky Lefkowitz, who used a tape measure to make sure his closet looked good, and who, if someone touched him on the arm, would pull away and say threateningly, "Don't touch my clothes." This was also a man who'd thrown a hair brush at me, causing a welt the size of an egg on my leg, because he'd found a wrinkle in a suit I'd packed for him.

So I washed the socks by hand. And I did a very good job of it for a couple of weeks. And, of course, I continued doing the rest of the laundry like a good girl. Each morning, in the darkened room where Chalky was sleeping, I'd pick up the shirt he'd worn the night before and put it into the hamper in the bathroom.

One morning, shortly after our third anniversary, a balled-up shirt I was carrying fell onto the bathroom floor and I saw it in bright light. It was covered with makeup. Not just a little pink smudge on the collar. Big-time makeup—green eyeshadow and brown highlighter and streaks of black and smears of red. The shirtfront looked like a Max Factor test swatch.

I was wild with rage. I was nauseated with hurt and upset. I had to take Jeffrey to school. I hurled the shirt at Chalky's sleeping head. He sat up. "You miserable creep!" I said and left the apartment.

When I came back, he was at the bathroom sink, stark naked, trying to scrub the stains out of the shirt with a wet washcloth.

"Don't bother," I said. "It won't work."

"I'm at a restaurant," he said. "People come in. Women kiss me on the neck. What's wrong with you?"

I went nuts. I was foaming at the mouth like a dog. I cried, I screamed, I broke things.

"Sandy, what's the matter with you? This means nothing. It's dumb. Let's not even talk about it. Listen to me, honey," Chalky urged. "Let's spend the day together."

Honey? What have we here, I wondered.

He took me to Lutèce for lunch and ordered champagne. He took me to Gucci and bought me a pocketbook. And one for my mother and one for my sister. We walked through Central Park and he bought me a balloon. It was honey, baby, sweetie all day long. And then I got it.

"You're in trouble," I said. We were sitting on a bench near the zoo. "You've got problems, right? You're under investigation, aren't you?"

"Yes," he said. "If things don't get better fast, I've got to leave town for a while. I might be subpoenaed. I might be summonsed. They might even be working on an indictment."

I handed him the balloon and lit up a cigarette. "And you're afraid if you're arrested, they might want to put me on the witness stand?"

He didn't have to answer.

"Don't worry," I said. "I wouldn't do that. I'm not made that way. Anyway, don't you know the law? A wife can't testify against a husband."

"You know something," said Mr. Generosity, blue eyes atwinkle. "You're a smart woman. You're a lunatic, a crazy lady, but once you get it out of your system, you're okay."

Well, I hadn't really gotten it out of my system. And how smart I was I couldn't say, but smart enough to know that I couldn't go head to head with Chalky. He was cheating on me. He was seeing someone else. He probably had a mistress. He probably had a mistress *and* he was seeing someone else. It was killing me. And little by little, as I scrubbed his little silk socks, I knew I had to do something.

I couldn't leave. The couple of times I'd threatened to, he'd pin me with those cold blue eyes, he'd say in that slow, scary voice, "I told you, Sandy. Nobody leaves me. I do the leaving." Or, again, "You can't walk without legs." That was his favorite.

Don't get mad, get even, Bernie used to tell me. Standing in the kitchen, hand-rinsing Chalky's expensive socks, it was like Bernie was right there at my elbow, whispering in my ear. The step I took that morning was a tiny, baby step, but it was in the direction of freedom.

I starched his socks.

Chalky had fabulous feet. No corns or calluses. Soft, perfect, pampered feet that he treated to only the best socks and softest leather.

Within the week, he was home scratching and complaining bitterly. "My feet are killing me," he said. "They're burning. They itch. I'm getting big red blotches all over them. They're killing me!"

It was the best I could do at the time.

That and begin to hope an indictment did come down for him.

Chalky was never home on Fridays. Never. He spent every Friday night with his girlfriend. He'd say he was playing cards. He'd even come home with a bag full of money on Saturday and make me count it for him. But toward the end, I knew he was seeing his mistress. Every Friday night. What a lucky girl.

Sunday he was all mine. It was another one of those great ideas he had about what normal people do. Sunday was family day. So he'd hang around the house with the football game on like Mr. America. Never mind that the man couldn't tell you the name of a team, let alone a player. He just liked the idea of it—lying around in pajamas on Sunday, with what was left of his hair sticking up every which way, rolling up the couch pillows and watching the game. And, every two minutes, he'd call out orders for something else he needed to eat or drink or wanted me to do. Then, in the late afternoon, he'd cook his famous jailhouse spaghetti sauce.

My girlfriends used to kid me about what a great diet it was—I could eat as much sauce as I wanted, because spending one Sunday with that man I'd lose seven pounds from aggravation.

On the advice of one of the mafia wives I knew, I started putting Valium in his coffee. It really worked, too. He was much quieter on Sundays after that. Very mellow.

That third year we were married, I became close to the wives of two of Chalky's pals. One was an Irish girl named Terry, who was married to this big, fat mob slob, who was a very rough guy but good to her financially. The other was Crazy Tina, who was married to Frankie, the nut case. Frankie was who they meant when they said he'll kill you first and ask questions later.

I met Terry and Tina at a wedding. We were at the same table and during a lull in the conversation about kids and lipstick, I noticed that Terry was tapping her fingernails on the table and Tina was tapping her cigarette lighter and the three of us were smoking like crazy.

I said to Tina, "Oh, you have the same habit I do." And she said, "Married to men like this, you develop lots of habits. I'm surprised we're not all junkies here."

We had a lot in common. Before I knew for sure that Chalky had a girlfriend, I knew that Tina knew her husband had one. In fact, Tina had threatened the girl once. But the girl had passed out and then Tina felt sorry for her. Terry's husband had a girlfriend of long standing whom he'd put into business.

The three of us exchanged phone numbers. Terry and Tina lived in Brooklyn but we were constantly in touch by phone—often at two or three in the morning, keeping each other company while our husbands were out. And we'd see each other at funerals. Funerals were a big deal for the wives. I mean, it was one of the sacred social events where the guys couldn't bring their girlfriends.

I remember Tina called me one day, all excited, and said, "What are you wearing tonight?" I didn't know what she was talking about. She said, "We're going out. Chalky'll probably call you soon. Didn't you hear, Little Georgie died. It's going to be the biggest event ever."

We got dressed to kill for the funerals and wakes. I remember once ruining a gorgeous pair of high heels walking to a funeral in the snow in Williamsburg, Brooklyn. You never parked your car near the funeral parlor. Nine times out of ten the FBI was there taking pictures and checking license plates. So everyone but the immediate family parked miles away and wore sunglasses, even if it was nighttime, so that they couldn't be identified in the photographs.

Chalky was a maniac about security. He was sure the FBI had our phones tapped, our car wired, agents following him, following me. I thought he was flattering himself. He'd yell at me for saying things on the phone like, "Chalky's going out tonight," or, "He's going to work in five minutes." And I'd remind him that he'd threatened to break someone's legs or have their mother shot on the same phone a couple of hours earlier when he'd come in drunk and spoiling for a fight.

He was always on the lookout for places the FBI wouldn't bug. When I was in the hospital to have a tumor removed from my ear, he showed up with flowers, candy, and four other guys. Everyone said hello, how you doing, Sandy? Then Chalky asked me to take a walk down the hall with him. I shlepped along in my bandages and bedroom slippers and sat down in a little plastic chair near the nursing station. "Wait here. I'll come and get you in a little while," he said. And he and his friends locked themselves into my private room and had a little meeting.

Nurses and orderlies were banging on the door. They were angry at me, telling me I wasn't supposed to be out in the hall. I wasn't supposed to be sitting up, I had to get back into bed right that minute. Fat chance. There was an Appalachian mafia conference going on at Doctors Hospital and no one was going to get those guys to budge.

When the meeting was over, they filed out. Each one, sweet as could be, kissed me on the cheek. "Get well soon, sweetheart." "Get into bed." "Take care of yourself, honey," they urged me.

At his mother's funeral, Chalky took over the funeral director's office and held a meeting there. He had me go outside into the street to check and see if the FBI was taking down license plate numbers. At his own mother's funeral!

Then, one day, he phoned me and said, "I'm having a meeting in the house. I don't care where you and Jeffrey go, but be out of there by six and don't come back for at least three hours." It was no big deal. It had happened before. But then he added, almost as an afterthought, "And, Sandy, before you go, make a meat loaf. Enough for seven guys. Get the best steaks you can find and have them ground up. I want you to make it like my mother taught you, with the egg slices in the center. And also, make a salad and some garlic bread and just leave it on the table."

"Steaks?" I said. "You want me to make meat loaf for you and your friends out of the best steaks I can find?"

Less than a week before, Chalky had come home drunk in the middle of the night, gone rummaging for ice cream in the fridge, and pitched a fit because he'd found two lamb chops wrapped in butcher paper in the freezer. Chalky decided they were too expensive. So he woke me up, at four A.M., by throwing the frozen lamb chops at me. "This is how you spend my money?!" he'd demanded.

"They're for Jeffrey," I had tried to explain.

"A kid doesn't need eight dollars' worth of lamb chops!"

Now he said, "Yeah, get steak. You make a good meat loaf. Make it out of steak. At least let me be able to show you off."

I hung up fuming.

Chalky ranted about money all the time. His son's lamb chops were too expensive. The phone bill was too high. The cleaning woman cost too much. But nothing was too good for his pals.

I paced the kitchen for a couple of minutes, unconsciously rubbing my arm where the bruise from the frozen lamb chops was beginning to turn from blue to yellow. Twice, I picked up the phone to call the butcher. Then I got a better idea.

I hurried downstairs to the supermarket and bought salad greens and bread. And then I bought two pounds of the cheapest chopped meat I could find. And then I bought six cans of dog food. Alpo.

A can at a time, I spooned the dark, almost purple, mystery meat into the bowl of cheap ground beef and blended and shaped the mixture with a vengeance. It smelled awful, like organ meat, like dead horse flesh. It smelled like what it was—dog food! While it was cooking, the whole house stunk. I had to open every window in the place and turn on the kitchen and bathroom fans. Finally, I sprayed everything with Lysol deodorant spray—even the meat loaf. But in the end it was gorgeous. Egg slices and all.

I didn't dare come home that night, until I looked up from the street and saw that the apartment was dark. Of course the dirty dishes were still there on the pretty dining table I'd set. And there was a little bit of food left—some salad, some pickles, but only a nibble of the meatloaf.

The dirty dogs, they loved it.

I called my mother, my sister, Terry, and Tina. We howled. But it was pathetic really. This was what I was reduced to. Childish pranks. Starching socks, putting Valium in his coffee, feeding him Alpo. It wasn't exactly the French Resistance.

* * *

A word about the FBI. Chalky was right. They were after him. They had our phones tapped. They had guys assigned to me. They had guys in the Garment Center watching him. He'd tip the door-man fifty bucks a shot and it paid off. They'd ring up and say, "Sandy, there are some guys asking around about your husband." Or "Sandy, the FBI is here. They're looking for Chalky. Is he around? Is he home?"

Of course, I'd say, "No, there's no one here." And the doormen would tell the FBI that they'd seen us go out or that they'd just tried to call and there was no one home. Sometimes the doormen would ring up and say, "There's a strange car circling the building. Tell your husband." Sometimes I think they enjoyed getting caught up in the excitement, the games, the racket club life.

Why not? You met a very interesting class of people in the life. Like Roy Cohn, the lawyer, whose name was in the papers every other day. You couldn't read a gossip column in the seventies with-out finding out he'd been at this society party or that new disco with Steve Rubell, with Liza, with Halston, with Bianca. So I was impressed when Chalky said he had a little problem with the Feds (and none of my fucking business *what* little problem) and that he was going to hire Roy Cohn to see if he could squash it. I don't know why, but he wanted me to get dressed up and go with him to Cohn's place in the East Fifties.

I've seen some gorgeous houses in my day, but Roy Cohn's three-story townhouse was to die for. Antiques, sculptures, paint-ings. He showed me around. He was shorter than Chalky, shorter than me, and gracious and gay. In his bedroom, he had an oversized king-size bed with a leopard throw on it and a bathroom you could've lived in. Everything sparkled. It was mirrored and had a hot tub and a separate sunken bathtub and a stall shower *and* a re-frigerator.

We all sat down together in Roy's study. While Chalky ex-plained whatever the problem was, I made sure to occupy myself looking around at the knickknacks and clocks from France and other elegant little furnishings. Finally, the meeting was over. Cohn stood up and told Chalky not to worry, he had the deal clinched. "You'll never have a problem," he said.

Chalky said, "Okay, Roy, what do I have to give you for this?" And he started reaching in his pocket for the dough.

Cohn looked up at him, looked him square in the eye. And in this very throaty, very quiet voice, he said, "Chalky, take an attaché case and just fill it up with hundred dollar bills until you can't close it anymore. That's my fee."

Chalky said, "You're kidding."

Roy said, "No, Chalky, I'm not."

Chalky paid up.

Months later, Jeffrey's second-grade teacher called me aside when I went to pick him up from school. She said the principal wanted to see me. It seems two men representing themselves as FBI agents had come into the school and they wanted to know how much it cost a year to go there. They said they were interested in Jeffrey Lefkowitz—and how much tuition his parents had paid for the year. The principal was shocked. She said it was free, hadn't they seen the sign outside that said public school? It was a big sign. P.S.—that meant Public School, she'd had to tell them. She said they were embarrassed. Shmucks.

Okay. A little time passed. All of a sudden I start getting credit-card offers from every department store in New York. Bergdorf's and Macy's want me to have their cards. Lord & Taylor sends me an application with a lovely letter offering me the world. Finally, I get one from Saks Fifth Avenue saying they've recently checked their records and found that I don't have a charge account with them and they think I ought to. So I called the number on the application and I asked the woman how they got my name. She said the Treasury Department had been there a week ago looking at their records. They'd said my husband was very wealthy. So Saks wanted me to have a line of credit with them.

One day I got a tip from a friend who worked in the post office. "Mrs. L., there's something you should know. We just got orders down at the post office to hold and X-ray all mail addressed to you before delivering it."

"Thank you very much." I said. As if a wise guy was going to send checks to Chalky or drop him a line about the nice little heist that went off last week or the union pension fund they skimmed.

Next they sent for us to come down to the Income Tax Bureau and discuss the cost of Jeffrey's day camp and where the money to pay for it had come from. They sat us in a room, which had a bulletin board at the front of it. And on the board were all these mug shots of tax evaders with little "Apprehended" stickers over their faces and the time and fines they were doing for their crimes. If the day camp cost a big $500, it was a lot. We answered their questions. They looked angry. They looked sad. They looked like the shmucks they were. And we left.

* * *

In the fourth year of my marriage to Chalky, the FBI gave me a boyfriend. He was an agent named Richard—not Richie, he'd correct me, not Richela. "Mrs. Lefkowitz, my name is Rich-hard," he'd say, exasperation creeping into his hard-working, just-the-facts-ma'am voice. Poor Richard. Sweet Richard. Every night between seven and seven-fifteen, he'd phone the house and say, "This is Richard Stanley of the OC Task Force." The Organized Crime Task Force. "Is Chalky there, Mrs. Lefkowitz?"

"Richie, he's not here. You know he's never here in the evening, Richela. So what are we going to talk about tonight?"

Sometimes it was Bernie Richard wanted to talk about. He knew all about Bernie. He knew about Jeffrey. He'd followed my life like a soap opera fan. He'd listened in on it, replaying the taped triumphs and tragedies with a fan's determination not to miss a single thrilling moment.

"You know, Bernie wasn't bad. He was a nice guy, really," he'd say, "compared to Chalky. Why do you stay with Chalky, Sandy?" We'd moved on to such familiarities. After all, he was the most faithful, most dependable man in my life. He'd earned the right to call me Sandy. To call my husband Chalky.

If he failed to phone for a night or two, I missed him. I'd say, "Richard, what happened to you?"

He had a cold. I told him what to take for it. Chicken soup, of course. Jewish penicillin, I told him.

He tore a ligament in his leg. I said, "You've got to keep your foot above your heart otherwise you'll get a bloodclot, Richela." He said his doctor had told him the same thing.

He'd call when I was busy. I'd say, "The baby's in the bathtub. I can't talk to you now." And he'd say, "Oh, I'm sorry. Go ahead, take care of him. How long do you think it'll take? I'll call you back."

One afternoon, I spotted a couple of guys following me. One of them was wearing a leather trenchcoat and gum-soled shoes. He was a tall, thin WASP, squeaky-clean looking even in black leather. I bumped into him and his partner as I was coming out of Gristede.

"Richard?" I said.

He blushed.

"Well, as long as you're going my way," I said, and I gave each of them a bag of groceries to carry. "You look like I thought you would," I said to Richard.

"Really?"

"A *goy*," I said, walking between them. "You know what a *goy* is?"

"Someone who's not Jewish," his friend, who looked Italian, said.

"That's it. So Richie, how's your foot? Did you do what I said?"

They walked along with me to the cleaners, to the pizza parlor. They walked me home.

On the phone that night, it was business as usual.

"What are you doing with a guy like him? You deserve better," he'd say. "When are you going to leave him?"

I didn't say, "Nobody leaves Chalky. Chalky has to do the leaving." I didn't say, "I can't walk out on him without legs."

And I didn't tell him the story of the last time Chalky had gone on the lam to avoid a subpoena. A man had come to my house in the middle of the night with a list of clothing to be packed. There was trouble brewing, he'd said, and Chalky had to get out of town for a little while.

What a list it was. Everything itemized, everything coordinated. Shirts, shoes, socks, and ties. The Lefkowitz Traveling Collection. And at the bottom of the list was a little note in the master's own neat scrawl, "Please pack everything nicely and fold things so they don't wrinkle."

Maybe I'd seen too many old gangster movies, but since when did a guy go on the lam with color-coordinated outfits?

I didn't see Chalky or hear a word from him for six weeks. My friends were commenting on how relaxed I looked, how happy I seemed. It must've gotten back to him that I was feeling fine. Next thing I knew, his friend showed up again and told me Chalky was in Florida and that he wanted me and Jeffrey to come down and join him. "It'll be like a second honeymoon," the guy said.

I didn't tell him I wished I'd passed on the first one.

"I don't want to go," I said. "I don't want to take Jeffrey out of school."

Next morning, two bruisers, two huge, young Italian *bulvons*, showed up at my door. They were enforcers, probably hit men. But they were very polite. Very uncomfortable. "Sorry," they said, "but we're here to help you pack and put you on the plane." Which is exactly what they did. At least they had the decency to be embarrassed about it.

For me, it proved again that there was no escaping Chalky. Not when all he had to do was make a telephone call and have me delivered to him like Chinese Take Out.

I never explained to Richard why leaving Chalky was not an option. But I did, occasionally, break down and cry with frustration. And sometimes, I'd say, "Do me a favor, Richie. Put him in jail already." Especially after they started telling me about Chalky's girlfriend.

It was during our last year together. "He has a mistress, you know," Richard said one night.

"Really? Great," I answered glibly. "It'll take the pressure off me."

"She lives in Queens," he said another time.

"Sure, you think he'd pay Manhattan rents for her?"

They didn't let up. And I didn't let on. But it got to me. And they must've sensed it. "He was at his girlfriend's again," Richard would say. "Yesterday. Three o'clock. We followed him to her house."

He had a mistress. He saw her regularly. The FBI knew about her before I did. Probably all my girlfriends had known about her, too. It got to me. It made me one of them. The final, full transition from picket-fence promises to racket club wife.

I started confronting Chalky with it. "You've got a girlfriend," I'd say, slamming down his morning orange juice.

"What's the matter with you? You're crazy," he'd answer. "When have I got time for a girlfriend?"

"How about Friday nights when you're never home. How about holidays when you send Jeffrey and me to the Catskills, while you're in town for business? How about every night when you stay out till two or three or don't come home at all?"

"You know where I am. I tell you. I'm busy. I've got people to see. I go to dinner, to restaurants. You know that. You see the matchbooks."

See them? They were driving me crazy. Late at night, he'd wake me up, reeling drunk. He'd throw a matchbook from a fancy restaurant at my head. "You see, if you were a good girl, you could've been with me at this fancy place tonight." If you didn't have such a big mouth. If you treated me nice. If you fixed my collar button like I told you. If you were a good girl.

For years, I'd tolerated this insanity. For years, I'd turned myself inside out trying to be a good girl and never quite making the grade. I was worn out. I rarely got a decent night's sleep because he'd wake me at all hours. Either he'd ring the doorbell till I woke up and let him in or he'd crash into the bedroom and turn on the bright light next to where I was sleeping. And, on top of it, he was throwing these matchbooks in my face, literally. Matchbooks from romantic, elegant restaurants where I now knew he'd been with his girlfriend.

Well, one night, after my FBI boyfriend Richard had given me an earful on the girlfriend, Chalky shook me awake and tossed a matchbook at me. He was bobbing and weaving and reeking of booze. He leaned over me, slamming his hand on the night table. "*You* could have been with me tonight," he was saying, "but no. If only you'd be a good girl and control that mouth, I'd give you whatever you want. But you've got a *big Jewish mouth*—"

I shook every time his angry hand slammed down, going flat, fingers spread out. I was scared, but I was also angry. I'd had it. I noticed the Christmas gift from one of the mob wives on the night-stand. It was a magnificent jewel-encrusted letter opener worth a couple of thousand dollars, standing in its own holder at arm's length from me.

"You don't know how to do anything right!" he yelled.

"Shut up and let me sleep," I screamed, amazing myself.

"You dumb bitch," he said. "You don't know how to be a wife."

"Shut up!" I screamed.

In one clean sweep, I pulled the letter opener out of its holder, grabbed his wrist, and stabbed his hand. I got him through the little fold of flesh between his thumb and forefinger. Blood shot out like Old Faithful. You'd never guess there could be a geyser of blood like that out of such a skinny slab of skin. When I saw what I'd done, I rolled out of his reach as fast as I could. He pulled the letter opener out of his hand and ran into the bathroom.

There was blood everywhere, on the headboard and the walls. I cowered on the floor behind the bed, then crept out and ran and hid in the kitchen.

I grabbed a knife and waited, quaking with fear. I figured he'd come in any second and try to murder me. When he didn't show up, I got scared. Oh, my God, I really killed him, I thought. There was enough blood around to convince anyone that it was possible. I tiptoed carefully back into the bedroom. The bathroom door was locked. "Chalky," I whispered. "Are you okay?"

I put my ear to the door. And I heard a very weird sound. Click, pop, click, pop, click, pop. I had no idea what it was but something was alive and moving in there, so I sat down on the bed and waited.

The door flew open and he charged out like a mad animal. This is it, I said to myself. He's alive and I'm going to be dead in one second. My son won't have a mother. Or he'll disfigure me.

There was blood all over him, all over his fancy suit and shirt and pants; all over the towel he had wrapped between his fingers. And all over the Polaroid camera he was brandishing in his other hand.

"Okay, you've had it!" he said to me. "This is it. I'm through. I'm leaving you. We're getting a divorce. I'm calling my lawyer and I'm taking you to court. And when the judge sees these pictures—" He threw a handful of Polaroid snapshots at me, color pictures of his bleeding hand! "It will be on record that you stabbed me! And it will be on record because I'm going to go to the hospital now. They'll give me a divorce instantly. And you won't get a penny!"

I became hysterical laughing.

He'd lost a lot of blood. He was turning very white.

"Come on," I said, "I'll take you over to Lenox Hill. I'll get a neighbor to stay with Jeffrey and then we'll go over to the hospital."

While I waited for the doctors to sew him up, I couldn't stop laughing. I kept thinking, an Italian would have grabbed a gun. Only a Jewish mobster would reach for a Polaroid to prove his case in divorce court.

He didn't divorce me. That would have been too easy. But the knifing had made him nervous. He stayed away more often, but when he was home he gave me, if not respect, at least respectable distance.

Coincidentally, the FBI started giving me distance, too. Richard's calls tapered off to once or twice a week. Then in the early summer of 1974, the calls stopped altogether.

And Chalky started treating me differently. It was almost as if he were courting me again. We went out to dinner a couple of times a week. He'd send flowers once in a while. Sex, which had always been good, got better toward the end of summer as we approached our fifth wedding anniversary.

"Something's going on," I told Tina. "Chalky's acting too nice."

"You probably should have knifed him years ago," she said.

I told my mother. "I have a premonition, a feeling. He's getting me ready for something."

"For what?" she'd ask.

"He's leaving," I said.

Of course, everyone thought I was nuts. I even thought so. But the feeling that Chalky was saying a long goodbye haunted me.

In late August, when Jeffrey came home from camp, Chalky announced that we were all going up to the Raleigh Hotel in the Catskills for a little vacation. He invited my mother along, too. Tillie had been diagnosed with cancer by then, but she'd just finished a series of cobalt treatments and seemed in good shape and terrific spirits. I was grateful that Chalky had asked her to join us. I started looking forward to a week in the country with the whole family.

My friend Crazy Tina called a couple of days before we were to leave. "I hear you're baby-sitting the Jaw's wife. You'll like her, Sandy. She's a sweet woman, very quiet though."

Giorgio the Jaw was a major player from Mulberry Street. His brother was a priest. It was a good thing, too. From what I knew of the Jaw's reputation, he'd need a close relative to intercede with God to get him into heaven. When it came to family matters— marriage *and* mafia—the Jaw made Chalky look like a liberal.

"What are you talking about?" I asked Tina. "I don't even know the woman."

"Hey, I didn't know her two summers ago when Frankie made me baby-sit her. Terry's done it, too. All the wives do it. They take turns. It's no big deal. Only you'll be pulling your hair out from boredom."

Sure enough, the day after we arrived at the Raleigh Hotel, he said, "There are some friends here I want you to meet." We went down to the dining room and at our table was a woman in her thirties, very quiet, very sweet. And three children, ranging in age from four to eleven. The kids were wild animals, *vilda khaye* running all over the place, whining, arguing, shoving each other. But the woman sat placid as a plaster Virgin. In fact, her name was Mary. Mary, wife of the Jaw.

That afternoon, I was given my assignment. Stay with her. Keep her company. Don't leave her alone. "This is important to me, Sandy," Chalky said, giving me the old familiar, cold-eyed squint to make sure I got the message. "I've got some business with Giorgio. I've got to leave for a couple of days."

Three days. Tillie and I made small talk with Mrs. Jaw. We sat side by side at the pool. We sat side by side at dinner. We went for a little walk side by side. And then, at about seven or eight in the evening, Mary would take the kids up to bed and lock herself in the room for the night. And, for three days, Tillie and I would put Jeffrey to bed and lock ourselves in our adjoining room. And we stayed like that, side by side.

By the fourth night, my mother and I were bored to death. We'd already watched television and played cards for hours, and it was only ten o'clock. Tillie said, "Come on, let's sneak down to the bar."

Like children.

We did. We were sitting there, at the bar in the lobby, chatting with a couple of other guests, when my mother laid an icy, air-conditioned hand on my arm and said, "Don't turn around. Chalky and another guy are coming toward you. And from the look of him, I think it's the Jaw."

It was. And Chalky went nuts. "What are you doing downstairs here? Where's Mary? I told you not to leave her alone." He was wild, ranting and screaming. "I go away and I gotta come back to find the two of you holding up the bar!"

"Yeah, with a Coca-Cola in front of me, and ginger ale for my mother," I pointed out.

The Jaw turned on his heels and went upstairs to check on his wife and kids.

"You're an embarrassment!" Chalky yelled at me in our room that night. "You disgraced me. I can't depend on you for anything! I've got things on my mind. Important things. I don't have time for you to fuck up now. I'm in trouble! There's an indictment coming down! They're looking to arrest me!"

An indictment? An arrest?

I knew it. I'd known something big was breaking. Ah, Richard, my telephone hero, I thought. He'd heard me all those times I'd begged him to put Chalky away. He and the other agents who'd planted bugs and harvested hundreds of hours of tape, who'd phoned and followed us in conspicuously unmarked cars and checked our credit-card status with Saks and our license plate numbers at cemeteries and tried to look casual at the supermarket in black leather coats—hooray for the whole hardworking lot of them. They'd finally found what they'd been looking for. Freedom was at hand.

Within a month of the failed babysitting gig, Chalky announced he was leaving. He'd spent weeks checking the closets and asking for things. "Have you seen that old key chain of Mama's I used to have? I kept it after she died. Find it for me and put it in my jewelry box." Or "Where are the ruby cufflinks?" Or "Get everything back from the cleaners. I need the gray double-breasted you brought in last week and the two pink shirts. Put them in the closet. Neatly."

He came home with an attaché case one night. "What's that?" I asked. "Nothing," he said. "For papers, for business, for the lawyers." Those blue eyes sparkled nervously. He put the attaché case, which had a combination lock on it, into his clothes closet. Neatly.

It's for money, I thought. He's taking his money with him.

That got me nervous. I didn't have much left of my own cash. And knowing Dr. Generosity's record on these matters, I could see trouble coming.

Finally, in the middle of September, he came home one afternoon and said, "Come into the bedroom. We've got to talk."

I did. I sat down on our bed. Chalky was pacing back and forth in front of me. He didn't look at me when he began speaking. "I'm leaving tomorrow," he said, catching a glimpse of himself in the mirror. "I'm going away—for a month, a year, forever. I don't know." He was pacing, brushing something off his shoulder, straightening the crease in his trouser leg. "I don't want this life and I don't want to go to jail. I feel trapped. And I want out. There are things happening. You don't know the half of what's going down."

"Tomorrow?" I'd watched him getting ready. I'd known this was coming. I thought I'd feel relieved, triumphant. Instead, his words hit me like an icy fist in the gut.

"I have to straighten my head out," Chalky said. He hadn't heard me. He hadn't looked at me yet. Which was okay with me because, much to my surprise, I felt tears coming. Old feelings, old fears. I felt again the aching hole in the heart I'd first felt when my father left. The sadness and dread of waking up without Bernie. At the moment I should have jumped for joy, the moment I'd been waiting and praying for, I felt sick and scared.

Next thing I knew, Chalky was dragging suitcases out of the closet. "Help me. Come here. Help me pack."

I took a Valium and we packed his things together. We must have filled eleven suitcases. I was very quiet. We packed quietly. Then he said, "Okay, now I'm going to leave you enough money to live on for a year." And he sat down at the dining room table and started figuring it out to the penny.

"What happens if the price of milk goes up?" I asked, trying to make a joke of it.

"Don't be funny, don't be cute," he said. "You're lucky to get this. Just be a good girl. For all I know I'll be back in a month. This is just in case."

He made love to me that night. He kissed Jeffrey goodbye when he went off to school the next morning. Then he went out to make a phone call. And I walked into the bedroom and took a look at the suitcases lying open on the floor, the neatly packed garment bags draped over the bed, the locked attaché case sitting on top of the dresser.

Old habits die hard. I strolled over to the dresser. I started fiddling with the leather case. It was full, nothing rattled inside, and it was fairly heavy. The latch was a combo lock. Hmmm, I wondered, what combination would Chalky choose? And I started trying some out. And the more involved I became in trying to break the combo, the more the icy knot in my gut loosened and the warmer and happier I felt.

151 First Street, I thought. Chalky's mother's address, the house he grew up in. I spun the dials. Click. Click. Click. The latch popped. I opened the leather attaché case carefully. It was filled to the brim with cash. Rubber-banded packets of big bills, thick as bricks. It was an awful lot of money. Chalky wouldn't have to worry about the price of milk for quite a while.

I lost it.

I burst into tears. The sight of all that cash, the realization that Chalky had been rich all the time he was crying poor to me, tore me up. He'd lied about money, picked fights with me about it—for nothing! For no goddamned reason, he'd made my life hell and Jeffrey's less than it should have been.

I was standing at the dresser, staring at the attaché case full of money, bawling my eyes out. And then I got mad. Really mad. Anger roared through me. I didn't shake my fist the way Scarlett O'Hara did when she swore, "God as my witness, I'll never go hungry again," but that was how I felt. Abandoned, betrayed, desperate, angry! I can't remember ever feeling as high or low at the same time.

Before I knew what I was doing, I ran into the kitchen and grabbed a pair of scissors. I had no idea what the hell I was going to use them for until I got back to the bedroom. I remember thinking, "What? Are you going to cut up the money? Are you insane?!"

Then I answered myself aloud. "Yes!" I yelled, because I *was* insane at that moment. I was having an insane little dialogue with myself. "Me?" it went. "I'm crazy? Why? Am I the one whose life is over if there's a wrinkle in my suit or a shirt button missing?"

And as I was saying these things, I was already standing beside the bed, in front of Chalky's unzipped garment bag, reaching behind the carefully laid out $500 sportcoat to the new $1500 single-breasted navy blue suit lying under it. Half-blinded by tears, I made one long cut in the sleeve, from wrist to elbow. Then I picked carefully through the suitcases, snipping a couple of buttons off a shirt here, a little piece of a cuff there. I cut through the fly of a pair of white linen pants. And, finally, I sliced the looped fringe off a gorgeous pair of shoes Chalky had recently brought home.

Then I neatly closed the garment bag and suitcases, and ambled over to the attaché case on the dresser. Because Jeffrey needed a mother, preferably one still breathing who could walk without crutches and hadn't had her face rearranged by fists-for-hire, I didn't give in fully to the insanity and rage for revenge I was feeling. I reached into the case and peeled off exactly four thousand two hundred and fifty dollars. The precise amount of money Chalky had swindled me out of the day he decided to marry me.

There was no doubt in my mind that he'd count the money once he got where he was going. I wanted him to. I wanted him to wonder and remember. Truth be told, I wanted to make a much bigger dent in Chalky's nest egg than that, but I pulled back my hand as if it had touched fire, and snapped the lid shut.

Case closed.

It was over. It felt over. The anger started to subside. The hole in the gut didn't feel quite as empty. I turned my back on the luggage filled with all that was precious to Chalky and left the bedroom. I could hardly wait for him to come back for the goddamned suitcases and money. I wanted it out of my house, out of my life, and Chalky Lefkowitz with it.

I lit a cigarette and went out to the terrace to wait. By the time Chalky returned with the two guys who were going to help him carry his bags down to the garage, to the limo that was taking him to the airport, I was practically a new woman.

He took one look at my face and said, "What's the matter with you? What're you smiling about?"

"I'm being brave," I said. "I'm just trying to be a good girl, like you told me."

I called Tillie about ten minutes after Chalky's limo pulled out of the garage. She was at my house with her little overnight bag in less than an hour. Crazy Tina showed up at my apartment about five minutes later. "Frankie sent me over," she said apologetically. "I'm supposed to baby-sit you for a couple of days."

"He must've told Frankie he was leaving before he told me," I said. "I'm glad to see you, but why do they think I need a sitter?"

"They must've thought you'd be so broken up about his leaving you might try something." She paused. "You don't look broken up," she said.

"Is it too early for champagne?" I asked.

The Strike Force agents showed up three weeks later at six-thirty in the morning. There were four of them, all pounding on the door and ringing the bell at the same time. "We're here to arrest Chalky Lefkowitz!" one of them shouted like a nervous wreck the minute I opened the door. Big boys, they were. There was one from the OC Task Force. Another one was from Treasury and there were two huge marshalls who looked like the lard-assed Southern sheriffs who gave guys like Cool Hand Luke a hard time.

One of the marshalls handed me a search warrant rolled up like a sacred scroll. On it was listed the indictments against Chalky— *twenty* of them. Shylocking, racketeering, income tax evasion. It was like a Torah of shame. I didn't even finish reading it. I was still married to the man, and the people who'd prepared this little scroll obviously knew him a whole lot better than I did.

"He's not here," I said. "You guys know Chalky's not here. You know everything, right?"

Tillie came in from the bedroom. She looked pale and fragile in her long nightgown. But she was a rock. *"Shah!"* she commanded. "Be quiet. What's wrong with you people? What do you want from my daughter's life? And my grandson. You'll wake my grandson."

"We've got to look around," the Treasury guy said. "We showed you the warrant. Okay." He gave the marshalls a high sign and they pulled out guns.

I said, "Are you insane? What are you going to do, shoot me?"

"Lady," one of the marshalls said, "this is a violent man. We know this man's background. If he's in the house, he's going to come out shooting."

I told them again that Chalky wasn't there, but they went from room to room, poking under beds, pointing their guns at the closet doors. Against my mother's protests and mine, they woke Jeffrey up and looked under his bed. He began to shake at the sight of the guns. He was crying. It was pandemonium. Finally, they left.

A month later, Chalky sent word through a lawyer friend that I

should begin divorce proceedings against him. He didn't say anything about the missing money, nothing about his wardrobe. He
just couldn't come back. He'd beaten the indictment by a couple of
weeks, but things were really hot now. It looked like the Feds
wanted him badly enough to wait him out. If he returned, he'd be a
cooked goose. So he was graciously cutting me loose. Go have a
life, was the message from generous Chalky Lefkowitz. And anyway, he didn't want to be married to me anymore.

He'd left me. He'd walked. His ego was intact. And I still had
my legs. And my life.

EPILOGUE
NEW YORK CITY
JUNE 1989

Almost from the day Chalky left, I'd been working in the Garment Center. I'd done all right supporting myself and Jeffrey. But I was always looking to trade up. And the doormen in our building knew that.

One of them said to me, "You know Briskin, from the twelfth floor? He's a big manufacturer of sports wear. You should talk to him."

I filed the information.

Then came the big day, Jeffrey's graduation. In my new linen dress and high-heeled summer shoes, I stepped onto the elevator. I'd put my makeup on carefully, but the real glow lighting my face was coming from joy, not cosmetics.

We'd made it, the Jab and me. There weren't too many people we'd known in the old days who would've put money on how well we'd do out on our own. I'd been earning a living like a regular working stiff for almost fifteen years. I had a son graduating from college. I felt great. I looked great. And as I stepped onto the elevator I could tell that Mr. Briskin from the twelfth floor thought so, too.

"Hi," I said. "Your name is Briskin, isn't it? I'm Sandy

Lefkowitz. The name used to be Barton. The doorman said that I should—"

Briskin nodded. "I know both your names," he said, starting to grin. "You still look good."

A lot of years and guys had come and gone. "Uh, did we ever . . . ?" I asked nervously. He didn't look familiar, but who knew.

"You were my first case out of the academy," he said. "I'm in *shmattes* now, the rag business. But I used to be with the FBI. In fact, I used to listen in on your phone conversations. When your first husband was sick . . . What was his name? Bennie?"

"Bernie," I said, stunned. "You were an FBI agent?"

"With the Organized Crime Task Force. That's right," he said, "his name was Bernie. Bernie Barton. What a character. We used to follow you to the hospital every day. I used to. It was my first assignment. God, you look terrific."

"Thanks. I feel terrific today," I said.

"How's your kid? You had just had a baby, right? A little boy?"

"Jeffrey. That's why I'm all dressed up," I said. "I'm on my way to his graduation. From John Jay College of Criminal Justice."

"You're kidding," Briskin said. "Bernie Barton's son is going into law enforcement? Well, well. Imagine that. *Mazel-tov!*"